T0326592

The
Political Economy
of **Reforms** in Egypt

The
Political Economy
of Reforms in Egypt
Issues and Policymaking since 1952

Khalid Ikram

The American University in Cairo Press
Cairo New York

Copyright © 2018 by
The American University in Cairo Press
113 Sharia Kasr el Aini, Cairo, Egypt
420 Fifth Avenue, New York, NY 10018
www.aucpress.com

All rights reserved. No part of this publication may be reproduced, stored in a retrieval system, or transmitted in any form or by any means, electronic, mechanical, photocopying, recording, or otherwise,
without the prior written permission of the publisher.

Exclusive distribution outside Egypt and North America by I.B.Tauris & Co Ltd., 6 Salem Road, London,
W2 4BU

Dar el Kutub No. 26252/15
ISBN 978 977 416 794 2

Dar el Kutub Cataloging-in-Publication Data

Ikram, Khalid
        The Political Economy of Reforms in Egypt: Issues and Policymaking since 1952 / Khalid
    Ikram.—Cairo: The American University in Cairo Press, 2017.
        p. cm.
        ISBN: 978 977 416 794 2
        1. Economic development
        2. Economics—Egypt
        330.0962

1 2 3 4 5   22 21 20 19 18

Designed by Adam el-Sehemy
Printed in the United States of America

For Shirin

Contents

Figures and Tables

Figures

Tables

Note: Unless otherwise specified, the figures and tables are based on the IMF and World Bank databases.

Preface

This book describes the interaction between politics and economics that went into dealing with some of the most important issues of economic policymaking in Egypt since 1952. A certain degree of overlap with my earlier book—*The Egyptian Economy: 1952–2000: Performance, Policies and Issues* (London: Routledge, 2006)—is inevitable. The major distinction between the two is that the earlier book contained a good deal of technical analysis and was lighter on the interaction with politics. The present work tries to rectify the imbalance. However, as before, the focus remains on the durable, structural issues that policymakers confronted, rather than on day-to-day problems.

I have been engaged with the Egyptian economy since 1975 as senior economist in the World Bank responsible for Egypt, as director of the World Bank's Egypt department, and as a consultant for international organizations and private think tanks. During these years of association, I have been fortunate to have had the opportunity to access many diverse sources of information and advice. Thus, in addition to published material, the present book draws on unpublished studies, background papers, memoranda, and back-to-office reports of the World Bank, the International Monetary Fund, and other international and national organizations.

It has also benefited from discussions with several present and past Egyptian policymakers, politicians of every hue, bureaucrats, scholars and students, members of Egyptian and foreign think tanks and civil society, bankers, lawyers, journalists, diplomats from countries providing assistance to Egypt, and of course with former colleagues in the World Bank and the International Monetary Fund. I am grateful for the candor and the detail with which they discussed their views, and for their unvarnished assessments of political and economic issues confronting Egypt and the country's policy responses to them. Many of the insights are directly quoted in the text and have been referenced. However, this book is not a journalistic exposé and confidences have been respected; where identification might breach confidentiality, or the source requested anonymity, comments have been paraphrased without attribution.

The Egyptian economy faces a number of difficulties. The proportion of young people in the population is expanding rapidly and their expectations for the future are growing. These developments are taking place in an environment in which world economic growth has slowed, in which the benefits of economic integration and free trade are being called into question, and in a region in which threats of terrorism have added to political uncertainty. History has shown that on many crucial issues, economics and politics are inextricably intertwined. Overcoming the economic difficulties will call on all the skill and the wisdom that Egypt's policymakers and citizens can muster, together with learning from the experience of successes and failures in the past. I hope this book can help in the task.

Acknowledgments

I n a previous book on the Egyptian economy (Ikram 2006), I wrote that "anyone who works on Egypt will recognize how quickly he incurs debts that beggar his ability to repay them adequately." The passage of time has only deepened my debt and increased my inability to discharge it. From prime ministers and cabinet members, through bureaucrats, academics, members of think tanks and civil society, politicians from all sides of the political spectrum, businessmen, journalists, and university students, numerous Egyptians have given liberally of their time to discuss economic and political events, no matter how sensitive. They all have helped to shape my thinking on economic issues and policymaking in Egypt. It is impossible to thank them all individually, but I must make an attempt to acknowledge those whose influence was the largest, even though several of them, sadly, are no longer among us.

My biggest intellectual debts concerning Egyptian economic development are to Robert Mabro, Hanaa Kheir el-Din, Heba Handoussa, Heba Nassar, Samir Radwan, Ahmed Galal, Galal Amin, Bent Hansen, Mahmoud Abdel Fadil, Adel Bishai, Gouda Abdel Khalek, Karima Korayem, Ragui Assaad, Nader Fergany, Heba el-Leithy, and John Waterbury.

Since this book is chiefly concerned with policy, the insights of policymakers, past and present, bulk large in the discussions; indeed, one might almost consider them as participants in its writing. I am grateful to many of them for so freely discussing the issues that they confronted and the reasons why they undertook the policies that they adopted, and also why they did not enact others. For the subject matter of this book, I learned much from Kamal al-Ganzoury, Abdel Moneim el-Kaissouni, Abdel Razzaq Abdel Meguid, Abdel Aziz Hegazi, Hilmi Abdel Rahman, Atef Ebeid,

Ismail Sabri Abdullah, Hamed el-Sayeh, Salah Hamed, Zaki Shafei, Hazem el-Beblawi, Sultan Abu Ali, Zaafer al-Bishry, Osman Muhammad Osman, Ahmed Abou Ismail, Ahmed al-Dersh, Nabil Fahmy, Mahmoud Mohieldin, Youssef Boutros-Ghali, Wagih Shindy, Ismail Hassan, and Ali Negm.

A major part of Egypt's economic strategy has rested on access to external aid, therefore it is vital to look at how bilateral donors and international agencies viewed Egypt's policymaking. From the donor community, I profited especially from the knowledge and sagacity of Hermann Eilts, Edward Walker, Daniel Kurtzer, Alfred Atherton, Sir Nigel Barrington, Sir David Blatherwick, Don Brown, Toni Wagner, John Westley, Edward Peck, and Henry Mattox.

Colleagues and friends from the World Bank and the International Monetary Fund have over the years been generous with discussions, notes, advice, information, and data. I am particularly obliged to Kemal Dervis, Masood Ahmed, Martijn Paijmans, Vinod Dubey, Azizali Mohammed, Ismail Serageldin, Nemat ("Minouche") Shafik, Arvind Subramanian, Daniela Gressani, Manuela Ferro, Inder Sud, Marcelo Giugale, Nadir Mohammed, Asad Alam, Christopher Jarvis, Paul Dickie, Matthew Simmonds, Lorenzo Forini, Yufei Cai, Nadeem ul Haque, and Farrukh Iqbal.

Archivists and librarians at the Joint IMF–World Bank library—especially Southamini Borlo, Becky West, Megan Sumner, and Sangeeta Sharma—were unfailingly helpful in providing a congenial environment for work, and procuring material that otherwise might have been impossible to obtain.

A number of scholars read the entire manuscript and provided important insights. I should like to express my gratitude to Ishac Diwan (Paris Sciences et Lettres), Tarek Selim (American University in Cairo), Ahmed Ghoneim (Cairo University and Center for Social and Economic Research, Warsaw), Ehtisham Ahmed (London School of Economics, University of Bonn, and Zhejiang University), Shahid Yusuf (George Washington University and the School of Advanced International Studies at Johns Hopkins University), and Zubair Iqbal (Middle East Institute, Washington DC). Constraints of time, commitments to other work, and the necessity of maintaining confidentiality, may have limited my ability to benefit fully from their advice, but my debt to them remains heavy.

I should like to express especial thanks to Nadia Naqib, my editor at the American University in Cairo Press. She suggested that I write this book, kept me in touch with sources in Egypt, supplied material that I was unable to locate in the United States, and responded to my queries with unfailing courtesy and promptness. I was also very fortunate in having Johanna Baboukis as my copyeditor, who went through the manuscript with a keen eye and sharp red pencil, paying meticulous attention to detail.

Over the years, many Egyptian friends have helped me to better understand, and greatly enjoy, Egyptian life, history, and culture. These friends are much too numerous to list in detail, but I would be especially remiss if I did not acknowledge Samir Koraiem, Wafik Hosni, Ismail Bedawy, Saad Barghout, Essam Rifaat, Hussein el-Gamal, Noorna ("Mickey") Sarofim, Hisham Fahmy, and Omar Mohanna.

The underlying premise of this book is that a government must provide a better life for its citizens and protect the country from external pressures. These goals require policymaking that ensures the best use of a country's resources, minimizes poverty, and maintains income disparities within socially acceptable bounds. My biggest intellectual debts are to Mahbub ul-Haq, who for many years in the Pakistan Planning Commission and the World Bank was my mentor in the formulation and analysis of policymaking in these areas; to Gustav Papanek, my thesis advisor at Harvard, who has counseled governments in Pakistan, Nigeria, Indonesia, and elsewhere on guiding individual greed into socially useful channels; and to Amartya Sen, whose wide array of writings on removing poverty and enabling the enlargement of human capabilities (to cite some of his work in only the economic field) have been recognized by the award of the Nobel Prize, and who has been teacher and friend from my student days at Cambridge and Harvard.

I remain deepest in debt to my family, who have borne the brunt of my preoccupations and absences with an amazing amount of patience and understanding. As I said in an earlier book, "What may have helped them is their profound attachment to Egypt, which quite rivals my own." Time has only strengthened our attachment. Shirin, Salima, Nicholas, Aden, Ana, Chase, and Cruz are a continuous font of love, joy, support, and inspiration.

My wife, Shirin, has been a particular source of strength. She never ceases to amaze me with how much she is able to accomplish. For more than fifty years she has maintained a family environment of cheerfulness and affection on three continents, while at the same time meeting the demanding requirements of a very successful legal career that spanned Pakistan, Egypt, and the United States. It is impossible to express the extent of what I owe to her, and this book is dedicated to Shirin as but a small acknowledgment of my profound debt.

Abbreviations

CAPMAS	Central Agency for Public Mobilization and Statistics
EGP	Employment Guarantee Program
ERSAP	Economic Reform and Structural Adjustment Program
ESA	Employee Shareholder Association
FAO	Food and Agriculture Organization
FPL	Food Poverty Line
GASC	General Authority for Supply Commodities
GDP	Gross Domestic Product
GNP	Gross National Product
GODE	Gulf Organization for the Development of Egypt
HIECS	Household Income, Expenditure and Consumption Survey
HIES	Household Income and Expenditure Survey
IDA	International Development Association
IFIs	International financial institutions
IMF	International Monetary Fund
JICA	Japanese International Cooperation Agency
LE	Egyptian pound
LFSS	Labor Force Sample Survey
LPL	Lower Poverty Line
MOED	Ministry of Economic Development
MOP	Ministry of Planning

NGO	Non-governmental organization
NPC	National Planning Committee
NTM	Non-tariff measure
ODA	Official development assistance
PCDNP	Permanent Council for the Development of National Production
PRIDE	Project in Development and the Environment
REER	Real effective exchange rate
RMSE	Root mean squared error
SCAF	Supreme Council of the Armed Forces
SMEs	Small and medium enterprises
TFP	Total Factor Productivity
UNCTAD	United Nations Conference on Trade And Development
UNDP	United Nations Development Program
UNICEF	United Nations Children's Fund
UPL	Upper Poverty Line
USAID	United States Agency for International Development
VAT	Value-added tax
WHO	World Health Organization
WVS	World Values Survey

Introduction

When a country has a continuous history of more than five thousand years, dating the genesis of an issue requiring reform can become a little arbitrary. It seems that in Egypt's case, no matter which date is chosen, it is almost always possible to look back to find pre-echoes of political-economy issues that are being discussed today. "This country is a palimpsest," wrote Lady Duff Gordon in 1863 "in which the Bible is written over Herodotus, and the Koran over that" (Gordon 1969).

Even the time of the pharaohs offers important instances of matters with which present-day administrations continue to grapple. A modern policymaker would be no stranger, for example, to wrestling with problems of controlling and distributing the Nile's waters; to managing an extremely centralized administration; to examining issues raised by the level of government intrusion in the economy; to assessing the consequences for the country's cropping patterns of farmers' not having to pay for irrigation water; to estimating the taxes to be levied in the coming year; to concerning himself with the role of religion in the polity; and many more questions that can trace their roots to pharaonic times.[1]

Or one could start with Napoleon's expedition to Egypt (1798–1801) because it marked the beginning of the most recent serious interaction between Egypt and the West and has political, economic, social, and cultural consequences that continue to unfold to our day. Moreover, the reign of Muhammad Ali (1805–49), who assumed power after the departure of the French, and his successors saw the introduction of many policies—such as those relating to the ownership of land; the expansion of the canal network; the steady replacement of basin by perennial irrigation in order to meet the requirement of increasing the country's limited cultivated and

1

cropped area; the government's sponsorship of industrialization; protection against imports and the consequences of removing it; the enlargement and modernization of the armed forces; the raising of revenues to pay for the policies of economic expansion; the construction of the Suez Canal and the resulting deeper integration of Egypt into the international economy; the rise of external indebtedness and the political vulnerability that it created; and several others that have molded much of Egypt's contemporary economy and society. These policies delivered many of the strengths that buttress the country but also initiated problems that continue to engage the attention of today's regimes.

This book has a more limited compass. The discussion focuses on the era since the Free Officers staged a coup on July 23, 1952, but refers back to earlier periods to show how an issue arose and how deeply, with time or reiteration, it has become embedded in the political and economic structures of the country. It discusses the principal economic challenges that Egypt faced and looks at the interaction of politics and economics that went into determining the policies devised to deal with the challenges. In discussing these policies, one must almost inevitably raise the question of whether other approaches would have been more effective.

Four points concerning the approach and the scope of the book should be stated at the outset. First, this is not a book about the politics of Egypt per se; rather, it deals with how political and economic variables interacted to produce the crucial economic outcomes for the country since 1952.

Second, its underlying assumption is that the most important responsibilities of a government are to create a better life for its citizens and to keep the country free from external domination. While many different elements go into the creation of a better and more secure life, the economic element is critical; this includes policies that would bring about a sustainable development of the economy and a better distribution of its fruits. These criteria are taken as the touchstone against which to appraise the effectiveness of economic strategies.

Third, much of Egypt's economic development since 1952 has involved the use of foreign resources, contracted bilaterally, multilaterally, or commercially. One could even say that a good deal of Egypt's political maneuvering since 1952 has been in the quest to obtain such resources. How providers of external resources reacted to Egypt's economic policymaking, and what the impact of their policy advice was, therefore requires scrutiny.

Fourth, there is no attempt to provide a recipe for dealing with an immediate situation, such as, for example, that resulting from the overthrow of the Mubarak regime in January 2011. The discussion of the way forward is on the enduring structural issues in the economic field that will have to be tackled by whatever regime is in power over at least the next two or three decades.

The Importance of Economic Health

Egypt's economic future matters. With a population that accounts for about 40 percent of the Arab world; with a preeminence in Arab culture, education, and media; with a large and well-qualified diaspora that underpins the economic and social development of many other Arab countries; with a strategic location where the Suez Canal provides the shortest passage between Europe and Asia; and with the largest armed forces among the Arab countries, Egypt should rank as one of the most important countries in the world. And yet there is a perception that the country's performance has fallen short of its potential.

While many reasons—historical, political, and other—have contributed to this state of affairs, economic weaknesses have been responsible for many of the country's most serious political ills. To take but one example: even 150 years ago, the failure to generate sufficient foreign-exchange earnings created both the need for Egypt to borrow externally for the construction of the Suez Canal and also its inability to service this debt. The default provided the creditor countries a pretext to set up the Caisse de la Dette Publique in 1876 that, together with the "advisors" imposed on the Egyptian ministries (especially after the British occupation of Egypt in 1882), dictated Egypt's principal economic policies and appropriated the country's financial and material resources for the benefit of the creditors. The occupation continued de jure until the ratification of the Anglo-Egyptian Treaty in 1936 and de facto until the withdrawal of the British troops in 1954. Economic weakness cost Egypt its political sovereignty.

Lest one think that this is all ancient history, more recent examples of the interactions of economics and politics impacting powerfully on Egypt can readily be offered. Thus, because Egypt could not mobilize sufficient resources domestically to pay for the construction of the High Dam at Aswan, it had to seek funds from abroad. When the foreign loans that had originally been expected were canceled, President Gamal Abd al-Nasser took the political decision on July 26, 1956 to nationalize the Suez Canal and use the transit fees to pay for the dam's construction. "The Canal will pay for the dam!" said President Nasser, according to two French eyewitnesses (Lacouture and Lacouture 1958, 472). This was a political policy undertaken in pursuit of an economic goal. The nationalization led to a war with the United Kingdom and France—the major shareholders of the Suez Canal Company—that in addition to damage inflicted on Egypt's infrastructure induced the country to reorient its political and economic relations away from the West and toward the Soviet Union. These political actions had long-term economic consequences. They cut off Egypt's access to the financial and technical resources of the West, thus potentially restricting the investment and growth rate of the country and constraining it to rely for its development on the less efficient technology of the communist countries.

Ironically, the political fallout from economic weakness did not impact only on Egypt—the British victory in the Suez episode was Pyrrhic. The uncertainty created in the region by the hostilities, the interruptions to trade caused by Egypt's blocking of the Suez Canal, and the spike in oil prices made investors very nervous and led to an attack on sterling. In order to defend the exchange rate, the Bank of England was compelled to draw down its reserves (between September and November the United Kingdom lost 15 percent of its gold and dollar reserves), which began to approach a level at which a devaluation of the British currency looked inevitable.[2] This alarmed the British government, which felt that a debased sterling "would probably lead to a breakup of the sterling area or (possibly even the dissolution of the Commonwealth) . . . and currency instability at home leading to severe inflation."[3] The government approached the United States for financial help, but the latter agreed to offer this assistance only under a number of conditions, such as complying with a U.S.-sponsored United Nations resolution that required Britain to quickly relinquish its military gains and withdraw its troops from the Suez Canal area. Subramanian (2011, 15) reports a senior advisor to the British government writing, "This was blackmail. . . . But we were in no position to argue." Economic vulnerability had enfeebled Britain's political hand and erased the country's diplomatic weight. Another case of economic weakness begetting political subservience.

Other examples can be offered where external pressures resulting from Egypt's economic weakness produced serious long-term results. With continuing inability to match government revenues and expenditures, Egypt was compelled to accept diktats from the International Monetary Fund (IMF) in 1977 to cut subsidies on bread and other consumer items. This resulted in the worst riots to take place in Egypt since 1952, with considerable damage to public infrastructure and production facilities. Perhaps even worse, the incident left scars on policymakers' psyches that have to this day made them very wary of undertaking reform policies.

Some Conclusions

The book covers too much ground to allow a simple summary, but some points are worth emphasizing.

First, the overriding issue during the period covered by this study concerns the role of the state in the economy. The state spent the earlier part of the period imposing an extensive set of discretionary controls on the economy, and the latter part in dismantling many of them. Neither experience was entirely satisfactory. The task defined in Ikram (1980, 8) still remains: "The government will have to continue trying to strike a balance between the conflicting objectives of *liberalization* for the sake of productivity growth and *intervention* for the sake of an equitable distribution of income."

Second, accelerating the GDP growth rate is imperative; Egypt's demographic dynamics do not permit an alternative.[4] Every two years Egypt adds a New Zealand or Ireland to its population; every three, a Denmark or Finland; every four, an Israel or Switzerland; and every five, a Sweden or Portugal. And while it adds the population, it does not add the capital assets, the technical knowledge, the institutions, and the governance of these countries.

Moreover, Egypt is not only experiencing a bulge in the population's working-age cohort, but it also has an even larger "echo" generation below the age of ten that will enter the labor market in the near future. In 2016 there were about 10 million Egyptians aged 25–29, but also more than 13 million below the age of five years. This age structure offers a potential dividend, but also creates a danger.

The dividend is provided by the rapid increase in Egypt's labor force and productive capacity, while the experience of countries that have passed through a similar demographic transition suggests that it could also raise the country's savings rate. But if the economy fails to create a sufficient number of meaningful jobs, the demographic dividend could turn into a demographic nightmare as hundreds of thousands of young men and women crowd Egypt's streets desperately seeking jobs, income, security, housing, and access to health and education for themselves and their families—a mouthwatering prospect for a recruiter for any extremist ideology.

Third, Egypt's experience since 1952 also shows the influence exerted by external forces in the country's development. These external forces have been foreign governments, international agencies, and commercial financial institutions. The influence can come from the financial resources they provide, from the technical advice they offer, or more generally from a combination of the two. The experience suggests that Egypt should have been more proactive in deciding which elements of the economic advice to act upon and which parts to decline. But "Who pays the piper calls the tune" remains the most compelling maxim of international politics, and Egypt will only be able to reduce external political pressure if it takes more serious measures to mobilize domestic resources and to correct the anti-export bias in its incentive structure.

Fourth, Egypt is ripe for "second generation" reforms. The distinction between first- and second-generation reforms is to some extent a semantic question and the two forms of reform can overlap. However, Naím (1994) provides a useful way of classifying the main differences. First-generation reforms can be undertaken relatively quickly, focus on actions that need to be taken (on "inputs," so to speak), and face political opposition that is largely diffused. Examples of first-generation reforms would be macroeconomic stabilization, reductions in import tariffs, budget cuts, changes in tax rates and coverage, privatization, and similar policies. These are technically easy to identify and, if the authorities are serious about economic policy, the policies need not take very long to implement.

On the other hand, as Navia and Velasco (2003, 265–68) point out, second-generation reforms are often "merely statements of desired outcomes (for example, civil service reform or improving tax collection), without a clear sense of policy design." Moreover, second-generation reforms frequently raise a different level of technical difficulty. As Navia and Velasco put it: "Any economist can tell you that curtailing inflation requires lower money growth; fewer are prepared to put forward a proposal for supervising operations in derivatives by banks and other financial institutions, or for solving failures in the market for health insurance." Thus, for first-generation reforms, identifying the outcome to aim at and the means to attain it are both, in principle at least, fairly straightforward; for second-generation reforms, the desired outcome may be discernible only in a rather general form, and the means of attaining it can be far from clear.

Moreover, second-stage reforms commonly take much longer to implement because they require fundamental changes in the organizing and/

or functioning of institutions—their chief aim is to improve governance. And the widespread experience is that faith-, ideology-, and culture-based attachments to institutional structures, or those rooted in a long history, are fiercely resistant, or even immune, to policy. Thus, for example, second-stage reforms generally require a reform of the bureaucracy. This is seldom easy and could be particularly difficult in Egypt. More than one-fourth of the country's labor force is employed in various parts of the government—in 2016 there was one government employee for every thirteen citizens (even this figure excludes the Armed Forces)—and is set in its attitudes and methods of working. The reforms might also require creating entirely new institutions or politically empowering existing ones, such as regulatory agencies that would actually restrain monopolistic or oligopolistic behavior by firms. They would also require fundamental changes in the functioning of the commercial judicial system in order to speed up judgments and to reduce the case burden on judges. And measures would also have to be put in place to ensure that judicial decisions were implemented promptly.

The two stages of reforms also raise different issues of political economy. Apart from some exceptions—such as businesses that might be compelled to compete against international firms because reforms had cut import tariffs—the groups affected by first-stage reforms are often too fragmented or too poor to carry much political clout and thus their concerns can be set aside more easily. But, as Navia and Velasco (2003, 268) put it, "By contrast, the set of interests potentially affected [by changes in governance] in the next stage reads like a *Who's Who* of highly organized and vocal groups: teachers' and judicial unions, the upper echelons of the public bureaucracy, state and local governments, owners and managers of private monopolies, and the medical establishment." Their resistance can prove lethal to the reform program.

Fifth, most of Egypt's GDP growth of the last fifty years has come from adding more labor and particularly capital; the contribution of total factor productivity (TFP), that is, the efficiency with which factors of production are used, has been very small. Productivity in this sense results not only from technology change, but also from any other changes that influence the efficiency with which inputs are converted into output.[5] Of particular importance are such factors as changes in regulations and the working of institutions that govern the economy. A discussion of the principal conceptual issues relating to TFP measurement and of Egyptian data problems will be found in Ikram (2006, 101–16); here only the main results from recent studies will be summarized.

A paper by Mohammed (2001) estimated that for the period 1965–2000, capital accumulation contributed about two-thirds of the growth in real GDP, growth in human-capital-adjusted labor about one-third.[6] Egypt was becoming a capital-intensive producer. The capital intensity of production is not surprising in view of the overvalued exchange rate and the negative real interest rates that prevailed in Egypt over much of the period. The contribution of TFP between 1965 and 2000 was mildly negative; this says that any combination of labor and capital would have produced less output in 2000 than it could have in 1965. Productivity growth appears to have been important mainly during 1975–80, when it accounted for about 14 percent of GDP growth. Estimates for more recent periods—for example, Boopen, Sawkut, and Ramessur (2009) and the Conference Board (2015)—continue to show the same picture of a very low contribution by productivity growth, including zero or negative contribution from 2007 through 2014. The IMF (2005) estimated the long-run (1961–2004) average contribution of TFP to Egypt's GDP growth at only 0.9 percent, and IMF (2015) put the growth of TFP between 2004 and 2010 at a mere 0.8 percent per year. World Bank (2015) estimated that during the ten years 2004–13, growth was mainly driven by capital, which on average contributed 70 percent of overall growth, while labor and TFP growth contributed 18 and 11 percent respectively. There is a wide consensus, therefore, that in the period from 1965 to 2016 as a whole, TFP growth contributed very little, if at all, to the growth of Egypt's GDP.

Pushing the story back to 1950 reaffirms the same finding. Maddison (1970, 53–54) calculated that in the period 1950–65, changes in productivity contributed only 20 percent to the growth of Egypt's income. However, Maddison arbitrarily assigned weights of 0.5 to both labor and capital. If we instead substitute the weights estimated from more recent studies, productivity improvements would account for barely 12 percent of the growth of GDP during that period.

These are very different from the findings for the fast-growing developing countries and the developed countries. The Nobel laureate Robert Solow (1957), who pioneered the technique of growth accounting, estimated that for the period 1909–49 capital accumulation contributed 11 percent to the growth of the United States' GDP, increases in labor contributed 38 percent, while the remaining 51 percent came as a result of technical progress. This pattern appears to have stood the test of time; for example, Denison (1962, 1985) came to broadly similar conclusions for the period 1929–82.

Egypt's experience with TFP growth also differs markedly from that of the fast-growing East Asian countries. Estimates of the contribution of TFP differ between various studies, but the broad conclusions are that for South Korea in the period 1960–2005, increases in physical capital accounted for about 40 percent of the GDP growth, increases in labor about 30 percent, while increases in TFP contributed about 30 percent. Over roughly the same period, the contribution of capital to the growth of output in Taiwan was about 46 percent, that of labor about 18 percent, while TFP growth contributed nearly 36 percent. For the high-performing East Asian countries (Hong Kong, Singapore, Indonesia, Malaysia, and Thailand, in addition to South Korea and Taiwan) as a group, the average growth of GDP between 1960 and 2003 was 6.5 percent a year; of this, capital contributed nearly 49 percent, labor 25 percent, and TFP growth 26 percent (World Bank 1993a, 60–70; Thorbecke and Wan 1999, 3–20; Kim and Hong 1999, 183, table 8-5; Stiglitz and Yusuf 2001, 16, tables 1.3 and 1.4).

The experience of China provides further confirmation of the importance of factor productivity to growth. The World Bank (1997b) estimated that TFP growth accounted for 30 to 58 percent of China's growth during 1978–95. A more recent and very detailed growth accounting exercise by Yueh (2013) for three decades from 1979 estimated that about 45 percent of the country's growth could be attributed to capital accumulation, and about 30 percent to TFP; the rest was contributed by increases and improvements in the labor force. A decomposition of the gains from TFP indicated that 8 percent of total GDP growth was explained by the transfer of labor and capital from public-sector enterprises to the private sector. About 20 percent of growth was explained by institutional improvements, such as providing greater flexibility for the internal movement of labor liberalizing the financial sector. This analysis therefore highlights the importance of the contribution of TFP to total growth, and within TFP, the importance of improving the efficiency of institutions (Yueh 2013).

The findings on Egypt's TFP growth indicate that GDP growth in Egypt has resulted more from using additional labor and capital than from using these factors more efficiently—"the result more of perspiration than inspiration," as Paul Krugman, another Nobel laureate, put it (Krugman 1997). If Egypt's TFP growth does not step up substantially, generating the required growth of GDP will require rates of increase in capital, savings, and in the quality of human resources that may not be feasible (Ikram 2006, 314–15; Hevia and Loayza 2011, 21–25 offer estimates of increases in investment and savings rates that would be required under different assumptions of GDP and TFP growth; the rates are about double those sustained by Egypt in the last fifty years). Indeed, this underscores that Egypt's major long-term economic challenge is to shift from a strategy based on factor accumulation (principally that of increasing the input of capital) to one that is based on productivity growth.

The failures of productivity growth inevitably impacted Egypt's competitiveness in the world economy. Between 2007 and 2014, Egypt's competitiveness ranking for the macroeconomic environment and major indicators deteriorated. Thus, compared with 148 countries, Egypt's ranking fell from 115 in 2007 to 140 in 2014; for government budget balance, from 119 to 146; for gross national savings (as percent of GDP), from 65 to 108; for general government debt, from 109 to 122; and for the annual percentage change in inflation, from 106 to 129 (World Bank 2015, 35, table III.1).[7]

A little more elaboration of the central message might be helpful. Thus, sixth, the essential messages of the book would be on the following lines.

1. During the past two hundred years, Egypt's policymakers have been confronted with challenges of which a surprising number have proved enduring and continue to resonate today. Some of these challenges have been dictated by nature, such as the relative fixity of the arable land and the declining per capita availability of water. Some are a combination of nature and human agency, such as the inexorable growth of the population. But many represent inadequate policy attention, such as the failure to strengthen institutions that would support the rule of law, boost competition in the economy, and mobilize more resources for development and thereby avoid the political and economic vulnerabilities associated with external indebtedness. The recurrent political-economy message from Egypt's experience is that concerns about regime survival trumped considerations of economic vulnerability in policymakers' calculations, and that economic reforms tended to be adopted only when a crisis had extinguished all other options.

2. If one were asked to sum up in a few words the reasons for Egypt's failure to perform to its economic potential, one could do worse than to say that its roots lay in the fragile political legitimacy of successive regimes, who sought salvation by continually increasing public consumption expenditures—between 1965 and 2016, real public consumption expenditures increased at an average rate of

about 4.4 percent a year, well ahead of the population growth rate. The survival strategy also required regimes to minimize resource mobilization from domestic sources. This meant that taxes, and in particular the personal income tax, could be touched only very gingerly. The ratio of tax revenue to GDP in 1952 was estimated at 14.8 percent (el-Edel, 1982, 140) and at 14.4 percent in 1965 (World Bank, 1977), rising to a peak of 26 percent in 1982, and declining thereafter to about 16 percent in 2016; over the period as a whole the tax ratio averaged about 16.2 percent. About two-thirds of the total tax revenue during 1965–2016 was provided by indirect taxes—on production, consumption, imports, stamp duty, and so on; another 30 percent on business profits; personal income tax provided only about 7 percent of total tax revenue. The reluctance to tap domestic resources for revenues in turn compelled rulers to rely unduly on external economic rents and exogenous resources, and heightened Egypt's vulnerability to foreign pressures.

There is a close convergence between the explanations offered by many writers for the political-economy behavior of successive Egyptian regimes. The reasons provided by, for example, Baker (1978, 167–68), Cooper (1979, 482–84), Roy (1980, 3–9), McDermott (1988), Springborg (1989), Waterbury (1983, 1985), Hansen (1991, 116–17, and 250–54). Wahba (1994), Marcou (2008), Soliman (2011), Kandil (2012), and others essentially boil down to the following paraphrase.

Egyptian regimes have felt exceptionally vulnerable because they lacked the legitimacy of a democratic election. The basic political-economy element in their survival strategy was to placate the population by offering an abundance of consumer and other subsidies (at times even cigarettes and *halawa* [a dessert] were subsidized); free education and health care; guaranteed employment; controlled rents for housing; redistribution of landholdings; regular increases in bonuses, industrial wages, and government salaries; ceilings on interest rates, and so on. The regimes also could not risk antagonizing the population by increasing taxes; hence they mobilized much of their resources from economic rents, whose burden for the most part fell on foreigners. The strategy for regime survival tended to be short-termist: a continual search for band-aids, most of which were to be provided by foreigners, especially in the shape of external assistance and debt forgiveness or restructuring. The Churchillian mantra of offering one's own "blood, sweat, toil, and tears" never caught fire among the regimes' leaders.

The political-economy strategy was threatened by two factors. First, the rapidly growing population and its continuing expectations of subsidized items required a constant expansion of public consumption expenditure. Second, Egypt's foreign policy initiatives, especially from 1952 to 1974, carried very substantial costs. Egypt had projected itself as the leader of the Arabs; a leader of the Muslim world; a leader of Africa; a leader of the "nonaligned" group of countries; champion of Palestinian rights; supporter of Algerian resistance to French rule; a bulwark of the Third World against the West. It had been involved in wars with Israel in 1948, 1956, 1967, and 1973, plus a "war of attrition" (March 1969 to August 1970) and a war in Yemen against Saudi Arabia from 1962 to 1967, and in hostilities against Libya in 1977. All these severely depleted Egypt's economic, financial, and human capital. The cumulative effect of these factors came to a head in the early 1970s.

The growing demands of the different constituencies could be met only by a continuous enlargement of the economic cake, that is, a sustained increase in the GDP. But the country's political-economic strategy contained two fundamental contradictions that caused it to founder. One, the rising consumption demands worked against the imperative of increasing domestic savings to pay for the investment that would propel GDP growth. This meant that Egypt had to look to external sources to finance the gap between investment and domestic savings. But, two, the anti-West stance adopted by Egypt until 1974 depleted Egypt's political capital in the world's biggest sources of finance and modern technology, and drastically restricted the country's access to these resources, especially those available on concessional terms.

In sum, *Egypt's failure to perform to its economic potential resulted chiefly from internal political pressures to maintain increases in public consumption while not mobilizing sufficient revenues from domestic sources and, especially until 1974, foreign policy overstretch. Major economic reforms tended to be introduced only in the wake of a military or economic crisis that eliminated all other options.*

Egypt was trapped in a "trilemma," or a political version of the "impossible trinity." The original version of the "impossible trinity" was formulated by Robert Mundell and concerns the pursuit of incompatible economic objectives. Mundell (1963) showed that it was impossible to simultaneously adopt an independent monetary policy, a fixed exchange rate, and free capital movements; policymakers could successfully pursue only two of these aims. The political version would say that Egypt's policymakers could simultaneously pursue only two of a policy of rapid GDP growth, prioritizing consumption over savings, and an anti-West political stance.

The political-economy strategy had become unsustainable. The continual enlargement of the cake required resources much in excess of what Egyptian regimes were willing to extract internally plus what foreigners were prepared to provide. Economic growth would be unable to meet the demands of the political-economy strategy, and this could jeopardize the survival of the regime. At least one element of the trinity would have to be abandoned.

The anti-West foreign policy was jettisoned in 1974. The financial rewards that the change procured enabled the regime to maintain the economic elements of the former strategy. The surge in the "Big Five" (Suez Canal dues, oil exports, tourism earnings, workers' remittances, and foreign aid) resulting from the greater political stability in the region, the return to Egypt of oil-producing facilities after the Arab–Israel war of 1973, the reopening of the Suez Canal, and the major inflow of Western economic assistance expanded the economic cake and made it possible to afford the subsidies and other benefits that formed the heart of the political-economy strategy.

But the increasing population and the policy of large-scale subsidization meant that consumption demands kept rising, necessitating more imports and also cutting into the exportable surplus of many commodities, especially oil. Moreover, the "kindness of strangers" has limits, and it was not possible for foreign aid to keep increasing. Indeed, between 1980 and 2015, annual economic assistance from the United States (Egypt's largest consistent donor) fell from $815 million to $250 million (and to even less in terms of purchasing power). See Sharp (2010).

Egypt had not taken advantage of the good years to adequately step up the investment rate, to strengthen the performance of key institutions, and to improve the productivity with which it used inputs. Policies will have to facilitate the structural transformation of the economy, that is, moving inputs from low-productivity sectors to those of higher productivity. The fifty-year period 1965–2016 saw only a slow transformation of the economy. Thus, for example, the ratio of exports of goods and services to GDP was 17 percent in 1965 and 14 in 2016; that of imports to GDP, 21 and 23 percent; of taxes to GDP, 15 and 16 percent. A study by Galal and el-Megharbel (2008) that looked at two indicators of structural transformation—increases in product variety and total factor productivity—within the key sector of industry for the twenty-year period 1980–99 found that in fact variety decreased, while total factor productivity remained stagnant. They argued that policy during this period did not help new activities; did not make assistance to firms conditional upon specified concrete goals (such as export performance); and did not provide clear indications to firms about when assistance would cease, thereby leaving alive the suggestion that it could continue indefinitely.

Without paying attention to the foregoing matters, it would become progressively more difficult to sustain the economy's expansion at the required rate, and the implicit compact—economic benefits in exchange for political quiescence—between the rulers and the ruled could unravel. This is not to suggest that purely political issues, such as the public's desire for democracy and the problem of presidential succession, might not have been important, indeed perhaps even the dominant, factors in the revolution of 2011. The point is that fundamental contradictions in the political-economic strategy were showing up and will have to be addressed by whatever regimes are in power during at least the next twenty or thirty years. To add to the problem, perceptions of inequities in the distribution of incomes were rising, and had been ignored by the authorities. Thus, despite impressive economic growth in 2005–2008, social and economic factors were fermenting a politically menacing brew beneath the surface. The mixture exploded in 2011 in the form of a massive uprising against the rule of President Mubarak.

3. If one had the temerity to try to sum up in a picture and a few numbers the critical reasons for Egypt's failure to perform to its economic potential over the last fifty years, they could be illustrated by figure 1 and the numbers quoted earlier for the contribution of TFP to Egypt's GDP growth.

The message is clear. *Egypt's investment rate was insufficient to expand the economy at a rate that would fully employ the labor force; the domestic savings rate fell short of even the inadequate investment rate; and institutional weaknesses inhibited productivity increases from compensating for the investment shortfalls.*

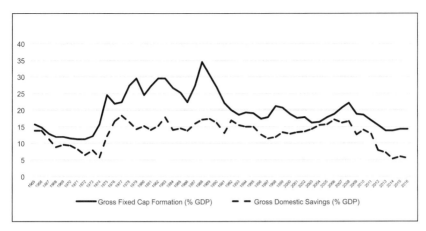

Figure 1. Investment and domestic savings, 1965–2016 (percent of GDP)
Source: World Bank, *World Development Indicators*

The persistent gap between investment and domestic savings also measures the extent to which Egypt relied on foreign savings to finance its investment and to cover its balance-of-payments deficits, which explains the continual piling up of external debt and the resulting exposure of the country to external political pressure. Of course, behind the savings–investment performance lie deeper institutional issues, such as matters of governance, the structure of incentives, the working of the bureaucracy and the commercial judicial system, implementation capacity, and the shortcomings of the education and training system.

4. What about future prospects? In view of the growth and age structure of the population and the approximate relationship between employment and GDP growth, Egypt's economy needs to grow at around 7 percent a year in real terms for at least the next two decades and probably longer in order to absorb the additions to the labor force and to reduce the rate of unemployment and underemployment from the past. This is particularly necessary in order to give the population, and especially the young, the possibility of fulfilling their capabilities and leading lives that they value.

The required GDP growth rate compares with a rate of about 4.7 percent that the country averaged over the fifty-year period between 1965 and 2016. The experience of fast-growing developing countries suggests that a sustained 7 percent growth rate is likely to require an investment rate in excess of 30 percent of GDP (compared with Egypt's 20 percent average of 1965–2016), and most likely even higher as the economy becomes more complex and has to produce more sophisticated goods and services. Moreover, if Egypt is to reduce its dependence on foreign savings and finance most of the investment from its own resources, the domestic savings rate would have to be of the order of 25–27 percent of GDP (allowing a manageable deficit on the external accounts). Raising the savings rate to this level could pose a stiff challenge, as Egypt's domestic rate of savings between 1965 and 2016 averaged barely 13.5 percent of GDP.

Seventh, while this might seem paradoxical in view of the shortcomings of past policies and economic performance that are discussed in this book, I would underscore that the most important message from Egypt's experience of the last fifty years is that one must not underestimate the country's resilience. Egypt has repeatedly surprised observers and confounded predictions of economic doom. As Hilmi Abdel Rahman, a former minister of planning who played a major role in devising economic strategies for the country, said: "Egypt will frequently not act on policy until the eleventh hour, but it *will* act. It would not have survived intact for more than five thousand years if it hadn't done this."

Consider some reasons for optimism. In 1947 the country had a population of some 19 million inhabitants; in 2016 the population of Greater Cairo alone was about that number. The *difference* between Egypt's present (2016) population of some 90 million and that in 1947 is equal to the *total* present-day population of the United Kingdom or France. These 90 million persons—four and a half times the number in 1947—have, on average, higher real incomes, are better fed, housed, clothed, educated, and connected to the rest of the world, and have longer life expectancies and much greater opportunities to fulfill their capabilities than their counterparts in 1947. Moreover, these improvements have taken place despite Egypt's being engaged in hostilities with Israel on a number of occasions and suffering an invasion by the United Kingdom and France. These facts attest to the strength of the Egyptian people and the resilience of the economy, and bear witness to the distance it has traversed and the obstacles it has overcome during the last seventy years.

If one has misgivings about Egypt's economic performance, the regret is for the country not performing to its potential. The reproach is that Egypt could have done better. If, say, South Korea and Taiwan, perched on the edge of Asia, destitute of natural resources, and rent for long periods by war (and in the case of South Korea, with its capital city occupied twice by enemy forces), could achieve so much so quickly, then it should not be impossible for Egypt, with its abundance of resources—to name but its strategic location, oil and gas deposits, fertile agriculture, myriads of tourist attractions, intellectual abilities and long tradition of learning, and large labor force—to achieve something comparable.[8]

In managing the future, policymakers cannot ignore the role and the weight of the past. Elements of continuity from earlier periods are pervasive. The Egyptian economy of today is in many respects the product of past molds. The capital stock of today in the productive sectors and the infrastructure are the result of past investments (in both good and bad projects); more importantly, the institutions, the administrative structure, the policy framework, the modes of production and organization, the vested interests, and the habits of thought and work are collectively an inheritance that defines many of the features of the economy today and colors much of its prospects. In shaping the future, policymakers will have to manage this legacy from the past.

The change in Egypt's economic future will not happen by itself. It will require conscious changes in many areas, but most importantly in people's attitudes and ways of thinking. The Holy Qur'an stresses this message: it says (8:53): "God never changes the favor He has bestowed on any people until they first change what is in themselves." This is reiterated (13:11): "God changes not the condition of a people until they (first) change what is in themselves." It is in the spirit of this injunction that this book seeks to identify some crucial economic challenges that confronted Egypt and discusses how politics and economics interacted to address them. Such a discussion might contribute to clarifying the course toward which changes in policymakers' attitudes and thinking might usefully be directed in the future.

1

The Political Economy of Reform: A Survey with Special Reference to Egypt

Central to the political economy of reform is the conflict of interests between economic actors in a society.[1] Changes in economic policies can drastically alter the distribution of winners and losers. A group that is in the winners' column has every incentive to resist being relegated to that of the losers. What makes policy reform particularly difficult in developing countries, including Egypt, is that the pre-reform group of economic winners has more often than not become such by virtue of its political strength, generally obtained through wealth or close association with centers of power, such as the monarchy, the military, or the religious establishment. It would be demanding too much of human nature to expect this group to willingly cede its economic privileges—turkeys do not readily vote for Christmas. For policies to be reformed, the built-in resistance of such interest groups has to be overcome. Various political-economy models and case studies of individual countries attempt an explanation. This chapter surveys and develops approaches that are most relevant to the political-economy experience of Egypt.

Following Haggard (2000, 22–39), these approaches can be roughly divided into two groups: one that focuses primarily on the role of interest groups, and the other that emphasizes the importance of institutional arrangements. In practice the distinction is not nearly so clear-cut and the conduct of economic reform, and especially the sustainability of reform policies, often requires a melding of these elements. Indeed, Williamson (1994a, 20–21) notes that "from a political standpoint, the most difficult part of a reform program is not introducing the reforms but sustaining them until they have a chance to bear fruit and thus generate political support from the potential beneficiaries."

The foregoing classification is not the only way of grouping different approaches. Roháč (2014), for instance, stresses two broad constraints on policymaking that could be used to classify the approaches: (a) the differences in incentives that voters, politicians, and bureaucrats face; and (b) the differences in the beliefs and mental models used by the public and the politicians. The discussion in this book largely follows the grouping proposed by Haggard.

Interest-group models emphasize the role of coalitions—how they can come together and how they can become influential enough to change the status quo. In order to do the latter, a pro-reform coalition has to be formed that can defeat the groups opposed to reform, or at least induce their acquiescence in the reforms. Such models have an impressive lineage, with Mancur Olson (1965, 1982) the best-known progenitor. Institution-focused models, on the other hand, emphasize the institutional and administrative restructuring to ensure that the economic reforms are efficient and have a better chance of surviving in the long run.

As Haggard points out, interest-group models face an important problem. These models can explain how a policy regime has come about after a struggle between different coalitions. If that policy regime has been in place for a substantial time, one might say that an equilibrium has been reached in that the coalitions have managed to optimize their political and economic strategies. Reform, however, is about policy *changes*. What would it take to upset the existing equilibrium and to change the dynamics between coalitions? If stakeholders are strong to begin with, how will their power be overturned? The best explanations in Egypt's experience emphasize the part played by crises and by the design of reform packages, especially their comprehensiveness, and the extent and speed of compensation. These issues have been of particular relevance to Egypt.

Interest Groups, Crises, and Economic Reforms

In Egypt's case, crises—military, political, and economic—have been crucial to empowering coalitions and triggering economic reforms that had a major effect on the economy. A few examples will illustrate the point.

On July 23, 1952 the Free Officers led a revolution and overthrew the monarchy. The principal motives behind the revolution were resentment against the corruption of the monarchy (also perceived as a major reason for the defeat in the 1948 war against Israel) and frustration with the failure of the politicians to rid the country of British occupation. The Free Officers did not have any well-defined economic philosophy or even a common political ideology (Nasser 1954; Vatikiotis 1961). They did, however, have a clear idea of who would be their foremost opponents—these would be the large landowners who formed the backbone of the former regime. The political and economic power of this coalition had to be broken, and new constituencies had to be created to support the revolutionary group. It was crucial to create these constituencies, because as Vatikiotis (1961, 218) notes, the Free Officers were an exclusively military group and "acceded to power without the active support of a single civilian group in Egyptian society."

The power of the landowning coalition was evident. In the parliament elected in 1950—the last before the Free Officers' revolution—landowners formed the mainstay of the regime, holding 63 percent of the seats (compared with only 14 percent by capitalists).[2] Before the 1952 land reform, a tiny elite of about eleven thousand landlords (0.4 percent of the total)[3] owned almost two million *feddan*s (34 percent of the cultivated land);[4] in fact, the two thousand largest landowners possessed nearly 20 percent of the agricultural land. At the other end of the spectrum, 2.6 million owners (94.3 percent) possessed 2.1 million feddans (35 percent) (Mabro 1974, 61, 73). However, once the army seized control of the country, the balance of power between the two competing coalitions—the Free Officers and the landowners—tilted decisively toward the former, and thus the existing equilibrium between the winners and losers could be altered.

The determination of the landowning faction in parliament to defend their privileges was made evident by their relentless opposition to any measure that tried to improve the distribution of land. For example, in 1945 a bill had been introduced that prohibited future acquisition of more than one hundred feddans of land. In 1950 another bill proposed breaking up, with adequate compensation, all holdings over fifty feddans. Another bill in 1950 provided that newly reclaimed agricultural land owned by the government should be sold only to peasants who owned less than two feddans. All these measures were decisively rejected by the parliament. "The most that could be wrung out of the landlord-dominated Parliament," notes Issawi (1954, 135) "was a law requiring owners of large estates to provide better housing and health and social services for their tenants." And what constituted better housing and other services lay in the eye of the landowner.

Similarly, a bill abolishing *waqf* (land and property gifted to an ecclesiastical or other corporation) had been introduced in 1937, but this also had been rejected by the parliament. (Family *waqf* amounted to nearly 600,000 feddans—about 11 percent of the cultivated area—and vested the use and enjoyment of the land in the heirs in perpetuity.)

The Free Officers recognized that the immediate order of business was to break the power of the landowning coalition. This led to the promulgation on September 9, 1952—barely a month and a half after the seizure of power—of a law on agrarian reform that limited individual ownership to two hundred feddans. The reforms had had a mixture of political, social, and economic objectives. First, it was to eliminate the power of the large landowners. Second, it aimed to improve the living conditions of the rural population. The reform measures did succeed in improving the condition of the tenants, whose disposable incomes increased as a result of the reduction in rents and by the greater security offered to their tenancy by the Agrarian Law.[5] Third, it was to stimulate the movement of capital from the agricultural to the industrial sector by discouraging further land purchases and by permitting landlords to invest the government bonds (with which they had been compensated) in approved industrial enterprises. Fourth, it was to raise agricultural output, in the belief that an owner would put more resources into improving the land than would a tenant.

Of the stated objectives, the first was crucial. The reform measures stripped the rich landowners and contributed to ending the power that the class formerly possessed, and stopped it from obstructing other policies that the revolutionaries might want to implement. Writes Mabro (1974, 56), "The political implications did not escape the civilian Prime Minister, Ali Maher, a man of the past, who objected to the [agrarian reform] project and was asked to resign."

This early move by the revolutionary government found support not only in Egypt, but also abroad. The United States moved quickly to establish relations with the Free Officers. Roussillon (1998, 2:354) states that the Americans were the first to be notified that the coup was imminent and "taking into account the discreet contacts made with the officers through their representatives, in July 1952 they had many reasons to think that 'their men' had seized power on the banks of the Nile." He notes that United States aid to Egypt within the framework of Point Four (the forerunner of today's USAID) "shot up from less than $6 million before 1952 to $40 million only a few weeks after the coup, and Dean Acheson, the U.S. Secretary of State, asserted that Egypt could henceforth count on the United States' 'active friendship.'" The honeymoon hit turbulence in 1955 after Egypt's purchase of weapons from Czechoslovakia.

The British moved more cautiously. However, based on the messages from their ambassadors (Jefferson Caffery of the United States and Sir Ralph Stevenson of Britain), both countries were in favor of the land reform. Indeed, Gordon (1996, 166) reports that Winston Churchill scribbled "Down with the Pashas, Up with the Fellahin" on a note to Anthony Eden and dispatched experts to advise the Egyptians.

Another crisis, another major set of reforms. In 1956, Britain, France, and Israel attacked Egypt following President Gamal Abd al-Nasser's nationalization of the Suez Canal. Because of these hostilities, the coalition of British and French interests in Egypt could be defined as enemies of the country and thus easily be overcome; British and French assets in the country consequently were sequestrated.[6] Joan Nelson (1990, 3–32, 321–362) analyzed the politics of reforms between 1979 and 1988 in a sample of nineteen countries in Latin America, Asia, and Africa and found that it had been easier to introduce reforms in countries and periods in which the opposition was discredited, disorganized, or repressed. The changes in Egypt's economic framework in 1956 conformed to this finding.

The Suez crisis of 1956 also triggered a fundamental change in Egypt's political-economy environment. Egypt's external policies tilted toward the Soviet bloc, with collateral effects on the economy. The principal impact of the crisis was a drastic increase in the role of the government in economic matters and a vigorous move to "Egyptianize" the main arteries of the national economy.

These matters are discussed further in chapter 4. For our immediate purpose, it is sufficient to note that these changes included the sequestration of British and French assets; the extension of nationalization to other sectors of the economy; and the introduction of comprehensive economic planning. Egypt's politics began to shift from the West toward the Communist Bloc; economic management started to move away from relying on the private sector; and state intervention and influence set about reshaping the economic landscape. The power of the British/French coalition as well as that of the Egyptian private sector was thus progressively overcome, and the country's economic structure came to be dominated by domestic public-sector organizations.

Yet another instance of a crisis strengthening the hands of one group and enabling it to effect substantive economic reforms occurred after the Egypt–Israel war of October 1973. Egypt's economic situation in the months leading up to the war and after had become dire. GDP growth had dropped to about 3 percent in 1973. Oil prices had fallen, and with the resulting fall in revenues, the deficits in both the budget and the balance of payments increased sharply. The external situation was made even worse by the requirements of servicing the foreign debt, especially as the country had resorted to financing earlier deficits through bank credit facilities that had an average maturity of only 180 days. The overall budgetary deficit in 1974 was estimated at 17 percent of GNP (Gross National Product), with much of the financing borrowed either from abroad or from the domestic banking system. This inevitably had a major impact on the money supply and domestic liquidity, and fueled inflation. A detailed description of the economic situation in 1973 and 1974 is provided in chapter 5.

These developments made it clear that Egypt could not continue with a "business as usual" approach to economic policy. In April 1974, President Sadat outlined a new direction in the *October Paper* that was presented to the People's Assembly. This document laid out the basis for a new strategy, in which the public sector would be responsible for implementing projects that other sectors would not or could not undertake, and for providing essential services, while the production of most goods and services would be the responsibility of the private sector. The new strategy has come to be known as the *infitah* or "open-door strategy." While the full effects of, and indeed the motivation behind, the strategy have been much debated (see chapter 5), the new direction clearly challenged the prevailing orthodoxy of Arab socialism.

Of course a crisis is not essential to enable one coalition to distort economic policies in its favor to the detriment of even a much larger group. Such outcomes can also be created by differences in the organizing ability of the coalitions and the vigor with which they pursue their aims.

A standard example is provided by international trade theory. Egyptian producers would benefit from tariffs on imports because they would be able to sell their products domestically at higher than international prices; however, Egyptian consumers would benefit from lower prices if such tariffs were not imposed. The grounds for a clash between the rival interest groups were clearly demarcated. Whether the pro-tariff or the anti-tariff prevails depends on the political weight of the respective groups and the strength with which they are able to press their demands in the political process. Crucial ingredients in this strength are the ability and incentive to organize and to raise the finance necessary for effective lobbying. However, "consumers" are a very large and ill-defined group scattered all over the country, and thus difficult to organize into a coherent coalition. Moreover, as Frey (1985, 146) points out, "Protection constitutes a public good affecting all the members of a particular economic sector or occupation. There is an incentive not to join the interest group or to contribute financially, because one may profit from the outcome by free-riding [that is, benefiting from an activity without paying for it]." As against this, compared with the number of consumers, industries or importers that benefit from the higher prices constitute a minuscule group; they would thus be much easier to organize and also have a strong incentive to contribute financially to a lobbying effort because the benefits from import restriction would be concentrated in a very small number.

The tariff example is but one instance of a wider issue. Pareto put it in more general terms.

> In order to explain how those who champion protection make themselves heard so easily, it is necessary to add a consideration that applies to social movements generally. . . . If a certain measure *A* is the case of a loss of one franc to each of a thousand persons, and of a thousand franc gain to one individual, the latter will expend a great deal of energy, whereas the former will resist weakly; and it is likely that, in the end, the person who is attempting to secure the thousand francs via *A* will be successful.
>
> A protectionist measure provides large benefits to a small number of people, and causes a very great number of consumers a slight loss. This circumstance makes it easier to put a protectionist measure into practice. (Pareto 1927, 379–80)[7]

Military and Economic Crises

Although in Egypt revolutionary and military crises have paved the way to drastic restructurings of the economy, a crisis does not necessarily require bloodletting. On many occasions economic crises have changed the dynamic between coalitions and compelled the acceptance of major policy changes.

Why would it take a crisis to induce reform? An early, and still perhaps the most influential, answer was provided by Olson (1965, and especially 1982). He argued that economic performance created powerful groups who would resist reform policies that might impair their interests. Their strength would enable them to block socially desirable reforms. This would freeze the status quo, making society, in Olson's term, "sclerotic." If reform required overturning the power of such groups, something drastic would have to occur to break their hold. This could be a political disaster for which the group could be held culpable—such as the Egyptian monarchy being held responsible for the country's defeat in Palestine. Or it could be economic deterioration of such a magnitude that a sufficient number of groups decided that the country could not continue with "business as usual" and that a different set of economic policies had to be tried. This section of the book concentrates on the role of economic crises in inducing reform; other explanations have also been suggested, and Drazen (2000, 44–54) elaborates a discussion of a number of them.

Different economic situations have been proposed as crises that triggered reform—for example, Krueger (1992, 81–2) notes that "the majority of policy reforms are initiated in what are perceived as crisis situations," and identifies them as taking two forms. The first, and which she judges to be the more frequent, is when a country finds it difficult to meet its foreign exchange obligations. The second occurs when the rate of inflation reaches unacceptable levels. Other writers add different crisis situations, but foreign exchange dearth and raging inflation figure in all the lists; see, for example, Bruno and Easterly (1996), Lora (1998), Drazen and Easterly (1999), and the several studies of individual countries edited by Bhagwati and Krueger in the National Bureau of Economic Research's project on "Foreign Trade Regimes and Economic Development;" the volume on Egypt is Hansen and Nashashibi (1975).

But the literature cautions us that an economic crisis is defined not simply by the fact that an economic variable is present, but critically by the degree to which it is present. "A first problem is to determine what is, and what is not, [an economic] crisis," writes Krueger (1993, 124), and goes on to say, "No satisfactory answer has yet been given: rates of inflation that in one country provoke immediate policy responses are not even criticized in other countries, and the absence of critical goods such as medicines and petroleum has been withstood for years in some countries, while inducing an immediate response in others." This book is not the place to delve into the complexities of the issue, but we must note two critical factors that have emerged from the debate and are most relevant to the Egyptian case.

First, Krueger (1993, 126) concludes that successful reform in the face of deteriorating economic conditions requires a government that "has the political resources to undertake action *and the technocratic support to take appropriate actions.*[8] Second, after examining a host of studies, Drazen (2000, 445) concludes there needs to be an *extreme* deterioration of the status quo before a reform is adopted that is, "things need to get *very* bad, and not just bad, to induce reform."

In the political-economy literature, "crisis" is generally measured by the value of some macroeconomic indicators matched against a comparator; for example, real per capita income or inflation in year $t + y$ compared with that in year t. "Reform" is gauged by a change either in the selected macroeconomic indicators or in policy variables.

Thus, Bruno and Easterly (1996) defined a crisis rate of inflation as that above 40 percent annually for two or more years (that is, a severe deterioration), and examined the effects on growth and inflation in a large number of countries in subsequent years. Their study found that growth dropped sharply during a crisis caused by high inflation and rose above the pre-crisis level after inflation had been brought down. They also found that high-inflation countries *were* motivated to undertake reforms and they subsequently kept inflation below the 40 percent threshold. Drazen and Easterly (1999) widened the foregoing study by examining the inflation experience of 123 countries between 1953 and 1996, considering more variables, and using alternative levels of inflation to define a crisis. Their results echoed those of Bruno and Easterly and supported the view that sustained high inflation was likely to beget reform.

The importance of crises in stimulating policy reforms is not confined to Egypt. An exercise by Lora (1998) for the Inter-American Development Bank is succinctly described in Drazen (2000, 453–54), and further elaborated in Lora and Olivera (2004). Lora developed policy indices for trade reform; financial system reform; tax reform; privatization; and labor market reform for nineteen Latin American and Caribbean countries over the period 1985–95. He then examined a number of political and economic factors that might lead to a reform, such as the time in office of a government; compensation mechanisms for losers in the reforms; capital flows; and economic crisis. The last was measured by macroeconomic indicators, such as the gap between real per capita income and its previous highest level, negative growth, high or variable inflation, and government budget deficits. The study considered the reforms taken individually as well as overall structural reform, the last being measured as an average of the five individual reform indices.

Lora found that of all the factors he examined, the most important factor for reform was a crisis. For the total index, the best crisis indicator was how far per capita income had fallen from its peak. The individual reform indicators reacted to different metrics; for example, trade and labor market reforms were especially sensitive to negative GDP growth, while financial sector reform was most responsive to the level and variability of inflation. Conversely, Lora found that privatization and tax reform were only weakly related to a crisis, even a fiscal crisis. The purely political variables that Lora used did not much affect the reform indicators.

The foregoing studies are useful in tracing connections between economic reforms and variables that are largely economic in nature. However, each country has its own institutions and particular historical experience. I suspect that for Egypt the purely political factors might carry more weight than they did in Lora's study.

Thus, the Egyptian agrarian reform followed a military coup (that is, a political crisis) and the necessity for the coup's members to break the power of the opposition and to build up a constituency for the revolutionaries. The nationalizations and sequestrations of British and French assets in 1956 followed the invasion of Egypt (a political crisis) by the United Kingdom and France and strengthened the government's role in the economy, which, down the road, led to large-scale nationalizations and the move toward "Arab socialism." Conversely, the deteriorating economic and mounting external debt situation in the 1980s did not compel the government to introduce major reforms; these were introduced in the 1990s following Egypt's political decision to participate in the war with Iraq. The participation responded to a political decision by the United States and other Western donors to offer a compensation package of generous debt write-offs and economic assistance to induce countries to join the anti-Saddam Hussein campaign.

After surveying a number of studies, Drazen (2000, 454) concludes that "empirically, crisis is important in inducing or facilitating reform." This conclusion, however, should be read in conjunction with his caveat that "much work remains to be done on matching of theory and actual experience."

Political Institutions and Policy Reform

The second broad approach to the political economy of reform looks at the incentives that policymakers face within the political framework in which they operate. This family of models examines questions such as whether reforms are more likely under authoritarian governments or democracies. They also investigate the characteristics of electoral rules, the structure of political parties, the number of "veto gates" in the system, whether the ruling party in a parliamentary system has a dominant majority or is part of a coalition, the extent of power accorded to the president or the prime minister, and so on.

For a number of reasons, this approach may be more useful for discussing the sustainability rather than the initiation of economic reforms in Egypt. First, theoretical or a priori arguments can be produced in favor of both democracy and authoritarianism as an engine of reform. Second, the large number of empirical case studies has thrown up no convincing or definitive relation one way or the other; for a survey see Maraval (1997). Several reviews have argued that authoritarian regimes are more likely to be successful reformers, because they can override the power of interest groups that had held back reforms in the past—instances adduced include China, South Korea, Taiwan, Hong Kong, and Singapore. But an equally large number of reviews point to instances where authoritarianism has only created crony capitalism or sclerotic bureaucracies—instances cited include Russia, Haiti, Zaire, North Korea, and Romania.

The advocates of democracy rely on the argument that this system of government increases competition and increases the number of voices to which policymakers must listen and to whose interests they must cater (Haggard 2000, 39). However, after setting aside the a priori arguments and examining the data, Alesina et al. (1996) show that, on average, the economic growth performance under dictatorships and democracies is indistinguishable. The worst economic outcomes, compared with both established democracies and dictatorships, occur in countries that are transiting to democracy (Haggard and Kaufman 1992), because they show the greatest amount of instability and consequently discourage investment and growth.

Third, for Egypt in the period from 1952 to 2011 this approach is of limited relevance, because for the entire period the country was under only three regimes, all of them authoritarian. The more interesting questions, therefore, concern the attitudes of the incumbent president and his principal advisers to economic reforms and the capability of the ministers and bureaucrats to implement them. Three broad issues are crucial to shaping these attitudes: (a) the pace of reform; (b) the content of reform (especially which groups will benefit and which will be disadvantaged); and (c) the design of the compensation package (especially its size, its distribution among different groups, and its speed of delivery).

The Pace of Reform: "Big Bang" versus Gradualism

An issue that frequently comes up in the discussions of policymakers as well as in the literature on the political economy of policy reforms is the pace of reform. Would it be better to institute reforms simultaneously in several sectors of the economy (the "Big Bang" approach), or would it be better to introduce reforms gradually and test their acceptability before moving on to further reforms? Theoretical arguments have been advanced for each of these approaches. Both sides can claim successes and concede failures in practice, and the empirical studies do not confer a decisive victory on either strategy.

Four principal ideas underlie the "Big Bang" approach. First, an economy functions as an interaction of different sectors; therefore acting on several of them simultaneously will make a policy package more efficient because the reforms will reinforce each other.

Second, the most common danger with implementing reforms is that the government will lose heart before the policies begin to take effect. Advocates of the "Big Bang" approach argue that simultaneously undertaking a wide range of policies is more likely to bind the government to the strategy, because it will have committed itself to too many areas to back down without seriously damaging its credibility. Thus the "Big Bang" approach is more likely to entrench the reform process and to make it sustainable.

Third, proponents of the "Big Bang" strategy believe that it avoids another weakness of the gradualist approach. The latter, by introducing reforms in a piecemeal manner, potentially creates several stages with different distributions of winners and losers, and thus offers incentives to the winners at each stage to resist further reform. Hellman (1998) uses the experience of reforms in the previously communist countries to point out that further reform can then be blocked not by those who lost from changes in the initial situation, but from those who gained from the partial reform and the inefficiencies in the economy that were left uncorrected (and were presumably to be corrected in subsequent stages of the reform). This group would be concerned that the subsequent corrections would eliminate the opportunities of capturing economic rents (unearned profits).[9] A step-by-step introduction of reforms would create multiple stages at which different interest groups could mobilize opposition. Milton and Rose Friedman in *Tyranny of the Status Quo* similarly urged political leaders favoring reform to act quickly after election to counter the inevitable closing of ranks of people threatened by change (Friedman and Friedman 1984). This line of thought thus also supports the idea of doing as complete a set of reforms as quickly as possible.

Fourth, champions of the "do all reforms as soon as possible" approach argue that partial reforms often fail to provide sufficient clarity to economic agents. Employers can be deterred from creating permanent jobs because they are left uncertain whether they will be able to shed labor if they have to and what this would cost. Investors hold back because they are uncertain about what will be even the medium-term shape of the regulatory environment. "We don't know when the other shoe will drop and on whom it will land," is how an Egyptian businessmen responded to a World Bank questionnaire on the investment climate. Thus, for the proponents of the "Big Bang" approach, the foregoing difficulties taken together provide compelling reasons for getting the reform process over and done with as soon as possible.

So much for the essence of the theory; it is worth looking at arguments that have held special appeal to practitioners. The case for a swift and comprehensive reform is cogently argued by, among others, a former minister of finance of New Zealand, Roger Douglas, drawing on the experience of the very successful reforms carried out by New Zealand after 1984. Krueger (1992, 115) notes that the program was so successful that it came to be known as "Rogernomics."

Douglas (1990, 2–6) argues that the authorities should not try to advance one step at a time; otherwise interest groups that oppose the reform will have time to mobilize and drag down the government. He asserts that "speed is essential; it is impossible to go too fast. Even at maximum speed, the total program will take some years to implement, and the short-term trade-off costs start from Day One."

Douglas reiterates that the basic reason for urging speed is that the economy is an interlinked mechanism, and acting simultaneously on a wide range of structural reforms will improve the quality of the interactions within the whole. This will help win wider public acceptance of the reform. He argues that in order to win public acceptance, the policymaker has to demonstrate that opportunities for people as a whole are being improved, while the most vulnerable groups in the community are protected. The important point is that the public will accept short-term pain if the costs and benefits are seen to be shared "with visible fairness across the community as a whole."

Douglas makes an important argument about mobilizing support, even from coalitions that initially oppose the reform. *Before* the privileges of a protected sector have been removed, it will tend to see structural change as a threat that has to be opposed. However, *after* the government has removed the group's privileges and demonstrated credibly that they will not be restored, that group will resent the privileges that still accrue to other groups and which boost its own costs, because "wherever a group manages to hold onto a privilege, an avoidable cost is imposed on those who are facing up to an adjustment process." The de-privileged group will then lobby to remove the privileges of groups that still possess them, and thus become an ally of the government in the reform process. The crucial ingredients, in Douglas's view, are speed and the government's credibility, procured by "an unwavering consistency in serving medium-term objectives."

The gradualist approach, on the other hand, rests on the idea that the reform process can only be sustained if there is a "buy-in" by the major stakeholders. "Sustainability" is the exception rather than the rule. Krueger (1993, 132) notes that "more countries have experienced a reversion to their earlier economic difficulties within two or three years after the beginning of a reform program than have successfully entered a period of long-term improvement in economic performance." Moving slowly, at least in the earlier stages of policy reform, gives the authorities the opportunity both to persuade stakeholders by pointing to the successes obtained in the area of reform and to reassure them by being able to pull back on tactics that have not worked. It would be difficult to do this if the government were acting simultaneously all across the economy. A World Bank minute reported an Egyptian minister defending his country's gradualist approach with the words, "You do not test the depth of the Nile with both feet."

Generalizations have proved difficult because the viability of either of these approaches depends on too many factors, in particular: the initial situation, that is, how much economic pressure the country is under; which groups most affect the economic decision-making process; the technical strength of, and the political backing received by the economic team; whether the incentive system has created groups that would give continuity to economic policy; the resources that can be conjured up to cushion the almost inevitable austerity at the start of the reform program; and how long the economy can withstand shocks to its interdependence with other economies.

Moreover, a government is not a monolithic unit.[10] Even when different cabinet members agree on a common objective, for example, accelerating the GDP growth rate, they may hold substantially different opinions regarding the means of attaining the objective. One faction is usually not sufficiently dominant in cabinet to determine policy outcomes in all areas; if it were, policies would be much more consistent and coherent than is actually the case. Chapter 5 describes in some detail the differences between the approaches of Egypt's Ministry of Economy and Ministry of Finance to the policy reforms proposed by the International Monetary Fund in 1976, and the tactics that they employed in the cabinet to ensure the triumph of their views. The gap between the methods supported by the two ministries turned out to be unbridgeable, even though they both agreed on the ends.

A complicating factor is that policymakers can and do change their policy preferences depending upon their shifting views of the country's circumstances or their assessments of what would be best for the survival of the regime. Such "time inconsistency," as it is known in the literature, can be perfectly logical. As Keynes is famously reported to have said, "When the facts change, I change my mind. What do you do, sir?" Let me offer an example from Egypt's experience to illustrate the point.

A key issue in Egypt's approach to economic development concerns the respective roles of the public and private sectors. Ever since the nationalizations after 1956 (and especially from 1961), the public sector's role had metamorphosed from supporting the private sector to dominating the economy. However, in a far-reaching program of reforms starting in 1991, Egypt began to tilt the balance back toward the private sector.

Some leading policymakers viewed the change in the relative roles of the public and private sectors as a logical response to the stage of Egypt's development and the state of the international economy. Kamal al-Ganzoury (minister of planning 1982–85, deputy prime minister 1985–96, prime minister 1996–99 and 2013) regarded the change as a pragmatic response to evolving conditions; it was important not to be blinkered by ideology, but to respond in a pragmatic manner to what was best for the economy in a given situation. From 1956 and especially immediately after the 1973 war, the main task facing the Egyptian economy was the building or rebuilding of a large amount of infrastructure. The domestic private sector did not have the financial or human resources to undertake this task (could the Egyptian private sector have run and maintained the Suez Canal after its nationalization, or built the High Dam?). Moreover, in view of the uncertain Middle East situation, foreign investors were chary of committing the required resources. The challenges, therefore, had to be met by the Egyptian public sector.

Three major changes had occurred since the 1990s. First, much of the infrastructure had been built and the more urgent challenge for the country was to create productive jobs for the rapidly expanding labor force. This private enterprise could do more efficiently than the public sector. Second, the private sector was now also much bigger and able to mobilize sizable amounts of capital; given the proper economic incentives and legal safeguards, it could now undertake large projects both in the infrastructure and in the directly productive sectors. Third, the more stable situation in the Middle East had reassured foreign investors. In order to take advantage of these changes, Egypt had to create an environment that would be more friendly for the private sector, both domestic and international. In Ganzoury's view, therefore, the redirection of strategy was necessary to making the Egyptian economy viable for the twenty-first century.

Dr. Ganzoury emphasized that the government was not going to disappear from the economy—the strategy called for a recalibration of the government's role, not its extinction. The revised emphases in its functions in fact made its role much more important. In addition to the crucial functions of providing internal and external security and managing the administration of the country, the government had the responsibilities of funding education and health, providing infrastructure (by itself or in public–private partnerships), dispensing justice, managing externalities, regulating monopolies and ensuring a level playing field for private enterprises, developing the lagging regions of the country, protecting the most vulnerable elements in society, and ensuring that the distribution of incomes did not exceed bounds that would create dangerous social tensions. The government was also best placed to take a holistic view of the economy, and thus to judge whether regulations were light or onerous; taxes competitive or punitive; incentives insufficient, excessive, or just.

Ganzoury's view was that decisions in many sectors could be taken only by the government, because those taken by a profit-maximizing private entity might not be optimal for society. For example, in the vital electricity sector, it was important to maintain a certain amount of excess capacity, because disruptions caused by electricity shortages cost the economy much more than maintaining the excess capacity. But a profit-driven private sector would have no incentive to create excess capacity. Similarly, even when the financial sector was privatized, major decisions concerning the size of banks and the activities that they could engage in would have to be taken by the government. This would help avoid the "too big to fail" syndrome, in which very large financial institutions could not be allowed to fail because of the immense collateral damage that their failure might inflict on the rest of the economy, and consequently these institutions would have to be bailed out using taxpayer money. Moreover, in order to avoid financial crises, the government would have to set banks' capital requirements far above what these profit-seeking institutions might aim at if they were left unregulated. In the transport sector, the government was best placed to consider the needs of the country's security and its economy to strike the balance between air, road, river, and rail transport. The government also had the crucial responsibility of perfecting the "software" of development: strengthening institutions, monitoring incentives, maintaining equity, and reinforcing governance to ensure that the private-sector economy performed in a manner that was both efficient and socially responsible. The issue was thus not of the government's withering away, but of ensuring that it made good decisions.

Returning to the choice between a "Big Bang" and a gradualist approach, the strategy adopted (especially in an authoritarian regime) might simply reflect the personality and preferences of the political leader. Having described Douglas's advocacy of a "Big Bang" approach, it would only be fair to put the case for the gradualist side, especially as for several decades this has been the preferred route for Egypt. Here I will provide only a very brief outline of President Mubarak's explanation of his views; the reader is referred to chapter 6 for a fuller exposition extracted from my minutes of his meeting with James Wolfensohn, the president of the World Bank.

President Mubarak said that he favored a "step-by-step" approach. He offered two reasons in support of the strategy. First, he said that people had to be carefully prepared to accept the reforms, and this required time. One could not simply ram reforms down the throats of people who were living close to the margin of subsistence, especially as reforms often initially require a significant amount of belt-tightening. The government had to persuade people that the alternatives were inevitable and worse. The government also had the responsibility of creating a safety net for the most vulnerable members of society who would be impacted by the reforms—even the most efficiency-obsessed government had to recognize the political wisdom and the humanity of tempering the wind to the shorn lamb.

The president credited the gradualist approach for his success in pushing through reforms that were much more stringent than those attempted in 1977 by President Sadat. Moreover, the blowback against President Sadat's reforms had caused the entire package to be annulled, and the public had absorbed the unfortunate lesson that if it resisted, the government would back down. This had not only set back reforms in 1977; it had also made it virtually impossible to undertake them for several years thereafter.

The president's second reason for favoring a gradualist approach was that it did not require an all-or-nothing package. The government could introduce a set of policies, and if they "stuck," then the government could add another policy or two. If the public resisted, it was much easier with the step-by-step approach to identify which policies the public had found the most unpalatable, and to modify only them. With a "Big Bang" strategy, that is, when a host of reforms were introduced simultaneously, the set of reforms tended to be viewed as a unit, and so if it were resisted, the entire parcel would have to be scrapped. This is what had happened with President Sadat in 1977.

Mubarak's cautious attitude conditioned his officials' approach to policy reform. More than one Egyptian minister confided that Egyptian policymakers follow a precautionary principle: if you cannot be confident of the results, do not experiment. And since it is in the nature of economics that one cannot offer precise and infallible assurances of the outcomes of reform policies, the evidential burden on the advocates of change becomes too great and thus the bias of Egyptian policymakers tends to favor the status quo. Egyptian policymakers gamble on economic transformations only if there is little alternative. This might help to explain why policymakers generally accepted reforms only in response to a crisis.

Moreover, knowing that the United States would be reluctant to risk threats to Egypt's stability enabled ministers to ward off pressures for policy change by cloaking their defense of the status quo in the mantle of national security. The resistance became particularly strong after the 1977 riots (described later). Ali Lotfi (a former prime minister) said that whenever a discussion on rationalizing the subsidy system came up in cabinet, "Up would go the Minister of Interior's hand and he would insist that he could not be responsible for the security situation in such circumstances." This sufficed to snuff out any debate.[11]

While one might feel that Egyptian policymakers could have acted with greater urgency, one must remember an important asymmetry between their fate and the results for the counselors from abroad. If the program imposed excessive austerity on the country, Egypt's policymakers would have to face the music; this could take the form of sacking by the president or perhaps stoning by an incensed populace. The counselors, on the other hand, would simply go off to ply their trade in Tunisia, Turkey, or Timbuktu.

That Egyptian officials had had the same thoughts is not mere speculation. During the 1977 bread riots, Wagih Shindy, at the time a deputy minister in the Ministry of Economy, and I drove through the parts of Cairo that had been the worst affected. While viewing the burnt buses, the demolished government buildings, the shattered glass that was everywhere, and inhaling the stench of teargas that still hung in the air, Shindy kept repeating, "See what those *boys* have done!" It is almost impossible to convey the anger and loathing that was expressed in the word "boys." He described a meeting of undersecretaries of the economic ministries that had taken place a day earlier at which everyone present had lamented that Egypt's fate had come to rest in the hands of a group of inexperienced youths from the IMF who could unwittingly destabilize the country, but who would neither individually nor collectively pay any price for their mistakes.

Shindy and his colleagues complained that the Fund's policy prescriptions were merely lifted from elementary textbooks that assumed an ideal economic world, and that its staff members on the mission to Egypt were entirely innocent of any real-world political-economy experience. "Have these 30-something year-olds ever functioned in roles that acquaint a policymaker with the full range of governmental work and the political constraints within which economic policies must be devised?" was in effect the rhetorical question they asked. Heikal (1983, 90) and Sadowski (1991, 155, 353n45) describe the "Dickie memorandum" outlining the IMF's conditions, the acceptance of which led to the riots.[12] (See also Tignor 2016, 138.)

In fairness to Egyptian ministers, I must point out that it was not unknown for the president to possess a hotchpotch of irreconcilable instincts on economic issues, and in the country's extremely centralized regimes since 1952, inconsistent aims or policies could be decreed or suggested (and the "suggestion" would have the force of a command) by the president, who would in effect be asking for a square circle. The ministers and the bureaucracy were then left with no choice but to construct the squarest circles that their ingenuity was able to devise in the circumstances.

President Mubarak was not alone in emphasizing the importance of convincing the public that the government would carry out its announced policies. President Chung-Hee Park, the initiator of South Korea's economic miracle, also made sure that announced policies were carried out. Policies were implemented through a rigorous structure of rewards and punishments that included compulsion and administrative discretion. The result was a sharp increase in the public's perception that the government meant what it said. A major study of how South Korean businessmen perceived the firmness of the government's resolution found that only 20.4 percent of the respondents considered that under Syngman Rhee (the previous president) decisions were "always implemented" or "almost always implemented." In the Park period the comparable figure was 94.8 percent (Jones and SaKong 1980, 136–37 and table 22). This shift in perception made it much easier for the Park government to execute its policies without having to apply extreme measures.

The foregoing comments underline the importance of a government's rigorously carrying through its announced policies. They do not, however, demonstrate that these policies must necessarily be carried out slowly or in a piecemeal fashion. President Park's regime was distinguished not only for the firmness with which it adhered to its declared policies, but also for the speed with which they were implemented.

The overriding lesson from the foregoing discussion is that there is no unique approach to implementing a successful program of structural economic reform. The literature, however, emphasizes that indispensable constituents of a program's success are a strong and visible government commitment and a general perception that the pains and gains under the program are shared in a fair manner. It is also very helpful to provide a cushion to protect the basic needs of the most vulnerable elements of society, and to ensure that the public believes that the compensation package is adequate and will indeed be delivered quickly.

"Tragedy of the Commons" and the Impact on the Environment

The political economy of Egypt highlights other outcomes that reflect the power politics of self-interest versus the collective (social) interest. Public resources are vulnerable to the familiar "tragedy of the commons" problem. Where there are no property rights over a resource, individual users have an inducement to independently maximize their use of that resource. There is therefore an incentive for individuals to use the resource beyond limits that are justified by the sustainability of the system. This overuse can lead to a deterioration or destruction of the resource, making its benefits unavailable to all users—the unregulated pursuit of private profit can and often does lead to a substantial social loss.

A classic case is the discharge of chemical waste into the Nile by the numerous factories situated along the river. This behavior on the part of powerful industrial groups renders Nile water impotable without being treated (so consumers have to bear the costs associated with the treatment), reduces the catch and increases the cost of production of downstream fisheries (so fishermen have to spend much more time on the water to catch a given amount of fish), and increases the possibility of spreading gastrointestinal and other illnesses.

Such outcomes are not limited to the Nile. A study for USAID (PRIDE 1994, 1:III–7) estimated that industry and hospitals in Cairo alone produced up to 65,000 tons annually of hazardous and infection wastes that received no special management but were simply dumped. The study (1994, 2:D–28) also estimated that because of exposure to lead from smelters in Cairo, an average of 4.25 IQ points was lost per child, and that more than eleven thousand heart attacks and premature deaths could be prevented annually in older adults if the blood lead levels in Cairo were reduced to those in the United States.

A report by the World Bank (2002) estimated the damage cost of environmental degradation in 1999 at up to 6.4 percent of GDP. Sarraf (2004) found that as a share of GDP this was about two times higher than in high-income countries and, indeed, substantially higher than in other developing countries in the region.[13]

Policies for dealing with the tragedy of the commons are well known. If the situation is one in which property rights can be assigned, they should be clarified and enforced. The owner of those rights will take steps to limit the usage of the resource at a sustainable level by imposing a suitable charge. In cases in which private ownership is not feasible, such as the Nile waters or the streets in which garbage is dumped or the air that is polluted by the emission of lead particles, an agent (such as the state) with the power to coerce users of the resource to pay an appropriate tax or fee would prevent the overutilization of the resource. The proceeds of the tax or fee would also provide finance for investing in maintaining or expanding the resource, which the private user of a public resource has no incentive to do. No such policy has been enforced. It is a measure of the political strength of groups engaged in the degradation of the Egyptian environment that they are permitted to inflict major health and economic damage with impunity.

The Costs and Benefits of Policy Reforms

Attempts have been made to estimate the costs and benefits of policy reform. In view of the difficulty of controlling for all factors that are involved, conclusions cannot be definitive. Moreover, the estimates relate only to economic, and not to political, costs. Even where economic costs are concerned, estimates of the costs and benefits of reform policies undertaken simultaneously in several parts of the economy are more difficult to compute and will be less secure than measures for particular sectors. It might, therefore, be useful to examine some results for more restricted areas of the economy.

The sector that has received the greatest amount of attention regarding the costs and benefits of reform policies is that of external trade—in particular, the benefits and the adjustment costs likely to result from trade liberalization.[14] These investigations looked at this problem from a number of angles—the trade sector as a whole, economy-wide levels of employment, the percentage of the labor force that might have to change occupations as a result of the reforms, the impact on particular industries,[15] the costs of capital equipment becoming idle during the adjustment period, and so on.

Since the methodologies used differ from study to study, the estimates span a very wide range. Depending upon the assumptions—concerning, inter alia, the number of jobs lost compared with the normal amount of job turnover in the economy, the length of unemployment, the cost of capital idled by the reforms during the period of adjustment, the discount rate used to compute present values of costs and benefits—the benefit–cost ratios range from 1.3 for iron and steel (Mutti 1978) to 153 for footwear (Takacs and Winters 1991). Matusz and Tarr sum up their review of the studies as follows:

> In studies where such comparisons are possible, it seems to be the case that each dollar of adjustment cost is associated with several dollars' worth of efficiency gains. . . . [A]djustment costs are the largest in the period immediately after the implementation of reforms, disappearing after a period of one to five years. By contrast, the efficiency gains of liberalization grow over time and continue indefinitely. (Matusz and Tarr 2000, 381–82)

However, given that with only a minor tweaking of the assumptions, Matusz and Tarr (2000, 381n21) can raise the Takacs and Winters benefit–cost ratio to 2193 (!) suggests that some estimates can be far from robust, and that their acceptance should be garnished with the proverbial pinch of salt.

If the effects of policy reforms are generally positive, why have so many countries, including Egypt, been reluctant to embrace them wholeheartedly? Banerjee (2000, 58) provides the best response: "Reforms necessarily involve cobbling together a package that is only part economics. . . . The rest of it is part institutional design, part public relations, part rhetoric. A successful reform involves coming up with the right combination of all these things in the context of the particular country."

Given the diversity of political, social, economic, and institutional conditions between countries, it would be futile to search for an unequivocal, universal answer. The empirical literature does, however, suggest some recurring issues that impact on policymakers' decisions.

Four issues appear to be the most critical.

1. *Disjunction between the timing of the costs and the benefits from reform.*
   Most of the cost of adjustment will have to be borne immediately, while the benefits could take perhaps two years or even more to make their full appearance. As Rodrik (1996, 10) reminds us, "Good economics does often turn out to be good politics, but only eventually." Rodrik later argues that the data do not consistently show a significant lag between the adoption of the reform and the benefits flowing from it. However, his use of the word "eventually" would suggest that there is in fact a sort of J-curve effect—that is, that conditions first deteriorate and travel down the bowl of the J, before improving and moving up along the stem of the letter.

   This pattern is confirmed by other studies. Masera (1974), in a detailed analysis of the 1967 devaluation of the pound sterling, estimated that it took eighteen to twenty-four months for the current account to move into balance. Williamson (1983, 154) reports that the evidence shows that while trade may respond within months to changes in income, reasonably complete adjustment to price changes may take three years or so. The study by Matusz and Tarr quoted earlier (2000) also pointed out that adjustment costs would be largest immediately following the reforms and could take one to five years to disappear. Some calculations by the World Bank on Egypt's experience with exchange-rate depreciation indicated that it took at least eighteen months for a significant response by non-oil manufactured exports. However, the cost of imports would increase as soon as the currency was devalued and could have a serious impact on prices and consumer subsidies (the latter in Egypt have at times amounted to more than 20 percent of budgetary expenditures).

The inevitable time gap between suffering the costs and enjoying the benefits of the reforms can play havoc with ministerial futures. The rapid turnover of economic ministers, particularly evident during the days of President Sadat, reinforced the tendency for caution. One can hardly blame ministers for not wanting to submit themselves to immediate criticism for the sake of some uncertain felicity in the future when the evidence pointed to a rather short ministerial shelf life. Between 1973 and 1980 there were seven changes of finance ministers, seven of planning ministers, five of ministers of economy, and four of ministers of international trade.[16]

Wagih Shindy (deputy minister of economy and subsequently minister of tourism) summed up the quandary. He said that ministers knew what they had to do; what they did not know was how to be retained as ministers once they had done it. They would have to carry the burden for the immediate consequences of reform policies, even if the short-term consequences had been foreseen to be inevitable and all the evidence indicated that the reforms would bring substantial benefits down the road.

This is more likely to be the case in an authoritarian presidential system, under which the ministers are generally technicians and do not bring a political "dowry" for the regime. Hamed al-Sayeh, a minister of economy, said that ministers under President Sadat knew that they were, politically speaking, cannon fodder and easily disposable if policies turned out to be unpopular even if only in the short run. Weiss (1993, 66) noted that "a series of ministers was replaced every six months on average, and prime ministers changed almost annually." The matter was somewhat better, but perhaps not by very much, under Nasser. Thus, McDermott (1988, 103–104) remarked that Nasser in eighteen years formed eighteen cabinets with 131 different individuals, but under Sadat the ministerial merry-go-round became dizzying—in seven years he had eleven cabinets with a turnover of 127 members. "Ministers tended to last half as long under Sadat as they did in Nasser's time, and in the economic portfolios, the changes verged on the hysterical." With the cabinet merry-go-round spinning at this speed, ministers could barely begin to grasp the details of their portfolios before they were ejected from office, and while occupying it could at best do little more than execute variations on existing policies rather than prepare well-considered ones to initiate.

This created an environment in which the cabinet might want the ends, but was reluctant to supply the patience that would be required for the policy measures to attain the ends. This is unfortunate. After reviewing reforms in several Asian, African, and Latin American countries, Krueger (1992, 69) notes that a successful reform normally spans several years, and that "time is one of its ingredients."

And therein lay the rub. Ministers were reluctant to support austerity measures unless they felt that they stood a good chance of being in office to see the benefits. But given the political mortality rate, the odds of this happening were distinctly unfavorable. The costs of policy reform were immediate and certain; the payoff was deferred in timing and unpredictable in amount. In their calculations, ministers heavily discounted the future. Consequently, the balance between risk and reward did little to encourage ministers (and even the president) to take the long view.

Dr. Abdel Aziz Higazi[17] described a meeting in February 1975 at which President Sadat had been urged to slow down the consumption boom following the infitah. The argument was that policy measures taken up front to restrain excessive consumption would lead to increased investment and incomes, and thus permit high and more sustainable consumption a little later. The president had dismissed this view out of hand, responding sarcastically, "*Ya'ni bukra fi-l-mishmish?*" ("In your dreams!"). The tendency of the government to concentrate almost exclusively on immediate benefits was much discussed among donors. At one of the monthly donor meetings in Cairo, the British representative remarked that the preoccupation with the short term made it appear that the government's main strategic principle came from FitzGerald's *Rubaiyat of Omar Khayyam*: "Ah, take the cash, and let the credit go,/Nor heed the rumble of a distant drum." Or as Hamed al-Sayeh (minister of economy) confided more prosaically, "Ministers do not necessarily support reforms; they just want the results of reform."

The focus on the short term was not limited to a particular cabinet. In early 1981 the deputy prime minister for economic affairs, Abdel Meguid, tabled at a cabinet meeting a range of proposals dealing with the exchange rate, consumer and fuel subsidies, the restructuring of loss-making public enterprises, and the injection of competition into the financial sector. Detailed papers, coordinated by the Ministry of Planning, had been circulated concerning the likely effect on the price level, the budget, and employment in the public enterprise sector. Abdel Meguid had discussed his ideas with the ministers concerned, and he was confident that they were all on board. At the meeting he asked for their formal assent to begin drafting appropriate legislation. The response took him by surprise.

He said that ministers had "hopped from one 'however' to another" and that the cabinet had not been able to reach any decisions. As Abdel Meguid put it, "Everyone was ready to go to heaven, but no one was prepared to die." He added, "I suppose the most sobering thought for any politician is that *he* should politically die [because of authoring reform policies], while his successor should benefit from the outcome of those policies and go to political heaven." The clear political-economy lesson is that if ministers perceive the benefits of reform to lie beyond the electoral horizon or (especially under an authoritarian regime) the president's forbearance, reform policies will have few champions.

It is thus impossible to predict for how long a government is likely to persist with stabilization efforts or structural reform in the face of continuing austerity. Too many variables—such as the nature of the immediate economic crises, the economic trends of the previous decades, the political structure of the government (democratic, authoritarian, or dictatorship) and its strength, the state's capacity for efficiently implementing the program, the role of external agencies, and many others—all are in play. After reviewing the experience of nineteen countries in Latin America, Africa, and East Asia, Nelson (1990, 339) tentatively concluded that "some relief from economic hardship within, perhaps, a year usually is necessary to sustain confidence" to carry on with the program even where economic crisis may have convinced much of the public that drastic measures were required. The only stabilization program in Egypt that may be said to have attained many of its goals covered 1991–93. Much of the government's ability to stay the course resulted from the relief from economic hardship provided by the substantial write-offs and reschedulings of external debt, and the donor financing of support programs such as the Social Fund for Development (See chapter 6).

A further problem arose from Egyptian ministers' insecurity about their tenures. Kassem (2004, 27–28) points out that the constitutional power to appoint the prime minister and the other ministers (and to relieve them of their posts) gave the president absolute power over the political future of cabinet members; moreover, the economic ministers were almost exclusively technicians who were not backed by a political constituency. This situation is very likely to inculcate in them a strong feeling of loyalty to the ruler; indeed, "the issue of loyalty accommodates subservience to the ruler's policies. Consequently, [the president's] personal decision-making is less likely to be questioned, let alone challenged." Ministers could too often be unwilling to tell the president that some of his pet initiatives might not be workable.

McDermott (1988, 139–40) describes a meeting at which President Sadat was enthusiastically told by a minister of agriculture that he could carry out the president's directive to "turn the entire Sinai green within one year." This undertaking was given despite USAID's providing the minister with evidence that (a) there was virtually no water to irrigate the Sinai; (b) if water were diverted from other uses and pumped across the Suez Canal into the Sinai, the per-gallon cost would be about five to eight times that of delivering it to existing sites in the Nile Delta; and (c) improving the quality of soil in the Sinai to support even simple grass cover could take five years or more. Such instances could occasion some irony by international observers. McDermott recounts that at that meeting the World Bank representative asked if the minister intended to fulfill his promise by plastering the Sinai with Astroturf, since growing natural vegetation appeared to be out of the question. Of course the Sinai has not become any greener in the forty or so years since that meeting. "Never commit to a date and a number," would be sage advice to Egyptian policymakers, observed the USAID representative at the meeting.

These ministerial attitudes did nothing to encourage donors' belief in the government's seriousness. Moreover, such pronouncements debased public discussion by pretending that simple solutions existed for complex, and perhaps insoluble, problems, and corroded people's trust in the government when it became apparent that there were in fact no easy answers.

Perhaps the ministers' fears of their political ephemerality if they acted on sensitive subjects were not irrational. In a well-known paper, Cooper (1971, 28–29) analyzed the political effects of twenty-four devaluations between 1953 and 1966. He found that in about 30 percent of the cases the government lost office within one year, compared with only 14 percent in a random control group of similar countries that did not devalue. Ministers of finance suffered even worse fates: nearly 60 percent of them were dismissed in the year following devaluation, compared with 18 percent in the group that did not devalue.

2. *Disjunction between private and social profitability.* The cost–benefit ratios discussed above have all referred to social benefits or profitabilities, that is, the gains from policy reforms that accrue to society as a whole. However, the calculation that interest groups typically make does not refer to this wider concept of benefits, but rather focuses on private profitability—the gains or losses that would impact their own coalition. And there frequently is a wide disjunction between social and private profitability. Therefore, what happens to the structure of the country's policy framework can depend crucially on whether the group seeking to advance social profitability can outwit, persuade, or overpower the group seeking to preserve private profitability that is created by inefficiencies in the economy. This is seldom easy. As long ago as 1513, in his classic study on the exercise of political power, Nikolai Machiavelli warned that "the reformer has enemies in all those who profit by the old order, and only lukewarm defenders in all those who would profit by the new" (*The Prince*, chapter 6).

Instances of the ascendancy of private over social profitability in the Egyptian experience and the effects this has had on policies are not hard to find. Let me describe some examples from different sectors.

For long periods Egypt's exchange rate was overvalued. A devaluation would provide an incentive to stimulate exports, increase tourism, and redirect workers' remittances from unofficial to official channels. All these would add foreign exchange, which has remained a key bottleneck to the country's development. The higher exports would also increase domestic savings while the greater availability of foreign exchange would require less foreign borrowing, which has compromised Egypt's sovereignty several times during the last 150 years. The social benefits therefore were evident. However, the overvalued exchange rate benefited importers, while the subsidies effectively increased the disposable incomes of consumers. The private benefits therefore were also obvious. The fact that Egypt maintained an overvalued exchange rate for long periods showed that the interest groups favoring imports and consumption retained a dominance over those that favored exports, savings, and investment, even though the benefits to the country would have been more aligned with the interests of the latter group.

The resistance by particular factions to protect their interests can make governments go through various contortions to make a policy package look like a reform, even when it does not alter the underlying reality. Krueger (1992, 80) describes the Egyptian reform program of 1962, in which the country sought emergency support from the IMF. As a condition of obtaining the funds, Egypt had to devalue its exchange rate by about 25 percent. However, "the authorities managed to remove a sufficient number of surcharges on imports and subsidies for exports so that almost no exporters or importers were receiving or paying more than 3 percent more local currency per unit of foreign exchange than they had earlier." The status quo was effectively protected. Indeed, Hansen and Nashashibi (1975, 90), whose data provide the basis for Krueger's calculations, say quite bluntly, "There is little doubt that the government, despite its commitments to the IMF, had no intention whatever to cut down domestic demand"; which continued to expand vigorously.

A further example is provided by policies that discriminate between Egypt's small and large enterprises. The small, and usually informal, firms account for 95 percent of the country's enterprises, but they lack the political access and the privileged entrée to policymakers that is accorded to the large firms. It is thus not surprising that trade, labor, locational, energy, competition, and other policies are devised primarily with an eye to benefiting the large firms. The effect of these policies is to artificially reduce the cost of, and thus to encourage the use of, capital- and energy-intensive methods of production, even though these are not aligned with the country's resource endowment or its comparative advantage. Concern for the private profitability of the politically influential 5 percent of the total number of firms trumps the social profitability of increasing labor-intensive production and creating jobs by facilitating the activities of the other 95 percent. The discussion in chapter 6 of crony capitalism illustrates the effects of this differential treatment on the country's employment and potential GDP growth.

Another long-standing example of private profitability outweighing social profitability is shown by the country's cropping pattern. The United Nations Food and Agriculture Organization (1999, 32–34) concluded that the cultivation of sugarcane was profitable for private farmers because they did not have to pay for water, but the resulting distortion of incentives encouraged the planting of sugarcane and imposed a substantial economic loss on the country. This occurred because, first, Egypt was not an efficient producer of sugar, and thus could not export it at international prices, but in many areas sugarcane competed for land with other crops, such as cotton, in which the country was internationally competitive. Second, water was the most binding constraint on Egyptian agriculture, and sugarcane is a very water-intensive crop; thus, the encouragement of sugarcane production led to a less than optimal use of the country's most valuable agricultural resource. Third, sugarcane is a year-round crop and the land is thus not available for double-cropping, so the country has to forgo the benefits of the displaced crop.

However, the government remained wary of upsetting the agricultural coalition. In discussions on agricultural strategy with the United Nations Food and Agriculture Organization (FAO), the government stonewalled any attempt to discuss water pricing. The FAO reported that the government's position remained that the kingdoms of Upper and Lower Egypt had been united under King Narmer (circa 3000 BCE) in order to better manage the waters of the Nile. Since that time, the farmer had not paid directly for the use of water. Any attempt to change the situation could be seen as striking at the basis of the country's foundation with unpredictable, and possibly dire, political consequences. The incentive system therefore remained tilted in favor of growing a water-intensive crop, such as sugarcane, that was profitable for the private farmer even though it entailed a loss for society as a whole. The origins of some political-economy issues in Egypt can go back quite far!

The agricultural lobby also resisted paying for drainage. A cardinal fact of economics is that "there is no free lunch." The costs of constructing and maintaining the vast irrigation and drainage infrastructure were thus pushed onto groups that were less powerful than the agricultural coalition. The foregoing examples reiterate a general political-economy truth: some powerful political forces will fight to preserve their private benefits (in the shape of economic rents) that arise from an inefficient allocation of resources, regardless of the cost to society.

3. *Differential impact of reforms between sectors and between individuals.* The empirical investigations show very wide differences in the benefit–cost ratios for different sectors. Many of these studies found that even if the countrywide benefit–cost ratio was impressive, the costs (especially declines in unemployment) tended to be concentrated among a few industries. If the worst-affected sectors are politically important (for example, if they are large employers of labor or have strategic value), policymakers will not pay too much attention to overall benefit–cost estimates but seek to protect these sectors by abstaining from or slowing down reforms.

Private adjustment costs, such as the dislocation of workers, also differ between groups of workers. The private losses borne by workers depend on individual characteristics, such as their skills and experience. Workers with the training or experience required by the market are likely to find another job relatively quickly. However, workers not so endowed may continue to swell the ranks of the unemployed for long periods. Thus, even if the social benefit–cost ratio is very favorable, the private costs borne by a dislocated worker may amount to a significant fraction of his or her lifetime earnings.

Studies that focus on countrywide estimates of benefits and costs tend to ignore or downplay the distributional impact of reform policies on individuals. Academics in ivory towers (and their international advisors) can make an intellectually rigorous case for reform measures on the basis of the benefits that would accrue to the country as a whole; political representatives who will bear the wrath of their unemployed constituents will feel the pressure to tread more circumspectly. This can be seen, for example, in the manner that the Egyptian government handled the privatization program of the 1990s.

Studies had repeatedly shown that public enterprises suffered from massive overstaffing. The Public Enterprise Office estimated employment in public enterprises in 1993 at just over one million. Khattab (1999, 12–13) reported that before the main restructuring began in 1996, public enterprises employed 932,404 workers, and that the Ministry of the Public Enterprise Sector estimated that about 300,000 of them were redundant. It was unlikely that private investors would rush to purchase public enterprises in which one-third of the workers were unnecessary. The excess labor would have to be shed. Mindful of the political danger of antagonizing labor, the government undertook reforms in the public enterprise sector only after donor governments and international institutions put together a substantial financial package to cushion the impact of the job losses. The government's measures (such as early retirement, not replacing workers lost through normal attrition, and so on) succeeded in reducing employment in public enterprise to less than 600,000 by the middle of 2000, and to about 400,000 by 2009, when the privatization program was frozen.

The crucial ingredient making the reduction politically possible was that donors offered substantial resources to support compensatory measures that would mitigate the dislocation. Distributional issues—who will benefit and who will lose—are at the core of groups' resistance to reform. The political-economy lesson is that the size and design of the compensation package, the speed with which it can be delivered, and, most importantly, credibility that the government will actually implement the package are crucial to passing a successful reform over the resistance of opposing coalitions.

4. *The perception that the burden of reform policies is shared equitably.* The literature points out that austerity is almost invariably an initial outcome of major reform policies. It also emphasizes that austerity is likely to be accepted by the population and reform policies supported if there is a clear perception that this burden is equitably shared (see, for example, the earlier discussion of "Rogernomics" (see page 31).

A necessary implication of this finding is that reform policy must be rigorously evidence-based. Facts have a way of getting their revenge. Overall growth may look robust and average (per capita) incomes apparently growing, but the averages may conceal substantial pockets of people and regions that have been left behind. The Gini index and other measures of income distribution have to be scrutinized carefully in order to ensure that they are not systematically affected by influences that cause the indices to show spuriously equitable outcomes. Such an effect may have been a factor in Egypt, as pointed out by the World Bank (2015b). The report argued that the Gini index might have been truncated at both ends—with high-income groups under-reporting their consumption and income in order to avoid attracting the attention of tax authorities, and low-income groups underreported because survey enumerators found it difficult to access poor neighborhoods (for reasons mentioned in chapter 8 of this book). It is also clear that Upper Egypt, especially its rural areas, has benefited much less than the rest of the country from the development process (World Bank 2009). Thus, although aggregate growth and average incomes in Egypt were rising much faster from 2005 until 2008 (when the international financial crisis occurred) than in the decade before, a widespread perception that the fruits of growth were largely captured by the richer classes connected with the political regime (see the discussion of crony capitalism in chapter 8) proved toxic to reform efforts and, indeed, fatal to the political regime.

The "Insider–Outsider" Conundrum

For much of the period after the nationalizations of 1961, almost one-third of Egypt's labor force was employed by the public sector (excluding the armed forces). In 2015 the compensation paid to government employees consumed 35 percent of budgetary revenues and accounted for 8 percent of GDP. The aggregate burden on revenues of salaries, pensions, and bonuses is thus very heavy. Moreover, numerous studies have shown that virtually every public-sector organization suffers from overstaffing and that many of their employees are simply involved in "make-work" activities.

A few examples might help convey a flavor of this problem. I have already quoted the Ministry of the Public Enterprise Sector's estimate that in 1996 (before the Egyptian authorities had agreed to a restructuring of the public enterprise labor force under an IMF/World Bank program), almost one-third of the more than 900,000 workers employed in public-sector enterprises were redundant. Earlier, Waterbury (1983, 246) quoted an official report on overstaffing which noted that in 1975 the Ministry of Human Resources asked the Ministry of Agriculture for the number of graduates that it would need in the following year. The answer was 261 university graduates and 495 with secondary agricultural diplomas. Facing this demand was a supply of eight thousand graduates of agriculture faculties and higher institutes, and eleven thousand holders of agricultural secondary school diplomas. One can only guess at the frustration suffered by graduates who were unsuccessful in getting one of the advertised jobs, and also by those who were forced by circumstances to accept jobs the requirements of which fell well below the graduate's qualifications.

The problem is durable. Nearly a quarter of a century after the incident described by Waterbury, a headline in the *Egyptian Mail* (December 5, 1998, p. 2) blared that "3 Million Employees Get Paid for Doing Nothing." The report quoted the state minister of administrative development complaining that "there are 5 million [public] employees in Egypt, but there are only 2 million jobs. It means that 3 million employees are doing nothing, not to mention that they can slow down the progress of the work." He urged the country to stop appointing ten persons where there was work only for one. As yet another instance, Galal (2002) reported a government announcement of the availability of 170,000 jobs being confronted by a tsunami of more than 5 million applications.

The Egyptian bureaucracy has shown itself to be a powerful group that will strongly resist attempts at reform. In part, the strength derives from its sheer size—the civil service expanded from 350,000 in 1952 to 6.37 million employees in 2014 (excluding military personnel); this works out at one civil servant for every thirteen Egyptians (World Bank 2015, 16n28).

The size, growth, and structure of the bureaucracy has attracted a good deal of unfavorable comment. Thus, for example, McDermott (1988, 122–24) described the bureaucracy and its growth as "a deadly combination of Ottoman complexities, Eastern European inflexible committee rule, a touch here and there of British and French secretive intrigue, and Egyptian indiscipline. . . . Nasser may have purged the state apparatus, but he basically did not restructure it. It could be said that the revolution... bypassed the civil servants almost as much as it did the fellah."

The crux of the problem was that governments tended to make the bureaucracy and the public enterprise sector perform a social welfare function, namely, to act as repositories for the rapidly growing labor force. Budgetary constraints meant that the numbers involved could only be accommodated at appallingly low salaries, made even worse by price inflation. Handoussa and El Oraby (2004, tables 3 and 4) reported, for example, that the top of the salary for the highest grade (First Undersecretary) increased by only 30 percent in nominal terms between 1964 and 1999, a period of 35 years.[18] Similarly, in 1964 prices, the salary range for Grade 6 (the lowest grade after 1978) dropped to LE11.86–21.01 in 1999 from LE330–600 in 1964.

The low salaries sap morale and encourage civil servants to work (illegally) at two or more jobs. The numbers involved can be daunting. Palmer et al. (1988, 61–2) reported that 89 percent of the respondents in their survey admitted to holding such second jobs and defended it as an economic necessity. Moreover, 84 percent of those respondents holding second jobs said that they spent between three to five hours a day (that is, half a normal working day) on this supplemental job. Ayubi (1980, 507) points out that government officials were not technically ignorant of how to do a job; they were simply not socially motivated as to why they should do it. Matters change when the pay increases. "The same ministry employees who sit idly most of the days," writes Weinbaum (1986, 115), "are examples of industriousness in hustling to make extra cash once off the [government] job."

The employment issue poses a delicate political-economy conundrum—the creation of large numbers of essentially artificial jobs at low salaries works against the government's aim of mobilizing sufficient savings to invest in accelerating GDP growth that would create sufficient numbers of more meaningful jobs. However, there are time lags between mobilizing the savings and investment and achieving the output and sustainable job growth, and the political-economy of successive regimes gave priority to the short-term.[19]

Government attempts to increase flexibility and to improve efficiency have not gained much traction. Thus, for example, in 2005 the government attempted to make it easier to hire temporary contract employees and to discipline poor performers. However, the vehement opposition of civil servants and public employee unions compelled the government to withdraw the proposed amendments to the civil service legislation.

The question of labor in the public sector has attracted particular attention. Measures to shed the excess labor in public enterprises form part of the conditions attached to virtually every IMF program or World Bank policy loan, while measures to make labor markets more flexible are the subject of numerous discussions between donors and the Egyptian authorities. Simulations are run and spreadsheets flourished, all purporting to show large benefits to the economy of "resizing" or "rightsizing" (other euphemisms for firing workers are not unknown) the labor force in the public sector. The argument that the econometric exercises make is straightforward: If the public sector were to reduce its excess labor, the savings could be invested, which in turn would raise the GDP growth rate and create productive employment of numbers that would substantially exceed those that the public sector had eliminated. The country as a whole would benefit.

Why, then, is the government loath to take this seemingly straightforward and socially beneficial measure?

The political-economy answer lies to a considerable extent in the "insider–outsider" problem. The point is that although the number of jobs created would outweigh those abolished, those fired and those hired would be different persons. Those who stood to be fired would be "insiders," those already employed and whose positions were protected by laws and by the costs of labor turnover (such as advertising the jobs, screening applicants, training the new hires, and so on). The "outsiders" would be those who were working in the informal sector of the economy or were unemployed; in either case they would not enjoy the protection that the insiders did.

Public enterprises would be discouraged from firing workers because of the legal costs involved in separation and because of the costs involved in training their replacements. Lindbeck and Snower (2002) discuss some other reasons that might also discourage this replacement of workers. They point out that, for example, insiders who have been working together for some time are known to form groups or factions and cooperate with each other in the production process and thereby raise each other's productivity, but could threaten not to cooperate with newcomers and thereby reduce overall productivity and increase costs. Moreover, Egypt's stringent legal protection against dismissals (and a drawn-out legal process in case it occurs) makes the costs of firing an insider significantly higher. Furthermore, insiders are generally unionized and thus able to exert a degree of political power; outsiders of course would be unable to do the same.

Finally, uncertainty about the shape of the post-reform environment plays an important role in the resistance of the insiders to economic reform, including those who are in no danger of immediate dismissal. Once a long-lasting, not to say sclerotic, structure of public-sector employment is threatened by the possibility of a reform policy being introduced, a great deal of uncertainty is created as to whether the initial reform is only the thin edge of a process that will keep on being repeated in the future. The IFIs' studies underpinning the 1991 reforms contain references to workers asking whether the tradition of stable public-sector employment was to be abandoned. There was much concern about the terms of the employment of the retained workers and of the size of the compensation package of those deemed redundant, because workers wanted to be compensated for the loss of the value of their (sure) position in the pre-reform situation, for the loss of what the literature calls their *situation rents.*

For all the foregoing reasons, the Egyptian government proceeds cautiously in dealing with questions of labor in the public sector. Its most successful episode of reducing jobs in public enterprises (it did not touch the general bureaucracy) occurred in the second half of the 1990s and for about five years in the early 2000s under an agreement with the IMF and the World Bank. An important part of the arrangements was the provision of a "golden handshake" equivalent to three years' compensation to workers taking early retirement, and the creation of the Social Fund for Development that paid for retraining workers and provided funds for micro- and small-business startups to which the exiting workers (and others) had access. The IMF (1998, 53) pointed out that the elimination of these jobs in public enterprises was possible because the low wages and benefits paid in the public sector made the retirement packages affordable.

Apart from the overstaffing issue with public enterprises, there are substantial labor problems even with private enterprises. The legal protection against dismissals is, in practice, quite rigid not only for the public sector but also for the private. Background papers for the World Bank's studies on private-sector development described repeated complaints by businessmen of how difficult it was to dismiss unproductive and even dishonest workers. They also described some ingenious methods that businesses had developed in order to circumvent these rules. The most popular techniques were hiring on temporary contracts, or obtaining signed but undated letters of resignation from workers at the time of hiring; these were then dated and presented to the authorities should the worker have to be dismissed.

However, such methods impose costs on the worker, on society, and on the employer. The temporary worker does not get all the benefits (such as a pension) that a permanent one would. These and other handicaps push an increasing number of workers into the informal labor market, in which wages are lower and benefits nonexistent. The informalization of employment imposes a cost on society; for example, the exchequer loses the revenue that it would have collected from formal enterprises. Costs are also imposed on employers. Businessmen who made use of the undated resignation letters reported in World Bank questionnaires that they had to bribe local authorities or representatives of the Ministry of Labor to accept the letter without delving too deeply into its background. Getting around the rigidity of the market thus creates transactions costs that hurt the interests of all the parties involved.

Political Economy and Dictatorships

The question whether a democratic or an authoritarian regime is more conducive for economic growth has been widely debated but has received no clear answer. The difficulty is that a priori arguments can go both ways. Thus, for example, a democratic regime may be said to be better for growth because it is buttressed by institutions that provide greater security for property rights, and hence better incentives for investment and innovation, that are the engines of growth. On the other hand, as Przeworski and Limongi (1993) show, it has also been argued that universal voting rights bestow power on groups that have little or no property. The acquisition of the franchise by such groups could shift the balance of political power toward them and enable them to overturn property rights in order to extract resources from the economically more successful. Thus, the enlargement of the franchise to a universal or very wide one would wither the latter group's incentive to commit to long-term investment.

Similarly, it has been argued that an authoritarian regime is better able to disregard immediate pressures for redistribution and focus on investment and growth. However, as Olson (1991) and Drazen (2000) point out, dictators' commitment to future policies must be viewed with skepticism— if there are no limits on the ruler's power, there is no way of holding him to any commitments he makes. And North and Weingast (1989) stress that the risk that the autocrat will subvert property rights for the benefit of himself or his allies will lower the expected returns from investment and reduce the incentive to invest. Investment entails long-term risks, and the incentive to invest thus requires the investor to be confident of the regime's long-term commitment to rights. More elaborate discussion of this subject will be found in Przeworski and Limongi (1993), Sirowy and Inkeles (1990), and Drazen (2000, 488–501).

Economic policymaking under authoritarian governments or dictatorships is an important subject for Egypt, because the country has been under such regimes almost continuously since 1952. However, the political-economy literature on dictatorships is limited and is generally concerned with discussions of whether dictatorship or democracy is better for economic growth.

Dictatorships are a very mixed group, and this heterogeneity makes it difficult to generalize. Moreover, being overthrown in a dictatorship is likely to involve much more severe consequences than in a democracy; it cannot be shrugged off as just a bad day at the office. Regime change would not only eliminate the dictator's office, but also jeopardize his liberty and possibly his life and limbs. Similar risks to his family and associates are not negligible. Regime survival in a dictatorship, therefore, is a much more compelling instinct and will suffuse the government's assessment of any reform proposal.

Alesina (1992) reports that, empirically, one cannot distinguish between the average growth performance of democratic and authoritarian regimes. He makes a distinction between "strong" and "weak" dictators. The former are those whose survival is not seriously threatened. However, this group itself is heterogeneous. Some "strong" dictators or authoritarians—such as Chung-Hee Park of South Korea—put economic development at the forefront of their agenda; others (for example, the Duvaliers in Haiti, Mobutu in Zaire, Ceaucescu in Romania)—indeed, probably the great majority—have been predatory and despoiled their countries.

"Weak" dictators are those in danger of being overthrown. Alesina argues that when such a dictator is in danger, his incentives are likely to be similar to those of an incumbent political leader in a democracy who faces an uncertain election. In such a situation, therefore, one would expect to see fiscal policies that are generally "loose," in the sense of increasing budgetary expenditures, especially on items such as consumer subsidies, and "opportunistic," targeting budgetary expenditures toward constituencies (such as the armed forces and the security services) that would shore up the ruler's support.

Egypt's history provides examples of such political-economy decisions. Chapter 5 describes how, when confronted with unrest following an attempt to rationalize some consumer subsidies, President Sadat chose to jettison the prime minister who had argued for reform in favor of the minister of interior, who was in charge of the security services. Again in 1977, following the riots over the cut in the bread subsidy, Sadat rapidly rescinded the price increases and asked the prime minister to personally take charge of the Ministry of Interior.

Egypt's leaders are not alone in the opportunistic use of fiscal and military policies. Several Latin American dictators followed opportunistic policies, especially by using public expenditure to benefit key constituencies, particularly the military, when the ruler felt he might be overthrown (Alesina 1992).

An allied question is whether authoritarian/dictatorial governments are able to push through reforms more quickly than more participatory regimes. Mau offers an interesting example that would not be entirely foreign to the thinking of many policymakers working under authoritarian regimes.

> Count Sergei Witte, a prominent reformer under the Czars,[20] used to say that there were two essential elements for radical reforms in Russia: absolute monarchy, because you need not pay attention to your critics if His Majesty supported you, and speed, because somebody might persuade the Czar to change his mind before the reform could be made irreversible. (Mau 1994, 6)

There has been a fair amount of discussion in the literature on the subject. A useful distinction is made by Haggard (1994, 467–71) between the initiation of reform and its consolidation. He argues that initiating reform is facilitated by an independent or autonomous executive, while consolidating reform requires the support of institutions, such as legislatures and even interest groups. The application of such criteria in Egypt's case is a little problematical. Although the country was ruled almost continuously by authoritarian regimes since 1952, reform proceeded only slowly, and generally only when the economy was in extremis. A fruitful focus of research in Egypt's case, therefore, would be what circumstances made the ruling autocrat risk the change that a significant economic reform would inevitably bring. Some answers are attempted in this book, but the matter requires more exhaustive examination.

The Role of the Foreign Patron

A factor that complicates the political-economy response, and one that probably occurs more frequently in developing-country dictatorships, is the role played by a foreign patron. In Egypt's case, the latter was the Soviet Union in President Nasser's era and is the United States at the present time. The interests of the foreign patron and its attitude toward the client country's political economy can be quite complex, and the interplay of their interests and powers can be a major determinant of political-economy outcomes. The general experience is that if the patron has to decide between pressing the client to adopt reform policies or to support him in resisting reform because of a fear that otherwise the client will lose office, the patron will opt for support even if the client is undeserving. The attitude of the patron is epitomized most colorfully in the remark attributed to President Franklin D. Roosevelt in *Time* magazine (November 15, 1948) concerning the Nicaraguan dictator Anastasio Somoza: "Somoza may be a sonofabitch, but he is *our* sonofabitch."

The client dictator wants the patron's unconditional support. The patron may be willing to support the client, but may want the client to adopt certain reforms. However, sensing that these might not be welcome and would therefore damage the bilateral relationship, the patron may seek indirect ways of influencing the outcome.

Let me give two examples from Egypt's experience of this complex relationship and the political-economy outcomes to which they led.

At the height of the January 1977 bread riots in Cairo, I had a discussion with Hermann Eilts, the U.S. ambassador to Egypt, who was the best-informed diplomat I have met in Egypt.[21] He urged the World Bank to press Egypt on subsidy and other reforms, because Egypt desperately needed such reforms. He suggested that the World Bank make the disbursement of the Bank's loans conditional on actions on subsidies and the budget. I answered that the World Bank was disbursing only $60 million while the United States was disbursing about $600 million. Would the United States hold back even a penny of this amount if Egypt did not go in for the recommended reforms?

The ambassador responded that the United States believed President Sadat to be a force for moderation in the Middle East, and that so long as he continued to be such a force he merited the United States' support. *Translation*: So long as Egypt adhered to its peace treaty with Israel and refrained from creating any nuisance that would interfere with the West's access to Middle East oil, it would get the money no matter what it did or failed to do in the way of economic reform.

I replied that the laws of physics did not permit the tail to wag the dog, and neither did the laws of arithmetic suggest that a hint to hold back some part of $60 million would terrify the Egyptians into taking the recommended actions, especially as they knew that at least $600 million would be available and that the United States was pressing the G-7 and other countries to join the aid program for Egypt in order to increase the total amount. (The first Consultative Group for Egypt, consisting of about twenty-five aid donors, in fact met later that year and pledged $3.4 billion in aid for the coming year.) I could not therefore in good conscience recommend to the World Bank's management to join the IMF with any hints to withhold disbursements, particularly as Egypt had been fulfilling its contractual commitments on the World Bank's projects. After some further discussion, Ambassador Eilts accepted my position.[22]

Thus, on the one hand the United States agreed that the policies proposed by the international financial institutions (IFIs) were necessary to deal with Egypt's economic predicament. On the other hand, publicly agreeing with these institutions might harm the United States' bilateral relationship with Egypt. The solution seemed to be to urge the IFIs from behind the scenes to press Egypt on reform while publicly remaining "understanding" of the country's difficulties.

The Egyptians sensed the Americans' dilemma, and were quite prepared to take advantage of it. Ministers said that the cabinet would trumpet the "understanding" statements in order to glue the United States to its public posture. The Americans understood that abandoning a position that Egyptians applauded as being sympathetic would drain much of the popularity that the United States had garnered because of its (well-publicized) helpful stance. The political costs of a retreat would be too great.

The presence of the patron also enabled Egypt to play the "American card" in its dealings with the IFIs, in which the United States was the principal shareholder. Several examples of Egypt's co-opting the United States to pressure the IMF are documented by Richards (1991) and in various issues of the *Middle East Economic Digest*.[23] Some instances are also described in later chapters of this book.

A telling example is provided by the experience of the Consultative Group of aid donors for 1979. In September of that year it appeared that the World Bank was reluctant to hold a meeting of the Consultative Group for Egypt. I was invited to join a discussion between Hamed al-Sayeh (the minister of economy) and the United States ambassador (Alfred Atherton) at which the minister asked the ambassador to have Robert Strauss (at the time President Carter's special envoy to the Middle East) call on the World Bank's president, Robert McNamara, and prevail on him to hold a meeting of the Consultative Group within that calendar year. The minister drew attention to the fact that meetings of the Group had been held in 1977 and 1978. Not holding one in 1979, after the Camp David Accords between Egypt and Israel,[24] and in response to which the Arab countries had cut off their aid to Egypt, would send an unacceptable political signal, namely, that the West also had abandoned Egypt. In these circumstances, how could the public accept a continuation of Sadat's pro-West policy? As matters turned out, Robert Strauss's intervention was not required. That evening Ambassador Atherton telephoned to let me know that Assistant Secretary of State Richard Cooper had called McNamara, who had assured him that a meeting of the Consultative Group would take place before the end of the year. The meeting was held in Aswan on December 20.

The result of this interplay of interests between donor and patron was that the signals from the United States could often appear ambiguous. This sometimes led to confusion on the Egyptian side as to what was really wanted, but more frequently to Egyptian policymakers dissecting the United States' messages and highlighting elements that conformed to their own views and would buttress their own position.

Egyptian officials had also become more adept at getting the United States to put political pressure on the IFIs to moderate their conditions. Hamed al-Sayeh said that the cabinet had realized it should not jump to accept IFI prescriptions. If direct discussions failed to convince the IFIs of Egypt's concerns, then it was the "absolute duty" of Egyptian policymakers to use the route through the U.S. State or Treasury Department to make the IFIs understand what the feasible boundaries of reform were. He added that after the experience of the 1977 bread riots, Egypt's policymakers were adamant that it would be "insane" on the part of donors to insist on, or for Egypt to agree to, major subsidy cuts. He had little doubt on whose side the United States would come down if it had to choose between maintaining its Middle East policy or subscribing to the purism of the IMF's economic ideology.

A picture of the ambiguous situation between client and patron was brought out by Abdel Meguid, deputy prime minister for economic affairs. He said Egypt's policymakers were quite aware that in the relationship between Egypt and the United States the economic dialogue would be eclipsed by the political narrative. In any such relationship, the key decisions are always determined by political leaders, not economic technicians.

He maintained that Egyptian policymakers would argue that for political reasons they could not implement a number of the IMF's conditions without risking the government's fall. They would therefore indicate that they would have to withdraw from discussions with the IMF or to ignore some parts of an agreement with it. The United States had built up a solid relationship with Egypt in order to secure two of its principal policy goals in the Middle East—peace between Israel and the largest Arab country, and unhindered access to oil. The United States would be reluctant to risk the possibility of an unknown regime's coming into power in Egypt and perhaps placing the foreign-policy gains in jeopardy. The Americans would therefore use their leverage as the largest shareholders to encourage the Fund to water down the conditions that Egypt found most unpalatable or to find a fudge around them—there were many ways of making the IMF's precepts more accommodating. Egypt would not find it too difficult to slip the IMF's fiscal leash.

Abdel Meguid highlighted the irony in the situation: if domestic politics pointed Egypt toward the exit from an IMF program, geopolitics would work to keep the country in a watered-down agreement. The United States would have to weigh the strategic cost of risking an Egyptian government collapse against the diplomatic cost of leaning on the IMF. According to Abdel Meguid, these issues had frequently been discussed in cabinet, which had concluded that the "dilemma" was a non-issue. The threat of political turmoil in Egypt would compel the Americans to find ways of getting the IMF to adjust its conditions. "Never underestimate the power of weakness," said Abdel Meguid, adding that seven thousand years of survival had left the Egyptians well instructed in the art of turning weakness into an element of strength. Egypt was too big to be allowed to fail.

This situation highlights another political-economy conundrum, namely, the difference in objectives that can crop up between principal and agent, even though they may be working for a common goal. The tactics described by Abdel Meguid were so transparent that it would be astonishing if U.S. representatives did not see through them. Indeed, I asked a U.S. ambassador if he really believed that the apocalypse was around the corner and that the Middle East would hurtle toward it should an Egyptian government fall.

He replied that of course the United States was aware of the Egyptian strategy, but there was a danger, even if very small, that if an unfamiliar regime replaced a government with which the United States had built up a solid relationship, it just might cause the United States to lose the foreign-policy gains that it had so painstakingly assembled. No U.S. official was willing to jeopardize his career by being stigmatized for Egypt being "lost" on his watch. Officials were thus willing to go very far to avoid this possibility; if it required pressuring an IFI or putting the best face on policy lapses by Egypt (in the economic as well as the political field), then so be it.

An example of the extent to which the American card could be made to work was demonstrated by events relating to Egypt's 1987 agreement for debt relief with the Paris club of creditors. Pressure on the IMF by the United States gave birth to an agreement that was described as "probably the feeblest in recent memory." Moreover, the easy terms, said by Cairo diplomats to be "unprecedented" in their leniency, drove a senior IMF executive to resign in protest.[25]

Over the years, I have discussed aid issues relating to Egypt with a number of ambassadors from donor countries. The discussions naturally concentrated on assistance from the United States, because of the importance of the country in the total aid picture and its weight in the IFIs. Let me summarize some of the key points from the discussions.

In the ambassadors' view, the basic problem was that the IMF and some countries were happy to propose drastic change, but shirked the burden of showing that it was safe for Egypt. Unless Egypt could be reassured on this point, it would fight very hard to maintain the status quo. Egyptian policymakers regarded the status quo as a lot better than many plausible alternatives—better the devil you know than one you don't know.

However, the ambassadors were concerned that the foreign-policy stances of both Egypt and the United States concealed a substantial amount of impermanence that could lead to problems down the road. They described two major weaknesses in Egypt's strategy to obtain external assistance. Let me summarize the substance of our discussions.

First, they said that the Egyptian negotiating strategy in dealing with the IMF was to concentrate on the center of gravity, the United States, and to let that country use its weight in the IMF Board to bring the other members around to its point of view, which was to "go a little bit easier" on the policy conditions applied to loans for Egypt. This was a very short-term view, and likely to be counterproductive:

(a) It encouraged Egypt to avoid adopting the policies that would enable it to stand on its own feet. It would not correct the distortions in the borrower's economy, and was thus likely to set up a continued cycle of its recourse to the Fund's resources.

(b) While the United States might for a while be able to prevail upon the IMF to soften its policy conditions, it could not do this unilaterally for the long term; it would have to shepherd other IMF board members along the same path. This would not be simple. The 1987 experience should not be seen as a precedent that could be repeated indefinitely. The conditionality for Egypt set down markers which would be used as precedents by other borrowers from the Fund. Repeatedly easing conditions for Egypt might require the Fund to offer similar dispensations to all borrowers. These concessions could make the whole point of IMF lending futile, because the watered-down conditions would not attain the objectives of restoring external and internal balance in the borrowing country.

Second, Egyptian politicians acted as if the narrative of apocalyptic peril had been hardwired into the United States' DNA and that the United States would never rebut this storyline. This premise was wrong. A country's foreign policy could not be taken as a constant. A foreign policy was only an instrument to further a country's interests. These interests not only altered over time, but the methods by which they could be attained could also change. Unless Egypt took measures to strengthen its economy, its requirements for foreign assistance would keep increasing and a time would be reached when democracies that supported Egypt would find it impossible to persuade their taxpayers to continue to foot the bill. "Donor fatigue" was very real. Egypt could not act as if there were an unlimited treasury of donor grace. The United States' strategy toward Egypt was not calcified, but could change with changing circumstances. Egypt's long-term political-economy strategy thus might be built on sand, because it mistook political expediency for permanent truth. A review by donors of their aid budgets and their overall foreign-policy goals might well show that they could attain their objectives more efficiently by measures other than shoveling money into Egypt.

The ambassador highlighted another important reason why patience with foreign aid was running low in donor countries. Foreign aid was the transfer of incomes of taxpayers in donor countries to a recipient country. In the donor countries, citizens at most income levels had to pay taxes. On the other hand, in the recipient countries, including Egypt, the taxation systems contained huge loopholes, inefficiencies, and corruption whereby the higher-income groups avoided paying their fair share of taxes. However, they benefited fully from the assets and other advantages created by the foreign aid their country received. The decline in the ratio of taxes to

Egypt's GDP had not gone unnoticed in donor capitals. Taxpayers in the donor countries were getting increasingly weary of a situation in which their middle- and even lower-income citizens were having to transfer a part of their incomes to subsidize the lifestyles of the rich in recipient countries.

They warned that the day of reckoning may be not be too far off. Egypt was a big country, its resource requirements were correspondingly large, and thus the burden on donors was substantial. Political circles in the United States were already grumbling that with around two-thirds of the aid budget preempted by Israel and Egypt, it left little scope to use aid as an instrument of U.S. foreign policy in the many other countries with which it had dealings. The United States had already seen glimmers of this issue and had sought to widen the circle of support, and thus lighten the load on individual donors, by appealing to the G-7 and encouraging the World Bank to set up a consultative group of donors. However, the results of these exertions could not be guaranteed, because they depended on whether other countries considered that their commercial and strategic interests justified providing support to Egypt. Thus Egypt should not regard foreign assistance as an eternally available or a continually expanding resource.

From the viewpoint of 2016, the ambassadors' analysis was prescient. It would be useful to briefly review the course of U.S. assistance to Egypt, and to bring out some of the political implications of its trajectory.[26]

After the Camp David Accords that cemented the peace between Egypt and Israel, the United States agreed to give Egypt $1.3 billion in military assistance and $815 million as economic aid, a total of $2.15 billion, annually. This contrasted with over $3 billion in total assistance provided to Israel. Commentators in Egypt were unhappy that on a per capita basis, Israel was getting ten times the assistance that Egypt was getting. However, $2.15 billion was still a substantial amount, and Egypt could not afford to reject it.

This state of affairs continued for two decades. Then in January 1998, Israel, mindful that a country with per capita income approaching $20,000 should not be a supplicant for economic assistance, negotiated with the United States to change the mix between economic and military aid. The former was to be reduced over a ten-year period and the latter increased. The United States applied a 3 to 2 ratio, similar to total U.S. aid to Israel and Egypt, to the reduction in economic aid. This reduced Israel's share annually by $60 million and Egypt's by $40 million, but military assistance to Egypt was not increased. As a result of these measures, economic aid from the United States to Egypt steadily dropped from $815 million in the fiscal year 1998 to $250 million from fiscal year 2009 onward. Military assistance remained at $1.3 billion, so total U.S. assistance to Egypt in 2016 was about $1.55 billion.

At the same time, Egypt's GDP has been increasing. In 1980 it was about $23 billion; total U.S. aid therefore accounted for somewhat more than 9 percent of GDP. Egypt's GDP in 2016 had reached about $300 billion; total U.S. aid today accounted for less than one-half of 1 percent. This greatly changed the calculus—9 percent of GDP can buy you a very comfortable armchair at the table; one-half of 1 percent would hardly pay for a two-legged stool (especially as the purchasing power of the $1.55 billion was much less than it was thirty-five years previously). The leverage that the United States can obtain by virtue of its aid program has substantially eroded.

The leverage is further diluted by U.S. procedures that greatly extend the gap between the promise of aid and its fulfillment, a fact recognized by the U.S. secretary of state John Kerry in testimony before the House Appropriations Subcommittee on April 17, 2013. After detailing the aid Egypt had received from Arab countries, Kerry went on to say:

> We promised $1 billion and until I took the $190 million that you kindly helped us to be able to provide, we didn't provide them with a dime, not a dime. We gave them a promise and a year later, we've given them zero. . . . I'll tell you, if you're not helpful to people in their time of need, if you're not there, part of the process, it's very, very difficult to have the kind of leverage to say, a diverse pluralistic politics is critical to us when they say, what's it matter to you? You don't really care. You're not helping us. The other guys are helping us. Thank you, we'll, you know, do what we want to do.[27]

Second, there have been suggestions in the U.S. press and from some legislators that more conditions should be added on the assistance. This produces a blowback from Egyptian policymakers. The latters' narrative goes on the following lines: "The contract with the United States was that Egypt would maintain the peace with Israel, and not do anything to impede the West's access to Middle East oil. Even in the face of strong public opposition, we have delivered on this understanding. Now the Americans are asking for more conditions—you must free the press, you must expand democracy, you must increase human rights, you must not be beastly to political dissenters, you must permit NGOs to operate without restriction, and so on and so forth. All these have nothing to do with the original agreement."

The Egyptian response is thus on the lines of "we already gave at the office." In the officials' view, if the United States wants Egypt to do extra things, it should be prepared to come up with more money—one-half of 1 percent of GDP doesn't begin to cover the bill. The pity is that most of the reforms supported by the United States and the international organizations would be to Egypt's benefit. However, the two countries are looking at these issues through different lenses, and it is not surprising that the outcome is a muddle and satisfies neither party.

In view of the foregoing analysis, it is difficult to resist the conclusion that the United States has given up direct, meaningful support of the Egyptian economy. It appears to have decided that its strategic goals can be most effectively pursued through its relationship with the Egyptian military combined with some pressure on the IFIs. The United States' approach takes the form of continuing the carrot of the $1.3 billion in military aid, while wielding the unspoken threat of withholding spare parts, specialized paraphernalia, munitions, training, and maintenance for the hardware supplied. This can be a powerful foreign-policy tool, as Egypt has largely switched its dependence for advanced military equipment from Soviet to American sources. For economic support, Egypt may increasingly have to look to other patrons.

This may not be altogether easy. The ambassador with whom I had the discussions on foreign assistance remarked that for historical, political, and cultural reasons Egypt naturally looked toward the Arabian Gulf countries for assistance. It had helped that many of the rulers and senior officials from these countries had had long-standing ties to Egypt by virtue of being educated in the country and having respect for its culture. However, this was not necessarily true of the younger generation, which increasingly looked to Europe and the United States for these matters. There was a limit to how long the Egyptians could act as Greeks to the Gulf Arabs' Romans, purporting to provide wise, experienced counsel and the benefits of their superior culture to the Middle East's new powerhouses. Egypt's stock of 'soft power' was rapidly waning.

The Political Economy of External Assistance

Since so much of modern Egypt's development has been associated with external aid inflows, it is worthwhile to examine some of the key political-economy discussions that Egyptian policymakers and external donors engaged in concerning this issue.

The economic case for seeking external assistance is straightforward. A country requires a certain rate of investment in order to raise its GDP growth to the targeted level. It may also want technical assistance to upgrade its institutions or stock of human capital. The country is unable to finance these requirements from its own savings, and it may be unable to afford or to access international financial markets. It therefore seeks foreign savings on concessional terms to fill the gap between the required investment rate and the domestic savings rate. The foregoing is the general justification for *project assistance*. In addition, the recipient country may generate insufficient domestic revenues and thus have a deficit in the budget. The country may therefore seek *program assistance*, which, in the simplest case, consists of receiving commodities from a donor on grant terms and which the recipient sells in its home market at the market price and thereby acquires the required domestic resources for its budget.[28] The recipient may also have a shortfall on its balance of payments for which it requires foreign exchange; this may be provided by a bilateral donor (generally the Arab Gulf countries in Egypt's case) or the International Monetary Fund.

This simple story, however, can mask a variety of political and economic intentions. The recipient may want resources purely in order to develop the country; or its interests may be narrower and may have more to do with securing the longevity of the regime. An associated motive is to obtain these resources without burdening the regime's constituencies with additional taxes so as to retain the loyalty of these constituents. The bilateral donors' motives are equally diverse: they may be altruistic in wanting to help countries that are less fortunate than their own; they may be commercial in wanting to capture a market for their exports; but most bilateral aid is likely to be provided for strategic purposes, that is, in order to acquire political influence in the recipient countries. Multilateral institutions may wish to increase their disbursements in order to maintain their relevance in the global order and thus to persuade their shareholders to finance an enlargement of their capital base.

The multitude of aims on both sides can make for a very complex mix of politics and economics. Moreover, while donor and recipient objectives may coincide on many points regarding aid, they may also diverge on several important issues. Thus, as an example, aid may fail to boost the recipient's GDP growth rate or reduce poverty in that country, and yet be counted a success by the donor if the purpose of the aid was to purchase strategic influence.[29]

In Egypt's case, if one takes as given that policymakers regard the offer of more aid as preferable to that of less, five issues recurred with sufficient frequency to warrant serious discussions in cabinet and with international agencies and bilateral donors.

The first was the composition of aid between project and program components. Egypt argued for a larger proportion of program assistance in the mix, for three reasons.

1. It is disbursed much more quickly. The World Bank estimated that typically between 50 and 100 percent of amounts committed as program assistance is disbursed in the twelve months following commitment, compared with only 3–5 percent for project assistance.

2. It called for much less intrusion by donors compared with project aid. The latter required an extensive process of project identification, feasibility studies, reviews, and lengthy contracting procedures, to be followed by supervision missions at least once or twice a year. The process not only consumed a good deal of time, but also grated politically on the Egyptians. The resentment was focused largely on assistance from the United States, which was not only the largest single donor but also, as Weinbaum (1986, 102) noted, because of the "comparison between the supervision of U.S.-sponsored projects in Egypt and U.S. economic assistance to Israel that is delivered without an AID [later known as USAID] mission."

3. It enabled existing manufacturing and other capacity to be utilized more fully by providing the necessary raw materials. It also increased the Egyptian government's ability to generate domestic resources by selling to the private sector some of the commodities imported under program aid. This was an important benefit. The Egyptian budget was chronically short of resources, and projects were held up because donors tended to finance only the foreign-exchange component (which on average accounted for about 30 percent of a project's cost), leaving Egypt to provide the domestic currency portion of about 70 percent. Speaking of Egyptian ministries and agencies, in late 1976 Mahmoud al-Imam, minister of planning, expressed his problem as, "They bring me a button from abroad and expect me to provide a coat to sew it onto."

The second area that gave rise to concern among policymakers was the *costs of aid tying*. Studies pioneered by Mahbub ul-Haq (1967) and Bhagwati (1967) had shown that commodities obtained under conditions in which the procurement was tied to the donor country typically tended to be priced higher than international prices. Some of the price differences obviously resulted from the use of what was effectively monopoly power by the donor. A few resulted from what might well be viewed as rather dubious practices. Haq gives an instance of a subsidiary firm in country A obtaining air compressors from its parent company in country B, marking them up by 30 percent, and including the higher-priced item as part of the aid package from country A.

The Egyptian government examined the question of aid tying in detail in 1979, after two meetings of the Consultative Group had greatly increased the number of donors, the offers of assistance, and multiplied the range of terms on which the assistance was offered. Let me paraphrase the findings of a rather discursive study for the cabinet on this subject. The study concentrated on assistance from the United States, since that country was by far the biggest provider of economic assistance to Egypt. The paper found that many items procured from the United States were priced 30–50 percent higher, and at times even more, than if purchased in the international market. However, a closer look at the facts would exonerate the United States from deliberately following a predatory pricing policy for items financed under aid. The price differences resulted chiefly from a mismatch between the items that Egypt wanted and the areas in which the United States was an efficient producer.

The United States was most efficient at producing what one might call the most "modern" items; studies showed that the more technologically advanced the product, the more efficient was the United States in producing it. Thus, the United States was more efficient at producing bicycles than donkey carts, motorcycles than bicycles, motor cars than motorcycles, jet planes than motorcars, and so on all the way to, say, space rockets and satellites compared with jet aircraft. The problem was that most of the commodities that Egypt required lay closer to the donkey-cart than to the space-rocket-and-satellite end of the technological spectrum. It was unfortunate that, to quote Weinbaum (1986, 51), "U.S. aid programs normally stipulate that concessional financing be tied to U.S.-made products, regardless of more competitive prices elsewhere and irrespective of Egypt's ability to produce the same items." The effect was that the real value of aid in terms of purchasing power could be substantially less than the nominal value. Moreover, while Egypt might in real terms receive only 50–70 percent of the nominal value, the country had to repay 100 percent of the non-grant element in the aid package.

The government of course wanted to mitigate the effects of aid-tying, and the paper drew on work by UNCTAD to offer some proposals. It recommended that Egypt negotiate with the principal aid donors to accept some or all of the following suggestions.

1. In cases where the tied nature of credits raised the prices of imported commodities and equipment above their international prices by some specified figure, donor countries should write down the credit to the extent of the difference between the international prices and the domestic price, and treat this part as a measure of their domestic export promotion.
2. Where possible, credits could be tied to larger areas, such as the Common Market in the case of European countries, so that Egypt could take advantage of procurement in the region as a whole.
3. Aid-giving countries should accept the principle of tying at least some portion of the payment of tied credits to exports of manufactured commodities from the recipient country. This could lower the financial burden on Egypt, and also help the development of a quality-conscious manufacturing sector.

Nothing came of these proposals, but it shows that Egyptian officials were concerned from an early date with the paying back of foreign aid that was provided as loans.

Third, policymakers were concerned about the conditionality attached to some external inflows. This was a serious matter, because the conditions on the disbursement of aid determined the amount of pain imposed on the economy. The favored response of Egyptian policymakers was to argue for a more gradual implementation of the conditions so as to lessen the pain on the public and thus to give the authorities more time and make it easier to persuade it to accept the conditions.

Concerns with what might happen if the conditions imposed a sudden shock to the economic system could bring down wrath from the highest levels in the land. Sadowski quotes some comments of President Mubarak in 1988 regarding the IMF's prescriptions. He compared the Fund to a quack doctor, and went on to say:

A patient, for example, needs a treatment for one month. Instead of this doctor telling the patient to take the medicine daily for one month, he tells him to take all the medicine today and tomorrow and that he will recover the day after. Of course, he will take the medicine to go to sleep at night and will not wake up in the morning. He dies. This is the IMF. It writes a prescription for those who require prolonged treatment, just as for those who require short treatment. . . . I tell the IMF that economic reform should proceed according to the social and economic situation in the state and according to the people's standard of living. One should not come and say increase the price by 40 per cent. Surely, no one will be able to live. This will not be an IMF process: it will be a slaughter. (Sadowski 1991, 252–53)

Another reason for Egyptian policymakers' antipathy to conditionality was skepticism regarding whether the policy conditions would in fact achieve their aims. Many studies showed that conditionality frequently worked very poorly; see, for example, Spraos 1986; Cornia, Jolly, and Stewart 1987, 1988; Harrigan and Mosley 1991; Mosley, Harrigan, and Toye 1997; Collier 1997; Dollar and Svensson 1998; Easterly 2003, 2006; Easterly et al. 1993; Boone 2006; and some from the World Bank itself, such as World Bank 1990a; Corbo, Fischer, and Webb 1992.

These studies showed that conditionality was liable to fail because of two principal factors. First, it targeted instruments rather than outcomes, and the designated instruments might not be sufficiently effective to produce the desired results. Second, in the case of aid provided for strategic purposes (most frequently by bilateral donors), recipients seldom believed that it would be cut off. Terminating this type of aid would lose the donor all the strategic capital that had been built up; therefore, aid cutoff as an instrument for enforcing conditionality was rarely credible and hence seldom feared.

The aid relationship became more complicated as the Egyptian economy expanded and its financing requirements increased. The net transfer of concessional resources steadily decreased as a percent of Egypt's GDP, and with it the donors' leverage to impose conditions also eroded. At the same time, donors' budgets came under increasing strain, especially when the West was hit by a series of financial crises, and raising aid allocations to Egypt became unlikely. Egypt therefore began looking toward the Arab capital-surplus countries to provide assistance that was significant in amount and burdened with few, if any, conditions. Of course, Egyptian policymakers were aware that there is no free lunch, and that Egypt would have to repay the Arab aid in political, if not economic, currency. Such conditions are more implicit than explicit, but they are no less real for being invisible. Moreover, aid from Arab countries could be very generous, but also could be very volatile—for example, in 2014 Egypt received $20 billion from the Gulf countries as budget and balance-of-payments support, amounting to some 5 percent of GDP; the following year it dropped to 1 percent of GDP (Government of Egypt 2015a, 11). However, given the state of the Egyptian economy in the 2008–2015 period, the country's policymakers considered this route, despite the volatility, the least bad option.

The fourth issue, which became especially important after Egypt's debt crises of the late 1980s and early 1990s, concerned the terms of aid. In the early years of the aid relationship with the West, the Egyptian authorities did not define explicit criteria for discriminating between loans in order to decide which to accept and which to reject. The criteria evolved over a number of years and ultimately comprised three elements: (1) the currency in which the loan was denominated; (2) the phasing of the debt service; and (3) the concessionality of the loan.

1. Concern with the currency in which the loan was denominated came to the fore when the Japanese yen appreciated by about 70 percent against the U.S. dollar (which was the currency in which much of Egypt's foreign-exchange earnings were denominated). Until that time, loans from Japan had appeared attractive because of their low interest rates. However, the appreciation of the yen sharply increased the value of these loans and the cost of servicing them in terms of Egyptian pounds. Resource inflows that had been regarded with much favor began to be looked at askance. The cabinet demanded a more careful analysis of the prospects of the currency in which the loan was issued.

2. Egypt had previously suffered a "bunching" of its debt service payments; a temporary problem of liquidity faced with such a spike in servicing obligations might seriously damage perceptions of the country's solvency. Zaafer al-Bishry, the minister of planning and of international cooperation, initiated an examination of the time profile of external debt service so that loans that would worsen this profile could be rejected or renegotiated.

3. The next minister of international cooperation, Ahmed al-Dersh, established rules for comparing the concessionality of loans and set a minimum hurdle that the terms of a loan would have to clear before it could be accepted. The bar was set at a grant element of at least 40 percent with the stream of repayments discounted at 10 percent a year.[30]

Fifth, a Marshall Plan for Egypt? On a number of occasions, Egyptian policymakers raised the argument that what Egypt required from donors was a "Marshall Plan" for the country; indeed, variants of this idea were formally put forward in 1979 and 1986 for consideration to the G-7 (the group of the biggest industrialized countries). The notion continues to resurface from time to time, perhaps because its proponents have not paid due regard to the underlying premise of the Marshall Plan. Let me elaborate.

After the Second World War, the economies of the European countries had been destroyed and it was imperative, for humanitarian and political reasons, to rebuild them as quickly as possible. The United States was the only country that possessed the necessary resources, and it prepared a plan for the rebuilding of Europe.

As assistance under the European Recovery Program (which came to be called the Marshall Plan), the Europeans asked for $22 billion over four years; the U.S. Congress agreed to consider $17 billion over that period. From April 1948, when the Marshall Plan began, until December 31, 1951, when it ended, the United States provided about $11.8 billion in grants and $1.14 billion in loans to the sixteen countries covered by the plan. This amount in late-1940s dollars was estimated to be equivalent to about $108 billion in 2006 dollars[31] and to about $125 billion in 2015.

At the start of the Marshall Plan period the combined population of the eligible countries amounted to roughly 280 million. If Egypt's 90 million were to receive the same per capita amounts in 2015 dollars as disbursed under the Marshall Plan, it would require Western countries (assuming that, unlike the Marshall Plan, the United States would not be the sole donor) to transfer about $40 billion over four years. Given the state of the European and Japanese economies—which have undergone several years of recession and run up mountains of debt—would their taxpayers be willing to support the implied levels of external charity? One might note that the United States' allocation of economic aid to Egypt in 2015 was $250 *million*(!), that is, a mere 2.5 percent of the $10 billion that would have to be transferred under the presumed Marshall Plan.

Equally to the point, could Egypt productively absorb the targeted annual amount? The crucial assumption underlying the Marshall Plan does not hold in Egypt. The plan was predicated on the basis that while the capital assets of the Western European countries had been destroyed in the war, their human capital and fundamental institutions remained largely intact. Thus, if the United States replaced the destroyed physical capital, economic growth in these countries would proceed rapidly. This, in fact, is what occurred.

In Egypt, however, the human capital base is much smaller, of generally lower quality than in Western Europe, and a substantial part of it continues to be lost through emigration. Moreover, many key institutions remain weak or dysfunctional (see, for example, the discussion in Ikram, 2006, 287–308, el-Mikawy and Handoussa, 2002). This does not, of course, mean that the shortcomings cannot be remedied, but it does mean that it will require time, effort, and considerable political will. Many aspects of the program for Egypt must therefore be qualitatively different from those applicable to Western Europe; simply throwing money at the problem will not provide a solution.

Apart from Financial Resources, Egypt Requires Strengthening of Governance

Quite apart from the unlikelihood of a resource transfer of this magnitude, it may also largely be unnecessary. Many of the fundamental economic problems of Egypt have resulted not so much from a shortage of financial resources as from failures of governance—unclear property rights, a sluggish bureaucracy, an overburdened judicial system, a weak and unbalanced taxation system, corruption, uneconomic pricing of scarce resources (such as electricity and water), an education system that that does not deliver the skills and especially the quality demanded by an internationally competitive market economy, the prevalence of crony capitalism, oligopolies and reduced competition in many sectors of the economy, significant overstaffing in public enterprises, a perceived lack of accountability at many levels of government, and the list goes on. These impediments raise the cost of doing business and thereby discourage investment, and they also lower its productivity. Fixing these problems does not call for mounds of money, but requires analysis, implementation capacity, and above all, the political will to subdue the factions that benefit from economic rents created by inefficiencies in the economy.

Discussions and data on these issues appear in World Bank (1992), el-Mikawy and Handoussa (2002), Ikram (2006), and World Bank (2016).

Donors' Views

This survey of political-economy issues impacting the aid relationship would be unbalanced if it did not, even if briefly, refer to some problems raised by donors. The chief complaint of multilateral donors was obviously the slow implementation of the policy conditions in the agreement (the experience of the early 1990s was an exception).

The complaints of bilateral donors, at least on the economic side (one assumes they were getting sufficient strategic returns because they continued their politically oriented aid programs), generally concerned the insufficiency of good projects, slow implementation, and the mismatch between what the donors could do and the expectations of the Egyptians.

Bilateral donors often complained that there was a paucity of "spade-ready" projects that they could quickly incorporate into their aid programs. This led them to raise questions about Egypt's "absorptive capacity." Egyptian policymakers did, in fact, attempt to respond to this issue. Even as far back as the first meeting of the Consultative Group in 1977, the Egyptian delegation worked with the World Bank to prepare a list of projects divided by sector and distinguished by state of readiness—that is, whether it was an extension to an existing project, whether it was a new project and a feasibility study was ready, or whether it was as yet only a gleam in a ministerial eye. However, constructing a substantial portfolio of aid-worthy projects, backed by high-quality feasibility studies and with financing assured for the domestic currency component, undoubtedly represented a major challenge for a country unused to such procedures for receiving aid, and progress initially was slow.

There was also the pressure on donors to disburse their aid budgets within their country's financial year; donor bureaucrats were aware that this was the most certain way of ensuring an adequate replenishment of their department's budget in the following year. Depending upon the flexibility within a particular country's regulations relating to external assistance, the pressure for quick disbursement could switch assistance toward non-project ends. Taking the United States as an example, in the period 1974–86, the Commodity Import Program disbursed about 80 percent and the PL-480 program almost 100 percent of the amounts allocated, while the project aid component disbursed barely 40 percent of allocated funds.

Weinbaum (1986, 111) reports that even attaining this level of disbursements for projects required the USAID mission to make special efforts and seek approval from Washington for costly, expanded infrastructure projects and to provide support for several peripheral programs.

Dissatisfaction with the pace of the implementation of projects was an issue that caused some unhappiness among donors, especially in the earlier years of the Western aid programs (commencing from about 1974). In part, this should have been expected and was simply the result of the Egyptians' inexperience of dealing with new procurement and other procedures and of starting work with countries and institutions from which they had largely been isolated for two decades. However, an important factor was the pressure on the Egyptian budget and the insufficiency of domestic resources to complement the foreign-exchange component provided by the donor. Donors felt that Egypt should be making a bigger effort to mobilize domestic resources so that it could fully benefit from the foreign assistance that was on offer.

Some bilateral donors, in particular the United States, felt that their Egyptian counterparts had unrealistic expectations about how much resources could be made available. Don Brown, the first director of USAID after the resumption of the aid program, said on more than one occasion that he had to keep reminding Egyptian officials that he had a large but not bottomless wallet. These remarks were occasioned because the Egyptian counterparts often appeared to think that most objectives could be attained simply by having the donors provide more resources. Commenting on this facet of the relationship between Egypt and USAID, Weinbaum (1986, 121) writes, "This notion of development during much of the [early] history of the program expressed itself in 'build us this.'"

The third aspect of the relationship was the thorniest. The United States ambassador Hermann Eilts (1985, xv) described the attitude of Egyptian officials "as though there were some kind of an obligation on the part of foreign donors to provide them with economic help." He noted that there was "usually little sign of appreciation on the part of Egyptian officials and an obvious reluctance to give public credit to the foreign donor for the burden borne by the latter's taxpayers," and that "their [the officials'] attitude often brought to mind Pharaonic friezes showing subject peoples bringing tribute to Egyptian rulers."

Dissatisfaction with Egyptians' apparent lack of appreciation of foreign aid was not confined to Ambassador Eilts, but also figured prominently in discussions among representatives of donor embassies in Cairo. I recommended that they read George Orwell's *Down and Out in Paris and London*, especially the part concerning Orwell's experiences in London, saying that it might help to disabuse them of any rose-tinted view they might harbor of the donor–recipient relationship. After reading it, one of the ambassadors commented that he had thereby acquired a much greater sensitivity concerning the relationship, but felt that Egypt in turn should be made aware that foreign aid had become increasingly hard to "sell" to donors' constituents. Ambassadors would thus have to make strenuous efforts to ensure that recipients, regardless of what they actually felt, made appreciative noises that could be relayed back to parliaments in donor countries.

The fundamental question, however, was left unresolved: Did the recipient country accept that the resource transfer was a "gift," for which it should be grateful, or did it view the transfer as simply part of a transactional exchange, to compensate the recipient for some service that it had provided? Examples of such incongruity of perception are not difficult to find: what the United States considered "aid," the Egyptians regarded as but a due reward for recognizing Israel and not impeding the West's access to Middle East oil, and thus did not feel any obligation to tug at their forelocks; during the war in Afghanistan, what the United States considered "aid," Pakistan tended to view as rent for the use of Karachi port and the country's road and rail network by U.S. military and support units. The donor and the recipient can be viewing the same transaction through different lenses, and that can create substantial misunderstandings.

Foreign Aid to Egypt: Benefit or Bane?

A question frequently asked in political-economy discussions in Egypt is whether foreign aid has had a beneficial or a baleful effect on the Egyptian economy. The answer might help to clarify whether or not aid should be accepted, and if it is, on what terms, in what amounts, and for what purposes.

The question whether aid supplements or displaces domestic efforts and whether it has succeeded in facilitating economic reform has generated an extensive literature. A settled conclusion, however, has not been reached. This is perhaps unavoidable; as Rodrik (1996, 30) remarks, "external resources reduce the costs both of reform [that is, by providing finance for some sort of cushion] and of doing nothing—that is, avoiding reform [that is, by continuing to provide finance for the status quo]." The studies tend to examine the experience of different countries and different time periods, and can use different criteria for judging success, so it is almost inevitable that they encompass a wide range of conclusions. In fact, as Adam and Dercon (2009, 173–74) point out, since Robert Barro's (1991) paper on cross-country patterns of growth sparked the surge of research on the empirics of growth, "perhaps only one broad conclusion emerging from the wealth of growth regression results commands universal support. This is that 'institutions matter.'"[32]

Proponents arguing for the success of aid (at times with nuanced caveats) can point to, among many others, Papanek (1972, 1973), Cassen (1994), Burnside and Dollar (2000), Sachs (2005), the U.N. Millennium Project (2005), Sen (2006), and Tarp (2010), while critics of aid can find much ammunition in (again among others) Bauer (1971), Boone (2006), and the writings of Easterly (for example, 2003, 2006). The increasing availability of data and the application of more refined models have at times cast doubt on the robustness of earlier findings and led to some to-ing and fro-ing between proponents and critics as they sought to attack others' positions or to defend their own. Tarp (2010, 43) is not far off the mark when he quotes the singer Bob Dylan to say that with all the uncertainty concerning aid effectiveness, it might appear that "the answer, my friend, is blowin' in the wind." However, the conclusion of Tarp's study is that "a substantial part of the modern aid-growth literature does suggest that aid has a positive impact on per capita growth," but he cautions that "no excessive claims about parameter sizes and total aid impact should be made."

In view of the unsettled nature of the general debate, it should surprise no one that examinations of the impact of aid on the performance of the Egyptian economy have been inconclusive. Critics of foreign aid argued that much foreign assistance harmed Egypt's economy or was wasted, and that large donors imposed their own preferences on Egypt's development pattern and distorted Egypt's priorities.

These critics can find support from a variety of sources. Thus, Weinbaum (1986, 52) reports USAID officials in Cairo acknowledging privately that their analyses showed food aid had a negative impact on domestic Egyptian wheat production. Springborg (1989, 275–76) presents an embarrassing litany of failed USAID-associated projects, such as "U.S.-built buses that rapidly and noisily disintegrated on Cairo's pot-holed streets;[33] a cement factory that required a decade to construct; automated bakeries that did not bake bread; fish farms that produced no fish but did give rise to embezzlement charges against the U.S. project director and some of his Egyptian counterparts; a housing project that consumed more than $100 million without producing a single new dwelling unit; a sewage project in Alexandria that dumped effluent on the city's beaches; pumping stations along the length of the Nile that remained uncompleted years after the pumps had been delivered; and various other embarrassing debacles that received greater or lesser attention in the Egyptian and U.S. media." Critics also claimed that inadequate donor funds were committed to industrial investment, that too small a contribution was made to building up Egypt's productive capacity, and that the deluge of concessional funds enabled policymakers to take the soft option and to abstain from structural reforms that would have improved the efficiency of the Egyptian economy.

Supporters of foreign aid to Egypt retort that some U.S. aid might indeed have been wasted, but the cost of this to Egypt was minimal because much of the assistance was in the form of grants. But the main point of foreign-aid advocates was that their opponents' principal argument rested on a demonstrably dubious assumption, namely, that the absence of aid resources would have compelled policymakers to restructure the economy. They point out that in the fifty years since 1965, the Egyptian economy had seen periods when the economy was under resource pressure (as for example in 1982–91 and 2000–2004), and in neither episode had policymakers shown any appetite for structural reform. The response to a curtailment of external inflows had been to turn to international capital markets, even if Egypt had to pay on hard commercial terms. For aid advocates, the experience of the last fifty years only nurtures the suspicion that smaller aid inflows would simply have triggered more commercial borrowing, not economic reforms.

The idea that Egypt's investment pattern was significantly distorted because of the predilections of donors also gets short shrift from aid advocates. They argue that Egyptian policymakers are adults whose vocabulary includes the word "no." Whether to accept or to reject aid for a particular activity, project, or sector was ultimately an Egyptian decision. Aid was actively pursued by Egypt, not thrust down the country's resisting throat. At bottom, Egypt had to seek external assistance because the country had opted for a political-economy stance that privileged groups who favored consumption over savings and imports over exports.

Moreover, there is no necessary reason why total investment in the presence of foreign assistance should be less than in its absence, and there was nothing to prevent Egypt from using its own resources to support its priorities. If total investment from Egypt's own resources plus the very substantial foreign assistance was still inadequate to meet Egypt's aims, it raised questions about the vigor of the country's efforts to mobilize domestic savings and the strength of the country's desire to move toward economic independence. Over the period 1960–2016, the domestic savings rate averaged only about 13.5 percent of GDP, showing that in the preferences of policymakers, consumption counted for more than savings. Exports of goods and services over the period averaged about 21 percent of GDP, compared with 29 percent for imports of goods and services, making it clear that the groups benefiting from imports retained an ascendancy over those championing exports.

The basic issue of Egypt's receiving foreign aid is not technical, but political-economic. As numerous analyses have reiterated, Egyptian regimes since 1952 have maintained an implicit compact with citizens: the regimes would provide a mixture of subsidies and other benefits (garnished with the threat of coercion), the citizens would remain politically dormant. With the population growing and wants expanding, the GDP had to keep increasing in order to sustain the compact. A shrinkage or severely reduced growth of the GDP could imperil the regime. Therefore, if Egypt could not finance the expansion with its own resources, then these had to be obtained from abroad, be it in the form of concessional assistance or of borrowing from capital markets on commercial terms.

The role of foreign aid in Egypt's development merits a serious discussion drained, as far as possible, of ideological prejudices. Foreign aid—whether from the West or from the Soviet Union—permitted Egypt a wider range of options. It enabled consumption, investment, and imports to be higher and exports lower than they would have had to be in its absence, and supported a military buildup and an expansive foreign policy. Those who argue that foreign aid has been a toxin coursing through the veins of Egypt's economy need to be explicit about the political-economy trade-offs. They need to address questions such as: What economic and/or political elements would or should the country have been prepared to give up in exchange for reduced dependence on external resources? Which groups would bear the cost, in terms of reduced consumption and higher taxes, for self-reliance? How far could the living standards of the people have been compressed and/or what elements of its foreign policies should the country have abandoned in order to live within its means?

The cheerleaders for external assistance are under an equal obligation to analyze the effectiveness of that assistance, to consider who were the main winners and losers from the availability of the additional resources, and to explain whether the price that Egypt had to pay in a political coin was adequately compensated by what it received in an economic one. A discussion of such matters could help policymakers and the voting public to pick their way through the thicket of political and economic issues that surrounds the question of economic growth and external dependence, and perhaps to reach some conclusions that could help to guide future policy in this area.

2
Challenges and Performance
1952–2016

E gypt's policymakers face a number of challenges that are sui generis to the country and others that are generic and appear in most developing countries. Some of these challenges, such as the scarcity of water and the resulting difficulty of enlarging the cultivable land, are imposed by nature; others, such as population growth, result from a combination of nature and human agency; while still others, for example, weaknesses in the country's international competitiveness or the insufficiency of domestic investment and savings, are the consequence of inappropriate policies.

This chapter provides a bird's eye review of Egyptian economic performance between 1965 and 2016, with forays to earlier years. It surveys the most critical economic issues that Egypt's policymakers confronted since 1952 and offers a brief discussion of the politics and economics that went into dealing with them. Of course, political decisions affecting the economy are taken almost every day; the intent in the chapter is not to be encyclopedic or to offer a day-to-day commentary, but to focus on those whose effects were durable. The chapter thus provides an overview and a context for the discussion in the rest of the book. In order to be meaningful, the discussion must describe examples from different periods in Egypt's experience; thus a degree of overlap between this and chapters 4 through 7 is unavoidable. The issue of population is particularly important, not least because population is both a consumer of the GDP as well as a producer, and is discussed separately in chapter 3.

In assessing economic policies, this book takes as its point of view that the fundamental duty of a government is to improve the life of its citizens and to reduce the country's vulnerability to external pressure. A key (but of course not the only) element in a better life is a higher income, because it enables persons to obtain greater command over goods and services that help them to live a life that they value. A main responsibility of Egypt's policymakers, therefore, is to adopt policies that would expand the country's production of goods and services, that is, its Gross Domestic Product (GDP), while keeping its external debt within manageable bounds. Moreover, in the interests of political harmony, there must be a socially acceptable distribution of this GDP and the incidence of poverty minimized.

Economic Growth
Gross Domestic Product
One cannot make bricks without straw, and one cannot formulate evidence-based policies without accurate, timely, and consistent data. The quip of the Nobel laureate George Stigler, that "the plural of anecdote is data," may not be entirely applicable, but one must recognize that the quality of economic data in many developing countries, including Egypt, can be variable. Some numbers, such as exports, imports, tax collections, the main categories of public expenditure, public debt, and monetary data are generally reliable. However, some of the most common measures of economic performance, such as the Gross Domestic Product (GDP) in real terms, which measures the value of all goods and services produced by the economy after adjusting for price changes, or the country's savings and investment, are less robust and have larger margins of error. These figures have to be used, because they are the best that we have and they are continually being improved. However, it is well not to obsess over decimal-point differences in the performance of these indicators from year to year. A short note on the estimates is annexed to this chapter; a more detailed discussion of Egypt's economic data will be found in Ikram (2006, 108–16).

The GDP growth story is broadly as follows. Between 1947 and 1952, the economy grew rapidly as it recovered from the effects of the Second World War; Hansen and Nashashibi (1975, 11–15 and table 1-1) estimate the growth of real GDP in this period at 5 percent a year. Growth slowed between 1952 and 1955, dropping to about 2 percent a year. After the Suez war of 1956, the government's emphasis on development aided by expansionary fiscal and monetary policies drove up the growth rate to almost 6 percent a year. These estimates are also in line with Mead (1967, tables I-A-6 and I-A-8), who puts the average growth of the GNP between 1945 and 1963 in constant 1954 prices at about 4.3 percent a year. Thus, Egypt's economy looks to have expanded at an average rate of between 4 and 4.5 percent a year in real terms between 1945 and 1965, with of course significant year-to-year variations. Pushing the figures back to earlier years requires a number of conjectures. On the basis of some generally plausible assumptions, Hansen and Marzouk (1965, 3, table 1.1) estimate that real GNP per capita in 1914 was about the same as in 1952—roughly LE45 in 1954 prices. The average Egyptian was probably no better off in 1952 than in 1914.

The behavior of the GDP from 1965 to 2016 is shown in figure 2. Measured in constant 2005 prices, the GDP increased from $13 billion in 1965 to more than $140 billion in 2016. The growth rate over this entire period averaged about 4.7 percent a year, but the year-to-year fluctuations were substantial. The coefficient of variation (a measure of the fluctuations in relation to the average) for the five decades as a whole was 57.9 percent.

Decomposition of growth on the supply side shows that it was based primarily on low value-added output consumed internally. The most dynamic sectors in Egypt were nontradables, with the exception of the manufacturing sector. The sectoral composition of growth also indicates that modern technology was not incorporated in significant amounts, except perhaps in some manufactures. Data on the allocation of investment by sector are patchy, but the high growth in construction suggests that this sector may have been the beneficiary of significant amounts of such funds. The World Bank (2001a, 11) also suggested that the country's investment went predominantly into new buildings rather than retooling or investment in plant and machinery. See also Mohammed (2001) and World Bank (2014a).

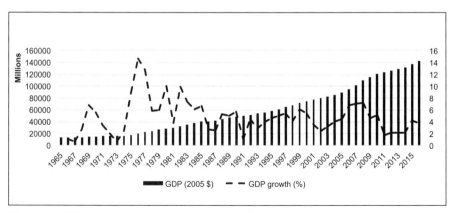

Figure 2. GDP and growth rate, 1965–2016; $ million in 2005 prices and percent

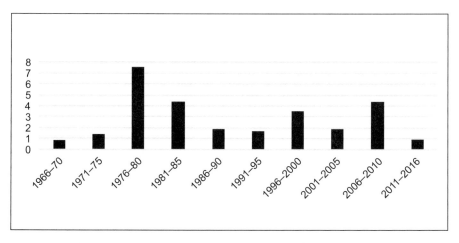

Figure 3. Growth rates of GDP per capita in 2005$, 1965–2016, percent

Per Capita Income

Developments in income per head are affected by both the growth of the GDP and that of population. Hansen and Nashashibi (1975, 14) estimate that between 1947 and 1952 GDP per capita may have increased by about 3 percent a year. From 1950 to 1956, per capita income probably fell slightly, while from 1957 to 1964 it increased at 3.0–3.5 percent a year.

GDP per head in constant 2005 prices increased from $406 in 1965 to about $1,630 in 2016. This series takes into account changes both in prices and in the population, and its growth rate should show greater fluctuation than that of the GDP. Indeed, in certain years—such as 1966, 1967, 1973, and 1991—real per capita income fell, creating negative growth rates (that is, rates of decline). For the period as a whole, the coefficient of variation was 97.6 percent, much higher than that for the GDP growth series. Figure 3 shows the growth rates for per capita GDP between 1965 and 2016 as averages for five-year periods.

Structural Changes

Growth in the GDP was accompanied by changes in its structure, a natural result of the sectors' growing at different rates over the fifty-year period. The biggest change between 1965 and 2016 was a halving in the share of agriculture from 29 percent of the total to 15 percent, and a corresponding increase in the share of industry from 27 percent to 39 percent. A substantial part of the increase represented the emergence and

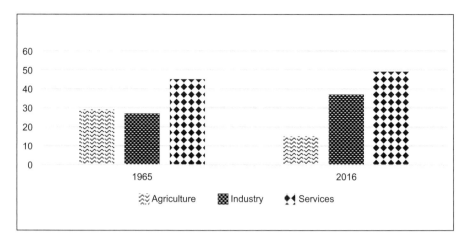

Figure 4. Structure of GDP, 1965 and 2016, percent

growth of the petroleum sector. The share of the services sectors fluctuated a little between 45 percent at the start of the period and up to 52 percent in some years, but by 2016 had more or less returned to its share in 1965. See figure 4.

Investment and Savings

Economic growth is driven by a combination of investment, financed mainly by domestic savings, and improvements in productivity. Between 1947 and 1957 gross fixed investment remained low, accounting for only 12–13 percent of GDP, and from 1957 to 1964 it increased to about 19 percent. Starting in 1964, the cutbacks in demand required to curb inflation and improve the balance of payments substantially decreased the share of investment in the GDP, while the June 1967 war intensified this fall. At the end of the 1960s, the share of investment in GDP was almost as low as in 1947 (Hansen and Nashashibi 1975, 14–15).

For about two-thirds of the period between 1965 and 2016, the investment rate remained below 20 percent of GDP; see figure 5. This rate was much below that sustained for periods of three or more decades by fast-growing countries in Asia. Thus, to put matters in perspective, South Korea, Taiwan, Malaysia, Singapore, and Hong Kong maintained investment rates of around 35 percent of GDP during their decades of rapid growth, while the rate for China was frequently in the 40–45 percent range. The discussion in the introduction showed that improvements in total

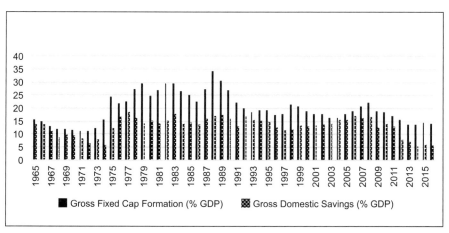

Figure 5. Investment and savings, 1965–2016, percent of GDP

factor productivity, representing the efficiency with which factors of production are combined, played a minor role in the growth of Egypt's GDP. The insufficiency of the quantity of Egypt's investment was not compensated for by improvements in its productivity.

The financing of investment raised its own problems for policymakers, as Egypt's domestic savings consistently fell short, frequently by a large margin, of the investment rate. Over the fifty-year period as a whole, the average ratio of investment to GDP was 20.2 percent, while the domestic savings rate averaged 13.5 percent. This savings ratio might make the picture look a little worse than it probably was. Largely because of remittances from expatriate Egyptians, the country's *national* savings are higher than its *domestic* savings.[1] However, there still remained a large gap between total savings and investment. Moreover, national savings, that is, savings generated by Egyptian nationals working outside the country, are vulnerable to political interference (including the expulsion of Egyptian workers) by the host country. This has happened on more than one occasion: for example, after President Sadat's trip to Israel; during the mid-1980s when oil prices fell and development programs in the major oil-producing states slowed; during the two Gulf wars; during Egypt's conflict with Libya in 1977; and during the political unrest in Iraq and Libya following the collapse of the "Arab Spring."

The shortfall was financed through inflows of foreign aid or by commercial borrowing from abroad. The borrowing obviously added to Egypt's external indebtedness, as did the amount of foreign aid that was not provided as a grant. The failure to mobilize sufficient domestic savings meant that Egypt's economic growth remained critically dependent upon the willingness of foreign institutions and countries to provide resources, while the buildup of external debt preempted an increasing amount of the country's foreign-exchange earnings to service this debt and was thus not available to pay for essential imports. Figure 5 illustrates the behavior of investment and savings from 1965 to 2016 as a percent of GDP.

Population, Labor Force, and Unemployment
Population and Labor Force
Egypt's population increased from about 26 million in 1960 to 90 million in 2016. The growth rate of the population of course fluctuated from year to year; the average over the period as a whole works out to about 2.3 percent a year. The labor force is estimated to have increased from 7.8 million in 1960 to 30.8 million in 2016. The bulk of the labor force is male; roughly 75 percent of males between the ages of 15 and 64 participate in the labor force, compared with only 23 percent of women. Issues relating to Egypt's population are elaborated in chapter 3.

Unemployment
Figure 6 shows the unemployment rate for selected years from 1960 through 2017. Although the data are continually being improved, and the

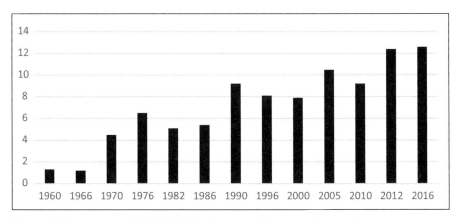

Figure 6. Unemployment, 1960–2016, (percent of labor force), selected years

Sources: 1960–2000 (except 1982) Ikram (2006, table 4.3 and sources cited there [with 1976 corrected]); 1982 from Ministry of Planning; and 2005–2016 from the IMF/World Bank database.

analyses of employment deepened (in which the work of Samir Radwan, Ragui Assaad, Caroline Krafft, and Nader Fergany figures importantly) the reliability of the figures for the earliest years may be suspect, and the IFIs tend to use data chiefly from the 1990s.

Two cautions must be kept in mind regarding the unemployment data. First, the data do not capture the "discouraged unemployed," that is, those persons who would have liked to search for a job had they had the money and the means to do so, and those who have got so fed up of looking for a job (because they have been unsuccessful so far) that they did not "actively search" for one in the reference period covered by the Labor Force Sample Survey. These groups are effectively excluded from the definition of the labor force, and the result is to understate the extent of unemployment.[2]

Second, policymakers, in particular, should take note of another short-coming of the unemployment rate. Krafft and Assaad (2014b, 1) point out that the official unemployment rate is most likely to capture the labor market status of the young, educated first-time entrants who seek formal (and generally public sector) employment. Because of its education, this group is likely to get public sector employment in due course, and also is likely to have the means to remain unemployed until it obtains such employment. The poor and less educated groups, on the other hand, do not have this staying power and are therefore compelled to take any job available in the informal economy. "By focusing exclusively on the unemployment rate, policymakers are thus limiting their attention to the plight of a relatively privileged group at the expense of much more vulnerable groups that suffer more severely in an economic downturn." They argue that unemployment in Egypt results primarily from structural conditions—the growth in the educated labor supply, and the marked divide between the public and private sectors regarding benefits and security of tenure. Krafft and Assad (2014b, 3) thus conclude that, "[T]he unemployment rate, being primarily driven by demographic rather than economic forces, is a poor measure of labor market health," and that therefore "signs of labor market distress during economic crises must be sought beyond the unemployment rate" (Krafft and Assaad 2013b, 17).

Some of the principal signs of labor market distress that are not captured by the unemployment rate point to a deterioration in the quality of employment, rather than to an increase in the unemployment rate. An important sign is the shift in the structure of employment toward irregular wage employment, which is closely associated with poverty. To make matters worse, unemployment in Egypt is principally a problem for new entrants into the labor force, and the trend starting from the 1980s is that the first jobs obtained by new entrants are mainly in informal wage employment. Krafft and Assaad (2013a, 2). The precariousness associated with such employment (that is, when the youths even do manage to obtain a job) and the political dissatisfaction that it is likely to engender, should be a cause of concern for policymakers. The problem of youth unemployment (estimated in 2015 at around 30 percent of the 15–24 age cohort), and of the poor quality of first jobs they find (when they manage to find one) is a critical political-economy matter for Egypt. Issues in the labor market are discussed further in the final chapter of the book.

Structure of Employment

Changes in the structure of employment followed the pattern of the GDP. Employment in agriculture dropped from 54 percent of total employment in 1960 to 42 percent in 1980 and by 2016 had been reduced to 28 percent. Employment in industry increased from 10 percent to 25 percent between 1960 and 2016, while the services sectors also registered significant gains, rising from 36 percent of total employment in 1960 to 47 percent in 2016. These progressions are illustrated in figure 7.

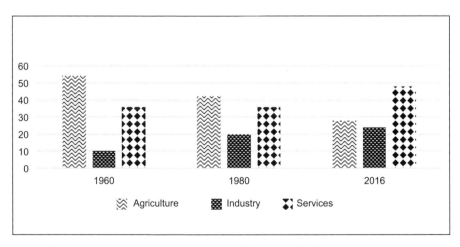

Figure 7. Structure of employment, 1960, 1980, and 2016, percent of total employment

Source: Ikram (2006); World Bank database.

Public Finance

In Egypt's history, the economic failure to generate adequate public resources has a substantial history and has had serious political consequences. Developments in this area of the economy therefore merit some attention.

Egypt's financial problems started to become serious with the khedives Said and Isma'il, who focused more on spending than on raising resources. The country became unable to service the debt incurred for constructing the Suez Canal. In 1875 Isma'il was compelled to sell the bulk of Egypt's shares in the Suez Canal Company to the British government, thereby stripping the country of a valuable financial asset. Continued inability to service debts forced him in 1876 to accept a British–French debt commission that supervised Egypt's fiscal affairs and oversaw the country's economy; Egypt's interests were thus subordinated to those of the two European powers. In 1882, Egypt was occupied by the British and effectively lost its sovereignty. The occupying British troops were withdrawn only in 1954; economic weakness exacted a heavy price from Egypt for seventy-five years. The story of the nationalization of the Suez Canal in 1956 and the war that it led to also had its ultimate cause in economic matters; this matter is described in the introduction and chapter 4. In more recent times, Egypt came under severe pressure in 1986 and 1991 because of inability to service its external debt and was compelled to accept a variety of economic measures, several of which were not to its liking.

After the Suez Canal war of 1956 and the sequestration of British and French assets, the public sector began to permeate many aspects of the economy, and public finance issues correspondingly increased in importance. The state's domination of the economic system is reflected in the proportion of GDP originating in the public sector; this increased from an estimated 13 percent in 1952 to about 40 percent in 1973 (the eve of the infitah; see chapter 5), to 50 percent in 1981. It dropped thereafter, but in 2016 it was still around 30 percent. Government expenditure reached nearly 60 percent of GDP in 1982, and even in 2016 was almost 30 percent of GDP. Moreover, government interventions through laws and regulations in many sectors remained so widespread that they virtually determined the level and composition of output, even though formally these sectors remained in the hands of private decision-makers. The "footprint" of the government in the Egyptian economy is much more extensive than might be inferred from traditional criteria, such as the ratio of government expenditure to GDP.

Overall Fiscal Developments

The role of Egypt's public finances and its impact on the country's political economy merits attention for a number of reasons. First, a major factor in the country's lackluster savings performance during 1965–2016 was that the government's expenditures exceeded its revenues by an annual average of more than 11 percent of GDP. Weak public savings diluted the savings efforts of households and businesses and thus pulled down the country's overall savings rate. Figure 8 summarizes Egypt's fiscal performance from 1965 to 2016.

Second, the resulting pressure on the budget forced the country to turn to external aid to acquire the required domestic resources, exposing it to external political pressures. The behavior of the external sector and foreign indebtedness is discussed below.

Third, the budget is not a mere bookkeeping device, but an important instrument for directing people's behavior into channels that society considers beneficial and discouraging it from those it deems noxious or less desirable. As Ganesh (2015) puts it, "A country's tax code is not just a mesh of rules and rates. It is a secular bible of moral signals. When the state taxes one thing and exempts another, raises this levy and cuts that one, it offers an account of what is and is not noble conduct." It is not just the size of the budget but, just as importantly, its composition, on both the revenue and expenditure sides, that determines vital political-economic outcomes.

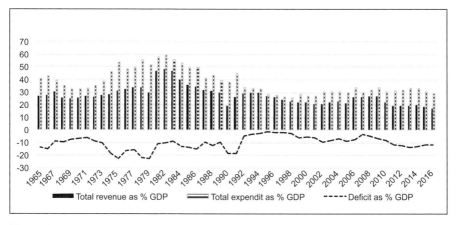

Figure 8. Revenue, expenditure, and overall deficit, 1965–2016; percent of GDP
Source: Ministry of Finance and World Bank

Throughout the period 1965–2016 the overall balance of the central government's budget remained in deficit, the shortfall at times exceeding 20 percent of GDP at current market prices.³ The deficit as a proportion of GDP fluctuated widely around an average of about 11.5 percent for the period as a whole, varying between 22.6 percent in 1975 and 1.6 percent in 1995, and close to 12 percent in 2016. Over the entire period, the ratio of total revenue to GDP at market prices averaged 26 percent, that of total expenditures to GDP about 37.5 percent, prompting one of the IFIs to remark that Egypt's fiscal problems resulted from "earning in Centigrade and spending in Fahrenheit."

The persistent gap between revenues and expenditures meant that the government's indebtedness increased relentlessly. The political-economy calculus evidently indicated that even sharply rising public indebtedness posed a smaller threat to regime survival than would restraints on public consumption. With the large forgiveness and restructuring accorded to external debt at various times (described below), the overwhelming amount of the government's indebtedness was to domestic sources. As of June 30, 2016, Egypt's public debt had reached nearly 95 percent of GDP— 87 percent to domestic sources and about 8 percent to foreign.

Until the late 1970s, two major themes ran through Egyptian public finances. First, Egypt had been in a state of war from 1948, and this meant heavy expenditures on defense. Second, the adoption of the National Charter in 1962 and the move toward "Arab socialism" led to a major realignment of political-economy objectives. The principal goals of this policy were to promote equity in the distribution of income and in consumption capability (to be obtained largely through fiscal measures) and to increase the country's productive capacity, especially of manufactured goods. With the economy dominated by the government, the latter aim required an increased diversion of public resources toward investment.

The relative importance of these two factors differed over time. In 1960, the official figures for defense expenditures put them at about 5 percent of GDP; in 1970, at 16 percent; and in 1978, at about 9 percent.⁴ After the peace treaty with Israel and with an annual $1.3 billion in U.S. grants for defense following the Camp David Accords, the official figures show a decline in the share of defense spending in GDP to about 1.7 percent in 2016. However, the published figures for defense spending are widely considered to be underestimates.

With defense and administration costs assigned the highest priority on the revenues, public investment had to accommodate itself to what was left of the resources. The impact on the resource allocation process can be seen by the gyrations in the rate of public investment (which represented about 80 percent of total investment). Public investment in 1960 was about 11 percent of GDP, rose to 19 percent in 1964, fell to 12 percent in 1970, and increased to 27 percent in 1978. A secular decline followed, with public investment dropping to about 10 percent of GDP in 2000, and further to 5 percent in 2016. Private investment did not rise commensurately to offset the public-sector decline, and remained for most years at 10–12 percent of GDP. Thus the declines in public-sector investment dragged down the aggregate investment rate. Moreover, the Ministry of Economy (1981) pointed out that a number of expenditure items that in Egypt were defined as "investment" would in many other countries be regarded simply as repairs and renewals. Egyptian figures for investment are thus likely to be overstated.

Politics injected a further long-term change into the fiscal picture. After the Arab–Israeli war of 1973, President Sadat sought to buttress his popularity by offering a "peace dividend" (facilitated by the infitah). Many consumer commodities were subsidized. These cost-of-living subsidies became an important item in the budget and a major driver of public consumption expenditure. Thus, if during the 1960s and early 1970s defense needs had competed with investment for resources, after 1973 an aggressive, and persistent, new claimant appeared on the scene. Total subsidies rose from less than 2 percent of GDP in 1971 to about 5 percent in 1973 and 10 percent in 1978. They generally hovered around this figure and even by 2016 they accounted for 9 percent of GDP. The main culprit was energy subsidies, which the World Bank (2016, xi) reported as reaching over 7 percent of GDP, and were more than the combined spending on health, education, and public investment. These subsidies were also regressive, with the richest 20 percent of Egyptian households capturing 60 percent of all energy subsidies.

Public Finance Issues
Revenue issues
In assessing Egypt's resource mobilization during the last fifty years, three important questions of political economy arise: (1) Is the effort adequate? (2) Is the system structurally robust? (3) Is the system equitable?

1. *Is the effort adequate?* "Adequacy" of resources can be assessed only in relation to the demands on them. Judged by an average budget deficit in excess of 11 percent of GDP over the fifty years from 1965 to 2016, the low rate of public savings, and the necessity of resorting to external aid for budgetary support, the answer must clearly be no. Domestic resource mobilization has not met the demands that society has mandated. In certain years, Egypt required extraordinary assistance from Arab countries, generally in the form of grants, to meet the gap between budgetary revenues and expenditures. This special assistance could be very substantial; for example, Government of Egypt (2015a, 22) puts it at 5 percent of GDP in 2014 (more than 20 percent of the revenue mobilized by Egypt itself). To paraphrase Robert Browning, Egypt's reach consistently exceeded its grasp.

2. *Is the system structurally sound?* The answer must again be in the negative. Figure 2.6 shows that the budget deficit was generally high and fluctuated widely during the period 1965 to 2016. This behavior resulted from a basic structural weakness—expenditures responded to domestic inflation while revenues were sensitive to influences from outside the country. Expenditures on consumer subsidies, public-sector salaries and pensions, government purchases, and interest on domestic debt rose in line with inflation and the expansion of government employment; since the base kept increasing, expenditures tended to be inelastic downward.

Revenues, however, marched to a different drummer. The exogenous influences were transmitted through the growing dependence of the budget on "economic rents," that is, payments in excess of those required to keep a factor of production in use. The definition is sometimes used in a more elastic sense; the World Bank (1983, 4) for example, calls them "exogenous" resources "in the sense of their having very little to do with the productivity of Egypt's domestic labor force." The point about Egypt's becoming a "rentier" state has been made by several writers and in World Bank and IMF documents dating from at least 1974, and is virtually a staple of an analyst's Egyptian toolbox.[5] The main rents for Egypt are considered to be foreign aid, Suez Canal tolls, a part of the payments received for petroleum exports, and a part of the receipts from tourism. In his pioneering article, Mahdavy (1970, 466–67) points out that "a government that can expand its services without resorting to heavy taxation acquires an independence from the people seldom found in other countries. . . . In political terms, the power of the government to bribe pressure groups or to coerce dissidents may be greater than otherwise."

The burden of the "economic rents" garnered by Egypt falls on foreigners and not on Egyptians. The political strength of this rent-seeking behavior is that it enabled successive Egyptian regimes to raise resources without alienating their own constituency. The concomitant economic weakness is that the generation of these resources is largely outside the control of Egyptian policymakers. Suez revenues are determined by traffic through the canal, which in turn depends upon the health of the international economy. Tourism is a luxury item and expenditure on it is highly responsive to the economic state of the countries from which tourists originate and to their perception of the security situation in Egypt. Revenue from petroleum taxes is contingent on oil prices that are determined by cartels and producers outside Egypt, while the amount of external aid is decided in foreign capitals. Workers' remittances depend upon the health and attitudes of the host economy, in which decisions are taken on how many Egyptian workers to hire and how much to pay them. There have also been periods when for political reasons the host country has expelled Egyptian workers. The exogenous and unpredictable nature of these major sources of revenues can introduce a substantial measure of uncertainty into revenue mobilization.

The political-economy choice to minimize the effort required from the domestic constituency restricted the amount of public-sector savings that could be mobilized. A World Bank background paper for one of its economic reports claimed that Egypt's fiscal strategy was, as far as possible, simply to tax the foreigner. The budget's vulnerability to very different factors on the revenue and expenditure sides, and the different amplitude and timing of the fluctuations in the two series, created serious difficulties in policymakers' efforts at short-term economic management. With expenditures continually outpacing revenues but with policymakers reluctant to antagonize the domestic constituency, both Abdel Meguid (deputy prime minister for economic affairs) and Salah Hamed (minister of finance) said that cabinet discussions during the preparation of the budget tended to dwell much more on the expenditure than on the revenue side.

In discussions with the World Bank, Abdel Meguid (deputy prime minister for economic affairs) was frank about the authorities' quandary: two crucial elements of the political-economy strategy—not antagonizing the domestic political base and warding off pressures from external sources—were in conflict. The former requirement meant that the authorities could not raise appreciable amounts of domestic resources; the latter that they could not *not* raise the necessary domestic resources. The authorities had to choose from two unthinkables. The choice almost invariably tilted in favor of maintaining the support of the base, which meant seeking the external resources while trying to minimize the accompanying conditions. The ministers tended to accept this as a fact of life, and concentrated their attention on the expenditure side.

The nature of taxes and the reactions to them of different political groups also impacted policymakers' sensitivities. Thus, a value-added tax (VAT), which was recommended a number of times by the IMF as a more efficient and equitable method of raising revenue than many of the measures in place, was regularly rejected.[6] Ministers of finance said that much of the resistance was sponsored by businessmen, and that the real objections of this group rested not on the rate of the tax, but with the group's unease with the documentation that the VAT required. Businessmen did not want to disclose as much information as the tax authorities required for the operation of the VAT, because it could show how little of their incomes they actually paid in taxes. After much vacillation over several years, the government accepted introduction of a VAT as a condition in the agreement between Egypt and the IMF on an Extended Fund Facility for $12 billion that was approved by the IMF's board in November 2016 (see chapter 7). How effectively the tax is implemented remains to be seen. Tax revenue fell from a high of nearly 26 percent of GDP in 1982 to less than 15 percent in 2016.

3. *How effective was the tax system in furthering equity?* Not very. First, one could look at the overall structure of tax revenues. Between 1965 and 2016, roughly two-thirds of the tax revenue was raised through indirect taxes, principally taxes on foreign trade and on goods and services. Direct taxes, that is, on personal incomes and business profits, accounted for about one-third, of which the overwhelming share was provided by the tax on business profits; the

personal income tax accounted for barely 7 percent of the total tax revenue. The heavy reliance on indirect taxes gave the system a markedly regressive structure.

Second, how does the taxation system measure up against the two fundamental criteria of judging the equity characteristics of a taxation system, namely, horizontal and vertical equity. The former requires that people in equal positions be treated equally for tax purposes; the latter requires that the tax system should distribute burdens fairly according to people's ability to pay.

Some studies, such as Ahmed (1984, 36–37) and Dinh and Giugale (1991, 17–18), pointed out that the principle of horizontal equity requires the tax rate to vary according to the level rather than the source of income. But in the Egyptian income-tax system the rate depends on the source of income—a higher rate on "earned" income (for example, that from wages), a lower on "unearned" income (such as that from dividends or bonds), while taxes on property are insignificant. Moreover, large tax exemptions have been granted for various purposes, for example, to stimulate private investment. These factors plus the substantial tax evasion have eroded the tax base for particular income groups.

The progressive rate structure of the tax system would suggest that the principle of vertical equity is supported. However, reality offers a different picture. The extremely low collections of personal income taxation (stagnating at less than 7 percent of total tax revenue during 1965–2016) show that the tax system, because of exemptions and evasions, was flawed in terms of vertical equity as well. The announced rate of tax was irrelevant. Musgrave's (1959, v) tart comment in *The Theory of Public Finance* that "the effects of a tax depend upon what it is, not what it is meant to be" is particularly applicable in these situations. The composition of tax revenues is shown in Figure 9a.

The equity principles were further violated because a significant amount of revenue was raised from taxes the burden of which both impacted on particular sources and was not related to the income of the taxpayer (the latter violated the "ability to pay" principle). The principal such taxes were the inflation tax and the taxation of agriculture.

The "inflation tax"[7] refers to the real revenue obtained by the government when inflation erodes the real value of its nominal liabilities. Keynes ([1926] 1972, 52) had argued that "what is raised by printing notes is just as much taken from the public as is a beer duty or an income tax." Inflation reduces the real value of the public sector's domestic debt and is equivalent to a tax because, like other taxes, it lowers the private sector's real disposable income. Keynes ([1926] 1972, 37) commented that "it is the form of taxation that the public finds hardest to evade and even the weakest government can enforce, when it can enforce nothing else."

Because it is a tax that a parliament does not have to vote for and requires no agency to administer, it appeals to governments wanting to raise revenue while avoiding the inconvenience of transparency and a parliamentary debate on the subject. It has obvious political-economy appeal to governments wary of raising revenues from the more explicit forms of taxation; the yields from the inflation tax in Egypt accounted for well above the average rate found in developed and in most developing countries. Revenues from the inflation tax during 1975–91, when the inflation rate was nearly 18 percent annually, averaged more than 4 percent of GDP, about 20 percent of total revenues. After 1991 the stabilization program brought down the inflation rate, and by 1997 the inflation tax yielded only 1.3 percent of GDP, about 6 percent of total revenues.

The high rate of inflation may have helped the government by maintaining the inflation tax, but it introduced some important distortionary effects into the economy. It made real interest rates negative, because nominal interest rates on domestic currency accounts had been kept low, principally to reduce the cost of the government's borrowing to finance its budget deficits. Governors of the Central Bank of Egypt had been given little choice in this matter; indeed, an IMF memorandum described the Central Bank as only a "satrapy of the Ministry of Finance." The IMF's frequent recommendations to make the Central Bank independent were met with a very deaf government ear.

The negative real interest rates also meant that, in effect, lenders to banks (that is, the depositors) were being made to pay the banks for the "privilege" of lending to them! It is apparent from these outcomes which groups were in the political ascendancy; it certainly was not the savers. Moreover, because the inflation affected only domestic currency bank accounts, it encouraged the "dollarization" (holding balances in foreign currency) of the economy; by 1990 almost 50 percent of money and quasi-money was held in foreign currency.

The government's resource mobilization efforts were also hampered in other directions. Agriculture, although accounting for about 20 percent of GDP, contributed very little to tax revenues. It was argued that because of the low level of literacy among the large number of persons involved in the agricultural sector, trying to impose direct taxation on their incomes would be impractical. What was perhaps more to the point, the larger landowners wielded considerable political influence. Thus the "direct" taxation of agricultural income took the form of a proxy, namely, a tax on landholdings. The yield from this tax was derisory, amounting to less than 1 percent of value-added in the agricultural sector.

Moreover, water was distributed free, with irrigation costs being partly paid from the public budget. Chapter 1 described the government's hesitation in pricing irrigation water. The government tried to recover some of the costs indirectly by imposing a uniform land tax based on rental value. However, assessments of rental values were few and far between, and the system was riddled with exceptions and bore little relation to water supply. The political-economy consequences of not confronting the agricultural faction thus bear both on mobilizing resources and on improving equity.

It was not that the government did not receive suggestions to reform the taxation system; IMF and World Bank papers on the subject go back to at least 1975. One or two of them did genuflect in the direction of (and quote) Adam Smith's (1776, 825–27) four "maxims with regard to taxes." In general, however, the papers accepted that they would have to be satisfied with proposing policies that advanced efficiency and equity only modestly, but would be easy to implement by a taxation service not celebrated for its dynamism.

The reasons for the business coalition to resist the VAT have already been mentioned. The chief obstruction to reforming the income tax and making its implementation more effective predictably came from the better-off classes, whose resistance was made more potent because their numbers included many of the individuals who would be responsible for legislating the tax or executing its provisions.

Expenditure issues

Budgetary expenditures remained high throughout 1965–2016, approaching 50 percent of GDP in some years with an annual average of about

37.5 percent of GDP over the period as a whole. The expenditure side was dominated by current expenditures, which accounted for two-thirds of the total. Most of these expenditures consisted of payments for salaries and cost-of-living subsidies (fig. 9b). For much of the period between 1965 and 2016, nearly one-third of the labor force was employed in central and local governments and the public-service authorities, and wages and salaries accounted for about 28 percent of total budgetary expenditure.

Over the fifty-year period, subsidies accounted for some 12 percent of total expenditures in the budget. In certain years they could be much higher; for example, in 1975–81 subsidies took an average of about 22 percent of budgetary expenditures. The weight of the cost-of-living subsidies decreased over the period as the number of subsidized items was gradually reduced from eighteen in 1977 to only four by 2016. In 1965–90, that is, before the stabilization program described in chapter 6, subsidies absorbed 18 percent of total expenditure; in the next decade the average fell to 7 percent.

In 1991, the stabilization program became the centerpiece of economic policymaking, and mandated a substantial reduction of the budget deficit. In order to comply with this condition, the increase in expenditures was held back below the growth of GDP. Total budgetary expenditure dropped from 38 percent of GDP in 1990 to 29 percent in 1995. Unfortunately, the main impact of expenditure cuts fell on investment: budgetary expenditures on investment accounted for about 32 percent of total budgetary expenditure in 1965, and reached a height of 39 percent in 1990; with the

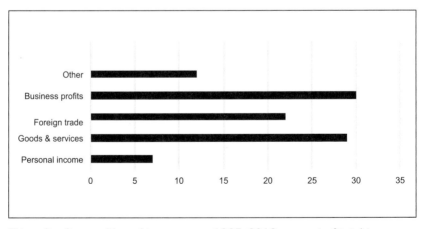

Figure 9a. Composition of tax revenue, 1965–2016, percent of total tax revenue

stabilization and privatization programs in effect from 1991, expenditures on investment started to decline and by 2016 accounted for only 9 percent of total budgetary expenditures. The composition of expenditures over the period 1965–2016 is displayed in figure 9b.

Other structural changes in budgetary expenditures also occurred. The costs of administration, as shown by the figures for central, local, and service agencies, were brought down from their levels in the 1960s, but even by 2016 they consumed close to 48 percent of total expenditure. Another notable change was the sharp rise in interest payments on government debt, which over the period accounted for 11 percent of total budgetary expenditures. About 70 percent of these payments were on domestic debt, reflecting two developments. One, the stock of domestic debt had increased rapidly in the 1980s and early 1990s in order to finance the budget deficits of those years. Large budget deficits reemerged from 2002, becoming very large in 2011–16 (more than 10 percent of GDP); the accumulated budget deficits caused the stock of domestic debt to increase rapidly. On the other hand, a substantial part of the external debt stock had been written down in the rearrangements provided to Egypt in 1991–96. Two, much of the external debt had been contracted on concessional terms and the debt rearrangements further eased the terms; domestic debt had been incurred on much harder terms.

Revenues and expenditures responded differently to the changes in the variables on which they were levied or expended. Ikram (2006, 165–77, 173–74) shows that almost all the expenditure items were more

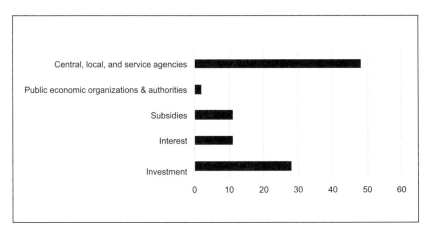

Figure 9b. Composition of expenditures, 1965–2016, percent of total expenditure

responsive—that is, the percentage increase in expenditures tended to be more than the percentage increase in the underlying variable[8]—than those on the revenue side. The consistently higher buoyancy values for expenditures tend to confirm that Egypt's budgetary problems were largely structural, and arose because expenditure items increased faster in response to the growth of the economy than did revenue sources.

Poverty

It almost goes without saying that for policymakers in a developing country perhaps the most essential goal is the reduction of poverty, and Egyptian policymakers are not exempt from this imperative. Modern investigations of poverty and income distribution in Egypt go back to 1977 and have proliferated in recent years.[9]

The Measurement of Poverty

There is no unique definition of "poverty," and that leaves room for a variety of approaches to its measurement. In order to maintain some uniformity, the data and definitions used in this book reflect those of the government of Egypt and the World Bank. These show much greater consistency from the 1990s; thus, even though the discussion touches upon earlier years, most of the focus is on this later period. Detailed discussions of measurement and conceptual issues relating to the poverty situation in Egypt are laid out in (among others) el-Leithy, Khawaga, and Riad 1999; World Bank 2002b; Ikram 2006; Fields 2003, World Bank 2007; and World Bank 2011; hence, only a brief description is offered here.

Three measures of poverty are generally computed.

1. The Food Poverty Line (FPL). The usual procedure is to choose a food bundle that reaches some predetermined calorie requirements (using information from the World Health Organization) with a composition that is consistent with the consumption behavior of the poor (proxied, say, by the second decile of the income distribution). The cost of the required calories is then computed using prices for the food items in each region. This procedure establishes an FPL.

    Households whose total expenditure falls short of the FPL are referred to as the "extreme poor." In other words, these are households who cannot afford even the food consumption to meet the targeted caloric requirements.

2. The Lower Poverty Line (LPL). Households whose total expenditure equals the FPL, but who choose not to spend it all on food but allocate a certain amount to nonfood items, are said to be in the category of the "poor" or "absolute poor." In other words, these are households who could afford the minimum food consumption if they bought nothing else. Since they do have to spend money on other essential items (such as rent, clothing, medicines, transportation), their food expenditure falls short of that required to meet the caloric standard.

3. The Upper Poverty Line (UPL). This measure permits a larger nonfood component of the total poverty line. Some studies compute this by scaling up the total poverty line by an arbitrary factor, say, 20 or 50 percent. The World Bank's procedure is to estimate the nonfood component of the poverty line as the nonfood expenditure of households whose food expenditure equals the food poverty line. Households whose total expenditure falls between the LPL and the UPL are said to be "near poor." These are households that spend just enough on food to purchase the caloric target and are also able to spend additional amounts on other items.

The three groups of the poor—extreme, absolute, and near—together make up the "all poor."[10]

The foregoing discussion shows that the choice of a poverty line involves a number of arbitrary elements and thus itself is ultimately arbitrary. However, the degree of arbitrariness is constrained because, in order to be generally acknowledged, the chosen poverty line must be accepted by society and thus must be compatible with society's norms of minimum requirements.

Trends in Poverty

Ikram (2006, 247–64, plus table 9.1 and figs. 9.1 and 9.2) summarizes and discusses estimates from investigations by the government of Egypt, the World Bank, think tanks, and individual researchers of overall as well as urban and rural poverty between 1959 and 2000, and the reader is referred to it for details. Each of the studies offers useful insights; however, they differ in approach and methodology and thus the findings are not always comparable. Nevertheless, a number of broad conclusions can be derived. Some of the main trends in poverty since 1982 are displayed in figure 10.

The overall trend from 1982 to 2015 shows an increase in total poverty, but there were fluctuations in the metric caused by different factors.[11]

Poverty increased between 1982 and 1991 and then dropped quite sharply until 2000 as a result of rapid economic growth. The subsequent slowdown in growth increased the incidence of poverty in 2005.

Between 2004 and 2009, poverty outcomes were subjected to contradictory forces, the net result of which was to increase poverty by 2009. The steady *rate* of economic growth between 2004 and mid-2008 assisted a substantial number of households to move out of poverty and near-poverty. However, the *pattern* of economic growth moved outcomes in the other direction. The pattern of growth was dominated by a reduction in the rate of employment and a change in its composition (the fast-growing sectors were those in which the poor did not participate) and an abrupt fall in overseas workers' remittances. The effect of these factors swamped those of the overall growth, and raised the incidence of poverty.

A period of very high inflation (especially of food prices) worsened the situation, particularly in 2008–2009. In these years, high inflation and rising food prices eroded the purchasing power of the population and increased the incidence of extreme poverty (the part of the population whose expenditure fell short of that required to meet basic food needs). Between 2004 and 2009, the Consumer Price Index increased by 47 percent, while the food index rose by 64 percent. Since food products accounted for 74 percent in the weight of the poverty basket, these developments pushed an estimated additional 10 percent of the population in rural areas into extreme poverty.

These trends also pulled up the incidence of total poverty from 19.6 percent in 2004 to 21.6 percent in 2009 (on the basis of the lower poverty

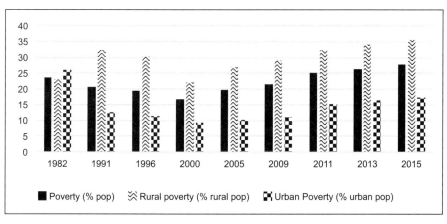

Figure 10. Poverty headcount, 1982–2015

line). The World Bank (2011, i–iii) estimated that as many as 5.1 million Egyptians were severely food deprived in 2009 (double the number in 2005). If the upper poverty line were used as the criterion in 2009, nearly 40 percent of the population would be classified as "poor" or "near poor." The sudden economic slowdown during the year of the financial crisis (2008–2009) also reduced employment rates within the family. A panel study showed that this was driving more than one-third of the households surveyed into poverty.

Political instability in subsequent years continued to drag down the GDP growth rate and with it the rate of job creation. The World Bank (2015, 41, box III.2) reports official government figures estimating that the poverty headcount increased to 26.3 percent of the population (about 22 million persons) in 2013, again using the lower poverty line at the criterion. Continuing lackluster growth pushed up the poverty headcount in 2015 to 27.8 percent (from 26.3 percent in 2013 and 25.2 percent in 2011) meaning that about 25 million persons fell below the poverty line.[12]

Characteristics and Determinants of Poverty in Egypt

As a broad generalization, the poverty profile for Egypt shows that the poor are rural, and more likely to live in Upper Egypt, be less educated, hold irregular informal jobs, and be members of families with more dependents. The following paragraphs highlight the principal elements of Egypt's poverty profile.

1. *Poverty was relatively "shallow," meaning that a large number of households were clustered around the commonly used poverty lines, and small differences in the level of the line could significantly change the numerical estimate of the poor.* Many Egyptians are only a single shock away from poverty. Such a clustering around the poverty line thus makes large numbers vulnerable and the country may quickly lose the gains in poverty reduction that it might have made in several years of robust growth. This might have occurred in 2009, when because of the sharp rise in food prices, Egypt may within the space of a few months have lost all gains in poverty reduction it made between 2005 and 2008, the three years of rapid economic growth.

2. *The incidence of poverty was greater in rural than in urban areas.* More than half the population in rural areas remained poor and near-poor, a statistic that the World Bank (2011, 2) described as "a dishearteningly stable share over the last 15 years."

3. *Poverty had a strong regional dimension.* The incidence in Upper Egypt was substantially greater than in Lower Egypt. Moreover, while in recent years poverty declined sharply in the urban parts of Upper Egypt, it stayed virtually unchanged in the rural parts. As an illustration of the concentration of poverty in Upper Egypt, the World Bank (2011, 4) reported that rural Upper Egypt accounted for 72 percent of all extreme-poor in the country, 56 percent of the poor, and 33 percent of the near-poor, although its share of the population was only 27 percent. In fact, almost one-third of all the Egyptian poor were located in just three Upper Egypt governorates—Minya, Asyut, and Sohag. World Bank (2009, 2012) provide detailed discussions of the geographical dimension of Egypt's development.

4. *Poverty was associated with self-employment and employment in casual activities.* Income from work (wages and earnings from self-employment) remained the first source of income among the poor and the near-poor. Wages were the most important source of income for the poor in both urban and rural areas, followed by agricultural income in rural areas.

5. *Poverty in rural areas was closely linked to lack of access to and/or ownership of productive assets, especially agricultural land, and to agricultural infrastructure services, such as irrigation.* Income from transfers, including outside-village remittances, was an important source, especially in rural areas.

6. *The most important determinant of poverty was education, which was also the most important influence in the intergenerational transmission of poverty.* This is true both in urban and in rural areas; see Datt, Jolliffe, and Sharma 1999; el-Leithy, el-Khawarga, and Riad 1999; World Bank 2007; World Bank 2011.

7. *Rapid economic growth was the only sustainable way to help people move out of poverty.* World Bank (2011, 33–34) showed that the majority of households that managed to climb out of poverty in 2005–2008, a period of high GDP growth, were resilient to shocks and stayed out of poverty despite the high rate of inflation.

8. *Employment status and occupation matter.* The composition of employment is important because the opportunities for productivity increases influence the wage rates offered in the sector.

9. *Food subsidies played a critical role in the living standards of the population.* The World Bank estimated that if there had been no food subsidies, an

additional 7 percent of the population would have been poor in 2005, while in 2009 the incidence of poverty in Egypt would have been one-third higher—31 percent of the population instead of 22 percent.

10. *Poverty characteristics remained relatively unchanged for most of the period 1982–2015.* The World Bank (2011, iii) presents estimates showing that about half of poverty in Egypt was chronic or near chronic, while the other half was transient. (For two reference periods, "chronic poverty" refers to households whose average [per capita] expenditure was below the established poverty line in both periods, whereas "transient poverty" refers to households whose average expenditure was above the poverty line in one period, but below it in the second.)

Income Distribution

According to CAPMAS (Central Agency for Public Mobilization and Statistics) data, income distribution showed a general improvement between 1991 and 2015, but the improvement was not uniform over the period (fig. 11). The distribution improved between 1991 and 1996; Kheir el-Din and el-Leithy (2008) attribute this to a sizable rise in agricultural incomes resulting from the implementation of the stabilization effort and the liberalization of the economy. The distribution worsened considerably in 2000, before improving in both 2005 and 2009. This was followed by a slight worsening in 2013 and 2015.

Income distribution data in developing countries need to be interpreted with caution, and Egypt is no exception. When aggregated to the

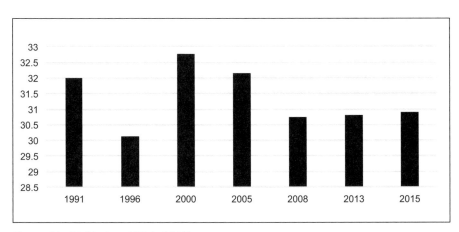

Figure 11. Gini index, 1991–2015

national level, income and expenditure figures provided by the Household Income and Expenditure Survey (HIES) are generally lower than those provided through national income accounts.

Thus, scrutinizing the 1996 survey data, Fergany (1999) pointed to the truncation of the distribution at its upper end, noting that richer households frequently are excluded from the survey, either because they refused to participate or because of underreporting. The exclusion of the rich from the survey therefore results in (a spuriously) greater homogeneity in income and expenditure levels among the non-rich, or a more equitable distribution that is skewed toward lower expenditure levels. The following paragraphs suggests that the lower end of the income distribution might also have been underenumerated.

Poverty and Equity in Egypt: A Cautionary Note

Some important caveats have to be attached to the official estimates of poverty and equity. It has been recognized that the conventional household income and expenditure surveys often miss or under-cover the richer classes, because of non-response or under-reporting of income or both—recent literature is surveyed in Atkinson, Piketty, and Saez (2011). Attempts have been made to solve this problem by using data from income tax records to estimate the top tail of the income distribution. This estimate, combined with an estimate of the bottom part of the distribution from the household survey, is used to obtain an estimate of the complete distribution. When the two sources of data are combined in this way, the Gini index has been shown to increase for several countries, including the United States, Columbia, South Korea, Ecuador, and Chile.[13]

Egypt's poverty numbers, as calculated from the HIES data collected by CAPMAS, are not immune to such issues, and could reflect problems at both tails of the income distribution. Problems at the upper end are not unusual in survey data in developing countries; they arise from the better-off classes not responding to the survey, or underreporting their consumption in order to shield the inferred income from taxes. Underreporting of non-wage income is especially problematic for estimates of income inequality. Various attempts have been made to adjust for these difficulties, but they rest on assumptions that may not be valid in the circumstances of a given country or time period, and call for data, such as income tax records, that often are not available.

The latter problem is particularly acute in developing countries. In order to overcome this problem for Egypt, van der Weide, Lakner, and Ianchovichina (2017) used data on house prices to capture the top incomes. On the basis of generally conservative assumptions, they found that the Gini of household per capita income for urban Egypt in 2009 worked out at 51.8 compared to the HIES estimate of 38.5; an increase of 13 points; thus inequality as measured by the HIECS was likely to have been significantly underestimated.

Other studies, for example, World Bank (2014) highlighted the likelihood that in Egypt the lower tail of the distribution based on CAPMAS data may also be underestimated. The principal difficulty lies in sampling some of the "informal" populations or difficult neighborhoods in the metropolitan areas. It can be challenging for conductors of CAPMAS surveys to penetrate these areas and conduct meaningful surveys. The World Bank study pointed out that ill-defined property rights and the threat of draconian punishments for unlicensed construction (including the demolition of dwellings without compensation) offered an incentive for dwellers to resist the intrusion of CAPMAS enumerators, while strong community organizations in these areas provided the means to repel such unwelcome attention.

The truncation of both tails makes the distribution appear more compressed and thus more equal than might actually be the case. This can lead the government to misdiagnose the situation and to ignore real problems or to follow inappropriate policies. The pattern of inequality is crucial to understanding the dynamics of poverty, especially in the 2004–10 period, that is, the years leading to the 2011 revolution. As the World Bank (2014) stresses, with rising average incomes and constant or falling inequality, the poor would have benefited from the growth. However, with rising inequality, the gains are likely to have been appropriated largely by the rich. The same World Bank report pointed out that the official perspective on inequality and poverty was at variance with nutritional data that suggested a sharp increase in stunting, wasting, and severe wasting among the under-five age group during 2003 and 2008.

The report also raised some questions concerning the estimates of poverty between areas officially defined as "urban" and "rural." The boundaries of Egypt's "urban" areas are defined in administrative terms, and the rapidly growing informal populations of the urban metropolitan areas tend to form agglomerations on land surrounding the core central areas. As the discussion in chapter 3 indicates, according to criteria (such as land use or the size of the population in the agglomeration) used in most other countries, these agglomerations would be considered simply extensions of the area designated as "urban" and would thus themselves be regarded as urban. However, since they are outside the areas that are defined in Egypt as urban, poverty in these agglomerations would be categorized in CAPMAS data as rural. Given that informality in Egypt has increased significantly— one estimate considers that the informal inhabitants of the metropolitan area of Cairo increased from virtually none in 1960 to almost 65 percent in 2010— it is likely that actual urban poverty and the rate of its increase are underestimated. Chapter 3 includes a discussion of some of the special issues that urbanization brings.

The World Bank (2014a) thus raises some important questions about official assessments that poverty was low and stable, and concentrated in the rural areas of Upper Egypt. The report highlights the possibility that because of definitional and access issues, the extent of urban poverty in Egypt has been underestimated. The errors in economic estimation are not simply exercises in academic or semantic nitpicking, but may have had serious political consequences. The CAPMAS estimates correctly identified poor households in Upper Egypt, but the likelihood of their missing out the rising numbers and the increasing vulnerability of informal migrants in urban areas may have led the Mubarak government to misread the extent of urban disquiet and underestimate the intensity of the Arab Spring, and thereby make policy mistakes that contributed to the regime's overthrow.

The political-economy lesson is obvious: while the Egyptian government's move toward increasingly using data-driven policies is to be much welcomed, such policies will be effective only if the data accurately reflect reality.

The External Sector
Overview
One major issue impacting the growth performance of the Egyptian economy, namely, the gap between savings and investment, has been discussed above. The other major impediment to growth was the gap between foreign-exchange earnings and requirements.

The Egyptian balance of payments has persistently been in deficit since 1950. The years of the Second World War saw substantial deficits on the merchandise trade account. The available shipping was directed toward the logistics of war; this made exports more difficult, but imports continued to surge, principally because they were required to supply Allied troops stationed in Egypt. During the war years Egypt's cumulative merchandise trade deficit was of the order of LE100 million, which was more than offset by an estimated inflow of LE550 million to finance expenditures of the British military. Thus, despite the large trade deficit, Egypt ended the war with sterling balances of approximately LE440 million, which Mead (1967, 158) puts at more than 80 percent of GNP in 1945. Until they were exhausted in the late 1950s, these balances helped to cover deficits on Egypt's balance of payments. The availability of these balances may partially explain policymakers' complacency and why they did not act earlier and with greater dispatch to boost exports.

For most years between 1965 and 2016, Egypt struggled to simultaneously achieve both internal equilibrium (that is, a balance between domestic demand and supply at an acceptable level of inflation) and external equilibrium (that is, a level of current-account deficit that could be sustainably financed). The policymakers confronted problems of both timing and amount. Imports responded much earlier and in larger amounts to GDP growth than did foreign-exchange earnings, and the resulting deficit added further to the debt and increased the resources required for servicing it. Policymakers were under pressure to control the external deficit, because it could not exceed the ceiling imposed by Egypt's foreign-exchange earnings plus the available external financing. Their principal efforts at control relied on restricting imports, but this left the capital stock underutilized (for want of raw materials) and labor unemployed. The balance of payments was thus the ultimate constraint on Egypt's growth during this period.

Over the five decades from 1965 to 2016, Egypt's earnings from the export of goods and services fell short of the country's imports, even though the latter were constrained for long periods precisely because the government was aware of the financing difficulties. (See figure 12.) Between 1965 and 2016, exports of goods and services paid for 73 percent of Egypt's imports of goods and services. The gap was met through foreign aid, workers' remittances, external borrowing, and running down foreign-exchange reserves.

The principal factor inhibiting the growth of Egypt's exports up to the 1960s was that they were dominated by a single commodity, namely, raw cotton. The product accounted for about 95 percent of total Egyptian exports in 1907–1909 and still accounted for 85 percent in 1950 and 45 percent in 1970. This degree of export concentration left the trade balance vulnerable to fluctuations in the supply and demand of this single item. From the 1960s, a number of other items, such as cotton textiles, rice, fruits and vegetables, and other manufactured products began to gain in importance. After the recovery of the Sinai and the Gulf of Suez oil fields, export earnings came to be dominated by petroleum exports. However, a characteristic of the Egyptian balance of payments was that merchandise exports covered only 30–40 percent of total foreign-exchange earnings, and that the overwhelming portion of the earnings came from so-called "invisible" items, comprising Suez Canal tolls, tourism, workers' remittances, and investment income.

Major Political-economy Issues Affecting the External Sector

Egypt's balance-of-payments difficulties resulted largely from an incentive structure that was biased against exports. During the entire period from 1952 to 2016, the coalition of import interests monopolized the ear of the government to the disadvantage of the interest group of exporters.

The major impeding factors in the incentive framework included: a frequently overvalued real exchange rate that acted as a significant export tax; high nominal and effective tariffs, which increased the profitability of producing for the home market rather than for export; significant non-tariff measures (particularly customs procedures and administrative controls on imports) that reinforced the incentive of producing for the domestic market; and inefficient systems of duty drawback and temporary admissions that raised transaction costs for exporters and failed to provide them timely access to imported inputs at world prices.

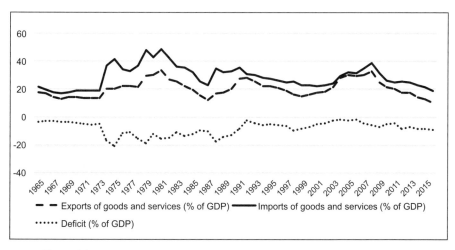

Figure 12. Exports, imports, and external balance, 1965–2016, percent of GDP

Three elements chiefly underlay the anti-export bias.

1. There was what might be called a "philosophical" misunderstanding of the basis of export growth in a modern economy. It appeared
   axiomatic for Egyptian policymakers that exports could only be based
   on materials indigenous to the country—hence the dominance of raw
   cotton and cotton textiles in the export lists for more than a century,
   and of petroleum thereafter. In 1981, oil exports accounted for over
   75 percent of earnings from merchandise exports, and even by 2013
   they accounted for almost half the value of merchandise exports and
   about a quarter of total foreign-exchange earnings. There was little
   effort to diversify the export basket.

   The philosophical misunderstanding missed the point grasped
   by the fast-growing East Asian countries, namely, that a spectacular
   export drive can be founded on imports. Many of these countries with
   the most rapid growth rates in history—such as Japan, South Korea,
   Taiwan, Hong Kong, and Singapore—are almost entirely bereft of
   natural resources. The "East Asian miracle" consists in essence of
   importing raw materials and semi-finished items, adding value by an
   educated labor force, and exporting them at a competitive exchange
   rate. No element of this strategy should be beyond the wit or dexter-
   ity of Egyptians. The East Asian growth strategy and what it would
   require for it to be adopted by Egypt are discussed in more detail in
   the final chapter of this book. There is also a significant literature
   on the lessons from the East Asian experience for other countries.
   Accessible overall accounts are World Bank (1993a) and Stiglitz and
   Yusuf (2001), while detailed discussions of the lessons in the context
   of particular countries that would have relevance for Egypt include
   Panagariya (2008) for India and Ikram (2011) for Pakistan.

   The result of not diversifying Egypt's export structure was that
   her export basket contained too few of the commodities whose share
   was expanding rapidly in international trade. A decomposition of the
   trade performance by Kouamé (2000) showed that Egypt not only
   did not trade sufficiently in products for which global demand was
   increasing, but it also lost market share in its traditional exports. The
   study further demonstrated that when Egypt did diversify its export
   basket, it was seldom toward the products with the fastest-rising
   international demand. These findings were confirmed by a study by

Mohammed (2001) for a joint Government of Egypt/World Bank advisory committee for the prime minister. An earlier study by the World Bank (1997a) calculated that if Egypt's exports had grown at world rates from 1983 through 1993, then her exports should have reached $6.3 billion rather than the actual $3.1 billion. It attributed the "loss" of the $3.2 billion in 1993 to: (1) a failure to direct exports toward faster-growing markets (this represented a loss of $0.7 billion); (2) a failure to shift the structure of exports toward faster-growing items (a loss of $2.3 billion); and (3) a residual that measured the loss of international competitiveness ($0.2 billion).

Egypt consequently continued to lose her share of the international market. Out of every $100 of world exports in 1950, Egypt accounted for $1; in 1965, Egypt's share dropped to 37 cents; by 2016 it shrank further to 14 cents. World trade had surged ahead, leaving Egypt well behind. The political-economy decisions that tilted incentives in the direction of imports rather than exports imposed a heavy cost on the country's foreign-exchange accounts.

2. The strategy of import substitution that dominated Egypt's thinking for most of the period overlooked what the Nobel laureate Robert Mundell reminded policymakers of at a conference in Cairo in 2003: "A tax on imports is a tax on exports." Imposing a tax on an import permits an Egyptian producer of that or a similar item to sell it in the home market at higher than international prices; it is therefore more profitable to sell it domestically than to export it.[14] The import tax thus bears down on exports. Moreover, its effects can be durable—the profitability of import substitution activities diverts resources (including investment resources) from both actual and potential export sectors and can thus reduce the future production of exportable products.

From 1965 to 2016, import duties were an important component of tax revenues, accounting for around one-quarter of the total. For revenue reasons, therefore, the government was reluctant to reduce these taxes. However, the protective effects of these measures distorted the country's incentive structure. They created high rents that encouraged producers to expend their energies in lobbying for increased protection against imports; it was more profitable than competing in the international market for exports. Nathan Associates (1998, i–ii) reported that the average effective rate of protection in manufacturing in the mid-1990s was more than 34 percent, with some rates well over

80 percent.[15] Producers were able to set domestic prices well above international prices of the same items, giving them a substantial incentive to target the home rather than the international market. According to the study, the tariff structure provided an average premium of 21.7 percent to potential exporters for selling manufactured goods domestically rather than in the international market.

The Nathan Associates study estimated that the average tariff of 31 percent was equivalent to a tax on exports of 19.4 percent—a considerable disincentive. Indeed, Kheir el-Din and el-Shawarby (2002, 15–16) estimated that if the average import tariff were reduced to 20 percent, the equivalent export tax would still be 13.9 percent; even a sizable reduction of the tariff rate would significantly penalize exports. The impact of the tariff structure on discouraging exports was confirmed by other investigations. Thus, for example, the World Bank (2001a, 27) estimated that fiscal barriers (tariffs and levies) on imports added 32.3 percent ad valorem on average to their cost. Recalling Mundell's admonition that a tax on imports is a tax on exports shows how the fiscal system played a major role in distorting the incentive structure against exports.

Import protection was not confined to tariffs. Throughout the five decades from 1965, an extensive system of non-tariff measures (NTMs) reinforced the structure of direct tariffs. These NTMs were generally cloaked as quality control or health protection measures. Even by 2015, more than one thousand tariff lines (about a fifth of the tariff schedule) consisted of items that were subject to inspection for quality control, and a sample of every consignment of such goods was examined. The stated reason for these measures was to ensure compliance with Egyptian standards. "In practice, however," commented the World Bank (1998b, 32), "quality control has become [another] means to protect local industry." The NTMs, although aimed at restricting imports, predictably had the same disincentive effect on exporting as the overt tariffs. Nathan Associates (1998, 5) estimated that in the 1990s, the increased protection that the quality control measures provided to imports resulted in the reduction of exports by at least 9 to 12 percent and of GDP by more than 1 percent.

There is no need to labor the point. Many of the policies that impacted economic incentives intensified the bias of the structure against exports. Foreign-exchange earnings and GDP growth were held down below their potential, large deficits persisted on the external accounts, and Egypt had to continually borrow from abroad in order to fill the gap. The relative political influence of the protectionist groups, who benefited from the inefficiencies thus created in the economy, versus that of exporters may reasonably be inferred from these outcomes.

3. Many policymakers and others believed that the foreign demand for Egypt's exports would not respond to depreciations of the exchange rate. Technically speaking, these "elasticity pessimists" looked at estimates of the elasticity (that is, the responsiveness) of foreign demand to the exchange rate for Egyptian exports and concluded that the Marshall-Lerner-Robinson conditions for a devaluation to improve the trade balance were not met.[16]

Two developments have not been kind to this belief. First, it has become apparent that the elasticities had been calculated in a manner that systematically biased the estimate downward—the econometric issues are discussed in Ikram (2006, 135–39). More methodologically sound studies—for example, Pearson (1997), Nathan Associates (1999)—showed that when the elasticities were correctly estimated, the Marshall-Lerner-Robinson conditions were comfortably satisfied. A currency devaluation *was* likely to improve the balance. Depreciation of the exchange rate in the early 2000s did, in fact, produce a healthy response of exports. In the decade 1990–2000, exports grew at an annual rate of 5.6 percent; after the exchange-rate adjustments, the growth rate between 2000 and 2011 doubled to 11 percent, when the political upheavals intervened. Even so, the growth between 2000 and 2016 averaged about 7 percent a year.

Second, the experience of high-exporting countries has poured cold water on the notion that rapid export growth can accompany an appreciating real exchange rate. The policymakers in all the East Asian high performers (Japan, China, South Korea, Taiwan, Thailand, Malaysia, Singapore, Hong Kong) labored mightily to keep their exchange rates undervalued. But inflation in Egypt remained higher than in its competitors and consequently the country's real exchange rate (RER) appreciated steadily,[17] especially for most of the final two decades of the twentieth century and into the next. The impact of the appreciation became even worse after the East Asian financial crisis of 1997, when Egypt's RER appreciated by more than 40 percent against the exchange rates of its main East Asian competitors (South Korea, Thailand, Malaysia, and Indonesia).

There is no reason to suppose that Egyptian exports are exempt from, or that her foreign customers are immune to, the connection between lower prices and increased demand. Most of Egypt's foreign-exchange earnings derive from tourism, workers' remittances, and other services, and studies—such as Nathan Associates (1998)—and experience have shown that these items are sensitive to the exchange rate. Moreover, the issue for policymakers is not simply of producing a once-for-all jump in exports; for a growing economy the issue is to produce a *sustained* increase in exports. This requires a continuous rise in the production of exportable goods and services. An export promotion policy must therefore signal to entrepreneurs that it would be profitable to increase the supply of exportables. An assurance that the exchange rate will be maintained at a competitive level has been an essential signal for investment allocations in the high-export countries. Through their reluctance to use the real exchange rate for stimulating exports, Egyptian policymakers denied themselves a weapon that plays a major role in the export success of many countries. If they had wished to use the real effective exchange rate (REER) as a policy instrument, they could have adjusted the nominal rate of the Egyptian pound against the U.S. dollar to produce the desired path of the REER. However, the policies concentrated on the nominal exchange rate, keeping the rate against the dollar constant for long periods, and letting the trajectory of the REER develop by chance.

Egyptian policymakers also argued that keeping the nominal exchange rate stable would encourage foreign investment, because a stable rate protected the investor against foreign-exchange risk; in effect, it meant that the Central Bank of Egypt had taken out the foreign-exchange risk. However, foreign investors were perfectly aware that the Central Bank had only a limited amount of foreign-exchange reserves, and thus could not maintain a fixed rate indefinitely; pressure on the reserves would compel the bank to abandon the parity. Investors' view of such a risk would be factored into their expectations of the returns on their investments. For long periods, the Central Bank of Egypt lost substantial amounts of foreign-exchange reserves in order to prop up the exchange rate at an ultimately unsustainable level. A particularly striking example was the period 2011–12.

In 2010, Egypt's foreign-exchange reserves amounted to $36 billion; by the end of December 2012 they had dropped to $15 million; in other words, Egypt hemorrhaged almost $1 billion a month of reserves. Much of this represented capital flight—Government of Egypt (2016a, 18) estimated that of the drop, $12.8 billion reflected capital flight from the government's treasury bill market, stock market, and banking system. An unrealistic exchange rate that played to the interests of importers left the country increasingly vulnerable.

Foreign Aid

If a country's foreign-exchange earnings cannot pay for its imports, then it must finance the gap through foreign investment, external assistance, or borrowing on international capital markets. Egypt has used all these methods, and while they may be necessary, each of them carries some collateral danger.

Several major political-economy issues bearing on the role of foreign aid in the Egyptian context were discussed in chapter 1, which should be read in conjunction with the present section. It is only necessary here to add how dependent Egypt's investment rate, and thus the future GDP growth rate, was on foreign savings. Figure 13 shows net official development assistance (ODA) as a percent of gross capital formation. It is quite striking that between 1971 and 1996, net ODA equaled at least 20 percent of gross capital formation, with peaks touching 70 percent (in 1973 and 1991); see figure 13. The idea implicit in comparing foreign aid with investment is that consumption is primarily the responsibility of the recipient government. A government that did not have the resources to feed its people and yet diverted a significant part of the sparse available amount to investment would, at least in the civilized world, find it very difficult to survive, except perhaps in exceptional circumstances, such as a war.

Relying on foreign aid to the extent that Egypt has done carries risks. The main collateral dangers with foreign aid are that: (1) the amounts are uncertain, because the recipient country must rely on "the kindness of strangers" to finance its current-account deficit, which in Egypt's case averaged around 11 percent of GDP in the period 1965–2016; and (2) the aid may have to be repaid in a political, if not economic, coin, and the former can turn out to be much more costly. Both methods of financing—external borrowing or foreign assistance—can leave the recipient vulnerable and restrict the ability to follow independent policies.

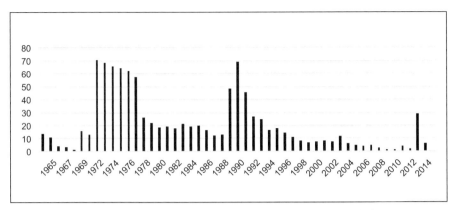

Figure 13. Net ODA as percent of gross capital formation, 1965–2015

The average share of gross capital formation in GDP between 1965 and 2016 was about 20 percent; the GDP growth rate was 4.7 percent a year, giving a rough capital–output ratio of 4.25. The average share of ODA in GDP was of the order of 5.2 percent. Had the ODA not been available, other things being equal, the investment rate would have been about 15 percent and the GDP growth rate about 3.5 percent. The difference, compounded over fifty years, is very substantial. Thus, one dollar growing at 4.7 percent compounded over fifty years would amount to about $10 at the end of the period; growing at 3.5 percent it would amount to $5.7—about 40 percent less.

The idea behind these back-of-the-envelope calculations is the Harrod-Domar growth model. The model is, of course, subject to some caveats: for example, it assumes that investment is the key constraint on growth and that there is a linear relationship between investment and growth. However, the model can provide a useful first approximation, especially since it was shown in the introduction that the growth of Egypt's GDP has been driven primarily by investment. Without these inflows—and the figures quoted underestimate the actual inflows because they do not include the substantial military assistance from the United States and the Soviet Union and understate the considerable economic aid from Arab countries—the GDP growth rate would likely have been one-fourth lower,[18] and that, compounded over a fifty-year period, amounts to a sizable loss. Alternatively, one might say that external assistance permitted Egypt to live beyond its means for long periods and to maintain consumption at higher levels than it could have paid for from its own earnings.

The point of raising the issue is not to debate the decimals of the growth rate, but to get one thinking about the vulnerability of Egypt's GDP growth or consumption levels to decisions taken outside the country, as decisions regarding foreign aid are. The outcomes are not mere scratchings on a piece of paper—a lower investment rate is likely to decrease the GDP growth rate and create a smaller number of jobs, with consequences for personal incomes and standards of living. A squeeze on consumption could provoke serious political repercussions, as the "bread riots" of 1977 bloodily demonstrated. One has therefore to face up squarely to the role of foreign aid in the performance of Egypt's economy and the importance of the political-economy decisions required to construct a strategy that would best manage these inflows.

External Debt

Do not rely on another's goods,
Guard what you acquire yourself;
Do not depend on another's wealth,
Lest he become master in your house. (Lichtheim 1976, 2:139)

Thus counseled the Eighteenth Dynasty scribe Anii, appealing twice to matters of economic independence in one verse. While Anii's remarks were intended for Everyman in circa 1300 BCE, they could have served as a text for Egypt's rulers from the mid-nineteenth century, and were equally relevant counsel for Egypt's economic policymakers during the last thirty years of the second millennium CE. Egypt's experience with economic development during this period was dominated by the insufficiency of nationally generated resources, especially of foreign exchange, and the consequent need to "depend on another's wealth." This dependence enabled others to become masters in the Egyptian house.

Origins of External Debt Issues
Current-account deficits must be financed, and one of the major sources of financing for Egypt was borrowing from abroad. External indebtedness strikes an important, and often rather somber, note in Egypt's history. Egypt's problems with servicing its debt provided a pretext to foreign powers to take over the country's economy in 1876 to be run for the benefit of creditors, and made it politically subservient from 1882 until the withdrawal of British forces in 1954.

Muhammad Ali, the founder of modern Egypt, at his death in 1849 left the country free from debt. He had borrowed relatively small sums for short periods, first from local merchants and then from commercial houses in Alexandria who had connections in foreign countries. He could not borrow long-period without the permission of his Ottoman masters. His successor, Abbas, left debt estimated at LE2.7 million. The debt, however, was domestic, chiefly comprising unpaid salaries to officials and amounts due to contractors. On the other side of the ledger, he left about LE800,000 as arrears in land tax that were to be collected by his successor.

The Egyptian debt saga properly begins with Abbas's successor, Said Pasha, on whom Hamza (1944, 263) bestows "le triste honneur" of having agreed to the issue of the first real state loan in 1862. Much of the debt contracted was for the construction of the Suez Canal. Of the 400,000 shares that were issued by the Suez Canal Company, Said ended up taking 182,023 at £20 each at a total cost of £3,640,460.

The Suez transaction had a number of important political-economy effects. The economic effects are obvious. The country was burdened with a very substantial amount of debt that had to be serviced regularly. For a long time the shares did not yield any return (since the construction of the canal took ten years), so Egypt's participation remained financially unproductive during this period. After the construction of the canal, Egypt was deprived of the revenue from the overland transit trade; a contemporary resource estimated this revenue was three-quarters of a million pounds per annum before the opening of the canal.

There was also a heavy opportunity cost. Under the terms of the agreement, Egypt had to provide a large amount of free labor to the Suez Canal Company for the construction. The total numbers involved imposed a huge burden. Karabell (2003, 170) reports that at its height the corvée (forced labor) involved more than sixty thousand fellahin. Nubar Pasha calculated that if one took into account the numbers of laborers traveling to and from the canal and those actually digging, 720,000 workers would be involved with the canal each year out of a total Egyptian population of less than 4 million. Moreover, this vast army of forced labor had to be pulled out of agriculture at a time when cotton prices were at their highest, during the American Civil War. Nubar claimed that the resulting labor shortage caused Egypt to lose 36 million francs a year (Karabell 2003, 200).

However, the political effects of this project outweighed the economic. As Hamza (1944, 26) puts it, "The construction of the Suez Canal compelled England, as Mistress of India, and as the Mother Country of Australia, to regard the ascendancy of Egypt or of any other European power in Egypt as a source of peril to her Empire." Hamza concluded that so far as Egypt was concerned, the canal proved a political and financial loss. While this might be too extreme a position when viewed from the long term, it is undoubted that the terms that Egypt's rulers conceded to de Lesseps imposed a heavy economic, financial, and human burden on the country, and provoked a deep and enduring intrusion into its polity and economy by European powers.

More borrowing and further difficulties with servicing external debt continued under the next ruler, Isma'il. Perhaps the final bitter pill concerning the Suez transaction was that by 1875 Isma'il was unable to pay the installments on the debt. He sold Egypt's shares in the Suez Canal Company for £4 million to the British government, which in November 1875 became the owner of 44 percent of the company and the largest single shareholder. The ownership of such a large proportion of the shares in foreign hands obviously limited the returns from the canal to Egypt, and the country's move to claim ownership of the waterway in 1956 led to the Suez Canal war.

The foregoing paragraphs point to the interplay of economics and politics in the origins of Egypt's external indebtedness. A detailed discussion of the evolution of Egypt's external indebtedness lies beyond the scope of this book. A number of very readable accounts are available, particularly Landes (1958) and Marlowe (1974), while Hamza (1944) provides a comprehensive account (including reproductions of several original documents) of the public debt of Egypt from 1854 to 1876.

Developments in External Indebtedness: 1952–2015

During most of the 1950s, Egypt's balance of payments was kept very close to equilibrium and deficits were generally financed from the country's foreign-exchange reserves. At the beginning of 1955, virtually all of Egypt's external public debt had either been converted into internal issues or paid off through the Debt Conversion Plan of 1943. The only amount known to be outstanding was approximately $482,000 due on the 4 percent City of Alexandria 1903–63 bonds.

From the early 1960s, three political-economy factors dominated the economic picture. First, Egypt's development strategy was based on import-substitution industrialization. The initial stages of such a strategy generally turn out to be import-intensive, because until the import-substituting facilities are up and running, the country must import not only the machinery and equipment required to set up the substituting facilities, but also the products that will ultimately be substituted. Second, the country's anti-West foreign policy had cut it off from the main sources of concessional assistance and limited its access to the largest capital markets. Third, a large proportion of Egypt's exportable commodities was tied up as payments to the Communist Bloc for weapons and for industrial equipment. The latter, however, was technologically inferior to Western equipment, and consequently its products were of lower quality than demanded by Western purchasers. Egypt's economic strategy and political stance thus limited the quantity of its exports to Western countries, although it had to purchase most of its food imports from them. This created a significant imbalance in its external accounts.

The First Five-Year Plan (1960–65) intensified the debt situation, because the import substitution strategy accelerated. As pointed out above, such a strategy in its earlier stages can actually increase the import bill. The plan's import requirements substantially exceeded Egypt's ability to pay from its own resources, and about 30 percent of the investment program had to be financed through external borrowing. Given Egypt's economic and political difficulties (the plan was initiated after Egypt's hostilities with the United Kingdom and France over the Suez Canal), access to long-term loans could be difficult and part of the borrowing had to take the form of short-term banking facilities on hard commercial terms. Ikram (1980, 356–57) reported that by the end of 1965, Egypt's total disbursed and outstanding external debt amounted to $1.516 billion, with an additional $103 million in short-term liabilities against banking facilities.

Arrears on external debt payments arose and payments on credits from commercial banks had to be rescheduled in 1966, followed by similar arrangements in 1968 with governments and major suppliers in France, Italy, Germany, Sweden, and the Netherlands, and again in 1969 with Mexico, Japan, and the United Kingdom. Anii's advice had been ignored, with predictable results.

Egypt increasingly had to borrow on commercial terms with very short maturities, which caused many of the repayments to fall due within a narrow time frame. As a result of this "bunching," even after the rescheduling arrangements, between 1969 and 1974 Egypt would have had to pay 74 percent of its existing debt.

The adoption of the infitah (the "open-door strategy" discussed in chapter 5) led to a liberalization of imports, which in 1975 (the first full year after the announcement of the infitah) jumped to two-and-a-half times their levels in 1973 (the last year before the infitah); as a share of GDP, the change was from 19.2 to 41.3 percent. Much of the import frenzy was for consumer goods. Although the much larger inflow of external assistance that became available after President Sadat's reorientation of Egypt's foreign policy helped in the financing, yet Egypt availed itself of considerable recourse to international markets, especially for very short-term banking facilities. From 1975 to 1980, external debt increased from $6.3 billion to $19 billion; the latter figure amounted to more than 80 percent of GDP and 270 percent of the value of exports of goods and services. An IMF comment summed up the outcome as the consequence of "maintaining champagne tastes on a beer income."

Very large arrears on debt mounted up; those on banking facilities alone reached nearly $1 billion by mid-1977. A financial catastrophe loomed. It was warded off only by sizable inflows of cash assistance, principally from the Gulf Organization for the Development of Egypt (GODE) set up in 1977 by Saudi Arabia, Kuwait, Abu Dhabi, and Qatar, that enabled Egypt to clear all payments arrears.

Egypt continued to borrow heavily in the 1980s. Even though in general Egypt received quite favorable terms on its foreign borrowing through the 1980s,[19] the failure of exports virtually guaranteed that another crisis would arrive. Egypt still did not have an effective policy for diversifying its export basket away from the reliance on oil exports. After the collapse of oil prices in 1986, the situation became critical. According to most of the widely used measures, Egypt's debt burden until 1991 was among the highest in the world. Debt-to-GNP ratio ranged between 100 and 150 percent through the 1980s (even reaching 175 percent in 1988). The servicing of the debt created severe liquidity problems; total debt service (including arrears) due in 1986 exceeded 100 percent of current-account receipts.

Political considerations were squeezing Egypt into an economic cul-de-sac. The political-economy dilemma leading to the debt crisis of 1987 was that—because of the compact between the regimes and the population for subsidies in exchange for political passivity—the economic cake could not be allowed to shrink. However, serious structural reform to stimulate economic growth and enlarge the cake through domestic efforts was also

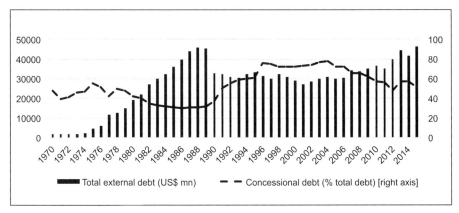

Figure 14. Total external debt and concessional portion, 1970–2015; $ million and percent

taboo. Either event risked alienating key constituencies. That only left external borrowing to finance the continued expansion of the cake, even if the loans were available only on hard terms.

Egypt had to seek another rescheduling of its debt payments. This was reached in May 1987, whereby outstanding arrears of $6.9 billion were rescheduled, together with all interest and amortization payments on public medium- and long-term loans falling due until June 30, 1988; these amounted to $4.4 billion.

The failure to sufficiently increase foreign-exchange earnings coupled with loose fiscal policies (the budget deficit reached 17 percent of GDP in 1991) rekindled pressures on the economy that culminated in a crisis in 1991. Fortunately for Egypt, the 1991 economic crisis occurred at a time when the donors, in recognition of Egypt's contribution in the Gulf War, offered a very large package of debt forgiveness and rearrangement. The total amount covered by the agreement was estimated at $28 billion, and was an economic reward for the political act of joining the Western-led coalition in the war (see chapter 6). A political *deus ex machina* bailed out economics.

Egypt's experience with external indebtedness in the period 1970 to 2015 can be broadly divided into two phases. Over the period as a whole, external debt grew at a rate of 8.1 percent a year, but this overall figure conceals two different growth paths created by different political-economy strategies. Between 1970 and 1989, external debt grew at a rapid pace, averaging 22 percent a year when, for most of the period, the brakes were taken off consumption. Between 1990 and 2015, Egypt capitalized on the debt relief and held down fresh borrowing; debt increased at barely 1.5 percent a year. The country also put greater emphasis on securing external funds in the form of grants and soft loans. The share of concessional debt increased sharply from less than 40 percent of total debt in 1990 to nearly 60 percent in 2015, with peaks exceeding 70 percent in 1997 and 2004. The combination of the politically motivated generosity of the debt arrangements and Egypt's more careful attitude toward fresh borrowing ensured that the pressure of external debt abated. Figure 14 displays developments in the amounts and concessionality of Egypt's external debt.

Why did Egypt's External Debt Increase Relentlessly?

Five factors accounted for the trend.

1. Egypt failed to accelerate the growth of non-oil manufactured exports and lost out on the expansion of international trade. The country's foreign-exchange earnings thus consistently fell short of its requirements.

2. Egypt's growth strategy was based on import-substituting industrialization. This strategy can tend for considerable periods to be import-intensive, because until such time as the industrial plants are fully functioning, the country must import both the capital goods required to set up the import-substituting facilities *and* the finished commodities.

3. Especially after 1973, Egypt had to import large quantities of equipment in order to refurbish an infrastructure that had been almost completely run down during the war years.

4. The growing population and the limited scope for agricultural expansion meant that large quantities of food and agricultural items had to be imported. Consequently, Egypt was faced with a growing import bill that was not covered by the country's foreign-exchange earnings, even when these were supplemented by external assistance. There is, however, another issue relating to debt that must be considered.

5. An important aspect of the debt situation is its political-economy background. There is an inherent asymmetry between which groups benefit from new debt incurred, and which bear the burden of its repayment. As Sherani (2015) points out, this issue has two aspects: (a) the difference between the effects on the elites and on the less

influential groups; and (b) the difference between those who would benefit from the additional resources and those who are likely to repay them.

First, the groups that benefit from the debt contracted are usually the elites, while those who bear the weight of the debt burden are usually the less affluent. The former, almost by definition, are or have privileged access to policymakers and are thus able to shape policies in ways that benefit them. Moreover, as political theory points out, the elites comprise a much smaller group and can thus be more easily mobilized in support of their interests. The less affluent groups do not enjoy comparable influence with policymakers, and constitute a much larger and more diffused group that is much more difficult to mobilize in support of their interests.

The elites benefit from the country's borrowing because their influence over the country's policies enables them to appropriate a disproportionate share of the borrowed resources and thus ease their budget constraint. The availability of additional resources also means that they need to pay lower taxes. Additionally, their influence over expenditure allocation allows them to increase spending on their own priorities. The consequences of these imbalances are shifted onto less influential groups. The consequences can be lower spending on public services, lower investment and growth in the economy.

The second aspect is that obtaining the borrowed resources and repaying them occur in different time frames. A government can contract the debt, benefit politically from growth or higher consumption financed by the borrowed resources, and pass the political unpopularity of squeezing incomes for repaying the debt on to a later government. Given the short-term horizon of many politicians, such a policy is not without its attractions. It is therefore not surprising that Egyptian regimes, which have been only tangentially accountable to the non-elites, have used external financing and debt as important instruments for mobilizing resources.

Issues of external indebtedness have been immensely important in Egypt's economic and political history. Moreover, external borrowing and/or soliciting external assistance has been a fundamental pillar of Egypt's political-economic strategy, whether or not this was made explicit. The fact that external borrowing in Egypt led to frequent crises and sometimes to catastrophic results also demonstrates that measures to boost domestic savings and implement a vigorous export drive appear to have attracted less of policymakers' attention than they should have. After all, one can look at instances of other countries that borrowed heavily but did not fall into the pit in which Egypt repeatedly found itself.

South Korea, for example, began the 1960s in a much weaker economic condition than Egypt. Its development strategy emphasized external borrowing rather than encouraging foreign direct investment, and in the 1980s South Korea became one of the most heavily indebted countries in the world. However, the country put in place incentives to boost investment, savings, and exports, and by 1995 had reached the position of offering significant amounts of development assistance to countries less fortunate than itself. In the early 2000s, South Korea had joined the list of developed countries. There are many lessons that Egypt can learn from South Korea's development experience; these are taken up in the final chapter of this book.

Annex: A Note on GDP Estimates

The quality of Egyptian economic data is variable. Data on tax collections, the money supply, payments for imports, receipts from exports, foreign-exchange reserves, and some other monetary and fiscal aggregates are generally reliable. However, in spite of a long history of estimations, data on national accounts and its principal components (such as investment, savings, public and private consumption) and the data on employment are less firm and are more useful as indicators of trends than of precise magnitudes.

The first attempt at estimating Egypt's national income was made by M.I.G Lévi (1922). This was followed by Baxter (1923); by Craig (1924); the United Kingdom's Department of Overseas Trade (1931); by Anis (1950); by Abdel Rahman (1959); and by the National Planning Committee (1958, 1960). For comments on these estimates see Issawi (1947, 50–54; 1954, 81–85), National Planning Committee (1958), Hansen and Mead (1963, 1965), and Mead (1967, 263–69). These earlier estimates used different databases, made different assumptions regarding missing data, and employed methodologies that were not consistent with each other. The estimates are to be lauded as pioneering efforts, but Issawi (1954, 83) rightly comments that "all of them are tentative."

More recent and methodologically sounder estimates for 1939–62 were prepared by Hansen and Mead (1963, 1965) and Hansen (1968). Currently, the national accounts are the responsibility of the Central Agency for Public Mobilization and Statistics (CAPMAS) with assistance from USAID's consultants for some years from 1998.

For the period 1965–2016 I have relied on the databases of the World Bank and the International Monetary Fund, not because they are perfect, but because they offer a comprehensive and generally consistent set of figures. They also form the basis of World Bank and IMF macroeconomic, sectoral, and project reports on Egypt, and thus provide a useful framework for examining macroeconomic as well as microeconomic issues. Since for the period before 1965 one is compelled to use different series of GDP data based on disparate assumptions, only general comparisons are possible and rates of change are likely to be more reliable than absolute levels.

The diagrams in this book, unless otherwise specified, have their source in the World Bank/IMF databases.

3

The Population and Related Issues

The center of political-economy concerns is people; indeed, a pioneer of the subject famously defined economics as "the study of man in the ordinary business of life" (Marshall 1920, 1). Much of the political-economic history of any country is concerned with what can be done for the people and, conversely, how they can contribute to the larger economy and society. This might seem a truism when applied to a democracy, but most authoritarian regimes also see the wisdom of providing at least a certain level of economic well-being to their citizens, even if only to mute dissent and to make control easier. Roman emperors are said to have followed a policy of providing "bread and circuses," with the idea that if the populace were kept fed and entertained, it would be less likely to challenge the rulers. It is therefore appropriate to begin with an examination of some key aspects of Egypt's population and the major issues that it raises for policymakers.

Five issues are crucial. The first is the size and the growth of the population. (See also Rivkin 2009, 95–105).

Egyptians have been said to be the most counted people on earth and, indeed, estimates of the country's population go back to pharaonic times; the Roman historian Titus Flavius Josephus provided a figure of 7.5 million, excluding Alexandria, for the first century CE (Bowman and Rogan 1999b, 6). The first reasonably reliable census of Egypt, however, took place in 1897, and thereafter censuses were conducted every ten years until 1947. The 1957 census was postponed until 1960 because of the Suez hostilities and there was a sample enumeration in 1966. The next complete census was taken in November 1976. Table 1 shows the population figures for the census years 1897–2006, and projections up to 2050.

The population of Egypt increased from less than 10 million in 1897 to 90 million in 2015, and the medium variant of the United Nations population projections puts it at 122 million in 2050 (the U.S. Census Bureau's projection is 169 million). Even if the projected slowdown in its rate of growth materializes, the population will have increased to twelve times its size in 1897. Policymakers thus have to deal with the implications for employment, income, food, health, education, law and order, housing, sanitation, energy, transport, communications, leisure, and so on, for a vast increase in numbers.

The dynamics of the demographic changes suggest that rapid population growth may be with Egypt for some time. Krafft and Assaad (2014a) show that by 2012 the peak of the youth bulge in Egypt was in the 25–29 age range and was starting to become parents. The increase in the size of this cohort together with the rise in the country's fertility rate was creating an "echo" bulge. "The number of children, especially young children, is unprecedented in Egypt's history. [Moreover] the increase in births has yet to level off, and all signs indicate that even greater numbers of children will be born, at least for the next several years" (Krafft and Assaad, 2014a: 2).

Second, the ability of policymakers to deal with these issues is severely constrained by Egypt's geography. Although the country comprises about one million square kilometers (386,000 square miles), nearly the size of France and Spain together, only a narrow strip in the Nile Valley and the Delta is, as Napoleon is said to have termed it, "usable Egypt." This area of 40,000 square kilometers (15,000 square miles), about the size of Switzerland and less than 4 percent of the total area of Egypt, is but an elongated oasis in the midst of desert. Without the Nile, which flows through Egypt for about 1,500 Kilometers (1,000 miles), the country would be part of the Sahara.[1] Crammed into the habitable area is 98 percent of the population, estimated at 90 million in 2015, giving a density of more than 2,000 persons per square kilometer (more than 5,000 per square mile) in the inhabited area. The problems that this situation engenders give rise to agricultural economist Hamdan's quip: "Our density is our destiny" (Waterbury 1983, 41).

Third, despite land reclamation and the attempt to develop a "second Valley" by constructing a canal to link Lake Nasser with a number of oases, the cultivated area has increased by only about 15 percent since 1947. More intensive cultivation has to some extent moderated the effects of the deterioration in the man/land ratio, but even so the cropped area (that is, the cultivated area multiplied by the cropping intensity) has increased only from 9.1 million feddans to about 14 million in the seventy years since 1947. Thus,

Table 1. Population, 1897–2050 (thousands)

Year	Population (000)	Average annual growth rate (%)
1897	9,715	
1907	11,287	1.51
1917	12,751	1.23
1927	14,218	1.12
1937	15,933	1.14
1947	19, 022	1.78
1960	26,085	2.38
1966	30,076	2.54
1976	41,213	3.20
1986	51,545	2.31
1996	58, 835	1.42
2006	72,009	1.98
2015	84,706	1.85
Projected*		
2020	91,062	1.48
2030	102,553	1.20
2040	113,000	1.00
2050	121,798	0.79

* Medium variant of U.N. projections.

Sources: 1897–2006: Census of Population. 2015–2050: United Nations 2012.

while the population increased by 350 percent between 1947 and 2015, the cropped area increased by only about 50 percent. A feddan in 2015 was expected to support nearly six persons, compared with 2.1 in 1947.

These two themes—the relatively fixed amount of the usable land and the snowballing requirements of a rapidly growing population—recur as leitmotifs in any discussion of Egypt's economic problems. They underpin issues with which Egypt's policymakers have had to grapple relentlessly, such as questions of agricultural productivity; the role of industry in creating the numbers of productive jobs that agriculture can no longer provide; the necessity of boosting exports in order to pay for imports of food (almost 60 percent of Egypt's wheat consumption depends on imports); the optimal use of Egypt's scarcest resource, namely, water; the importance of an urbanization strategy to restrain the continually expanding habitations from devouring the scarce agricultural land; halting the devastation of the environment; and many others.

Fourth, the population issue that is likely to claim much of the attention of Egypt's political and economic policymakers in the coming generation concerns not just the size or the growth of the population, but the changes in its age structure. Egypt has been undergoing a "demographic transition" characterized by falling birth and death rates. This gives rise to its own special problems, but also creates its own special opportunity, one that is sometimes labeled a "demographic dividend."

The changes in the age structure of the population at different periods create different problems, provide different opportunities, and call for different policy responses. For example, an increase in the younger age groups will require increased investment in health and education; a "bulge" in the age groups 15–64 will increase the potential for economic growth by enlarging the labor force; and as these groups grow beyond, say, age 65, the country will have to concern itself increasingly with questions of health and retirement income.

Demographers and economists have come to employ the term "demographic dividend" to describe a situation that arises when a decline in the birth rate lags behind that in the death rate and thus produces changes in the population's age structure. In due course, this increases the ratio of the working-age group in the population relative to the non-working-age group (the "dependents"). This outcome therefore can also be expressed as a fall in the "dependency ratio." A fall in the dependency ratio reduces the pressure on the labor force, because it means that each person of working age must support fewer nonworking persons. Figure 15 shows changes in the dependency ratio, actual and projected, from 1950 to 2050. It points to a steady decline in the ratio from 1990 to 2050, and thus identifies a potentially important source of growth for the Egyptian economy.

These demographic changes offer a "dividend" because the youngest and oldest age groups (the dependents) tend to consume more than they produce, while the working-age population produces more than it consumes. Thus an increase in the share of the working-age group in the total population provides the potential for a faster growth in aggregate output.

The expansion of the labor supply is but one effect of these changes in the population's age structure. Another important effect is the increase in

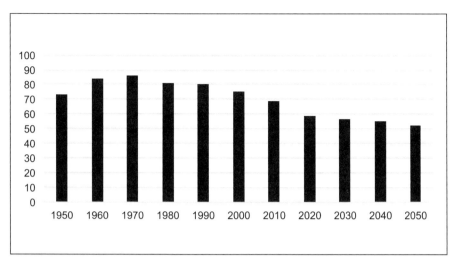

Figure 15. Dependency ratios, 1950–2050 (percent of population)
*Ratio of age groups 0–14 and 65+ to age group 15–64 (medium variant for projections 2020–2050)
Source: United Nations, World Population Projections: The 2012 Revision.

per capita savings. Studies on the effects of population growth on national savings suggest that people tend to increase their savings between the ages of 40 and 65 because during this period they have less of a need to invest in young children and because they need to accumulate savings in preparation for their retirement (Deaton and Paxson 1997; Bloom and Canning 1999). The higher savings can provide the wherewithal for higher investment and thus more rapid income growth. Increases in life expectancy also tend to increase the economic returns from education because these returns would accrue over a longer period. This encourages investment in education and training, and thereby produces more productive workers for the economy.

The combined effects can have very substantial results for aggregate output. Thus, for example, studies have estimated that the demographic dividend accounted for between 25 and 40 percent of East Asia's dramatic economic growth (Bloom and Williamson 1998; Bloom, Canning, and Malaney 2000; Mason 1988).

Two important caveats must be noted.

1. Changes in the population's age structure that produce a bulge in the working-age group offer only the *potential* for reaping a

dividend in the shape of more rapid economic growth. An Arabic proverb says, "With every mouth, God sends a pair of hands; with every pair of hands, God sends a mouth." This makes the point that an addition to the population potentially combines the roles of producer and consumer. However, a further point for policymakers is that in the highly competitive modern economy, a pair of hands without health, education, supporting infrastructure, and equipment to work with is not a pair of hands; one is left with only the mouths. The growing labor force will constitute an asset only if it is properly trained and equipped.

In short, the demographic dividend is not guaranteed. For the country to actually benefit from the increased supply of labor and for output to grow, policies would have to be put in place to increase investment, strengthen institutions, improve the education and training systems, and make markets more flexible and competitive so as to enable the additional labor to be employed in economically productive jobs. If this is not done, instead of receiving a demographic dividend the country might inherit a demographic nightmare, as its streets could be crowded with hundreds of thousands of young men and women desperately seeking jobs, education, health, and shelter for themselves and their families, and not finding them—creating a dire social situation and likely increasing the attractiveness of extremist ideologies.

2. The demographic dividend is not permanent. The bulge in the working-age group will inevitably pass into old age and thus lead to a higher ratio of nonworkers to workers, that is, to an increase in the dependency ratio. This makes it imperative for policymakers to use the window of opportunity created by the demographic dividend to prepare the economy and society for a time when a relatively smaller portion of the population than in the past will have to produce output, services, and taxes to support a relatively larger group of nonworkers.

Fifth, the population has become highly urbanized and is in the process of becoming even more so. This creates its own set of challenges and opportunities.

The definition of "urban" used by Egypt is based on administrative considerations rather than on criteria, such as the pattern of land use or the size of the conglomeration, that are employed in other countries.[2] Even on the basis of the restricted Egyptian criteria, about 45 percent of the population is said to be living in urban areas; this can create oddities such as "villages" of hundreds of thousands of inhabitants living in conglomerations possessing characteristics that in other countries would be clearly seen to be urban. The U.S. Census Bureau's definition of "urban" is based primarily on residential population density, while that of the United Kingdom defines an urban settlement as a conglomeration with a population of over 10,000. If similar internationally used definitions were adopted, two-thirds or more of Egypt's population in the census of 1996 would have been classified as urban (Denis 1999). On the basis of the Egyptian classification, the United Nations estimates that 60 percent of the country's population will be living in urban areas by 2050. However, using international definitions, that figure was comfortably exceeded as far back as 1996, and the urban share of the population in 2050 could approach 90 percent.

The foregoing is not simply a verbal quibble. Urban and rural conglomerations present some very different problems and opportunities for the politics and economics of a country, and muddling up the issue can blind policymakers to the dangers and also lead them to overlook the opportunities.

The scale and the increase in urbanization present four broad sets of issues.

1. The first is the cost of providing the infrastructure, such as water, sewerage, transportation, housing, health care, and educational services, to the rapidly expanding urban population. Moreover, the urgency and the scale of the required effort are much larger than in the past. The existing urban areas of the country evolved over a longer interval, involved fewer numbers during much of their maturing, and developed in circumstances in which they did not have to apply strict standards relating to labor, public health, safety, human rights, and the environment. The present situation is very different. Urbanization must take place in a situation in which standards in these areas are specified and over the next decades are increasingly likely to be enforced. This substantially raises the costs of urban development. Mobilizing resources to provide these facilities, at an acceptable level of quality, to the increasing urban population thus will be relatively more difficult than was the case in earlier periods.

2. The second important challenge thrown up by urbanization is political. Large concentrations of population make it easier to organize groups quickly and for them to voice their demands more assertively. This will require a strong base of local government organizations in order to respond swiftly and flexibly to rising expectations, to deal with problems, and to head off perceived grievances.

3. But, third, urbanization is not only a natural consequence of economic growth, it is also a major causal factor. Large agglomerations of people give rise to large and varied markets, and thus offer greater opportunities for innovation and enterprise. Large agglomerations also provide (a) a wide range of skills that could serve the market; (b) opportunities for division of labor and specialization of tasks that would reduce costs and serve the market more efficiently; and (c) facilities for persons with different ideas and aptitudes to interact and thus to increase the knowledge and skills that would make the production and distribution of goods and services more efficient.

A strong relation therefore exists between urbanization and prosperity. "There's no such thing as a poor urbanized country; there's no such thing as a rich rural country," said Edward Glaeser.[3] He also pointed out that "on average, as the share of a country's urban population rises by 10 percent, the country's per capita output increases by 30 percent. Indeed, per capita incomes are almost four times higher in countries where the majority of people live in cities than those in which the majority live in rural areas" (Glaeser 2011, 7).

4. The fourth important consideration created by urbanization is to require a more rational use of land. Egypt lacks an effective urbanization strategy, with the result that urban sprawl is making it difficult to provide services and is steadily eating away valuable agricultural land. Moreover, the location of industry and the creation of housing communities has been insufficiently coordinated, with the result that informal settlements closer to where employment opportunities are present have proliferated. The inhabitants of the settlements bear all the costs of informality—they cannot use the properties as collateral for loans (they represent "dead capital"), they are ill-served by public services, and they live on the fringes of the law-and-order network. Not being able to use their property as collateral is particularly burdensome—De Soto (1997, 11; 2000, 34)

estimated such dead capital in Egyptian real estate at $240 billion, which was thirty times the total value of all shares at that time on the Cairo stock exchange.

In view of the rapid increase in Egypt's population compared with the snail's-pace growth of the country's cultivated area, the question has often been asked whether Egypt is overpopulated, and how policymakers could best address this issue. Not surprisingly, the answer has undergone several changes of tone.

The assessment of one of the leading scholars of Egypt's economy, Charles Issawi, reflects these fluctuations. After posing this question, Issawi (1947, 50) concluded that "Egypt may just hope to maintain her growing population."[4] He added that any prospect of an advance from the very low standards of living of the time would require emigration or birth control on a large scale, together with industrialization and a "thoroughgoing" redistribution of land. In view of Egypt's economic performance at that time, this was not a very optimistic prognosis.

In his revised assessment, Issawi (1954, 242–45) adopted a more nuanced approach.[5] He examined the rise of Egypt's population in the light of density, level of employment, and level of consumption. On density, it was apparent that except for small portions of some of the river valleys of eastern and southern Asia, no agricultural region was as thickly populated as Egypt. On the level of employment, Issawi calculated that the existing agricultural output could be obtained with only half the rural population, even if no changes were made in technique and organization. He therefore judged about half the existing rural population to be "surplus." On the third criterion, namely the standard of living, Issawi concluded that "any attempt at raising the standard of living presupposes either an enormous expansion in production or a reduction in the population." However, perhaps somewhat surprisingly in view of the rather defeatist tone of the assessments against his three criteria, he expressed himself "convinced that Egypt's long-term prospects are good, because she will, in a not too distant future, be able to make much fuller use of her deserts."

In a further revision, Issawi (1963, 85–87, 298–302) stated that "Egypt's economic problems can be summed up in two words: poverty and overpopulation."[6] He reexamined the three previously adduced criteria and concluded that "Egypt may just hope to maintain its growing population but that, short of a technical break-through which would make it possible to utilize seawater for the cultivation of deserts, there is no prospect of an advance from the very depressed standard of living of today except through rapid industrialization and the immediate and energetic application of a birth-control program." This is less optimistic than his second evaluation.

He took solace, however, from an apparent change in government attitude toward family planning. In the *Draft of the Charter* of May 21, 1962, President Nasser had stated that "the problem of population increase is the most serious obstacle facing the efforts of the Egyptian people in their drive to raise the level of production." The president advocated family planning, and the first congress on family planning was held in Cairo in 1962.

The foregoing and other assessments of Egypt's capacity to support its population have correctly identified the problem but underestimated the economy's resilience. Some sources of its strength have come fortuitously, such as the remittances from Egyptian workers who have emigrated to the Gulf countries, the inflows of foreign assistance, the enhanced access to IFIs, the forgiveness of external debt, and the greater ease of borrowing from international capital markets with the reordering of Egypt's foreign policy toward the West. Many of these resources would be classed as "economic rents" (that is, unearned income) and their sustainability cannot be assured. Egypt cannot construct a secure economic future on the assumption of benefiting indefinitely from serendipity. The country's long-term economic health depends on combining rapid productivity growth with a strong family-planning program.

4

Political Economy in the Nasser Period
1952–70

On July 23, 1952 a group of army and air force officers—the "Free Officers"—overthrew Egypt's monarchical regime in a bloodless coup, and began the contemporary phase of Egypt's political history. On July 26, King Farouk was compelled to abdicate and go into exile. The monarchy was not abolished; Farouk's newborn son, Fu'ad II, succeeded him but was supervised by a Regency Council. The monarchy was formally abolished on June 18, 1953 and Egypt declared a republic.

The Free Officers were inspired by nationalism, not ideology. "It has often been said," wrote Roussillon in the *Cambridge History of Egypt* (1998, 2:338), "that the . . . officers forming the Revolutionary Command Council had no program, almost no ideology, and barely any 'philosophy.'" Tellingly, as Hopwood (1991, 38) points out, "the coup was announced in the name of the army on behalf of the whole of Egypt, not of a party, a revolutionary mass movement, or an ideology. The army's first aim was to purify itself and the government of corrupt elements; apart from that no firm plans had been made." Similarly, Vatikiotis (1961, 67–68) observed that "one finds few indications of any political program or plan of action. . . . There were perhaps as many shades of political belief as there were members of the Free Officers Executive." And Baker (1978, 34) commented that "the Egyptian revolution . . . was based on a vague nationalism rather than a coherent ideology," adding that "they [the Free Officers] had no action program that would have provided some conception of the society their revolution aimed at creating" (Baker 1978, 101).

Such views were not confined to foreign commentators; Mohamed Heikal wrote that "this movement . . . did not have an exact vision of the import and the profundity of the enterprise which it had undertaken."[1]

Indeed, in his memoirs Khaled Mohi el-Din (1995, 108–109), one of the original Free Officers and a member of the Revolutionary Command Council, said of a meeting of the officers one day after the coup, "We were meeting as rulers, but in fact we had not yet become rulers . . . because we ourselves did not know exactly how we would rule."

This was not surprising. The political and economic views of the Free Officers spanned an extremely wide spectrum. Sadowski (1991, 55) describes them as "an unusually diverse and cacophonous group, which included Marxists and Muslim fundamentalists, partisans of existing civilian parties and advocates of military rule, socialists and free traders, admirers of the West and violent anti-imperialists." The revolutionaries were motivated by resentment against the corruption of the monarch and his courtiers, and by frustration with the failure of the politicians to rid the country of British occupation.

Although the revolutionaries adhered to no clearly specified political or economic philosophy, their actions immediately after taking control showed that improving the economic situation was a priority in their mission, and they understood that political actions provided the most effective means of attaining this end. Their very first policy—the agrarian reform—was aimed at controlling the largest section of Egypt's economy and society and came within two months of their assuming power. Major political actions affecting the economy continued through the entire period of Nasser's rule.

The political economy of the Nasser era, 1952–70, was dominated by six principal issues, several of which were interlinked: agrarian reforms; the water issue and the decision to build the Aswan High Dam; problems with financing the Dam, leading to the Suez crisis; the Suez Canal war and the start of the nationalization wave; the expanding role of the state in the economy, including nationalizations and economic planning; and industrial development. Forming a background and permeating the other issues were structural problems, such as balance-of-payments crises and relations with donors and IFIs.

Agrarian Reforms

The first order of business for the Free Officers was to secure their regime. They had to subdue the opposition and create a constituency that would owe its loyalty to the revolution. The most potent resistance was expected to come from the large landowners who dominated the parliament, occupied the most powerful cabinet chairs, and resisted every attempt to correct the massive inequities in the ownership of land. The urgency with which the Free Officers felt they had to tackle this problem is evident from the speed with which they approached the issue—the land reform law was enacted on September 7, 1952, only a month and a half after their coming to power. The primary intent of the first land reform law was to politically and financially cripple the large landowners.

The seriousness with which the Free Officers regarded land reform was demonstrated in how they dealt even with the prime minister, Ali Mahir, whom they themselves had appointed. Ali Mahir, who was himself a wealthy landowner, argued that fragmenting the large estates and reducing them to smaller plots for distribution to the fellahin would reduce productivity and discourage foreign investment. He argued against putting a legal ceiling on land ownership, proposing instead the imposition of a heavier tax on landholdings above a certain (generous) limit, so that landowners would be encouraged to dispose of the excess land. The officers saw that this would only result in the transfer of land from the very large landowners to somewhat less large landowners (since these were the most likely to have the wherewithal to purchase the excess land) and thus would do nothing to create a political constituency that would support the military rulers. They swiftly rejected this proposal and insisted on enforcing a ceiling.

Not deterred, Ali Mahir suggested that the ceiling be five hundred feddans (as against the Free Officers' proposal of two hundred feddans), with the excess amount not confiscated but subject to an 80 percent tax. On September 4, Ali Mahir conferred with a delegation of twenty-two large landowners and associated his name with a warning drafted by them that the proposed land reform would "destroy the national economy. . . . It will make everyone poor for it will ruin the rich and the poor will not profit." The statement then went on to propose a ceiling of one thousand feddans, with additional exemptions of one hundred feddans per wife and fifty feddans per daughter (Gordon 1992, 66–67). For the Free Officers, this was the last straw. On September 6, Ali Mahir was summarily dismissed. Three days later, the Agrarian Reform Law was promulgated.

In 1952, before the land reform, less than half of 1 percent (0.4 percent) of landowners owned 34 percent of Egypt's agricultural land, while nearly 95 percent held only about 35 percent of the land (Mabro 1974, 61, table 4.1; Baer 1962 provides a historical discussion of landownership). The first agrarian reform law set a maximum limit of land ownership at two hundred feddans for a single person. Owners were permitted to transfer up to an additional one hundred feddans to their children, subject to a maximum of fifty feddans per dependent child. Land exceeding the ceiling would be appropriated by the government for redistribution among tenants and farmers owning less than five feddans of agricultural land. Further land reform laws followed: a law in July 1961 limited land ownership to 100 feddans for a single owner, while in August 1969 the maximum ownership was reduced to 50 feddans.

The redistributive aim of the law was important, but secondary. The 1952 and subsequent reforms could have had only a modest distributional effect, because not enough land was available for redistribution to satisfy the requirements of all tenants and landless workers. Waterbury (1983, 266–67) estimates that the series of reforms involved at most 16 percent of Egypt's cultivated land area, leading to the distribution of 13 percent of that land to about 10 percent of the country's rural families. In his view, "agrarian reform in and of itself did not lead to any major redistribution of land, and the object of the 1952 reform was above all political." Indeed, if every rural family had received an equal share of Egypt's cultivated land in 1969, its plot would have amounted to less than 1.8 feddans, a holding well below that required for subsistence. And with population growth and the inheritance laws, even this size would quickly diminish. Mabro (1974, 73) argues similarly that "the Egyptian land reform sought limited improvements in the distribution of wealth, and benefited the upper section of the low-income group." Baker (1978, 205) concurs, saying that the Egyptian land reform primarily benefited those who already had a stake in village society. The result was the elimination of the largest landowners and an increase in the size and affluence of the middling class of owners; as Kandil (2012, 62) says, "land reform shifted the balance of political power from large landlords to these new kulaks."

Nevertheless, the reforms did have a disproportionate impact on the largest estates, whose owners were the most powerful politicians in the *ancien régime* and who constituted the principal opposition to the Free Officers. After the 1952 agrarian reform, although the share of 94 percent of landowners had increased to only 38 percent of the total area, the share of the top 0.4 percent of landowners had dropped to 30 percent. By 1964, however, subsequent reforms had increased the share of the lowest 94 percent of owners to 55 percent of the land area and decreased the share of the top 0.3 percent to 13 percent (Eshag and Kamal 1968). The very large estates, which had accounted for nearly 20 percent of the area in 1952 before the land reform, entirely disappeared.

Perhaps somewhat to the Officers' surprise, the reform met with very little resistance. As Cooper (1979, 483) writes: "[The] ease with which it seized the economic structure (less than 2000 feudalists and 1000 capitalists had to be expropriated, and with very little bloodshed), reflects weakness in the system rather than power in the regime."

In addition to breaking the power of the large landlords, the economic weapon of the agrarian reforms had two further political aims. First, it was to obtain the support of a large constituency for the revolutionaries' cause, and to maintain the support by strengthening the regime's control over the rural population. This was accomplished through four principal means.

1. The distribution to the fellahin of the land expropriated from the large estates helped to create the sought-for class that owed the improvement in its living standards to the revolution.
2. The loyalty of this class to the revolution was further cemented by other provisions in the agrarian reform law and by additional concessions in subsequent years. A number of writers—for example, Warriner (1957) and Abdel-Fadil (1975)—have argued that perhaps the greatest impact was provided by changes in tenancy regulations. The agrarian law strengthened the position of tenants by various provisions: all leases were to be in writing; land could only be leased to those who cultivated it; the minimum duration of a lease was increased from one year (or even less) to three years; tenants could be evicted by landlords only if the latter intended to cultivate the land themselves; and the maximum rent was limited to seven times the value of the land tax. The last provision not only benefited the tenants by capping their obligations, but also reduced the former owners' income very substantially. Thus, Hansen (1991, 118) points out that even if the landowners had been paid all the compensation that the law allowed, "the expropriations would still have reduced the income of the old owners to about one-sixth of what they could have obtained at maximum rents from the confiscated lands." Financial enfeeblement would ensure political emasculation.
3. Additional financial concessions were provided. In 1958 the interest on beneficiaries' debts was reduced from 3 percent to 1.5 percent; the 15 percent administrative charge that beneficiaries had to pay in addition to the purchase price was reduced to 10 percent; and the repayment period was extended from thirty years to forty years.

But if the carrot did not work, the regime could resort to the stick—the agricultural cooperatives.

4. The reform of land tenure was supplemented by the introduction of agricultural cooperatives. In order to obtain seeds, fertilizer, machinery, or agricultural credit, a farmer had to become a member of a cooperative and follow its rules concerning crop rotation, output pricing, marketing, and so forth. This gave the cooperatives a vast amount of power over economic outcomes in agriculture. Thus, for example, the authorities instituted a system of compulsory deliveries for certain crops at prices much lower than those prevailing in the free market. The crops were then sold by the government at the market price. This mechanism enabled the government to impose an indirect tax on the cultivator, equal to the difference between the free market price and that paid on the compulsory deliveries.

The cooperatives also enabled the government to manipulate the structure of incentives by regulating the domestic terms of trade between agriculture and other sectors. Abdel-Fadil (1975, 89–93) shows that the government used the cooperatives to regulate the intersectoral terms of trade by purchasing all the cotton crop and disposing of large portions of other major crops; by state monopoly over the import and distribution of fertilizers and pesticides; and by providing supervised agricultural credit. The government was also able to pass laws mandating how much of a cultivator's acreage had to be sown to a particular crop; this provision was regularly applied to cotton cultivation.

In short, the land redistribution helped produce a class that was beholden to the revolution and which had an incentive to support it, while the cooperatives provided an instrument by which this class could be pressured to provide the support should the incentive prove insufficient.

Several writers have emphasized that there were important noneconomic aspects to the agrarian reforms. Vatikiotis, for example, observes that

sound economics was not the only rationale for agrarian reform. It was rather a means by which to strike a sensational political note with the Egyptian masses. Considering the premium placed on land by rich and poor Egyptians alike, agrarian reform with its redistribution of large estates to the *fellahin* was a potent psychological measure. It [also] gave the Free Officers their first political link with the peasant masses. (Vatikiotis 1961, 75)

Muhammad Naguib, the first president of the republic, also offers a psychological, almost poetical, justification for the agrarian reforms:

> A landed peasant is a man of spirit who will defend his land, if necessary, with his life. The difference between a landless and a landed peasant is the difference between a two-footed animal and a man. Too many Egyptian peasants have been reduced through the years to the level of two-footed animals. What Egypt needs for its renaissance is men, and we are counting on the agrarian reforms to help us to produce them. (Naguib 1955, 148)

And President Anwar Sadat (1977, 130) described the land reform as the measure that, more than any other, transformed the character of the Free Officers' movement from a mere coup d'état to a genuine revolution.

Second, by preventing or discouraging further purchases of land by the former landowning class, the revolutionary regime hoped to divert capital from agriculture to industry. This aim was unsuccessful. Farah (2009, 31–33) indicates the major reason for the failure—the industrial and landowning elites were overlapping classes. She points to a finding by Saad Eddin Ibrahim that "the same 12,000 families of big landowners who held some 50 percent of all cultivable land also included the 11,000 major shareholders who held some 40 percent of joint-stock companies." This class, once-bitten by the appropriation of their landholdings under the agrarian reform law, was twice-shy of investing in manufacturing enterprises, which could be nationalized. As Farah sums up, "The regime did not realize that the industrial entrepreneurs came from the ranks of the landowners. . . . They feared a government takeover of their industries." Issawi (1963, 163), while in general favorably inclined toward the agrarian reform law, agrees that this objective of the law failed, and that capital did not flow into industry but into high-income apartment houses. Kandil (2012, 63) estimates that of the LE45 million redirected out of agriculture (by the forcible sale of land by the large landowners), only LE6 million was invested in industry, while the rest was put into real estate.

The Cultivable Area: Water and the Aswan High Dam

The agrarian reform of 1952 improved the distribution of landholdings by confiscating and reallocating the existing cultivated area. However, the cultivated area per inhabitant had been steadily declining, and it had not been possible to provide land to all the landless living in the rural areas. If Egypt's agricultural output was to increase to meet the demands of a rapidly expanding population and to provide land to the substantial numbers who had not benefited from the land reform, the cultivated area had to be increased. The binding constraint on enlarging the cultivated area in Egypt is not land, but water.

The constraint is imposed by geography. Egypt is but an elongated oasis in the midst of a desert; rainfall is sparse and chiefly confined to a narrow belt along the Mediterranean Sea. The only large source of water is the river Nile. The Nile is formed by three tributaries: the Blue Nile and the Atbara River, which originate in the Ethiopian highlands and provide on average 53 and 17 percent respectively of the Nile's waters, and the White Nile, which originates in equatorial Africa and supplies the rest.

Egyptian policymakers have long understood that while the aggregate supply of water could not materially be increased, the available amount could be used more effectively by better managing the river's flow. In this, Egypt's policymakers had to contend with three principal problems.

First, the flow of the Nile fluctuated considerably from year to year, depending upon the rainfall in the areas in which its tributaries originated. There were also large seasonal differences within a given year, with the main flood coming in the winter and a low flow in the summer months; indeed, between 40 and 50 percent of the annual water supply was accounted for by only two months, August and September. Because of these fluctuations, the country could suffer from a drought if the river ran low, or undergo substantial agricultural and property damage if the inundation was too high. Mabro (1974, 86) mentions some extreme years: 1879, which recorded the highest discharge at Aswan in the previous 125 years at 137 billion cubic meters (BCM),[2] and 1913, when at 45 BCM the supply fell some 15 percent short of the country's requirements.[3]

Second, a major weakness was that the infrastructure of dams and barrages in Egypt could only control the water within one year. They could not supplement the supply if the flow of the Nile was insufficient, nor protect the country from damage to crops, lives, and property if the flow was excessive and the river overflowed its banks. Egypt lacked adequate storage to carry water over a multi-year period. Aswan was an important site, but it had only a barrage. The latter structure differs from a dam in that it has no storage function. It merely blocks the flow of water until the level is high enough for the water to flow into canals or ditches that are above the natural channel of the river or the canal.

Third, although Egypt is the principal user of Nile water, no part of the river originates in the country. This created a combination of political and economic problems, and required delicate handling with the other riparian countries, particularly Sudan.[4]

The Free Officers' response to the fluctuations in the supply of water, to the inability of the irrigation infrastructure to iron out these fluctuations, and to the need to ensure that an adequate supply remained under Egyptian hands was to abandon plans for using the great African lakes, Victoria and Albert, as places for storing the Nile's waters. Instead, they adopted an earlier plan for a high dam south of Aswan. The Free Officers were clearly in a hurry to address the water issue; Little (1965, 39) points out that they gave this project such high priority that they decided to pursue the High Dam scheme within two months of coming to power.

This structure would create the biggest man-made lake in the world (Lake Nasser) and would provide multi-year storage, thus eliminating Egypt's dependence on the annual Nile flood. It would also generate 10 billion kilowatts of electric power. The Free Officers considered that while the dam would certainly contribute to extending the cultivated area and permit additional cropping, much of the agricultural gains would be consumed by the rise in the population during the ten years or so that constructing the dam would require. As Little (1967: 258) notes, "The fact that Nile development can never again keep pace with population is at the root of Egypt's economic problem." A sustainable development strategy, therefore, had to emphasize diversifying the economy away from agriculture toward industry, and the massive amounts of low-cost electricity that were expected to be generated by the dam would support the required expansion of the Egyptian manufacturing sector.

The construction of the High Dam raised three issues that had a major impact on the politics and economics of Egypt. These were: (1) the effects on aggregate investment; and (2) the geographical pattern of trade. (3) The most important consequences for Egypt's political-economy arose from the problem of financing the Dam; indeed, they led to a crisis concerning the Suez Canal—war with the United Kingdom, France, and Israel—which in turn triggered fundamental changes in Egypt's external political alignments and domestic economic policies. These were so important that they are discussed in a separate section.

Effect on Composition of Investment

A project the size of the Aswan High Dam predictably had a significant impact on the composition of investment. The officially estimated cost of the dam was LE320 million, which Hansen (1991, 152–53) calculates would account for about 1.5 percent of average GNP during the eleven years of construction, with about one-third for the power station. Waterbury (1977, 112) puts the total cost at LE424 million (including LE141 million for the power station). See also Waterbury (1979).

Given the pressure on Egypt's resources, accommodating an allocation of this size would inevitably require retrenchment in other sectors. The housing sector bore the brunt of the cutbacks. In the period from 1960 to 1967, housing investment was cut back annually by more than 2 percent of GNP. "In this real sense," wrote Hansen, "the agricultural part of the project—the dam itself—was financed by a reduction of investment in housing" (Hansen 1991, 152).

Hansen (1991, 152–53) records a discussion with the Ministry of Planning which emphasized that cutting back on housing was reasonable because of the high ratio of capital to output in the sector. Gross fixed investment in the irrigation and drainage sector (which included the Aswan High Dam, except for the powerhouse and lines, which were included under electricity and public utilities), which had averaged 0.8 percent of GDP in the period between 1953 and 1960, more than tripled to 2.7 percent in 1961–65, and remained high at 2.1 percent in 1966–67. The electricity and public utilities sector also saw its share of investment to GDP triple between 1953–60 and 1966–67. A compensating slowdown was imposed on increases in industrial investment, which increased by only 1.1 percentage points of GDP in 1961–65 compared with 1953–60. Hansen remarks that "the Aswan Dam swamped everything in the early 1960s" (Hansen 1991, 153).

After Nasser had taken a personal decision to speed up construction on the High Dam, the available building materials had increasingly to be diverted to the dam project. This impression is reinforced by the fact that the first five-year plan did not make a holistic attempt to incorporate the accompanying consequences of the dam's construction. There were no plans for expanding the cement industry, and Egypt's substantial exports of cement ceased with the construction of the dam (Hansen 1991, 239n5).

The investment reallocations carried important social consequences. In the face of the rapidly increasing population and its urbanization, the reduced housing investment vastly increased the pressure of demand on the available stock of housing. The situation was made worse by various rent control laws (particularly Law 46 of 1962 that put a ceiling on annual rent of 5 percent of the value of the site and 8 percent of the value of the building) that discouraged private investment in housing and even in the maintenance of the existing stock. In the manner of King Canute, the authorities sought to control the resulting price increases by issuing more and more regulations.

The market paid as little regard to these pronouncements as the sea waves had to Canute's orders to stop coming in. A vast network of "advance sales" (that is, selling apartments before they were constructed), unofficial rents, "advance rents," and "key money" (a large upfront payment to compensate for the low legal rents) sprang up. The outcome was a badly fragmented market with very different outcomes for its participants. Tenants who managed to acquire housing at the official rate obtained huge windfall increases in their real incomes. Property owners who could use official connections or other means to evade the laws and obtain the unofficial rents made very large, untaxed profits. This did not markedly encourage private investment in housing, because the illegal rental transactions were very risky. However, the political gains from announcing rent controls overrode economic logic. As Thomas Sowell has written, "The first lesson of economics is scarcity: there is never enough of anything to fully satisfy all those who want it. The first lesson of politics is to disregard the first lesson of economics" (www.brainyquote.com/quotes/authors/t/thomas_sowell.html).

Effect on Direction of Trade

The construction of the High Dam, indirectly and directly, had an important political-economy consequence that persisted well into the future. After the cessation of hostilities in the Suez Canal war, the Soviet Union sensed an opportunity to benefit from the weakening of the West's influence in the Middle East and stepped in with the offer of a loan to pay for the construction of the dam. Egypt had also been compelled to turn to the Communist Bloc to obtain arms and other imports. These developments shifted the import pattern in the direction of the Communist Bloc, while exports had also to be redirected toward the bloc to pay for the imports.

Mabro (1975, 301) reminds us that Egypt was engaged in substantial commercial exchanges with many East European countries well before 1956. In 1948, these countries (including the USSR) accounted for nearly

10 percent of Egyptian exports and similarly of imports. In 1948, there was a spike in the share of the USSR in Egyptian exports, rising to 8 percent and accounting for 7 percent of imports.

At the same time, there was a sharp drop in Egypt's trade with the United Kingdom. This movement resulted principally from developments in the sterling area. Egypt was a member of the sterling area and had accumulated substantial sterling reserves in London, but Britain had restricted the amounts that Egypt could draw down in dollars and other hard currencies to pay for imports that could not be supplied by the United Kingdom or Western Europe. In 1947, the United Kingdom reestablished the convertibility of sterling, and Egypt took the opportunity to leave the sterling area.

Mabro points out that there was nothing abnormal about changes in Egypt's trading pattern in 1948. It was simply "the natural tendency of a trading country to search for new partners when difficulties are experienced in traditional foreign markets" Mabro (1975, 302). The transformation of the trading pattern before 1956, therefore, was a response to economic factors. After 1956, however, the change came about because of political factors, namely Egypt's having to purchase arms from the Communist Bloc because of the refusal of Western countries to sell them.

The trading pattern was also affected by changes in the pattern of aid flows. From 1959 until the mid-1960s, aid from the United States—consisting mainly of wheat and foodstuffs provided under Public Law 480—remained significant, even though the USSR was extending substantial assistance to Egypt. This was reflected in the United States' share in Egypt's imports. After Egypt entered the civil war in Yemen against the side supported by Saudi Arabia, the United States' attitude changed.

In order to persuade Egypt to withdraw from the proxy war against Saudi Arabia (a strong U.S. ally) in Yemen, the United States virtually terminated its aid program for Egypt in 1966. All of a sudden, the substantial amounts of commodities received under PL 480—Mabro (1975, 303) estimates the 1962 figure at £220 million—had to be paid for in foreign exchange. The United States thus used an economic weapon to try to attain a political aim. The aid cutoff put Egypt under great pressure; many economic activities had to be severely cut back in order to meet the current-account deficit (amounting to 7 percent of GNP in 1964). For reasons already discussed, public consumption could not be curtailed and the cuts fell heavily on the investment program. The squeeze on Egypt's resources was one of the factors that doomed the second quinquennium of the ten-year comprehensive plan.

These events imposed more durable changes on Egypt's trade pattern. In 1953, Egypt's trade with the Communist Bloc amounted to about 5 percent of its total trade. In 1958 this had risen to 32 percent. In subsequent years the figure came down somewhat, but throughout the 1960s it averaged about 25 percent. The figure is likely to have been even higher, because it is far from clear how imports for the High Dam and for military equipment are treated in the data. An interesting feature of these trade relations is that the Communist Bloc does not appear to have taken advantage of Egypt's dependence—Mabro estimates that in bilateral trade, export and import prices corresponded to world prices, often with a premium in Egypt's favor.

The main drawback to the shift in the pattern of trade toward the Eastern Bloc was certain long-term consequences. Egypt's industrial, transport, and communication sectors increasingly became equipped with technology that was markedly inferior to its Western counterparts. The results became apparent in the diminished quality of Egypt's manufactured products and in the productivity of the economy, with a consequent loss of shares in international markets.

Financing the High Dam and the Suez Canal Crisis

The story of financing the Aswan High Dam project and the relations between Egypt, the World Bank, and the Bank's principal shareholders involves a complex interplay of politics and economics and, at times, of politics masquerading as economics. Egypt did not have the resources for building the dam and had to look to external sources. Some of these, as it turned out, had agendas beyond the provision of financial assistance.

The West German government offered to finance the preparation of the High Dam project and assigned the design task to the Hochtief and Dortmund Union. This preparatory work was completed in two years, and was reviewed by a number of international experts. The availability of financing for the dam's construction would depend on the experts' verdict on the viability of the project. The World Bank also sent experts to Egypt to determine the technical and economic feasibility of the project. The Bank's final report was delivered in February 1956 and declared the project to be sound.

The total cost of the dam was put at $1.3 billion, to be spread over the estimated fifteen-year period of its construction. Of this amount, roughly $400 million represented foreign-exchange costs that Egypt looked to obtain from abroad, while the remaining $900 million for local currency expenditure would be met by Egypt itself. Negotiations for financing the project commenced with the World Bank.

Two other sources offered help. The United States and the United Kingdom agreed to seek approval from their legislatures for providing a grant of about $70 million ($54.6 million from the United States and £5.5 million [about $14 million at that time] from the United Kingdom) to cover the foreign-exchange costs of the first phase of the project. Mason and Asher (1973, 638, table 18-2), in the World Bank's authorized history of its first twenty-five years of operation, report that the Bank was expected to contribute $200 million out of a total foreign-exchange requirement of $390 million. For later phases of the project, Eisenhower (1965, 31n10) writes that the United States and the United Kingdom "would give 'sympathetic attention'—which really meant approval, given legislative authority—to a further loan of $130 million."

The financial offer was hemmed in by a number of stringent political and economic conditions. The most important were: Egypt would commit to allocating one-third of its own revenues to the High Dam project; construction contracts would have to be awarded through international competitive bidding from which communist countries would be excluded (the stated reason was that these countries were not members of the World Bank; however the political overtones are obvious); Egypt could not incur additional foreign debt without prior approval from the World Bank; and Egypt would have to reach a new accord with Sudan on sharing the Nile waters before any disbursement of funds from the United States, the United Kingdom, or the World Bank could take place.

These conditions were resented by Egypt's leaders, whose greatest dismay arose from the division of the financing into two phases, and by the contingent nature of the offer of finance for the second phase of construction. These maneuvers were seen as providing Western countries with an economic lever that could be used to coerce Egypt into settling the Arab–Israeli dispute on terms that were politically unfavorable to the Arab side. This idea was not far-fetched—Mason and Asher (1973, 642) acknowledge that "they [the Western powers] may have thought of it as potentially useful in this regard."

A series of negotiations followed, involving proposals and counter-proposals from the Western and Egyptian sides. Then on July 19, 1956 the United States abruptly, publicly, and without prior warning to Egypt announced its withdrawal from the financing of the Aswan High Dam. The declared reasons were that with the large-scale arms purchases from the Eastern Bloc, Egypt's economy could not absorb a project as large as the High Dam, and that no agreement between Egypt and Sudan over the dam had been reached (the lake created by the dam would extend nearly a hundred kilometers into Sudan, submerging many villages and the border town of Wadi Halfa). However, it was clear that the real reasons were that the United States had become incensed with Egypt's purchase of arms from the Communist Bloc and by its recognition of communist China.

The United Kingdom soon followed suit, with the cabinet deciding on July 20, 1956 that the country should withdraw from the project. Sir Anthony Eden, the British prime minister, writes in his memoirs that "we were informed but not consulted and so had no prior opportunity for criticism or comment" (Eden 1960, 422). It is not clear what "criticism or comment" the U.K. government would have delivered on the American action (except perhaps in support of it) since, according to Sir Anthony, "in mid-July, after the most careful canvassing of all the arguments, the Government came to the conclusion that they could not go on with a project likely to become increasingly onerous in finance and unsatisfactory in practice" (Eden 1960, 421). The conclusion that the United Kingdom should not proceed with the loan appears already to have been reached.

Selwyn Lloyd, the United Kingdom secretary of state for foreign affairs, asserts in his Suez memoir (Lloyd 1978, 71) that the decision was taken on economic grounds because "Egypt was undertaking other commitments (industrialization and continuing high expenditure on arms) which would prevent her giving to the dam project the degree of priority necessary to secure its success." This, however, is disingenuous. Lloyd had already stated (68–69) that he "had warned the Cabinet in March that we might have to withdraw offer of help for the scheme, and I had sent a message to Makins [the U.K. ambassador in Washington] at the end of that month saying that our feeling was that we should not give Nasser the money for the dam unless he genuinely changed his attitude towards Western interests in the Middle East." Selwyn Lloyd also describes a meeting in May at which he and Dulles (the U.S. secretary of state) had "agreed to let the Aswan Dam project 'wither on the vine.'" The reason for both countries' withdrawal from the project was thus political, dressed up as economic.

One is forced to conclude that the United States and the United Kingdom had decided at least as early as May to withdraw from the dam project, but delayed its announcement until July in the (highly unlikely) event that the Egyptians surrendered all their other vital goals, such as industrialization, procuring arms from the Eastern Bloc that the West would not sell them, and supporting the Palestinian cause. A classic example of saying "no" by saying "yes, but on impossible terms."

This is not to say that the Egyptians had handled the matter adroitly. Egypt had opened too many fronts and offended too many interest groups. As Lloyd points out,

> The China lobby had been infuriated by Nasser's recognition of Communist China in May. The cotton lobby were against the loan because of Nasser's deal with Russia over Egyptian cotton. The Israeli lobby were against it on the ground that it would strengthen one of their principal enemies. In addition, the United States was being bombarded with requests for aid from friendly countries in the Middle East. Their theme was that friendship should be better rewarded than enmity. The United States, they said, by giving aid to Egypt for the dam, was doing just the opposite. (Lloyd 1978, 69)

The World Bank's offer also lapsed, the stated reason being that with the withdrawal of the U.S. and U.K. offers, the financing for the project was left with a gap. In the Bank's view, it would be a waste to commit its resources to a project that was incompletely funded and therefore might never be implemented. Tying up resources in a project that might never be executed would not only not benefit Egypt but would also hurt other developing countries, because the committed resources would not be available for lending to them. However, with all the high politics involved in this episode, one might be forgiven for suspecting that some phone calls might have been exchanged between U.S. authorities and the World Bank that swayed the latter's decision. The Egyptians were not impressed by the Bank's change of heart. President Nasser, in his Alexandria speech nationalizing the Suez Canal, denounced what he called "mortgage colonialism," reported Jean and Simone Lacouture, two French eyewitnesses (Lacouture and Lacouture 1958, 472).

The Egyptians were also furious for another reason. Hopwood (1991, 47) quotes Zakariya Mohieddin, minister of the interior, telling the British ambassador, "It is not so much the withdrawal of the money which we mind. . . . It is the way in which it was done." And President Nasser in an interview with the BBC said, "I was surprised by the insultive [*sic*] attitude with which the refusal was declared. Not by the refusal itself."

The cancellation of the financing led Egypt to nationalize the Suez Canal. Since the West was prepared to allow politics to hold back Egypt's economic development, Nasser would play a political card to support this development. The president declared that he would use the revenue from transit tolls to finance the construction of the High Dam. "The Canal will pay for the Dam," he announced in front of a cheering crowd in Alexandria on July 26, 1956 (Baker 1978, 41).

The nationalization cocktail of politics and economics had further consequences, as it was used as a pretext by Britain, France, and Israel to invade Egypt. Providing a legal justification for the invasion required Eden to perform a series of verbal gymnastics. According to Tignor (2010, 266), "the Law Officers of the British Foreign Office acknowledged in an unpublished but widely read internal report, [that] the Egyptian government had a legal right to nationalize what according to the company's charter was a full-fledged Egyptian company." Eden himself grudgingly concedes that the Suez Canal Company was "technically" an Egyptian company (Eden 1960, 428), but then refers to it throughout the rest of the memoirs as an "international company." Moreover, he implies that the Egyptian action was illegal because it affected the interests of many countries, and it should therefore be put under international supervision. Eden has then to resort to further semantic contortions to defend the Panama Canal's exclusion from such an interpretation; this was necessary to keep the Americans on board with the United Kingdom's action (Eden 1960, 435).

In the event, it did not help. The Americans jumped ship after the British–French–Israeli invasion and compelled those countries to vacate the territory they had occupied. The second volume of President Eisenhower's memoirs (1965, 39–40) makes clear that from the beginning the United States differed from the British–French position on two principal grounds. First, the United States doubted the validity of the legal position that Britain and France were using to justify a possible resort to force. He noted that "the waterway, although a property of the Canal Company, lay completely within Egyptian territory *and under Egyptian sovereignty*" (italics in the original). Second, the United States believed that a resort to force before every possible resource of the United Nations had been exhausted in reaching a satisfactory solution would be unjustified and would weaken, perhaps even destroy, the United Nations. The United States was also skeptical of the British argument that no one except the European technicians then operating the canal were capable of doing so.

On October 31, 1956, in a broadcast to the nation, Eisenhower (1965, 81) said that he doubted that resort to war would serve the permanent interest of the attacking nations; that there would be no U.S. involvement in the hostilities; and that he would not call the Congress into special session. He added that the United States would take to the U.N. General Assembly the request that Israel withdraw and hostilities end.

Nutting (1967, 62) quotes John Foster Dulles, the U.S. secretary of state for foreign affairs, as saying that even if Egypt used force over the canal, "we do not intend to shoot our way through." The United States put forward a resolution in the U.N. Security Council that explicitly condemned the Anglo-French action (Eden 1960, 530, 554). Moreover, Eden (524–25) reports that in fact "the American Administration was urgently proposing to have Israel branded as an aggressor by the Security Council." Thus, although the United States agreed with the British and the French on the economic importance of keeping the Suez Canal open to international traffic, it differed strongly on the question of the ownership of the canal, and of the best way of ensuring that it remained open. The United States also refused to support the United Kingdom's application for a loan of $1 billion from the International Monetary Fund, thereby putting pressure on the British pound.

Eden went on to mislead the British parliament by stating that there had been no conspiracy among the United Kingdom, France, and Israel for their invasion of Egypt. Unfortunately for his reputation, this was revealed to be untrue. There had indeed been a conspiracy and its details were recorded in a document that has come to be known as the "Protocol of Sèvres" (after the name of the town in which the British–French–Israeli meetings took place on October 22–24, 1956). The papers confirming the collusion had been destroyed by the United Kingdom and "lost" by France, but preserved by Israel, and came to light several years later (see Nutting 1967, Troen 1995, and Shlaim 1997; the latter two references include the text of the Protocol).

The American reasons for withdrawing the loan were clearly political, and had to do with Egypt's increasing closeness to the Communist Bloc. The British reasons included a large dose of economics, in addition to bruised imperial pride and, indeed, to Eden's wounded ego. The

British prime minister had graduated from Oxford with an honors degree in Arabic and Persian and considered himself a specialist on the Middle East. To suffer a massive political defeat in that region was therefore especially hurtful.

Anthony Nutting, who had previously served as Eden's private secretary and since 1954 had been minister of state in the British Foreign Office, but then resigned as a matter of principle over the Suez invasion, writes that "Eden began to behave like an enraged elephant charging senselessly at invisible and imaginary enemies in the international jungle" (Nutting 1967, 32). Eden insisted that he did not want Nasser isolated or neutralized; he wanted him destroyed. Nutting cautioned Eden that the only result of removing Nasser would be anarchy in Egypt. Eden responded by shouting, "I don't give a damn if there's anarchy and chaos in Egypt" (Nutting 1967, 35).

Eden's memoirs highlight the dependence of Western Europe and the United Kingdom on Middle Eastern oil fields, and the economic factors behind the invasion of Egypt. These oil fields were producing about 145 million tons a year, of which nearly 70 million tons had passed through the Suez Canal in 1955. Another 40 million tons were transported through pipelines that ran through the territories of Egypt's then allies, Syria and Saudi Arabia. More than half of Britain's annual imports of oil came through the Suez Canal (Eden 1960, 429). Transport through the canal, for oil and other purposes, was vital to Britain's economy. Eden reports that in 1955 (the year before the canal's nationalization), 14,666 ships passed through the canal; three-quarters of them belonged to NATO countries and nearly one-third were British (Eden 1960, 426). Nutting (1967, 39) states that when the Russian leaders Bulganin and Khrushchev visited London in April 1956, Eden told them that oil from the Middle East was so vital to the British economy that "we would fight for it" if the need arose. President Eisenhower (1965, 22) also recognized the economic importance of the Suez Canal. In his memoirs, he pointed out that in 1955 more than 100 million tons of goods transited it, more than twice the amount that went through the Panama Canal. The canal's gross revenues of about $100 million produced an annual net profit of about $30 million.

The final result of the Suez Canal War must be seen as Egypt conjuring a very substantial political victory from the ashes of a military defeat. Cook sums up:

Washington's stand against Great Britain, France, and Israel bolstered Cairo's position on the Canal, essentially legitimizing the waterway's nationalization; effectively ending any further British efforts to directly influence the course of Egypt's domestic politics; and instilling Nasser with even greater self-confidence at home and on the regional and global stages. (Cook 2012, 71)

Changes in the Role of the State in the Economy

The Free Officers, on coming to power, were not wedded to a particular economic philosophy. In any case, Egypt's recent history did not provide a model that had proved unambiguously superior to all the alternatives. Since the nineteenth century Egypt had experimented with a variety of economic systems—ranging from complete state monopolies under Muhammad Ali to recognizably market economies following his reign. The period from 1880 to the 1930s was especially notable for the extent of free trade and laissez-faire. The state's role in the economy remained very important because of its investments and regulations in irrigation, drainage, and land reclamation, but economic activity was overwhelmingly conducted by the private sector.

The government's direct involvement with other sectors of the economy began to grow from the 1930s, when an escalating tariff structure intended to favor industry was adopted. The Second World War saw increasing government intervention, with the imposition of controls on foreign trade, supplies of necessities, prices, rents, and foreign-exchange transactions. After the war some controls were dismantled, but many others remained in place. The prices of basic consumer goods continued to be fixed, supported by government subsidies. In the late 1940s and the 1950s the import-substitution strategy was strengthened with the raising of import tariff levels. Mabro and Radwan (1976) judge that the overall economic environment remained relatively free, and that the benefits private enterprises derived from the protectionist policies are likely to have outweighed the cost of the price controls.

The Movement toward Arab Socialism

The revolutionary government did not move from a predominantly market to a socialist economy in one swoop. Three broad patterns can be distinguished in the movement, which was dictated as much by events as by intent.

Predominance of the private sector, 1952–56

In 1952, on the eve of the Free Officers' revolution, the economic role of the state was virtually confined to infrastructure (chiefly in expanding and maintaining the irrigation system) and social services. Agriculture and industry, and even key utilities such as electricity and water, were privately owned. Mead (1967, 272–73) estimates that in the year of the Free Officers' revolution the public sector contributed only 13 per cent of the country's GDP.[5]

At the beginning of their rule, the Free Officers favored private enterprise. In the first four years of the new regime, the government insisted that it would act as the partner of private enterprise and confine its own activities to heavy, or basic, industry. The rest of the manufacturing sector was explicitly reserved for private enterprise. Galal Amin (1968, 40) observes that the first four years of the revolution "from the point of view of the economic system may be regarded as a continuation of the economic system of the post-war years."

The official pronouncements were supported by actions to reassure private enterprise. The minister of national guidance, Gamal Salem, announced, "We are not socialists. I think our economy can only prosper under free enterprise." These sentiments were echoed by Abdel Moneim el-Kaissouni, minister of finance: "The state encourages private enterprise and aids it in every way." He added that his aim was to "create a favorable atmosphere for the investment of national and foreign capital."[6] The government regularly consulted with the Federation of Egyptian Industries, rarely intervened in the industrial field without consulting with the federation, and often accepted the latter's recommendations on major policies. Thus, the government agreed to the federation's demand for lower taxes and higher protection by lowering customs duties on raw materials and capital goods and by raising tariffs on items produced domestically. A number of measures designed to support domestic private investment were passed; for example, Law No. 430 of 1953 provided a seven-year exemption from profit tax for new companies that promoted economic development and for five years to existing companies that increased their capital. Taxes on undistributed profits and dividends were reduced by 50 percent.

The main theme of the economic policy debate during this period was not the respective responsibilities of the public and private sectors, but the role of foreign investment. In this area, too, the authorities proceeded cautiously. Until 1957 the state continued to woo foreign capital through laws providing tax holidays and generous provisions for the repatriation of profits. Under Law No. 156 of 1953 and Laws Nos. 26 and 475 of 1954, foreign capital was permitted majority control of companies operating in Egypt instead of the existing ceiling of 49 percent. In 1953 the Mining and Quarrying Law was passed, granting new concessions to foreign (and domestic) companies; in 1954 petroleum concessions were granted to four foreign companies. The government also partially reversed the Egyptian-ization policy of the former regime by allowing foreign shareholders to hold a majority interest and control in any domestic company (Issawi 1963, 53–54; Wahba 1994, 54–55; O'Brien 1966, 71–72).

The most significant restraint imposed on the private sector was the agrarian reform of September 1952, which limited individual ownership to a maximum of two hundred feddans. However, the law was not moti-vated by an ideological shift toward socialism. The expropriated land was distributed to landless peasants—the principle of private ownership was conserved. As stressed earlier, the principal aim of the reform was to break the power of the old ruling oligarchy that had its roots in big estates. The most radical component of the agrarian reform was the introduction of agricultural cooperatives, which controlled the most important agricultural activities. The cooperatives were directed by the government and were thus an effective method of control, but this did not rest on an ideology of the state's ownership of productive assets.

Decisions in 1952–54 thus did not attack private enterprise, but merely showed that the government intended to engage more actively in the econ-omy. Kaissouni and Higazi (finance minister, deputy prime minister, and then prime minister), both of whom had reviewed cabinet papers from that period, offered descriptions of the government's thinking, which might be paraphrased as follows.

The geographical constraints on Egypt's cultivable land mean that agriculture can provide Egypt's growing population only limited opportunities for employment, exports, and a decent income. The sector that best fulfills these requirements, plus offers the base for a strong defense against aggression, is manufacturing. Moreover, if the country is to take its due place among the advanced nations of the world, it will have to acquire the attitudes and methods of thinking of industrialized countries. Industry must therefore be prioritized.

Agriculture will still remain important, because it supplies raw materials and food, and the rural areas are home to most of the population. The cultivable area must therefore be extended, and this will require building the Aswan High Dam. However, population growth during the ten years required for the dam's construction will consume much of the benefits that it is expected to provide. Thus, agricultural growth, while necessary, cannot propel the economy at the rate required; it can only act as a holding operation. Thus another function of the High Dam becomes crucial. The Dam is designed to generate 10 million kilowatt hours (kWh) of cheap electricity that will provide a tremendous fillip to the industrial sector. The High Dam is the axis around which Egypt can maintain a satisfactory development of agriculture while pivoting toward an economic structure in which industry provides the main propulsion for growth. (Discussions with Kaissouni and Higazi)

With the government deciding to take a more active role to promote structural change in the economy, it was inevitable that it had to develop plans so that the movements could be enforced and monitored. Partial planning was introduced in 1953 through the creation of the Permanent Council for the Development of National Production (PCDNP), but this did not elbow out private enterprise and the council comprised representatives of both the government and the private sector.

Growing government intervention, 1957–60
The transition from a free, private enterprise system to a planned economy with a dominant public sector took place between 1954 and the early 1960s. The government took a small step by acquiring equity in two industrial companies established in 1954. The first significant expansion of the public sector occurred in 1957, partly through a fortuitous event, namely, the Suez Canal war, which prompted the nationalization of British and French economic interests, and partly through deliberate public investment in industry.

International developments also accelerated the movement toward greater government intervention. In the years following the Suez Canal war in 1956, Egypt lost much of its access to Western sources of finance. This was inevitable in the cases of Britain and France, which had invaded Egypt. However, with Egypt turning to the Eastern Bloc for arms and diplomatic support, the West began to increasingly view Egyptian foreign policy as hostile to Western interests. As a result, finance from other Western bilateral donors and Western-dominated international development institutions also dropped off sharply.

The phase of government policy in 1957–60 was described by Nasser as a "controlled capitalistic economy" (O'Brien 1966, 85). Government intervention in economic activity proceeded along four major paths.

1. Private-sector activity was still encouraged, but the government's laissez-faire attitude was starting to wear thin, and the new constitution of 1956 set out an ideological framework within which such private economic activity was to be conducted.

2. After the Suez Canal war, the government sequestered British and French assets, many of which were concentrated in banking and insurance. A special state Economic Organization was set up in early 1957 to manage these and other assets in which the government already had a share. The Economic Organization moved quickly and by 1958 it controlled all the specialist banks in Egypt, seven commercial banks, and five insurance companies. These and other sequestrations placed under the organization's control nearly half of all commercial bank loans, two-thirds of all insurance business transacted in Egypt, about one-third of aggregate output produced by the organized industrial sector, and nearly one-fifth of the labor force employed in that sector (O'Brien 1966, 90, 95). The Economic Organization thus became a powerful tool, channeling the resources of enterprises under its control into priorities determined by the government.

3. The government moved to "Egyptianize" the main sectors of the national economy. A five-year limit was imposed within which all foreign banks, insurance companies, and commercial agencies were required to be converted into domestically owned joint stock companies.

4. Comprehensive economic planning was introduced. The Permanent Council for National Development was abolished in January 1957 and replaced by the National Planning Committee, which was instructed to prepare a long-term plan for social and economic development that was to come into effect from July 1, 1960. However, a five-year plan for industry was launched in 1958. The industrial plan envisaged a rapid acceleration in investment, from the annual average of LE34 million of gross investment in the previous five years to an annual average of LE45

million of net investment between 1957 and 1961. The state would contribute 60 percent of the finance for this plan, with its contribution overwhelmingly assigned to heavy industry. Comprehensive economic planning is discussed in more detail below.

The years 1957 to 1960 were an important period of transition in economic management. Most economic activity still took place in the private sector, but state intervention and influence became increasingly important. This was most clearly reflected in the changing contributions of the public and private sectors to capital formation.

In 1952, the public sector accounted for about 13 percent of GDP and 28 percent of gross capital formation; by 1960, while still accounting for only 18 percent of GDP, the public sector undertook nearly 74 percent of gross investment.[7] The share of government both in investment and in economic activity generally continued to rise; Hansen (1975, 203, table 1) estimated that in 1973 the public sector accounted for perhaps 90 percent of investment and 63–70 percent of the total availability of resources.[8] The government's dominant share of investment was made necessary by the private sector's reluctance to run the risk of investing in the new (heavy) industries that were the government's priority, and the fact that the large amounts of capital that these industries required could be mobilized more easily by the government than by the private sector. However, Amin (1968, 41) points out that although the authorities had started to invoke a socialistic ideology, at this time most nationalization was still ad hoc and was justified on a variety of non-ideological grounds.

The introduction of a comprehensive five-year plan in 1960 required the policymakers to become more specific about the kind of economic system they wished to create. Thus the introduction of wide-ranging economic planning showed most clearly the change in the government's thinking about the relationship between the public and private sectors. The restrictions placed on private economic activity appear to be closely related to successive efforts to make the planning process more comprehensive. Widespread nationalization began in earnest in 1961, but even during the late 1950s the government had evidently begun to form the opinion that a high rate of planned investment, and especially its sectoral allocation toward heavy industry, could not be attained with an economy in which investment decisions were predominantly taken by private actors.

From the fundamental changes that followed in the wake of the Suez Canal war, it can be argued that 1956, the year of the war, was much more of a turning point for Egypt's economy than was 1952, the year of the Free Officers' revolution. Government intervention in the economy became more intrusive after 1956, but it should be noted that the sequestrations of that year and even the nationalizations of 1960 and of early July 1961 were defended in nationalistic rather than socialistic terms.[9]

Nationalizations and economic planning

The first hint of the government's new direction in policy came on February 11, 1960, when Bank Misr and the National Bank of Egypt were taken into public ownership. This action served as a portent, but did not signify a war against the private sector; Issawi (1963, 58) points out that the shareholders received compensation in government bonds based on stock-exchange prices quoted the day before nationalization. The significance of the step was that whereas previous nationalizations had been of foreign firms, these banks were owned chiefly by Egyptian nationals.

In addition to being the largest commercial bank left in the private sector, Bank Misr was also a most important holding company, whose twenty-nine affiliated companies accounted for an estimated 20 percent of Egypt's industrial output. There is some dispute concerning the reasons for the nationalization of Bank Misr; Wahba (1994, 80–81) reports a number of official explanations that appear to be self-contradictory.

An often-cited explanation points to differences between the government and the Bank Misr group concerning the targets allocated to Misr companies under the first industrial plan. The Misr group wanted to focus largely on the textile industry (in which it already accounted for nearly half of all production), while the government wanted it to invest in other sectors, especially in the engineering and chemical industries. The group had been assigned responsibility for nearly half of all activity undertaken under the plan by private enterprises, so it is possible that the government felt more secure about attaining its economic targets if it directly controlled the Misr enterprises (Hansen and Marzouk 1965, 171; O'Brien 1966, 92–93, 125; Amin 1968, 41–42; Mabro 1974, 127–31; Waterbury 1983, 72–79).

The moves against the private sector at this time are not necessarily evidence of some grand ideological plan to move the country toward socialism. The motives appear to be more nationalistic than ideological. Baker (1978, 49) reports that "Nasser had reached the fundamental decision that 'there is no alternative for us but to become an industrial power in the shortest possible time.'" This would suggest that an explanation based on the necessity to control and direct the Misr group's activities is more securely grounded than many of the alternatives. Several commentators have testified that the regime wanted to rapidly build up a wider manufacturing base with a major heavy industry sector, and the Misr group had balked. This group, and other industrialists, would have to be brought to heel if the regime's strategy were to succeed.

Thus, Waterbury (1983, 77–78) refers to a report in the periodical *Rose al-Yusuf* of a meeting in May 1961 between President Nasser and Aziz Sidqi (minister of industry) at which the latter saw on the president's desk an inventory of all Egyptian industries, in which various companies had been marked in pencil. The president then asked Sidqi how the state could plan anything if the industrial sector remained under the control of "individuals." Waterbury maintains that the nationalization decrees were not primarily motivated by economic factors but were designed to break the power of the larger industrialists and transfer their assets to the public sector. The regime would thereby not only acquire greater powers to plan the economy, but also the wherewithal by which to dispense patronage and thereby strengthen support for the regime. The move was thus rooted not simply in economics, but in a political-economy context.

Mabro (1974, 128) also notes that "nationalization [was] ultimately a political action related to Nasser's persistent drive for hegemony." There is little doubt that Nasser wanted to channel increasing amounts of power into his own hands, but nationalization and centralized control would also appear to be more effective means of bringing about the type of industrialization that Nasser had in mind. This political decision had long-term economic effects; indeed, Egyptian policymakers were wrestling with issues relating to public-sector industries even into the twenty-first century.

Sweeping nationalization of virtually all industrial and financial sectors took place in June and July 1961 in what is often referred to in Egypt as the "Socialist Revolution." The move began with the government's ordering the indefinite closure of the Alexandria cotton futures market and assigning the exclusive rights to purchase cotton to the state Cotton Authority. Further laws were issued requiring the Egyptianization of all companies dealing with the cotton trade and to bring all firms engaged in external trade under state control. Other measures brought the remaining banks and insurance companies under government ownership. The nationalization moves paid special attention to the industrial sector. The decrees brought into state ownership forty-four companies in industries that were regarded as "basic" (such as cement, electricity, and copper); expropriated half the capital of eighty-six firms, mainly in commerce and light manufacturing; and limited individual holdings to a market value of LE10,000 (shares in excess of that amount were confiscated by the government), which enabled the government to dispossess the shareholders of another 147 firms of a large part of their assets. The nominal capital of the companies affected by the nationalization laws of 1961 was estimated at LE258 million, which was about two-thirds of the total share capital of companies then registered in Egypt. The 1961 laws enabled the government to acquire LE124 million (that is, 48 percent) (Issawi 1963, 60; O'Brien 1966, 130–31, 153). Further nationalizations followed the secession of Syria from the United Arab Republic. In October the property of 167 wealthy Egyptians was sequestrated for political reasons, and in November that of about five hundred others. Issawi (1963, 58–61) provides examples of the companies that were nationalized and the laws under which the nationalizations were carried out.

After the 1961 nationalizations, the private sector was relegated to a minor economic role. Private property was not abolished—agriculture, small retail, service, and manufacturing enterprises, for example, remained in private hands—but the opportunities for private economic activity were severely restricted. The nationalizations were later justified as part of the "Arab socialism" that was a central pillar of the National Charter (al-Mithaq al-Watani) that President Nasser presented in May 1962 to the National Congress of the Popular Powers.[10]

A factor that facilitated the nationalization was the extreme concentration of ownership in the modern industrial sector. Wahba (1994, 74) quotes a report by the Bank of Alexandria in 1961 stating that prior to nationalization, 61.7 percent of all shares in Egypt were held by 9.1 percent of all shareholders, while 49.1 percent of shareholders held only 12.1 percent of total shares. Moreover, Wahba shows (table 3.3) that a mere 2 percent of companies accounted for 51 percent of industrial output in 1960.

Waterbury (1983, 74–75) writes that the initial wave of sequestrations affected 167 "reactionary capitalists" and the measures were later extended to another six hundred persons. He adds that, in all, about seven thousand persons were affected by the two land reforms and the nationalizations, or were accused of "political deviation" and their property sequestrated. Wahba (1994, 87n8) notes that if this figure were reduced by almost half to take account of property registered in the name of dependents, it would account for less than 0.015 percent of the population at the time. "It should not be too difficult for a government basking in the glory of 1954 and 1956 to achieve this," is his dry comment.

The charter argued that the country's economic development could not be left to profit-motivated efforts by private individuals, but must be based on socialism. It also provided a broad framework of principles within which socially acceptable economic activity should be conducted.

The main provisions were the following:

- The economic infrastructure should be publicly owned, as should the majority of heavy and medium industries and mining. These activities were strategically important, and also provided critical inputs to the rest of the industrial sector. Since so much of the economy depended upon these activities, their functioning could not be left to the whims of individuals.
- Banks and insurance companies should be exclusively in the public sector, for reasons similar to those advanced for the social control of infrastructure and heavy industries.
- The entire import trade should be in the public sector, as should three-quarters of the export trade; the private sector could be responsible for the rest.
- The private sector could retain ownership and control of internal trade, but the public sector should take charge of at least one-quarter of internal trade over the following eight years.
- The regime did not aim to take control of the entire economy; the private sector was permitted its own sphere. This area included internal trade, ownership of land, buildings, construction, and light industry. In order to prevent any "exploitation," the government had in reserve measures such as land reforms, rent control, and taxation that could be applied if necessary.
- Citizens had basic rights to social welfare, which would be provided by the state. These rights included access to medical care, education, minimum wages, and insurance benefits in old age and sickness.

Thus, in the decade after the Free Officers assumed power, the regime's economic policies moved in discrete steps. They progressed from encouraging and cooperating with the private sector, to gradually changing direction and reining it in by imposing restrictions and controls, and finally to sweeping nationalizations and policy interventions throughout the economy. Although this was later rationalized as "Arab socialism," the ideological basis was rather shaky. The process was often ad hoc and in response to chance events, such as the Suez Canal war in 1956 and the defection of Syria from the United Arab Republic in 1961; as Hansen and Marzouk (1965, 169) put it, much of it "just happened." The National Charter did, however, try to provide an *ex post* rationale for the new strategy and to fix the main lines of the economic structure that the government was aiming to create.

Central Economic Planning

Although the Free Officers came to power without a commitment to any particular economic ideology, they did recognize the importance of rapidly developing the country's economy. They also recognized the importance of diversifying the economy—agriculture was not to be neglected, but creating the required number of productive jobs required a vigorous push toward industrialization. In the very year of the revolution, a new institution, the Permanent Council for the Development of National Production (PCDNP) was created by Decree 213 of 1952 to study investment projects. The importance of its role was highlighted by attaching it to the cabinet office and having it presided over by the prime minister. The discussions in Mabro (1974, 108–13) and O'Brien (1966, 225–28) detail some of the principal efforts of the council at diversifying the economy, such as giving special emphasis to capital and intermediate-goods industries; expanding the capacity of existing oil refineries and constructing new ones; promoting entirely new industries such as rubber and iron and steel; and accelerating the construction of electric power stations.

Despite taking these initiatives, the government did not intend to be the sole owner or operator of the new industries; indeed, it was the policy of the council to associate private capital and enterprise with all its ventures. However, even with the incentives offered, the response of the private sector was tepid. Still more disappointing for the government, the private sector was not inclined to support the priority of heavy industry; private industrialists much preferred to place their savings in industries, such as food processing and textiles, that did not require large amounts of capital and produced quick returns.

To some extent, this was because the government's intended pattern of industrialization required managerial and technical knowledge beyond the experience of Egypt's private entrepreneurs—"steel mills are . . . more difficult to establish and run than cotton mills or jam factories," writes O'Brien (1966, 227). But perhaps the more important reason was attitude or propensity. Egypt's private investors continued to opt for the more traditional forms of manufacturing and projects that promised quick returns, and favored high profit margins on a small turnover. These margins owed much to protectionist measures, such as import tariffs imposed by the *ancien régime*, and should remind one that rent-seeking behavior by Egyptian businessmen is not a recent phenomenon.

The government noted that although it had offered many inducements—such as import tariff protection, tax concessions, reform of the company law—the private sector still continued to invest chiefly in consumer-goods industries and in housing; investment in the latter rose by 50 percent between 1954 and 1958. The government viewed this with some dismay and tried to discourage investment in real estate through a series of measures, such as strictly licensing the construction or improvement of buildings above a certain cost, and reducing rents by 20 percent on accommodation constructed after September 1952.

However, the government's measures labored under a critical asymmetry that is innate to private-sector-led growth—they could stop the private sector from investing in certain activities, but they could not compel it to invest in industry.[11] The government would therefore have to do that job itself, and to do that it would have to acquire the necessary resources. Where would these come from?

O'Brien points out that the distribution of savings among the different economic groups was such that it was much easier and more cost-effective to mobilize the savings of some groups than of others. Saving by households constituted a very small proportion of total domestic savings and was spread over such large numbers that it would be difficult and costly to appropriate them for the government's plans. A somewhat larger source of savings was the retained profits of the non-organized business sector—essentially the micro and small and medium enterprises (SMEs). These accounted for more than 95 percent of all Egyptian enterprises and were again too numerous, and their average amount of savings too small, to make the effort of mobilizing them worthwhile. The government may also have considered that this was rather a large constituency and it might be politically unwise to antagonize it. The biggest source of savings, which some estimates put at half of total Egyptian savings, was the retained profits of the organized business sector. These enterprises were relatively few and the administrative task of dealing with them would not be difficult. The calculus of both convenience and efficiency thus dictated that the organized business sector should be the main target for the government's appropriation of resources.

Although the government's thinking evolved over a period of years, it is possible to summarize the logic of it fairly simply. It would be on the following lines.

> The recurring theme in Egypt's development is the challenge between the relentless growth of the population and the scarce cultivable land. This sets a limit to the ability of the agricultural sector to provide rapid economic growth and generate the number of jobs that the country requires. Therefore, the country must industrialize as quickly as possible. But the industrial sector must be modernized if Egypt is to be able to compete effectively in the international economy. In the view of the revolutionary government, a "modern" industrial sector was one that contained a large component of heavy industry. The private sector was offered a role in developing heavy industry, but it refused. The public sector, therefore, had to shoulder the responsibility.
>
> Assumption of this responsibility required the government to find the necessary resources. The distribution of savings and the political imperative of antagonizing as small a constituency as possible meant that the confiscated resources had to come from the large private-sector firms. Therefore, in order to implement the desired industrial strategy and to finance it, the government had to take over the large firms in the private sector. The ideological justification of "Arab socialism" followed later.

Of course the foregoing description may make matters appear more coherent than they actually were and ignores the effect of fortuitous events, such as the nationalizations after the Suez Canal war to punish British and French interests; it simply lays out the bare bones of the thinking.

The First Five-year Plan
In January 1957 the Council for National Production was abolished and a new organization, the National Planning Committee (NPC) was established. The NPC was charged with drafting a comprehensive five-year plan

for the fiscal years 1960/61–1964/65 under the umbrella of a ten-year plan. Between the dissolution of the Council for National Production and the launching of the comprehensive plan, "partial planning" was to continue. In 1957, two sectoral plans (for industry and for agriculture) were prepared by the respective ministries. The outcome was not happy; Mabro (1974, 114–15) highlights several defects in this endeavor.

First, the sectoral plans were not fitted into a framework for the overall economy and thus did not take into account interdependencies between projects and the rest of the economy. Indeed, there was a tendency for the ministries to construct their plans in "silos" hermetically sealed off from each other. Mead (1967, 235) points to the "political problems of inducing jealous ministers to bow to the convincing logic of the computer." Second, the First Industrialization Plan, in particular, fell victim to the ambitions of the minister of industry, Aziz Sidqi, to push for as many projects as possible—according to Wahba (1994, 98), Sidqi boasted of building "one factory a day"—without paying too much attention to their quality. Mabro (1974, 114) dismisses the First Industrial Plan as "a confused and hasty document responsible for a number of disastrous ventures." Third, the partial plans were weak on policy recommendations, and tended simply to be lists of projects. Moreover, although resources were insufficient to finance the total number of projects, the plans did not propose clear criteria for prioritizing choices.

A "comprehensive" plan was then prepared. This was intended to span ten budget years from 1961 to 1970, and for operational reasons was to be divided into two five-year plans; the first would cover the five budget years 1961 to 1965, and the second those from 1966 to 1970.[12] A detailed discussion of the ten-year plan and its outcomes lies beyond the remit of this book; in any case, data to study the outcomes in a more or less reliable manner are available only for the first five-year period. More complete discussions of the data, the plan, and the mechanics of the planning process can be found in Hansen and Marzouk (1965, 295–316), O'Brien (1966, 148–98), Mead (1967, 233–56), Hansen (1968, 19–39), and several memoranda from the Institute of National Planning, such as Abdel Rahman (1962). Here the concern is chiefly with political decisions that had a major impact on the economic outcomes of this period.

The plan did not explicitly declare a movement toward a socialist pattern of society. It appears that the socialist pattern—in the sense of putting the bulk of the means of production into public ownership—was to be realized gradually by means of the public sector getting the lion's share of total investment for the plan.[13]

In the First Five-Year General Plan the public sector accounted for some 90 percent of total monetized investment throughout the 1960s, and this continued until 1973. This proportion did not decline very significantly, even after the liberalization measures of 1974, until the early 1990s. From 1965, annual investment programs became increasingly important as the main instrument of public investment planning. This was almost inevitable. The annual plans were the only part of the planning process that could be considered operational documents, because they were linked to the budget, and because one-year forecasts of revenue, foreign exchange, and so on were more reliable than multi-year projections.

Under the plan, the public sector continued to own most of the modern industry; all banks, insurance companies, and financial intermediaries; and a large proportion of construction firms, modern transport, and wholesale trade. The bulk of foreign trade operations remained in the public sector. In agriculture, old land remained privately owned within the ceilings defined by the agrarian reform laws, but the new land was largely in public ownership.

The principal objectives of the plan were:

1. To double national income over the ten years. Raising the standard of living of the population by increasing income and improving its distribution was the ultimate concern of the plan. The target was to increase national income by 40 percent in the first five years, with the remainder coming in the second quinquennium. The annual growth rates implied in these projections work out at 7.2 percent for the ten-year period; splitting the target into the two five-year periods gives 7 percent a year for the first and about 7.5 percent for the second.
2. To improve equity, especially through greater equality of opportunity and a more even distribution of income and property.
3. To employ almost all the projected increase in the labor force (not *all* the increase).
4. To effect a structural transformation of the economy. The planned structural changes would increase the share of the industrial sector from 21 to 28 percent of GDP and generate more than 50 percent of the intended increase in income.[14] The major part of this shift would affect not the share of agriculture, but that of services. The

plan projected nearly 75 percent of the total growth in income to be provided by the industrial and agricultural sectors. The services sector was expected to play a major role in the second five-year period of the comprehensive ten-year plan, when the growth of industry and agriculture would decelerate (in part because the base would have become much larger).

5. To raise investment from about 12.4 percent of GNP in 1960 to 18.5 percent in 1965 (Hansen and Marzouk 1965, table 11.4). Savings were projected to increase sharply from about 13 percent of GNP in 1960 (even though some estimates put the actual figure at less than 10 percent) to about 20 percent in 1965; domestic savings were forecast to exceed planned investment by the final year of the plan.

6. To boost exports and restrain imports (through a strategy of import-substitution in the industrial sector) so that the balance-of-payments deficit of 1960 should be converted to a surplus of LE40 million by 1965.

Political decisions played a major role in determining the targets and timings of the plan. Mead (1967, 236, 245) reports that the National Planning Committee had been studying plans with growth rates averaging 3–4 percent a year sustained over a twenty-year period. However, the country's political masters instructed the committee to adopt a target of doubling national income in ten years, which implied an average annual rate of 7.2 percent.

Nasser was quite explicit that the plan was expected to convey a political as well as an economic message. In his speech of November 12, 1964 to the National Assembly on the target of doubling the national income in ten years he is reported as saying:

Those in the planning said that it could not be done. They said it could be done in 18 years but we insisted that it should be 10 years. They said 15, but we said 10 again, they said 12 and again we said 10. Had we not worked on that basis, and had we not faced the problem in that manner, our efforts would have been to no avail.[15]

The outcomes of the plan were decidedly mixed. They could hardly be otherwise, given that some of the key outcomes, such as the national income target, appear to have been decided by a bazaar process of haggling rather than by a technical study. The process also compels one to wonder at the quality of technical analyses that underpinned the plan if these could first insist that doubling the national income required no less than eighteen years, and then with no further examination offer compromises of fifteen and twelve years and then accept the politically motivated target of ten years. This shows Sowell's "first law of politics" running amok.

In fairness, one must point out that Hilmi Abdel Rahman, who headed the group putting together the comprehensive plan, did not agree with the political time frame and asked to be relieved of his duties. He was transferred to head the Institute of National Planning. Recounting the events in 1975, Abdel Rahman (who was now minister of planning) said that he understood the importance of setting targets that were somewhat beyond what could be reached comfortably, so as to encourage the country to make a greater effort, but when targets were pushed to the point that the rulers had, the plan had ceased to be a plan and had become a fairy tale.

The plan's outcomes were also mixed because many assumptions had to be made concerning developments that were outside the government's control. There were moreover some unforeseen events, such as Egypt's participation in the war in Yemen (1962–67) and consequent increases in government consumption expenditure. Indeed, Tignor (2016, 133) reports Sadat's minister of finance, Abdel Aziz Higazi, saying that the war in Yemen had been little short of a disaster and had compelled the state to allocate no less than 33 percent of the nation's income to the armed forces.

The passage of time did nothing to mellow Higazi's views on the subject. In interviews with me he said that no matter for what reason Egypt had entered the Yemen war, persisting with it for five years was "an incomprehensible folly." Higazi was not the only minister to think that the Yemen war imposed an intolerable (and unnecessary) burden on the Egyptian economy. Nutting (1972, 381), in his biography of Nasser, indicates that Zakariya Mohieddin, the prime minister in 1965–66, insisted that ending the Yemen war was a prerequisite for improving the economy. At some point, Nasser himself appears to have accepted that his policy had been a mistake. McDermott (1988, 156) describes an interview Nasser had with *Look* magazine in March 1968 in which the Egyptian president said that his Yemen involvement was a "miscalculation; we never thought it would lead to what it did."

The second five-year period of the Comprehensive Plan also suffered from major disruptions—the war with Israel in 1967; the blocking of the

Suez Canal and the loss of transit revenue; the loss of the oil fields in Sinai and the Gulf of Suez; the loss of important productive facilities, such as the two oil refineries in Suez; the required rebuilding of the armed forces—and the cumulative impact of these put paid to any thought of completing the Comprehensive Plan. The second five-year period of the plan never became operational.

The first five-year period showed a number of encouraging developments. After correcting for some inconsistencies and biases in the official figures, Hansen (1968, 19–39) estimated the actual growth rate of the GDP in the five years 1961–65 at 5.5 percent a year. Although falling short of the planned 7 percent, this represented an acceleration over previous growth rates. Sectoral growth rates varied considerably: agriculture at 3.3 percent did not reach the planned 5.1 percent, and that of industry at 8.5 percent was well below the planned 14.6 percent. On the other hand, growth rates in the sectors of construction, electricity, and transport exceeded the planned growth rates by substantial margins.[16]

Since, in the first five years of the comprehensive plan, Egypt attained a growth rate of 5.5 percent, it might appear that the technicians had been too conservative. Perhaps so, but this observation is subject to some important qualifications. Egypt has never sustained a growth rate in excess of 7 percent per annum for any quinquennium, much less for two. Judging by the performance of the economy over the fifty years from 1965, it would appear that at the existing rate of investment and functioning of institutions, Egypt's potential growth rate is of the order of 4.5–5.0 percent a year; more sophisticated estimates (described, for example, in Ikram 2006, 277–79) also put it in much the same ballpark. Any plan that aims to sustainably raise the actual rate much above this level must be explicit about the policies that will be adopted to increase investment in the major sectors, and about what will be done to materially improve the functioning of key institutions, such as the bureaucracy, the commercial judicial system, the tax system, and the system of technical training and education, and must specify further measures that would reduce the cost of doing business and raise the efficiency of investment.

This the plan failed to do. It could be quite explicit on what would be the targets, but was much less so on how these would be attained. It thus lacked a realistic connection between ends and means. The key to the growth rate was a much higher investment rate, but the plan was quite vague on the policies that would produce this rate. Predictably, the main cause of shortfalls in sectoral outcomes turned out to be shortfalls in investment. This was particularly evident in industry, the sector that was billed as the main engine of growth; Hansen (1968, 30n2) suggests that net investments in the sector might have been less than two-thirds of the level envisaged by the plan.

The plan also was over-optimistic on several key assumptions. Perhaps the most critical was the assumption that the import-substitution industrial strategy would be so effective so quickly that by 1965 Egypt would run a balance-of-payments *surplus* of LE40 million (2 percent of GDP). In fact, the country ended up with a *deficit* of LE76 million (about 4 percent of GDP); the swing thus represented an error of nearly 6 percent of GDP.

The import-substitution strategy suffered from two major defects. First, it overlooked what has been observed earlier, that for several years the path to import substitution can be import-intensive. To repeat: The country has to import not only the machinery and ancillary equipment required to set up the import-substituting facilities, but also the commodities that these facilities would produce after a time lag. The cost of the equipment can be substantial and the time lags very long; consider, for example, that this was the period during which the High Dam was being constructed (this took a decade) and the iron and steel works set up. During these periods expenditures continued to be incurred, but no output was produced.

Second, the plan did not ask a fundamental strategic question: should a commodity be produced in Egypt, or should Egypt produce another one, export it, and use the proceeds to import the item the country needed? "The *leitmotif* for the Plan . . . ," remark Hansen and Marzouk (1965, 306), "has been import substitution and self-sufficiency." The political pressure appears to have been to make it in Egypt, regardless of whether it would have been more efficient (that is, would have required a smaller amount of domestic resources) to have produced an exportable commodity that could pay for the import of the required item. The ability to produce a particular commodity could be all-important, while the economic costs of producing it received only perfunctory attention.

From the late 1950s economic management had relied heavily on a materials-balance approach in planning, along the lines practiced in the Soviet Union. The planning process, therefore, made little or no use of market prices as allocative instruments and paid little attention to efficiency. El-Beblawi (2008, 11) notes that "industrialization became more of a political venture than an economic endeavor. . . . Costing, efficiency, and marketing were looked upon as of secondary importance. The viability, let alone the profitability, of these projects was of no concern." "Everything from the needle to the rocket," was the slogan that Sidqi, the minister of industry, associated with the industrialization strategy.

The autarkic attitude of policymakers—that is, produce something in Egypt without paying too much attention to cost—continued for a considerable time. An examination by the World Bank of a draft input–output table in the 1970s raised a concern that some production activities might not even satisfy the Hawkins-Simon conditions. These conditions on the Leontief input–output system (widely used as a planning tool in Egypt at that time) stipulate that the production of one unit of a good must not require, directly and indirectly, more than one unit of itself. The violation of these conditions obviously means that the activity is not sustainable. As Dorfman, Samuelson, and Solow write in their classic study *Linear Programming and Economic Analysis* (1958, 211), "A production process in which it took more than 1 ton of [say] coal to make 1 ton of coal . . . is not a method of production at all, but just a hard way of running down pre-existing stocks of coal."

Much of the continuing deficit on the balance of payments could also be traced to the impact of political factors, in this case impacting the domestic budget. Galal Amin (1968, 45–46) offers a perceptive discussion of the issue. It goes as follows. The revolutionary government needed the support of a large constituency. In a socialist regime the constituency would be the workers, who would be motivated to support the regime by a promise of an end to their exploitation. Amin points out that for an ordinary laborer the metric of "the end of exploitation" is "the end of poverty," and this requires a measurable increase in his real income. "It is easy for the Government to gain the support of a laborer who has experienced an actual rise in his real income as a result of development and Socialism. . . . It is very difficult for the Government to employ the slogan of rapid economic growth without a simultaneous promise of quick gains for labor." The "gains for labor" implied continuing increases in public consumption expenditure (by way of wage increases, bonuses, and consumer subsidies), a part of which would spill over into demand for imported commodities. This structural weakness persisted. Analyzing the cause of balance-of-payments deficits even well into the 1980s, Hansen (1991, 213) identified the "villain" as the huge budget deficit caused by high rates of public consumption expenditure.

The plan's employment strategy had a number of consequences. First, while the plan had initially envisaged the employment of most (not all) of the increases in manpower, political pressures compelled a change, and from 1962 the government offered university entrance to all graduates of secondary schools and assured employment to all university graduates. Since a university place in scientific, medical, and technological courses can cost up to four or five times that of one in the liberal arts, resource constraints made it inevitable that it was the latter disciplines into which most secondary-school graduates were shepherded. This created a marked imbalance between the skills demanded by private markets and those produced by the education system. It is therefore not surprising that most university graduates ended up in the government bureaucracy. Kandil (2012, 63–64) reports that state employment rates were 70 percent higher in 1969 than in 1962; in the latter year more than 60 percent of university graduates were employed by the state, and state salaries had increased by 102 percent. The sharp expansion in the numbers of university students also put considerable pressure on the government's budget and on university teaching staff and facilities, and was responsible for diluting the quality of the graduates.

Second, the need to produce a continuous improvement in the standard of living of large numbers employed by the government required the authorities to restrict savings more than consumption. The government-guaranteed employment, the access to free education and medical care, and the provision of cheap housing, transport, and consumption commodities ensured that public consumption in the use of resources would continue to grow.

Third, the increasing public consumption spilled over into imports, especially of foodstuffs, as the agricultural sector failed to expand as had been planned. This put pressure on the balance of payments, which in the plan period averaged an annual deficit of 5 percent of GDP. The result was a severe foreign-exchange shortage, especially from 1963. In order to cope with the situation, the government preferred to cut back on investment rather than to restrain current consumption. This, inevitably, jeopardized the economy's growth rate. The regime's need to build up a political constituency, therefore, had very significant economic impacts.

The argument here is not that the authorities should have refrained from trying to improve the standard of living of Egypt's citizens. The point is the scale and the speed with which it was done, especially in view of the other demands that impacted its fiscal resources, such as the costs of prosecuting the war in Yemen from 1962 to 1967 and rebuilding after the war with Israel in 1967. The benefits offered exceeded the country's ability to deliver them, given its resources and its ability to borrow externally. Moreover, squeezing investment in favor of current consumption only compromised Egypt's growth prospects and thus, ironically, struck at the very elements that would have enabled the country to provide these benefits a bit further down the road without leaving it vulnerable to external pressures. Egypt was trying to consume the fruit before the tree had taken root and, indeed, in some ways it was even axing these roots.

The political-economy lesson is that economics and politics routinely move on different tracks; what is politically attractive in the short term can pile up economic problems for the long. Politicians tend to be seduced by short-term gains because the rewards are immediate and tangible; future costs are discounted because they are distant and perhaps may not even arise, and, anyway, someone else may be in office and will have to bear the costs.

In view of the political motivations behind these economic policies, Kandil's (2012, 64) verdict was that "the poverty of its [the state's] economic policy clearly stemmed from the poverty of its politics. Rather than focusing on development, the regime was motivated by the need to curtail capitalist interests, on the one hand, and the need to 'bribe' society to excuse its dictatorial methods, on the other."

Egypt and the International Financial Institutions

The period under review also saw the beginning of interactions between Egypt and international financial institutions (IFIs), particularly the World Bank and the International Monetary Fund (IMF). The principal issue between Egypt and the World Bank concerned the financing of the Aswan High Dam, and has already been treated; this section touches upon the dealings during this period between Egypt and the IMF.

Egypt was hit by a major balance-of-payments crisis in 1962. The proximate cause was a fall in cotton production in 1961 of 40 percent (because of leaf worm infestation), even though the area sown to cotton, at nearly two million feddans, was a record. The result of the sharply reduced output was a steep drop in raw cotton exports from LE121 million in 1960/61 to LE75 million in 1961/62. Egypt's foreign-exchange earnings depended heavily on this commodity; for example, in 1960 it accounted for 70 percent of total exports. Thus, fluctuations in its foreign sales would have a tremendous impact on aggregate exports. As a result of the reduced availability of cotton, total exports dropped from LE204 million in 1960 to LE165 million in 1961 and further to LE145 million in 1962. The current-account deficit on the balance of payments in these years increased respectively from LE24 million to LE53 million to LE118 million. Net foreign-exchange reserves fell from LE62 million at the end of 1960 to LE16 million at the end of 1961.

Waterbury (1983, 94) points out that the sharp drop in export earnings from cotton was accompanied by pressures on foreign-exchange reserves imposed by other commitments. The principal such commitments included payments to the United Kingdom for property nationalized after the Suez Canal war of 1956, compensation to shareholders in the Suez Canal Company, and payments to Sudan to resettle Nubians whose villages would be covered by Lake Nasser after the construction of the Aswan High Dam.

The government had to seek assistance from the International Monetary Fund. In May 1962 a stabilization program between the IMF and Egypt was agreed. The IMF extended a credit of LE20 million; Egypt was to implement a package of reforms that included the unification and devaluation of the exchange rate from 35.2 to 43.5 piasters per U.S. dollar. There were additional commitments to restrain the growth of domestic demand.

After some discussions in the cabinet, the government felt that political compulsions forbade complete implementation of the agreement with the IMF. However, Hansen and Nashashibi (1975, 90) are skeptical about whether Egypt was ever serious about the agreement. They say quite bluntly, "There is little doubt that the government, despite its commitments to the IMF, had no intention whatever to cut down domestic demand. . . . The government refused to scale down its investment program; Arab socialism was taken to mean, in addition to the nationalization of big business, increasing wages. . . . And on top of it all, there were the rapidly increasing defense expenditures related to the Yemen war." After the devaluation, public expenditure as a percentage of GDP increased from 17.3 in 1960 to 18.9 in 1963 and to 22.0 in 1964.

The size of the devaluation was too small to boost Egypt's exports, while the continuing increase in public expenditure maintained the demand for imports. By 1964 an even more serious economic crisis was brewing.

Egypt tried to obtain financial assistance both from the Soviet Union and from the United States; a loan for $500 million in food aid over a three-year period was requested from the latter. Neither country was anxious to oblige. The United States was unhappy about Egypt's continuing participation in the Yemen war as well as its close relations with the Communist Bloc. The Soviet Union was feeling its own economic difficulties and appeared more ready to offer advice than money—Mabro (1975, 310) reports that Soviet assistance drastically slowed down, and the annual increment in 1966 was only $7 million. Waterbury (1983, 97) pointed to the irony that "Kosygin, Podgorny, and Brezhnev in their advice to the Egyptians advocated retrenchment policies not dissimilar to those of the IMF." Worse was to come. In May 1966, Egypt asked for a rescheduling of its debts to the Soviet Union but Kosygin's attitude became "bankerish," and he refused on the grounds that agreeing to a postponement would set a bad precedent and encourage all the other developing countries that were indebted to the Soviet Union to ask for the same concession.

The foreign-exchange crisis had become acute, and Egypt's economic fortunes were dwindling. It missed three monthly loan repayments to the IMF and renegotiated loan maturities with a number of European countries. In 1967, imports were some 25 percent lower than in the year before, and the investment budget even in nominal terms was no higher than in 1965. Real per capita income declined in absolute terms in both 1966 and 1967, dropping from $406 in 1965 to $392 in 1967, and remained at the same level in 1968.

Describing the experience of the years from 1965, Kaissouni said he sympathized with the dilemma in which Nasser found himself. If the president continued with his existing economic and foreign policies, Egypt would become bankrupt. If he abandoned the pro-USSR foreign policy and turned to the United States in order to protect the economy, he would lose the support of his armed forces, which were now equipped almost wholly by the USSR and whose higher officers had been trained exclusively in that country. It would also require fresh thinking on how best to support the Palestinian cause, because the United States would certainly pressure Egypt to accept the status quo as permanent.

Kaissouni gave priority to fixing the economy. He said that he had argued in cabinet that a strong military could only rest on the foundation of a strong economy. If Egypt continued on its existing course, not only would the people suffer extreme economic hardship and that would also create serious political problems for the government, but the weakened economy would also make it very difficult to maintain a large standing armed force. He also pointed out that no matter how much support the Soviet Union gave by way of weapons and training, Egypt still had to find the money to pay for the salaries of the troops, the expenses of maintaining the equipment, the manufacture of ammunition, the additional expenditures on training exercises, and so on.

Moreover, Egypt also had to deal with the problem of trade that was regionally unbalanced, a difficulty also emphasized by Abdel Aziz Higazi, another finance minister under Nasser. Egypt's transactions with the Eastern Bloc were generally in balance (if one included military purchases and debt service), but it ran a significant deficit vis-à-vis Western countries. Egypt purchased between one-half and two-thirds of its imports from Western Europe and the United States, and during 1963 to 1966 ran a trade deficit with these countries in excess of le150 million. Some part of this could be paid through Egypt's service exports, but the rest had to be financed through foreign aid and commercial borrowing.

There was no easy way out. Egypt was dependent on the West for much of its food supply, and the Eastern Bloc did not have the surpluses to meet the gap. If Egypt wanted assistance with meeting the balance-of-payments deficit with the West, it would have to restructure the economy in a direction that paid more attention to efficiency and quality. This would mean encouraging the private sector and creating a hospitable environment for investment by capital-surplus Arab countries. Egypt would also have to engage the West more. This did not mean abandoning the Palestinians; support for them was an article of faith for Egyptians. It only meant that Egypt's support would have to lay greater emphasis on diplomatic and political means. In fact, a strong economy would enable Egypt to stand up better to the political pressures of Western countries, and thus enable it to persist with support to the Palestinians.

Other advisors, especially of a leftist persuasion, offered a very different perspective. In their view, Nasser's regime would find it difficult to survive if the already impoverished masses were forced to tighten their belts further. They were also convinced that the Soviet Union would not let the goodwill garnered from its massive investment in Egypt, both economic (for example, the High Dam, the steel mill, fertilizer plants) and military, go to waste by not assisting Egypt to remain out of the "West's clutches." They were confident that, if the case were properly presented, the Soviet Union would come through with the resources that Egypt needed. They were convinced that going cap in hand to the West would spell the end of socialism in Egypt, and subjugate the interests of the country once again to those powers from whose yoke Egypt had only recently escaped. On the whole, they advised an expansionist economic policy that would create jobs and raise incomes.

Kaissouni's response to this view was that Egypt could not do everything at the same time. The country had many aims but limited resources, and it therefore had to prioritize. In his view, strengthening the economy was the top priority, and a strong economy would enable Egypt to attain its other objectives in due course of time.

Nasser vacillated between these diametrically opposed assessments, and no doubt he received advice from other sources as well. He permitted the government to approach the IMF, which in 1966 proposed a stabilization plan. This included devaluing the foreign-exchange rate by about 40 percent, as well as lowering subsidies on consumer goods and increasing some prices and taxes. The Mohieddin cabinet implemented some of these measures, but the president balked at devaluing the exchange rate. The cabinet was unhappy. In its view the exchange-rate adjustment was crucial to boosting Egypt's exports, which it considered the linchpin of any plan to help Egypt escape the repeated balance-of-payments crises to which the country had become subject. There also appear to have been serious disagreements between the president and the cabinet on other matters that affected economic policy; thus, Hansen and Nashashibi (1975, 121) write that "there seems to have been a clash between President and Cabinet about policy in general, and the Yemen war in particular. Mohieddin seems to have insisted upon a termination of the Yemen war as the only way of improving the economy."

The costs of the Yemen war have never been made public. Waterbury (1983, 94–95) summarizes some unofficial guesstimates: Nutting (1972, 379) puts it at LE500 million for the period between 1962 and 1965; Vatikiotis (1978, 162) at LE4 billion; Ibrahim Sa'ada[17] at LE1 million per day. Waterbury recounts how Nazih Daif (minister of finance) and Ali Gritli (minister of finance and economy in 1954), in interviews with him, quoted much more conservative figures of £20 million a year as the foreign-exchange costs. He considers these figures too low, in view of estimates that Egypt kept 20,000 to 40,000 men and a great deal of equipment in Yemen from 1963 to 1967. McDermott (1988, 156) has even higher figures—70,000 soldiers in 1965. I have already mentioned the comment by Higazi (Nasser's last minister of finance) in my interviews with him, namely, that persisting stubbornly for five years with the Yemen war was an act of "incomprehensible folly," and was a major factor in defense expenditures consuming one-third of total government revenue.

In the end, Nasser did not go along with the Mohieddin cabinet's views. He appointed a new cabinet on September 10, 1966, with Mohammed Sidqi Sulaiman as prime minister.

Industrial Development

This section is closely linked with those on the nationalizations in the economy and on planning and should be read in conjunction with them (see pages 165–83). Nasser outlined his vision of Egypt's role in the world in *The Philosophy of the Revolution*, which was issued in 1954. This assigned a central role for his country not only in the Middle East, but also in African and Islamic affairs.

> History is charged with great heroic roles which do not find actors to play them on the stage. I do not know why I always imagined that in this region in which we live there is a role wandering aimlessly about seeking an actor to play it. (55)
>
> We, and only we, are impelled by our environment and are capable of performing this role. (73)

To bring this sweeping vision closer to reality, Egypt's economy would have to be modernized, and Nasser regarded a modern economy as virtually synonymous with an industrialized economy. He was also conscious that because of Egypt's population density and limits on agricultural growth, industrial growth had to be a priority of national development if the growing labor force was to be employed. This point, indeed, had long been recognized. Waterbury (1983, 59) notes that Talaat Harb, Ismail Sidqi, and Amin Yahya, as members of the Commission on Commerce and Industry, wrote in 1918 that industrialization was the only protection against social discontent and perhaps even revolution. Waterbury adds that the 1929 Bank Misr report on import-substituting industrialization "differs little in its spirit from what Nasser brought forth thirty years later." While one may argue that some projects (such as the iron and steel plant, the military aircraft factory, the car assembly lines) were undertaken prematurely, and criticize a number of policies applied to the industrial sector (such as those requiring industrial firms to hire large amounts of superfluous labor, or the absence of export promotion), the basic tenet of Nasser's development strategy—the imperative of a strong push for industrialization—can hardly be faulted.

Soon after the agrarian reform was out of the way, attention turned to developing the country's industry.

Background

A brief review will put in context the state of Egypt's industry that confronted Nasser and highlight the issues that his regime faced.

Egyptian industrialization began under the rule of Muhammad Ali. Textile production dominated the manufacturing sector (as it does at present); food processing was important (as it is at present); and the regime paid great attention to foundries and to wood and metal workshops—the equivalent of the intermediate goods sector in modern industry.

Manufacturing industry in Egypt has tended to be inward-looking; since 1930 the dominant feature has been import substitution. This pattern prevailed whether the economic system was free private enterprise between 1930 and the early 1950s, the mixed system of the 1950s, or the planned socialist economy of the 1960s under Nasser.

Import-substituting industrialization had proceeded for barely ten years when the Second World War broke out. The disruption of foreign trade closed domestic markets to competition, thus further strengthening the incentives for import substitution, but it also prevented Egyptian industry from importing equipment and spare parts for new investment and replacing worn-out machinery. Thus the development of industry during the war was uneven—some sectors benefited and expanded, others were were held back, and some managed to attain varying degrees of success in meeting new demands with little means.

The war created conditions for the resumption of industrialization in 1945. Many firms had made significant profits and retained large liquid balances. Moreover, the Allied armies had trained an Egyptian workforce estimated at around 200,000 men that had been employed in various plants and workshops. Thus, although the physical stocks of equipment and goods were run down, significant amounts of human and financial resources were built up—the equipment could be upgraded, and trained labor was available.

During the war, entrepreneurs acquired a better knowledge about the demands of the market—they learned from experience that certain goods could be produced by domestic industry, and they discovered which domestic goods and in which quantity and quality could be absorbed by a market closed to imports. On the other hand, they had very little experience with the international markets and exports. These factors reinforced the impulses for import-substituting industrialization.

Nasser's Push for Industrialization

One of the principal aims of the agrarian reform was to divert capital away from being invested in agriculture and to encourage it to be invested in industry. Wahba quotes part of a speech by Nasser on July 27, 1958 on the occasion of the opening of the Iron and Steel complex:

> Private capital has always turned to agriculture in the past. Almost nobody used to invest in industry. . . . Our only aim in this is to direct private capital towards industry, and in this way private capital and government capital can share in the construction of the country. (Wahba 1994, 60)

In the event, the private sector showed no interest in investing in industry. This was hardly surprising; most of those who had the where-withal to invest in industry were also those who had lost substantial amounts of land in the agrarian reform. The reform was seen as an attack on large private properties, and it was never on the cards that a group that saw itself as the victim of such an attack would offer further hostages in the shape of large industrial concerns. The invasion by Britain, France, and Israel in 1956 presented the state with an opportunity to national-ize foreign industrial and commercial properties, and the breakup of the union with Syria in 1960 provided the pretext for wholesale national-izations (as described elsewhere in this chapter). The state became the dominant player in the industrial field.

The subject of industrial development under Nasser's regime merits a detailed study and lies beyond the scope of the present book. Almost all economic policies impact industrialization, and consequently a detailed treatment of the subject would occupy a large book. In the case of Egypt, policies dealing with agriculture, international trade, public finance, exchange rate, labor, education, technology, and privatization, together with the state of the infrastructure, the working of the judicial system, and indeed the politics of the period (such as Egypt's turn toward the East-ern Bloc and the growth of barter trade) have all at different times had a major bearing on industrialization. It is impossible to do justice to the subject within the confines of one section of one chapter of a book. Here the concern will only be with some of the main issues in which politics and economics interacted to have an impact on industrial development.

Planning Problems with Rapid Industrialization

The early attempts at developing public-sector industry were bedeviled by a number of planning and policy failures. Mabro and Radwan (1976, 69–70) provide a sampling. Investment criteria and methods of project appraisal were extremely crude. Departments differed in their degrees of competence and applied different procedures. Departments also prioritized their sectional interests, thereby making it impossible to follow a uniform set of priorities and objectives. In many cases, extra-economic objectives overrode economic considerations; for example, a plant for jet fighters that absorbed almost the equivalent of an annual investment in industry during the 1960s failed to deliver the fighters, and ended up being used as a workshop for repairs and for the production of consumer durables. The iron and steel mill and the automobile assembly plant are cited as other examples of extra-economic considerations trumping the economic. Further errors included the establishment of factories for dairy products in areas where they could not be supplied with milk; capacity in other food industries planned on a scale that far exceeded the availability of raw materials; and the neglect of building materials industries at a time when the High Dam and some of its complementary projects were being undertaken. Modernizing the textile industry was largely ignored, with the result that the extremely valuable long-staple Egyptian cotton was largely used to make coarse (and low-priced) yarn and cloth.

Pricing Issues

Price control originated during the Second World War but covered only a few essential commodities. Following the nationalizations of 1960 and 1961, the system expanded rapidly and affected all the major sectors of the economy. The government's increasing intervention in the economy led to the official determination of prices of goods produced by public or semi-public firms.

The stated objectives were to improve income distribution and resource mobilization. But these goals were sometimes contradictory. Price controls and subsidies were used to check possible rises in the cost of living, but price administration (such as selling commodities at prices higher than those at which they were compulsorily acquired) was also used as a tax to raise revenues for the treasury, and so did nothing to improve equity. Moreover, several agencies were involved in the exercise—such as the ministries of agriculture, industry, economy, supplies, and the Higher Committee of Prices, plus local committees of price determination. There was also continual intervention by foreign trade organizations and the treasury. All these bodies appear to have acted with a considerable degree of autonomy. Mabro and Radwan (1976, 71) quote a 1967 report by the Ministry of Planning that described the system as chaotic, with conflicting procedures adopted by the various agencies involved in setting prices, and with coordination between them almost totally absent. Rubbing salt in the wounds, Mabro and Radwan go on to say that the real situation was even more chaotic than suggested by the report, and provide several more examples of muddle to support their contention.

In the industrial public sector, prices were usually calculated on a cost-plus basis, but they were varied for many reasons—to increase revenues, to clear stocks, or to depress demand. Cost-plus pricing suffers from some well-known disadvantages. Principally, it does not penalize high-cost producers, because such producers can pass on their high costs without compressing their profit margins. Thus they have no incentive to improve efficiency, and this leads to a suboptimal allocation of resources; the pricing system is unable to perform its most important function, namely, to provide signals for the allocation of resources.

The pricing of items, especially of manufactured goods produced by the public sector, was an issue with both political and economic implications, and remained a live question. A faction in the cabinet argued that the primary purpose of public-sector enterprises was to serve the people. The political concomitant of this argument was that while these enterprises should not make a loss (because that would be wasting the nation's resources) they also should not generate excessive profits, which they could because of their monopoly position. To this way of thinking, the fairest procedure would be to fix prices at a level that would cover costs and add a specified percentage of profit.

Other voices pointed out that a rigorous application of cost-plus pricing would imply *raising* prices in a recession! What would be the political reaction to this? The economic point was that the total cost of a product comprises two types of costs—fixed and variable. The former—such as the rent of buildings, salaries of administrative, clerical, and financial staff, wages of certain kinds of workers (such as security guards), and the like—are incurred regardless of the scale of production. Variable costs—such as for raw materials, energy use, wages of production workers, and so on—move in line with changes in output. In a recession, the enterprise's production would be cut back and the fixed costs would have to be spread over a smaller output, thereby raising per-unit costs. A strict system of cost-plus pricing would therefore have to raise prices in a recession in order to cover these higher per-unit costs.

The outcome of these discussions was a compromise. It was recognized that price administration would generally adhere to a cost-plus system, but would allow flexibility to deal with "special situations" and special purposes, such as raising revenues when the usual mobilization methods could not produce the treasury's requirements.[18]

The authorities also attempted to use the pricing system to achieve multiple objectives. This was not technically possible; Tinbergen (1952, 27–30) showed that a necessary condition for economic policy to be effective is that there should be as many instruments of policy as the number of objectives. In fact, several writers recommend that because the effects of policy instruments are uncertain and may be associated with significant time lags, it is better to deploy more instruments than there are targets. Mabro and Radwan (1976, 72) say that after 1964 the government appeared to have recognized that the price system could not simultaneously handle the allocation of resources, provide incentives for better performance, protect welfare, and improve income distribution, and "prices mainly became an instrument of taxation and a means of curbing the growth of private consumption."

The arbitrary administered prices could create large disjunctions between private and social benefits. A prime example was that the textile industry did not yield an economic return when measured by the social opportunity costs of resources used. Hansen and Nashashibi (1975, table 8.4) estimated that the rates of return at international prices for yarn was 0.9 percent in 1960 and –10.2 percent in 1970; for cotton fabrics, –15 percent in 1966. The reason is straightforward: the main input for the textile industry, long-staple cotton, is of very high quality (and hence high opportunity cost).[19] Unless this raw material is used to produce a high-quality output, which commands a high international price, the activity will show negative value-added at international prices.

Technology Issues

The effects of erratically determined administered prices may have been made worse by the technology that Egypt's political turn toward the

Eastern Bloc compelled it to adopt. This technology was markedly inferior to that available from the West, but Egypt's foreign-exchange earnings from hard-currency areas were insufficient to purchase the food items (especially wheat) that the Eastern Bloc could not provide, and also pay for Western machinery.[20] The result was that Egyptian manufactures seldom attained the quality demanded by Western markets, and thus could either not be sold there or could only command very low prices.

Labor Issues

The government's labor policies unfavorably affected the industrialization process. From 1961 the government began the Employment Guarantee Program (EGP) as part of the extensive nationalization and employment drives of the regime, essentially guaranteeing employment to university graduates. This guarantee was later extended in 1964 to include graduates of vocational secondary schools and technical institutes.

A considerable number of workers were foisted onto industrial establishments, even if they were not required; estimates of over-employment were often in the 30 percent range. In effect, the EGP was a social welfare policy to cut down on unemployment and to provide benefits to a section of the population, rather than something to boost industrial production. The policy produced serious consequences for industry. The overstaffing meant that output per worker fell, that labor costs per unit of production increased, and that the international competitiveness of Egypt's industrial products weakened.

Productivity

The effects of inferior technology, excessive labor, and management not always appointed on merit were bound to coalesce in outcomes of weak productivity. Mabro and Radwan (1976, table 11.3) estimate the annual average rate of growth of total factor productivity in industry between 1954 and 1962 at 2.88 percent, falling to –1.90 percent between 1964 and 1970. There are a number of difficulties with the estimation, and the figures behind the decimal points need not necessarily be taken seriously. However, the trend is probably accurate, and it shows a steady fall. The growth of labor productivity—whether measured as output per man or output per man-hour—also shows a fast rise between 1945 and 1962 and a substantial fall thereafter (Mabro and Radwan 1976, 146–47 and table 8.6).

Studies of individual industries tend to confirm the foregoing pattern. Thus, for example, Hansen and Nashashibi (1975, 223) report "substantial over-staffing" in the textile industry, particularly in the 1960s, and estimate that labor productivity rose rapidly from 1956 to 1960, but quite slowly from 1960 to 1970. Overall, the efficiency of textiles deteriorated markedly, as measured by a substantial increase in the domestic resource costs per dollar earned. For the Helwan steel plant, they report that productivity was very low compared with steel plants in other countries, whether these countries were underdeveloped or highly developed, and that productivity deteriorated with the passage of time. The vehicle assembly plants exhibited similar problems. From their inception up to 1970, capacity utilization in the passenger-car sector was as high as 20 percent in only a single year; it was 15 percent in 1970 (the end of the Nasser period). The trucks and buses sector performed somewhat better, with capacity utilization generally around 30–40 percent; in 1970 it was 41 percent (Hansen and Nashashibi 1975, 300, table 9-10). The only new industry of note in which productivity showed an increase was the labor-intensive tire industry (Hansen and Nashashibi 1975, 277).

Mabro and Radwan (1976, 191–236), using a slightly different method, found that cement was competitive, and sugar and alcohol fairly so, in 1960. Cement and phosphates continued to do well in the calculations for the 1960s, as did nitrate fertilizers and rubber tires. However, their discussion provides a good deal of evidence to show that in many instances scarce resources were devoted to industrial projects that were either ill-conceived (wrong scale, wrong technology, faulty linkages) or ill-suited to the economic condition of the country.

Performance

The industrial drive achieved a number of goals, even if only partially. It broadened the industrial structure, increased industrial production, expanded employment (manufacturing employment increased by about 130 percent between 1952 and 1970), and greatly boosted manufactured exports (the value of which in 1970 was almost seven times that in 1953), whose share in total exports increased from 9 percent to about 30 percent between 1953 and 1970 (Mabro and Radwan 1976, 220, table 13.5; 300, table 13.4). However, because of the cumulative impact of a number of different policies, major inefficiencies and shortcomings accompanied the physical growth.

It is difficult to provide definitive estimates of the growth of industry in the Nasser period (1952–70) because of inconsistent procedures for arriving at estimates, changing concepts and definitions, unexplained revisions of older estimates, and the like. Mead (1967) reports that at constant 1954 prices, value-added in industry grew at about 6.2 percent a year between 1953 and 1960. Egypt's Ministry of Planning estimates that at constant 1959/60 factor costs, industrial value-added increased at an annual rate of about 5.7 percent. Calculations by Mabro and Radwan (1976, tables 5.2 and 5.3) suggest that over this period as a whole, industrial production expanded at close to 7 percent a year. The overall picture appears to be that between 1952 and 1970 industrial output grew quite rapidly, though at an uneven pace—thus, there were particular periods of high growth between 1954–55 and 1964–66, negative growth (that is, declines) in 1967 and 1968, and low growth (some describe it as relative stagnation) in 1966 and 1970.

Elements of a Summing Up

It would be presumptuous to attempt an assessment of the political economy of Nasser's regime after discussing the issues only within the confines of what, in view of the complexity of the subject, is a rather short chapter. Moreover, this chapter dealt only with issues in which politics strongly affected economic decisions and issues that continued to resonate beyond 1952–70, and not on day-to-day descriptions of political and economic developments during those years. The period of Nasser's regime was particularly active, one might even say hectic, in effecting policies that impacted the economy. It might, however, be useful to step back and take an overall view of developments during the years 1952–70 and rehearse some of the most important elements that would go into making an assessment.

1. The central issue in the political economy of this period concerned changes in the role of the state in the economy. After the Suez Canal war of 1956, this role vastly expanded. The state remained very important in agriculture, both because of its traditional responsibilities for the irrigation system, and because of the power it could exercise through the cooperatives by providing subsidized inputs and credit, and purchasing the major crops. Especially from 1961, the state took over large-scale manufacturing, the major transportation activities, the banking sector, and many important areas of internal and external commerce. But the private sector was not eliminated. It retained the ownership of agricultural land and Kandil (2012, 63) describes a report by Zakaria Mohieddin[21]in 1961 (before the nationalization measures of that year) which highlighted that two-thirds of

the economy was still in private hands (including 80 percent of commerce and 70 percent of construction and industrial projects), and that half the work force was employed in the private sector.

The public sector grew most rapidly between 1960 and 1965—indeed, Waterbury (1983, 423) considers that "the period of socialist transformation in Egypt's economy lasted no more than 5 years (1961–1966) and that of radical political mobilization at best two (1965–1967)."[22] In 1965, the public sector accounted for almost 40 percent of total output, 45 percent of domestic savings, and 90 percent of gross investment (Radwan 1974, 207). Increasing foreign-exchange pressure and expenditures on rebuilding the armed forces after the losses in the 1967 war diverted resources and policy attention away from economic development. The regime's concern to protect the public's consumption levels meant that the diversion of resources to defense were largely paid for by cuts in investment. Thus, at the end of the 1960s, investment as a share of GDP was no higher than it had been in 1947 (while public consumption had more than tripled and accounted for almost 25 percent of GDP).

2. The expansion of government control took a toll on efficiency. Hansen and Nashashibi (1975, 203–316) examined resource use in the Egypt's ten major industries, and found that they all showed increasing effective rates of protection and rising domestic resource costs of earning/saving a unit of foreign exchange.[23] Thus, from a social point of view, it was clear that investment in many of these industries was inefficient. For the country as a whole, large amounts of investment had been directed into branches of manufacturing industry that showed low social profitability,[24] while at the same time activities with higher social profitabilities had been starved of capital for investment.

The agricultural sector suffered from a similar malaise. Hansen and Nashashibi (1975, 158–94, table 7-6, and appendix A) estimated the separate effect of price distortions, direct government intervention with acreages, and the imperfection of market forces during 1962–68 on the deviation of actual acreage from the optimal acreage of Egypt's main crops. They found 7.9 percent of the total acreage to have been planted with the wrong crops. Of the 7.9 percent, they calculated that the imperfect response by farmers to prices was responsible for 3.5 percentage points, while government interference accounted for 4.4 points.

3. There are indications that some misgivings about the public sector's performance, and indeed of the management of the economy, had begun to creep into President Nasser's thinking. Baker (1978, 90–91) describes an attempt by the president to boost the economy through economic policies rather than administrative fiat. In October 1965 the president appointed as prime minister Zakariya Mohieddin, who favored a cautious budgetary policy and the improvement of relations with the United States. The Mohieddin cabinet agreed to some stabilization measures proposed by the IMF, and indeed implemented some price and tax increases and cuts in subsidies as well as in the planned investment rate. However, Nasser did not accept the cabinet's recommendation to devalue the currency, which the cabinet regarded as a key element in its policies, and consequently it resigned.

Nasser's doubts about the performance of the public sector and the state of the economy continued to surface. Waterbury (1983, 102n2) describes an interview that Abdel Aziz Higazi (minister of finance in Nasser's March 1968 cabinet) had with *al-Ahram*. In that interview Higazi said that Nasser had confessed to him his bewilderment concerning the state of the economy, whether it was on the brink of disaster or performing satisfactorily. The only instruction that Higazi received on his appointment was to assess the condition of the economy and to report back candidly to Nasser.

Higazi confirmed to me the substance of the *al-Ahram* report. He also went on to say that from March 1969, in particular, President Nasser began asking "serious questions" about the performance of the public sector. The president especially wanted to know how much of a drag the sector constituted on the economy and what could be done to mitigate it. Higazi emphasized that the president was becoming very anxious about the state of the economy and appeared to be quite open-minded as to the best measures for addressing its shortcomings. This did not, of course, mean that the president was willing to abandon the vision of a socialist economy for Egypt, but that he was open to technical ideas from any source, including the United States, to make such an economy efficient. He encouraged Higazi to make contact with the United States with a view to opening a substantive dialogue on economic matters.

4. The welfare-oriented policies of the first two decades of the revolution had two broad aims: greater equity in the distribution of income and

wealth, and increased consumption of goods and (especially public) services. These policies consisted primarily of agricultural land reform; nationalization of large industrial enterprises; labor market reforms; and social sector reforms, chiefly in the education and sectors.

The principal measure for redistributing wealth was (a) the land reform law of September 1952, and (b) the nationalization of industry.

(a) Land reform: The land reform law of September 1952 has been discussed above in some detail. From a political-economy viewpoint, the land reform had something of a mixed result. The 1952 land reforms broke the power of the old landowning elite and created a new one; the political goal was therefore achieved.

The distributional outcomes were a little ambiguous. The land that exceeded the law's ceilings was not appropriated by the state and distributed or sold among the peasants. The large landowners were permitted to sell the excess on the free market. This provision in the law permitted panic sales of about 150,000 feddans, and within one year Law 300 of October 1953 had to be issued removing this privilege (Waterbury 1983, 265–66). The excess land, of course, could only be bought by the financially solvent. These largely turned out to be small owners, who controlled between ten and fifty feddans, and middle-level owners, who controlled between fifty and two hundred feddans. The balance of power shifted from the large landowners to middle-level owners.

(b) Nationalization of the large industrial enterprises was another factor that worked to improve the distribution of wealth. Again, the primary reason appears to have been political—to break the power of groups that might have opposed the revolutionaries;[25] in Mabro's (1974, 222) phrase, the intent was "privative rather than distributive." Hansen (1991, 250) perhaps most clearly encapsulates this view. He writes, "Important though they were from an equity point of view, land reform, nationalizations, and sequestrations were primarily actions aimed at neutralizing or destroying actual or potential, real or imagined, political opponents or power contenders."

However, the nationalization of industry improved equity by reducing the concentration at the upper end of the wealth distribution. It also produced other social benefits, such as more opportunities for promotion and wider participation by those who had hitherto been excluded. Moreover, with full control over the nationalized enterprises, the government was able to legislate substantial benefits to workers and to enforce the legislation, and thus strengthen its political position by procuring the loyalty of another large group.

Although most commentators accept that cutting off the upper tail of the distribution of income and wealth contributed to improving equity, they also recognize that, even by 1973, large differences persisted between the incomes of landless laborers and owner-cultivators with the maximum holding of fifty feddans. Hansen (1975, 210–11) therefore concludes that "a certain exploitation of the peasants in favor of workers in modern enterprises had taken place." This should not be surprising, given that the government's development strategy of structural change and modernization involved a transfer of income from agriculture to industry.

(c) Labor market reforms: The urban constituency was not neglected. The minimum wage in industry was doubled in 1953 from LE0.125 a day to LE0.250. Although the wage legislation was seriously enforced only from the early 1960s, real earnings were raised by increasing fringe benefits. Hansen and Marzouk (1965, 141–42) estimate that the cost of fringe benefits for industry as a whole increased from virtually nothing in 1952 to about 10 percent of wages paid in 1960. For the larger establishments, the cost rose to almost 17 percent. They estimate that after 1961 the cost for industry as a whole rose to 13.5 percent and for larger establishments to 24 percent. The increase in costs was not accompanied by an increase in productivity (Hansen and Marzouk 1965, O'Brien 1966, Hansen and Nashashibi 1975, and Mabro and Radwan 1976). Abdel-Fadil (1980, 46–47) argues that the different elements of wage policy between 1952 and 1970 should not be regarded simply as technical devices, but must be set in the broader context of the government's social and economic objectives. He stresses that minimum wages were fixed so as to raise the levels of living of the lowest paid wage-earners. This could be seen from the fact that money minimum wages rose much faster than the cost-of-living index. Thus in the

1960s there was a relatively rapid rise in skilled workers' living standards. Moreover, the rapid increase in average earnings did not result from market forces. On the contrary, "Government influence on wages, both as an employer and through minimum wage legislation covering urban areas, ought to be regarded as a decisive factor in this respect."

Strikes were made illegal, but workers were compensated by improving their conditions in other ways. Important elements of compensation comprised an insurance scheme for industrial workers financed by contributions from the employer; profit-sharing schemes whereby 25 percent of the net profit was distributed among the employees; increased sickness leave and higher sick pay; and constraints on employers' ability to dismiss workers.

(d) Social gains were significant, with major expansions in the education and health sectors.

(i) Education: Government expenditure on education rose from about 0.5 percent of GDP in 1953 to about 5 percent in 1970, despite the increased diversion of resources to defense following the 1967 war. These increased expenditures created the possibility of vastly increasing the student intake. By the early 1970s, the education system was able to absorb a tripling of the number of primary and preparatory students; to increase by 165 percent in the number of secondary students; and more than quadruple the number of university students. These figures compare with a population increase of about 62 percent during this period.

The rapid expansion of the student body, however, had two drawbacks. First, it led to significantly increased pupil–teacher and pupil–classroom ratios and a deterioration in educational quality.

Second, the emphasis on numbers disregarded economic signals. Providing the infrastructure for a university place in the sciences or technology cost a substantial multiple of that of a place in commerce, law, or the liberal arts. If university places had to be vastly increased, then financial constraints virtually dictated that the bulk of the student intake would have to be channeled into the latter group of subjects. However, the government's aim to rapidly industrialize the country, especially with an emphasis on heavy industry, required that the education system produce very many more scientists and engineers. O'Brien (1966, 227) highlights the short supply of engineers, chemists, and other technicians as one of the reasons for the private sector's inability to support the government's plans for industrialization, particularly of the heavy-industry component.

(ii) Health: The health sector made considerable progress. Expenditures on health as a percent of GDP almost quadrupled, from about 0.5 percent of GDP in 1953 to about 1.8 percent (of a much larger GDP) in 1970. The higher expenditures enabled a large increase in the sector's physical plant and in the availability of medicines. The number of hospital beds more than doubled, from a little less than 36,000 in 1952 to about 75,000 in 1970; the ratio of beds to one thousand of the population thus increased from about 1.7 to more than 2.0 (for a significantly larger population) over the period. The availability of medicine at subsidized prices increased substantially, as did the number of pharmacies and public health centers also increased, although they remained much more accessible in urban than in rural areas.

5. For most of the two decades (1950–70), the economy faced a shortage of both foreign exchange and domestic resources. Since the end of the Second World War, Egypt generally ran a deficit in its balance of payments, which it financed by drawing down sterling reserves that it had accumulated during the war. Imports continued to outpace exports, and after the sterling balances had been exhausted, Egypt had to borrow from abroad in order to finance the deficit.

The foreign-exchange problem became more acute when the West stopped its assistance. The United States discontinued its assistance in June 1966, largely in an attempt to press Egypt to cease the war in Yemen against elements backed by Saudi Arabia (a staunch United States ally). After 1959, the World Bank and many of the potential Western European donors were constrained from providing resources to Egypt because of ongoing disputes over compensation for the nationalized foreign enterprises. Egypt thus began to borrow increasingly in the form of supplier credits that carried hard terms, and were largely instrumental in increasing the country's debt service obligations. One could say that, in essence, Egypt's foreign debt difficulties arose from the attempt to run a balance-of-payments deficit in excess of the available foreign aid.

The foreign-exchange situation deteriorated further after the war with Israel in 1967. Egypt's attempts to deal with balance-of-payments difficulties centered on restricting imports; a systematic and vigorous strategy to increase exports, especially to the West, was never undertaken. Imports were drastically compressed—for example, they were reduced by nearly 20 percent between 1966 and 1967, and in the first six months after the war they were another 17 percent less than in the corresponding period a year earlier. The squeeze on imports created severe shortages of raw materials and industrial spares, forced industrial plants to operate well below their installed capacity, and was largely responsible for increasing unit costs of production in manufacturing. The foreign-exchange crunch was also a crucial factor in aborting the second five-year period of the 1960–70 "comprehensive" plan.

6. The domestic savings rate remained well short of the investment rate, chiefly because of continuing budget deficits. Throughout the 1960s, increases in current expenditures outran those in revenues. Much of the increase in expenditure related to defense and the rebuilding and modernization of the armed forces after the 1967 war. According to the published figures, defense expenditures increased from 27 to 35 percent of total current expenditure; however, these figures are considered to understate the true position. But even non-defense expenditures grew significantly faster than revenues, principally because of larger allocations for the social services. The poor performance of savings took its toll on public investment, which dropped by one-third between 1964 and 1970. Once again, the implicit political compact decreed that consumption must be protected, and public investment had to bear the brunt of the cuts. This compromised the country's future growth, but in politics, short-term considerations usually eclipse longer-term ones.

7. By the end of the period, it was clear that Egypt's aims greatly exceeded its means. The country's economy could not support Egypt's

foreign and domestic ambitions. Egypt could not afford to maintain a military confrontation with Israel, to continue with the war in Yemen (and thus persist in hostility to Saudi Arabia, a potential source of financial assistance), to assume the responsibilities of a leader of the "nonaligned" group of countries, to champion the anti-colonial movement in Africa, and to set up a welfare state with guaranteed employment, free education and health care, and retirement pensions, while antagonizing the Western countries and the IFIs that were the chief sources of concessional capital and modern technology.

Something would have to give. President Nasser's successor, Anwar Sadat, took the decision to abandon the philosophy of a centralized economy and political dependence on the Communist Bloc. This development is examined in the next chapter.

5

Political Economy in the Sadat Period 1970–81

Nasser died suddenly on September 28, 1970 and was succeeded by his vice president, Anwar Sadat. The latter was generally regarded as a political lightweight and other, seemingly more powerful, contenders expected either to replace him or to rule Egypt from the background. However, Sadat managed to outmaneuver the others, dismissing them from office or imprisoning them. This "corrective revolution" of May 15, 1971 cemented Sadat's hold on the presidency.

During President Sadat's rule, the principal events with significant economic implications can be grouped under five broad rubrics.

1. The economic background on the eve of the infitah.
2. The infitah (often known as the "open-door policy"), or the move away from Arab socialism toward a capitalist economy.
3. The riots of 1977 and their consequences.
4. Relations with the IMF and the World Bank.
5. Attempts to articulate a strategy to address some of the underlying social grievances and economic weaknesses.

I must caution that while it may be convenient to analyze and comment on these events separately, many interrelations existed between them.

Economic Background to the Infitah

An account of the politics leading up to the 1973 war with Israel lies outside the remit of this book. The focus in this part of the chapter is on the economic situation that largely influenced and, according to several commentators, including Sadat himself, determined the timing of the war and led the president to seek a new economic strategy, the infitah.

The Economic Situation in 1973 and 1974

This section reviews the principal economic indicators in 1973 and 1974 to illustrate what the economic future looked like to Egypt's policymakers. A detailed description of the economic situation in 1973 and 1974 is provided in Ikram (2006: 13–17); only a brief summary is given here in order to sketch the background against which major political and economic events played out during the period; these included the war with Israel in 1973, and the major reversal of Egypt's economic strategy in 1974.

The economic picture was grim by any measure. The growth rate of the GDP in constant prices dropped from 3.4 percent in 1971 to 2.0 percent in 1972 and to 0.7 percent in 1973; in the last two years real per capita incomes declined. The GDP increased at 2.5 percent in 1974; this was about the rate of increase of the population, and per capita income was no higher than it had been four years earlier. Investment and savings were stagnating— the former remained at about 13 percent of GDP in 1971–73, thus dampening prospects of rapid future growth, while the latter fluctuated between 6 and 9 percent of GDP, reinforcing the need for Egypt to acquire foreign savings to finance even the inadequate investment rate.

The fiscal deficit, already high at 8.9 percent of GDP in 1972, increased to 10.5 percent in 1973, and even further to 18.3 percent in 1974 (and to 22.6 percent in 1975). A principal driver of the deficit was the increasing expenditure on subsidies; the consolidated subsidy bill had soared to $890 million in 1974, and was projected to increase by a staggering 85 percent to reach $1.64 billion in the following year. Much of the rise was attributable to increases in consumer subsidies (as measured by the deficit of the General Authority for Supply Commodities, which sold commodities deemed to be "essential" to consumers at prices lower than it paid to purchase them), which jumped from $28 million in 1972, to $228 million in 1973, reaching $845 million in 1974, and projected at $1.26 billion for 1975.

The budget deficits were financed by borrowing, internally and externally, which led to rapid increases in the money supply. In 1974, money and quasi-money increased by 29 percent; this followed a 40 percent increase in 1973. These increases fueled inflation. The official Consumer Price Index rose from 7 percent in 1973, to 10 percent in 1974, but even these increases were widely considered to be underestimates; unofficial estimates put the increase in 1974 at 20–25 percent.[1]

The outcomes on the balance of payments did nothing to lighten the economic picture. The current account deficit excluding official transfers increased sharply from 5.6 percent of GDP in 1972, to 7.8 percent in 1973, to 15.2 percent in 1974, and reached 20 percent in 1975. Even after the receipt of substantial official transfers, the deficit increased from 2.2 percent in 1972 to 3.5 percent in, and tripled to 11.3 percent in 1975. A substantial part of the deficit was financed by high-cost commercial borrowing on extremely short terms (180 days), which led to a "bunching" of repayments whose servicing created a major liquidity problem. The crisis was resolved in 1976–77 only by the intervention of a *deus ex machina* in the form of the newly created Gulf Organization for the Development of Egypt (GODE) set up by Saudi Arabia, Kuwait, Abu Dhabi, and Qatar. This organization provided Egypt with sufficient amounts to discharge the short-term debt liabilities and to import vital intermediate goods.

President Sadat offered a graphic summary of the seriousness of Egypt's economic plight.

> Let me tell you that our economy has fallen below zero. We have commitments (to the banks, and so on), which we should but cannot meet by the end of the year. In three months' time, by, say, 1974 we shan't have enough bread in the pantry! (Sadat 1977, 245)

> I wanted to tell them [the National Security Council] that we had reached the "zero stage" economically *(marhalat al-sifr)* in every sense of the term. . . . I could not have paid a penny toward our debt installments falling due on January 1, [1974,] nor could I have bought a grain of wheat in 1974. There would not have been bread for the people. (quoted in Scobie 1981, 31)

Economic desperation was one important element in the decision to go to war. However, in President Sadat's strategy the larger political thinking was to break the Arab–Israeli deadlock that had been frozen in Israel's favor after Egypt's defeat in 1967. Moreover, as Higazi (and others) stressed, Sadat had become very concerned that following the Nixon–Brezhnev meeting in May 1972, a détente between the United States and the Soviet Union could very well mean that the latter would implicitly agree to a freeze in the political status quo in the Middle East. The seemingly impending congruence of the interests of the two superpowers meant that Egypt itself would have to do something to break the standstill.

In essence, Sadat, who famously maintained that "America holds 99 percent of the cards" in the Middle East (Kandil 2012, 121; Tignor 2016, 146) and had declared that "the Russians can give you arms, but only the United States can give you a solution" (Fradkin and Lewis 2010; Phillips 2010, 56) decided that he had to demonstrate to the United States that Egypt and the Arabs could upset the political balance and disrupt the West's access to the region's oil supplies.[2] Sadat reasoned that this strategy would compel the United States to take notice of Egypt's concerns and help the country deal with its economic problems. His strategy was to wage a limited war that would get the United States' attention—Kandil (2012, 124) quotes the military specialist Julian Schofield describing the conflict as a "diplomatic offensive pegged to a military attack." Baker (1978, 133) describes it as "a war with political and psychological objectives that Anwar es-Sadat launched in October 1973, and in those areas the Egyptians registered important gains on both the global and regional levels." Kandil's conclusion captures the general consensus that Sadat "wanted to use the war to spark a serious-enough crisis to convince the United States that the regional situation was too dangerous to remain unresolved" (Kandil 2012, 129). Waterbury (1983, 127) goes further and concludes that "Sadat went to war in October 1973 in order to cooperate with the U.S. and to make his country safe for *infitah*."

The Infitah

The results of the war itself, and some ancillary measures taken by Arab countries (such as the movements in oil prices), convinced Sadat that the economic and political situation—internally, regionally, and internationally—had undergone a fundamental change. Egypt could take advantage of the new environment to revolutionize its economic prospects, but this could be done only if the country adopted a radically different economic strategy.

The president offered such an approach in the *October Paper*, which was presented to the People's Assembly in April 1974 and approved in May. The new approach has acquired the designation *infitah*, generally translated into English as the "open-door policy." Four key questions concern the infitah.

What was the Essence of the Infitah?

The *October Paper* outlined the case for a major redirection of policies in both political and economic spheres. The paper's argument was essentially as follows (United Arab Republic, n.d.).

- After the war of October 1973, Egypt had to prepare itself for the "construction battle" for modernizing the Egyptian society by the year 2000. The crucial element on which to base the modernization process was rapid economic growth. Egypt did not possess the resources to accelerate growth to the required rate. Consequently, it would have to obtain a considerable amount of external assistance, and this would be available only if the country adopted a policy that created a more hospitable environment for foreign investment. In addition, of course, Egypt had to unleash its own productive potential and make the most efficient use of its own resources.

- Such a policy required a change in the relative roles of the public and private sectors. In the future, the public sector would serve as the primary instrument for carrying out the development plan; undertake basic projects which other sectors would not or could not; and provide essential services to private and foreign investment. In the past, the private sector had been neutralized as a productive agent because of a number of "contradictory policies." It was now time to discard those conditions, and to provide the private sector with a stable framework of incentives and regulations, in order to encourage the sector to maximize production.

- Changes in the international environment made it extremely likely that, given the proper response by Egypt, the amounts of external capital that the country required would be forthcoming, especially from the vast increase in the financial power of the Arab world. Egypt was ready to grasp this opportunity, and was prepared to provide foreign investors with all the necessary legislative guarantees.

The foregoing represents what may be termed the official theory behind the infitah; it may also be useful to comment briefly on what the infitah, in practice, was not.

The infitah enunciated in the *October Paper* has attracted much attention as representing a decisive break with the Egyptian economy's public-sector-dominated past and providing a comprehensive guide to the future direction of the economy. While it did signal that the private sector would play the dominant role in terms of production and that foreign investment would be welcomed, the impact in terms of modernizing the structure of the economy was modest.

The basic reasons for the failure were that announcements of policies were not supported by ancillary actions that were necessary to make the new approach effective, and that many of the excesses produced by the infitah were not corrected. A competitive, private-sector-led economy would require the strengthening of many institutions, such as clear property rights; a commercial judicial system that delivered justice swiftly and economically, and whose judgments were implemented rapidly; an efficient bureaucracy that minimized unnecessary intrusions into private decision-making; a tax regime that functioned quickly, equitably, and transparently; and a system of education and training that produced the skills demanded by the market. Little was done to reform these institutions. Similarly, the socially damaging effects of the infitah for consumption and income distribution, and the rent-seeking behavior that it facilitated, especially by the politically connected, were disregarded. Whatever the economic rationale behind the infitah, ignoring the policy's collateral political damage virtually guaranteed that it would fail.

For nearly two decades after the pronouncement of the new direction (that is, well into the regime of President Sadat's successor), public enterprises continued to dominate the commanding heights of the economy. Their activities dwarfed those of the private sector in manufacturing, petroleum production, imports, exports, and infrastructure, as well as in large areas of distribution and other services. Their viability was assured through officially sanctioned monopoly power, backed by a soft budget constraint. Even at the beginning of the third millennium, the banking sector continued to be dominated by the big four public-sector banks—twenty-five years after the pronouncement of the infitah, they still provided nearly 60 percent of total credit from the banking system. The policy of guaranteed employment in the government sector to graduates of universities and other institutions continued and, if anything, expanded—Commander (1987, 26) estimated that the portion of the labor force in government employment rose from 9 percent in the early 1960s to 27 percent in 1976 (two years after the infitah was announced) to about 32 percent in 1981, the final year of the Sadat era. It remained at roughly that level for a further two decades. In a comment on the infitah,

Owen and Pamuk (1998, 37) claimed that "economists remain puzzled about the basic thrust of Egypt's liberalization."

But the mystification is unjustified. The writer I.A. Richards famously cautioned critics not to beat the cat for being the wrong sort of dog. Several policymakers who held key positions at the time of the infitah said that the policy should never have been regarded as intended to produce a tectonic shift in the Egyptian economic landscape. Some of them in fact argued that the infitah was a set of loosely related impulses rather than a coherent strategy—the latter would require the passage of legislation to restructure institutions, mechanisms to link aims with means, a clear view of how the public and private sectors would work together, and the monitoring of integrated policies. The infitah was supported by none of these elements. The actual motivation behind the 'opening' was much more prosaic.

Abdel Aziz Higazi was the first deputy prime minister at the time the *October Paper* was presented to the National Assembly (and subsequently prime minister). In half a dozen interviews he repeatedly described the infitah as being principally "an opportunistic tactic" intended to facilitate the inflow of Arab funds. He expressed surprise at the interpretation that Western writers had put on the infitah. He suggested that the West was eager to believe that Egypt was ready to make a 180-degree turn toward a free-market economy, and thus these commentators imbued the infitah with a host of qualities that it did not in fact possess. It was a case of the wish being the father to the belief. He moreover maintained that it had been in Egypt's interest to let Western commentators and aid donors swallow the "infitah equals a free market economy" line, and thus did nothing to disabuse them of their error.

It is true that a number of bilateral donors and even the IFIs were eager to embrace that interpretation, but not all Western writers were so gullible. Baker (1978, 168), for example, recognized that the infitah "was conditioned by an international configuration of power changed by superpower détente and Arab petrodollars," while Waterbury (1985, 76) summed up bluntly that "*infitah* is properly and primarily associated with direct foreign investment in the Egyptian economy."

The immediate aim of the *October Paper* was indeed to set up a mechanism that would encourage an inflow of capital from the Arab countries and the repatriation of additional amounts of the savings of Egyptians working in those countries into Egypt. These considerations provided the stimuli for enacting Law 43 of 1974, which eased the path for Arab and other foreign investment.

How did the Infitah Come About?

The move toward a more market-oriented economy did not appear out of the blue. Interviews with policymakers who were in office at the time of the infitah suggest that the story of the movement was as follows.

After Egypt's defeat in the June 1967 war with Israel, a number of policymakers had begun to question the wisdom of adhering to the country's socialist ideology and the efficacy of its economic strategy. Nasser asked some of his advisers to put forward ideas on the long-term direction of the economy. According to Ismail Sabri Abdallah (deputy minister of planning 1971, minister of planning 1972–75), the initial paper on a new approach was presented by Abdel Moneim el-Kaissouni, the minister of planning. This favored a larger role for the private sector and greater facilities for investment by Arab countries. Advisers from different parts of the economic and political spectrum commented on the document; for example, a group of "socialist economists"—Ismail Sabri Abdallah, Hassan Abbas Zaki (minister of economy and foreign trade), and Fuad Morsi (minister of supply and internal trade 1972–73)—provided comments that were critical of the Kaissouni proposals. These critics were skeptical that the private sector could do the job that the country required, and argued that the task really was to make the public sector more efficient by employing more up-to-date technology, better management techniques, and greater labor discipline in public enterprises.

After reviewing the conflicting advice, President Nasser deferred his decision. He was aware of considerable inefficiencies in the economy and may have had a measure of sympathy with the socialist economists' position, but was uncertain about the political and social risks of correcting the shortcomings too radically or too swiftly. He therefore temporized. He said that he was fully engrossed in rebuilding the armed forces after the defeat of 1967, and thus could not devote time to studying the complex issues that would be entailed in making fundamental changes to the economy. He said, however, that he would present his own views on the broad outlines of the economic strategy that the country would follow in the future.

The president's response was conveyed in the "30 March 1968 Paper," which sketched out the principles of his economic strategy for the immediate future. This strategy rested on three pillars: (1) priority to defense in resource allocation; (2) development to be maintained at a reasonable rate, with emphasis on economic and scientific administration of projects (this was a dig at the manner in which the public sector was being managed); and

(3) continuation of subsidies and of government-guaranteed employment to graduates. Thus, socialist policies would remain, but would be implemented in a more disciplined manner.

Higazi stressed that the president did not close the door to a policy shift; from 1969, in particular, he began raising serious questions about the performance of the public sector. Indeed, Cooper (1979, 488) quotes Nasser's *30 March Paper* as saying of public enterprises that "nonfulfillment by the unit of its activities on an economic basis, and consequent losses" should make it "imperative that such units be eliminated, or at least shrunk." Nasser also asked Higazi to think of how the public and private sectors could be made to work together so as to harmonize the greater efficiency of the latter with the social objectives of the former. Moreover, he changed his stance toward the Saudi and Kuwaiti regimes and accepted subsidies from them during the 1967 Khartoum Summit. This represented a significant change in Egypt's political stance, because the country had been at war with Saudi proxies in Yemen from 1962 until 1967.

Higazi said that the strength of the *30 March 1968 Paper* was that it not only spelled out the general policies that the president had in mind, but also that the president followed up by appointing officials who were charged to implement the program. Thus, for example, the economic team was changed in March 1968, with Said Gaballah being brought in as the minister of planning. The objective was defined—that gave it clarity; implementation responsibility was assigned—that gave it effectiveness. With President Nasser's sudden death in 1970 and the political maneuvering that followed, economic matters were pushed onto the back burner, and the next major economic initiative—the infitah—had to wait until 1974.

Some writers go further in assessing the effects of the *30 March 1968 Paper* and see it as initiating a reorientation of the regime. Cooper (1979, 486), for example, says that "one may wish to speak of a qualitative shift in this movement [toward the political right] after the accession of Sadat, but . . . the process had begun long before. Though most of the authors of the 1968 policy had been driven out of the regime's core constituency by 1975, it was they who had begun the process and set the basic conditions for its execution." Indeed, Cooper argues (1979, 481) that "there is a fundamental continuity between the Nasser and Sadat regimes and that an understanding of this continuity is vital to an understanding of the Egyptian political economy in the 1970s." On this reading, the seeds of the infitah were sown, or at least the ground prepared, in the *30 March Paper*.

Of course, Cooper's analysis relates only to the domestic political economy of Egypt; Sadat's foreign policy ventures with an economic payoff, such as the turning toward the United States and the rapprochement with Israel, were his own initiatives.

After the 1973 war, President Sadat asked his economic advisers for a paper on prospects for the future and the strategic changes that may be required to radically improve these prospects. A number of counselors agreed that Egypt should move forcefully toward a more mixed economy, because in their view the socialist structure in place in Egypt had failed to attain the country's goals. There were, of course, dissenting voices; Aziz Sidqi (minister of industry, petroleum, and minerals) was the most prominent opponent of any movement away from a socialist economy. Comments and suggestions trickled in sporadically, and both Higazi and Ismail Sabri Abdallah said that a consolidated paper setting out the pros and cons of the different possible strategies was never prepared, and nor were the issues discussed in a systematic manner. Moreover, President Sadat's modus operandi was to keep his cards close to his chest, and he did not share the progress of his thinking with his cabinet; thus, even key advisers could be unaware of much of the advice the president was receiving. The Ministry of Finance and Ministry of Planning also confirmed that they had not, *qua* institutions, been asked to provide inputs into the strategy or to comment on the proposals that had dribbled in from different sources.

Higazi was the principal economic expert associated with the change in policy direction that came to be called the infitah. Waterbury (1983, 126) reports that the very term *infitah* first acquired official sanction when it was used in Higazi's presentation of the government's economic program to parliament on April 21, 1973. Higazi's role in managing the new strategy was recognized by his promotions from minister of the treasury to deputy prime minister in charge of the economy in March 1973, to first deputy prime minister in April 1974, and to prime minister in September 1974. During the course of several interviews, he provided a much more nuanced and balanced view (aided perhaps by a degree of hindsight) of the infitah's genesis, aims, and achievements than many of the assessments that were common, particularly among Western commentators. Let me summarize the gist of these interviews.[3]

Higazi maintained that the open-door policy was intended more as an "investment promotion program" than as a blueprint for a free economy. Moreover, there was no "codification" of the strategy. The arguments and proposals remained scattered in various papers, because they had been put forward by different ministers in support of their own agendas. However, drawing on his notes, Higazi identified the following as having carried the most weight.

1. Egypt's balance of payments crises were caused principally by the imbalance in the country's trade pattern. Most Egyptian exports were to Eastern Europe, while most imports, especially wheat and other food items, had to come from the West, because the Eastern Bloc had no surpluses to offer. This imbalance created a serious shortage of hard currency, and had urgently to be redressed. Increasing the exports to Western markets was crucial.
2. Increasing the exports to the West was confronted by a structural problem. Egypt could not substantially increase the exports of its raw materials (particularly cotton) to the West, because the bulk of their production had been committed to the Communist Bloc in the trade agreements. It would not be easy to increase manufactured exports to the West, because the inferior technology obtained from the Eastern Bloc did not produce the quality required by Western markets. Egypt would therefore have to acquire technology from the West, but the question remained of how to finance it.
3. Egypt's chief political and economic supporter, the Soviet Union, was itself in economic distress. Indeed, after the meeting between Nixon and Brezhnev in May 1972, it appeared that the Soviets had recognized the weakening state of their economy and were signaling a readiness to open their doors to Western investment. The pursuit of economic objectives by the Soviet Union created a strong possibility that it might accept a political rapprochement with the United States and other Western powers.

    Egyptian policymakers feared that such a détente might undermine Soviet support for Egypt. It also appeared likely to the policymakers that a part of the bargain would be the Soviet Union's agreeing to freeze the existing Middle East situation, which favored Israel. In the circumstances, therefore, it was not prudent for Egypt to glue itself exclusively to the Soviet Union. Egypt had to diversify its alliances; indeed, Higazi stated that "You Must Not Put All Your Eggs in One Basket" was the title of an internal cabinet paper that had aroused particular interest among ministers. The paper also argued that Egypt's willingness to diversify should be clearly signaled. As a sign in this direction, Egypt canceled two large projects with the Soviet Union (the purchase of 500,000 textile looms and a phosphate project) and made attempts to acquire the equipment from Western manufacturers.

4. A large part of the "soft infrastructure" that Egypt would require for trade with the West had already been created. This consisted of a new generation of businessmen who had acquired financial resources and the experience of foreign trade issues in their dealings with the Soviet Union, and also had worked with Western businesses during extensive sojourns in the Arab Gulf countries.

5. After the oil price increase of 1973, the wealth of many Arab countries had vastly increased. It should be possible to persuade these countries that the enormous sacrifices that Egypt had made for the Arab cause over many years put them under an obligation to assist Egypt to repair its economy. Egypt, therefore, had to study measures by which some of the Arab wealth could be channeled into investment in Egypt.

Moreover, about two million Egyptians were employed in Arab countries, and the expatriate workers deposited the larger part of their savings in the West rather than remit them to Egypt. The expansion of oil revenues in the Arab countries and the large increases in the resources of Egyptian expatriate workers constituted "low-hanging fruit," and policies to tap these funds had to be developed.

Was a Change of the Existing System Inevitable?

As described earlier, the economic situation by 1973 had become grim, and has already been described. The flaws had become entrenched in the structure of the economy and would have had to be addressed by whatever regime was in power. Waterbury (1985, 66) argues that "many of the ills attributed to infitah are the consequences of other processes and policies, and, had the Nasserist 'socialist' experiment continued, it too would have been afflicted with these ills." Waterbury points in particular to structural rigidities in Egypt's import requirements that left it with no alternative to becoming more involved in the world economy.

The rigidities resulted in large measure from the country's large and rapidly growing population having to make do with a very limited cultivable area—less than 4 percent of Egypt's land area was cultivable, and this land area was also home to 98 percent of the population. The scope for agriculture was thus constrained and the ratio of domestic supply to total consumption of the main commodities continued to deteriorate. Bruton (1983, 703n10) notes that between 1970 and 1978 the ratios for cereals fell from 88 to 58, for sugar from 116 to 65, for milk from 97 to 66, for meat from 98 to 87, for vegetable oils from 64 to 52, and for fish from 98 to 62. No matter what imports cost, the rapidly growing population had to be fed.

Egypt's public sector was unable to meet the challenge of exporting sufficient amounts to convertible-currency areas, or even to socialist countries, and in the late 1960s Nasser had to call on the private sector to increase manufactured exports to the latter. Waterbury (1985, 66) points out that thus, no matter what domestic savings policies Egypt followed, "the need to generate foreign exchange and import food would remain as constants." Richards (1993a, 244) succinctly describes "food security" for Egypt in practice meaning "foreign-exchange security."

More broadly, Cooper (1979, 481–86) maintains that many of the reforms proposed by Nasser in the *30 March Paper* laid the basis for Sadat's policies; indeed, that "economic reform in 1968 was the jumping off point for economic liberalization in 1973."

The durability of Egypt's underlying problems and the limited room for maneuver that policymakers had to resolve them is elaborated by Waterbury (1985, 67–69). Nasser would have faced the same foreign-exchange problem that Sadat did. This would have required some sort of trade and investment liberalization; Waterbury observes that before the June 1967 war, Nasser had already drawn up legislation for establishing Port Said as a free industrial and trade zone. And as noted, he would have had to turn to the West for food imports, no matter what mode of payment—aid or foreign debt—was employed.

Moreover, given the great foreign-exchange pressure that Egypt was under, had Nasser lived, he would hardly have been in a position to reject the rents that supported the balance of payments, no matter what distortions they produced in the Egyptian economy. These "exogenous resources," as the World Bank (1983, 4) termed them, "are exogenous in the sense of having very little to do with the productivity of Egypt's domestic labor force that is overwhelmingly employed in agriculture, industry and services." In 1974, at the beginning of the infitah, the exogenous resources (Suez Canal tolls, workers' remittances, foreign aid, tourism receipts, and oil exports) accounted for 6 percent of Egypt's resources; by 1981 (at the end of Sadat's regime) they had risen to 40 percent. The availability of such resources, and the appearance of healthy macroeconomic indicators that they gave rise to, enabled Egypt to ignore reform of the fiscal system and to neglect measures to improve the productivity of domestic resources.

The genesis of Egypt's economic problems lay well before 1974. However, by that date the cumulative effect of five principal factors: (a) *geography* (the relative fixity of the cultivable land); (b) *demography* (the relentless increase in the population; (c) *military* (a decade of war—in Yemen 1962–67; with Israel in 1967, 1973, and the "war of attrition" 1969–70); (d) *diplomatic* (tying Egypt's trade to the Communist Bloc, which created a large imbalance between convertible-currency earnings and requirements); and (e) *political-economy policies* (the increasing financial burden of consumer subsidies, free education, health care, and guaranteed employment, the maintenance of a dominant public-enterprise sector that was unable to compete internationally, the suppression of a competitive private sector, and trade and exchange-rate policies biased toward imports)—had put the system under great stress, and made a major change of it unavoidable. The question is whether it necessarily required all the changes that were introduced or all the excesses that were permitted under the infitah.

What Were the Results of the Infitah?
The immediate results of the infitah probably dismayed even many of its most fervent adherents. The almost instantaneous result was the rapid and very visible expansion in consumption, which increased from 63 percent of GDP in 1973 to 75 percent in 1975. Imports in the same period tripled their share in GDP, rising from about 10 percent to over 30 percent (and quadrupling in value). Consumer goods accounted for the biggest increases in imports (largely because both the price of wheat and the quantities imported increased sharply), followed by consumer durables. The country's dependence on imports, even for the main items of consumption, increased sharply, as is shown by the steep fall in the ratio of domestic supply to total consumption for these items, described earlier in the chapter.

A part of the surge in consumer imports occurred because, for several years, foreign-exchange constraints had made such imports impossible or prohibitively expensive. The sudden availability of much more foreign exchange made it possible to accommodate much more of the pent-up demand.

However, the scale and speed of the change was dramatic. Imports, which for the first four years of Sadat's presidency had remained around 18 percent of GDP, doubled to over 37 percent in 1974 (the first year of the infitah) and climbed to even higher levels in several of the remaining years of Sadat's regime, reaching nearly 50 percent in 1981, his final year. Exports also increased, chiefly as a result of oil exports from the oil fields that had been returned by Israel following the peace treaty and because of higher oil prices, but the increases lagged well behind those of imports. The external deficit on goods and services jumped from the 5–6 percent of GDP that it had been in 1970–73 (the years of Sadat leading to the infitah) to nearly 17 percent in 1974 and more than 21 percent in 1975. In the remaining six years of Sadat's presidency, the external deficit fluctuated between about 11 and 19 percent of GDP. Figure 16 shows the sharp change in the series for imports and the external balance from 1973. The continuing deficits had to be filled in by borrowing from abroad; as a consequence, Egypt's external debt at the end of Sadat's regime was ten times higher than it had been at its beginning, soaring from $1.8 billion in 1970 to $22 billion in 1981.

It was not only the trend in the level of imports that was of concern; some leading policymakers also fretted over the social consequences of the changes in import composition and the beneficiaries of this change. Higazi, Kaissouni, and Abdel Meguid at different times said that when they expressed their concern to President Sadat, his response invariably was that the people had suffered much deprivation and now deserved "some joy" and

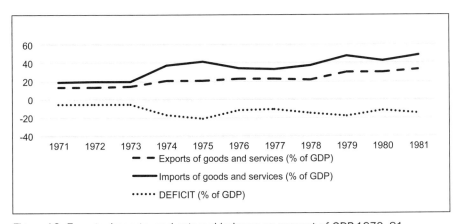

Figure 16. Exports, imports, and external balance as percent of GDP, 1970–81

a "peace dividend." The president was either oblivious to, or unconcerned by, the fact that the dividend accrued disproportionately to the group of the politically well-connected, who no doubt were supremely joyous at the way that things were turning out.

In two years (1973–75) imports of consumer durables increased from 0.3 percent of GDP to 1.3 percent of a much larger GDP; Cooper (1982, 115) observed that more cars, televisions, and refrigerators were imported into Egypt in 1975 than in the previous four years, and he commented that "commerce had truly become the focal point of liberalization." Moreover, the explosion of luxury imports raised questions whether this was the best use of foreign exchange. Weinbaum (1986, 40–41) saw Egypt's foreign-exchange earnings "severely drained for imports, much of it for luxury items," and reported that a large share of U.S.-supplied low-interest business loans went to Egyptian importers; many of these were middlemen who simply resold the goods they purchased to the Egyptian government.

World Bank memoranda of the period referred to the excesses of conspicuous consumption, particularly in Cairo. They cautioned that these indicated that the income gap between Cairo and other regions, especially Upper Egypt, was increasing sharply.[4] They pointed to international experience showing that regional income disparities had the potential of creating serious political dissatisfaction or exacerbating economic and social problems by encouraging massive migration from the low-income to the better-off regions. In the case of Egypt, this would mean from Upper Egypt to Cairo, and would put enormous strain on the infrastructure and social facilities of the metropolitan area. These points were even raised in a meeting in January 1978 between President Sadat and Robert McNamara (the World Bank's president), but do not appear to have made much of an impression on the Egyptian president's thinking.

Kandil commented that

in a country that had no millionaires in 1970, more than 17,000 sprang into existence by 1980, and 7000 of those simply became millionaires through land speculation. . . . Building construction in the second half of the seventies rose by 107 percent, more than 90 percent of which consisted of luxury apartments, villas, and vacation houses. . . . Between 1974 and 1979, 43 percent of the national investments, and 60 percent of the foreign aid and loans, were devoted to construction. (Kandil 2101, 161)

Heikal (1983, 86–88) gives several instances of Egypt's foreign exchange being squandered on luxuries, and sums up the situation with the tart remark that "Egypt was not being transformed from a planned to a market economy but to a supermarket economy." Plentiful details of the excesses of consumption and of misallocated resources following the infitah are provided in several works, including Cooper (1982), Waterbury (1983), Heikal (1983), World Bank (1983), World Bank (1990c), Hansen (1991), Amin (1995), Farah (2009), and Kandil (2012).

The "bread riots" of January 1977 (discussed later) occasioned some soul-searching about the infitah strategy in government circles and, indeed, the 1978–82 plan (the strategy of which is examined in some detail below) publicly discussed a number of these issues. Although the plan document recognized many of the failings of the open-door strategy, the overall tone of the argument was that the strategy had been misused, thus implying that there was nothing intrinsically wrong with it.

The official line promoting the strategy was that Egypt had been the champion of the Arab cause for justice in the Middle East and its economy had paid heavily for shouldering this responsibility. It would now be politically irresponsible for the country's leaders to require the Egyptian common man to continue to impoverish himself when the possibility existed of easing his burden by asking Arab countries that were flush with the oil bonanza to share some of their new wealth with those who had forfeited so much for so long in the service of the Arab cause.

This does not mean that there were no dissenters in Sadat's cabinets who were uneasy with the direction that policy was taking (Ismail Sabri Abdallah was a prominent one). However, the discipline of collective cabinet responsibility largely held; dissent was managed, and rancor and misgivings, while expressed eloquently in private, remained mostly contained in public.

Sadat had been strongly cautioned about the consequences of too rapid a liberalization. Several quarters, private and official, had expressed apprehension about the manner in which the open-door policy was being implemented. Journalists had lampooned the new strategy. Ahmed Baha al-Din, a well-known writer, had dismissed the policy as *"infitah sadah madah"*—a play on words that, in addition to meaning a state of utter confusion, suggests also a space with no windows, walls, or any boundaries at all. Prime Minister Higazi had described to the president how carefully the United Kingdom economy had to be nursed back to normalcy after the

Second World War. He said that he had briefed the president orally (the president's preference) and also provided written notes. Neither medium appears to have influenced the president's attitude. He was basking in the adulation of his close circle and of Western commentators, and was in no mood to do anything that might mute their applause.

The path that Higazi and some members of the cabinet and other advisors favored was to gradually loosen restrictions on consumption while at the same time to create incentives for resources to move into civilian investment, and to increase productivity by measures (such as lowering import tariffs and strengthening anti-monopoly laws) that would stimulate competition. A number of proposals were made by the cabinet to reduce bureaucratic interventions so as to reduce the cost of doing business in Egypt.

However, a populist group in the cabinet played to the president's weaknesses and supported an immediate increase in consumption to compensate the population for the years of privation before the October War. This group also continually reminded the president that the conclusion of the war had greatly heightened people's expectations of attaining an easier life, and that frustrating these expectations would carry political dangers. The warning of political hazard played to the president's deepest fears. Higazi said that whenever he tried to moderate consumption increases, rivals within the cabinet created street demonstrations against the proposed measures. He wryly described how demonstrators marched in front of government offices chanting rhyming slogans provided by dissidents in the cabinet, "*Hegazy beh, Hegazy beh/El-lahma ba'at bi-gineh*" ("Mr. Hegazy, Mr. Hegazy/Meat has become a pound [a kilo]") and "*Hukuumat Hegazy?/Walla hukuumat Nazi?*" ("A Hegazy government?/Or a Nazi government?").

Thus, far from functioning in a unified manner, the cabinet was acting as a coalition of competing factions. These factions were pursuing different agendas, so it is hardly surprising that advice to the president was contradictory and economic policies short on coherence.

Sadat was unwilling to risk any possibility of political disquiet. He therefore replaced Higazi as prime minister with Interior Minister Mamduh Salem (a former police general), and took the side of the "immediate peace dividend" faction in the cabinet. Mamduh Salem's appointment reflects the president's concern for security; Salem was the first police officer to be appointed prime minister. The subsidy bill also continued to swell; by the end of the Sadat era in 1981, the direct subsidies alone amounted to 10 percent of Egypt's GDP and more than 25 percent of the budget's current expenditures. A Western ambassador remarked that for the old Roman rule of governing by "bread and circuses"—keep the populace fed and entertained, and it will not make a nuisance of itself—the Egyptians had substituted a formula of "bread and surveillance"—keep the populace fed and under police observation, and it will behave itself.

The attempt to impose any caution or gradualism on market forces was aborted. Thus, at a critical juncture in Egypt's economic history, rivalries within the cabinet, coupled with the president's preference for the soft option in order not to risk rocking the political boat, opened the floodgates to the consumption binge by the higher-income groups (as they were the ones with the purchasing power). The flagrant conspicuous consumption by the rich and the widespread perception that that class had acquired its wealth by dubious means played havoc with the country's social harmony and was chiefly responsible for Sadat's steep loss of popularity among his countrymen. After the president's assassination on October 6, 1981, Heikal (1983, 5) graphically summed up the gulf between the international and the domestic reputations of Sadat: "He was taken to his grave by a most imposing galaxy of foreign statesmen, including three former Presidents of the United States and the Prime Minister of Israel, but with only a handful of his own fellow-countrymen as mourners."

As a contrast to removing the brakes on consumption, the infitah had only limited success in attracting investment funds. Higazi said cabinet studies estimated that between 1974 and 1990 capital transfers resulting from the open door policy increased by about 65 percent. The studies pointed out, however, that this figure had to be judged in the light of the very low base from which it started. These studies moreover estimated that about 75 percent of these transfers came from Egyptians who had invested their money abroad and were now repatriating it to Egypt; 15 percent from Arab countries (the expectation had been higher, but between 1979 and 1989 these countries had boycotted Egypt because of its peace agreement with Israel); and about 10 percent from European countries.

Higazi was very critical of what he termed the "open door to conspicuous consumption," and disappointed by the relatively small amount of capital inflows from non-Egyptian and non-Arab sources. He estimated that Law 43 inflows accounted for less than 10 percent of gross fixed investment between the announcement of the infitah and Sadat's death. Moreover, even by 1985, more than ten years into the infitah, two-thirds of Law 43 investment was in the services sector, while agriculture, manufacturing, transport, and communications had received less than one-third. He said that he had repeatedly pointed out to the president and the cabinet that capital would not flow into Egypt simply because it was permitted to do so. That permission, together with guarantees against expropriation, was a necessary condition, but it was not a sufficient condition; the latter required reducing the cost of doing business and thereby increasing the profitability of investment.

Several of the president's advisers (and not just those of a socialistic bent) had also pointed out that the political environment and the system of incentives created by the infitah favored activities that required short gestation periods and promised high rewards. These conditions were met by the sector of financial services (they did not require much hardware and therefore could be set up quickly, and would be difficult or impossible to nationalize) and by consumer-goods industries. The products of the latter were very profitable because they enjoyed high rates of protection against competing imports. It was therefore only to be expected that such infitah investment that did go into manufacturing, predominantly favored consumer-goods industries.

What Egypt had not done was to undertake structural reforms that would reduce the cost of doing business. In particular, Egypt needed to strengthen the working of institutions that supported a market-based economy. Higazi (and others, such as Abdel Meguid) pointed to the slow working of the commercial judicial system, the unpredictability of the taxation system, the misalignment of the education system with the needs of the market (especially where quality was concerned), and the failure to break down monopolies and strengthen competition, without which efficiency, especially in the manufacturing sector, could not be guaranteed and would put this sector at great risk. Without improvements in efficiency, it was idle to expect that manufacturing exports would increase rapidly. Since these conditions were absent, much of the capital that did flow into Egypt predictably went into commercial rather than industrial activities, because the former required smaller amounts of investment (and hence entailed smaller risk) and promised quicker yields. Indeed, Ismail Sabri Abdallah expressed fears that Egypt might well become "deindustrialized" if unconstrained international competition were abruptly permitted without the country first putting in place the required investments, and especially the institutions that would improve the manufacturing sector's productivity while providing due protection to social welfare.

This episode in Egypt's economic history provides an important political-economy lesson for development economists. This lesson is best summed up by Bruton.

> Economists have long emphasized foreign exchange as the one resource that holds back development, and its sudden relative abundance can understandably find a country unprepared for its effective use. What foreign-exchange-rich countries are now learning is that foreign exchange really is not the heart of the development matter. The heart must be the indigenous resources and their commitment to the nation's development. (Bruton 1983, 702–703)

One must conclude that the infitah failed to achieve its purpose, however defined. It was a failure even when measured against the modest interpretation of it as merely an investment promotion strategy to attract Arab funds. It may have had some merit in pointing to shortcomings in the performance of the public sector and in arguing that productive employment could more efficiently be created by the private sector.

However, merely highlighting the fallibilities of the public sector and trumpeting the putative strengths of the private does not constitute a strategy. There was a wide gap between articulation of the problem and implementation of the solution, between diagnosis and treatment. No account was taken of the effects, on the economy and society, of giving free rein to the private sector. A major strategic shift that gave the private sector the leading role in the economy required a parallel effort to improve governance so as to ensure that the incentives provided to the private sector obliged it to act in a manner that was consistent with society's values and priorities. These matters were not even attempted.

The most serious indictment of infitah is not its inability to provide the economy with the sustained fillip that was promised; the most severe charge relates to the impact it produced on society. The flagrant inequalities in income and wealth and the patently dubious manner in which they had been obtained; the flaunting of glaring differences in consumption; the ever-deepening cleavage between the sumptuous lives of the haves and the dismal ones of the have-nots, imposed unbearable strains on Egypt's social fabric. The people knew whom to blame. During the bread riots of January 1977—barely three years after he had been hailed as "the hero of the crossing"—President Sadat had to have a helicopter readied to fly him and his family to safety from the wrath of the public. The verdict on the infitah of most commentators has been severe.

Pressures on the Economy and the Riots of 1977

What was the performance of the economy in the decade after 1973, and to what extent was the infitah responsible for the performance? Ikram (1980, 2006) and Handoussa (1990) describe areas in which economic performance initially improved sharply. Thus, GDP growth between 1975 and 1986 averaged more than 9 percent a year in real terms; even with population growing at 2.8 percent a year, real per capita incomes increased at an annual average rate of 6 percent. The investment rate doubled from 13.7 percent of GDP in 1973 to 28.7 percent in 1985 and was accompanied by a rise in domestic savings from 8.3 percent of GDP to 17.8 percent. This decade witnessed the highest savings and investment rates in Egypt in the fifty years since 1965.

Social indicators also improved. The number of absolute poor rural households is estimated to have fallen from 51 percent in the early 1970s to 30 percent by the early 1980s; the infant mortality rate to have dropped from 117 per thousand to 93; life expectancy at birth to have risen from 50 to 58 years; the average caloric intake per capita to have increased from 100 to 128 percent of minimum standard requirements; and the primary-school enrollment ratio to have improved from 72 to 78 percent.

But these improvements had little to do with the infitah; they owed more to changes in Sadat's foreign policy than to his economic policies. The economic resurgence was based on a combination of events—the reopening of the Suez Canal, the return of the Sinai and Gulf of Suez oil fields after the 1973 war, the sharp rise in oil prices, the steep increase in workers' remittances, the increase in tourism because of the improved security in the region, the vast inflow of foreign aid, and the greatly improved access to international capital markets—that together provided Egypt with a much larger volume of resources. This made it possible to increase both investment and consumption. The more comfortable foreign-exchange situation also enabled a large expansion of imports, including those for intermediate goods that permitted the existing and new manufacturing capacity to be utilized more fully.

Bruton (1983, 682) argued that the foreign-exchange windfall—this was perhaps the only time in Egypt's recent economic history that foreign exchange was not a constraint—did little to affect the productivity of the "real" (as opposed to the financial) economy, and that the elimination of the foreign-exchange constraint enabled the government to avoid taking the difficult decisions that were necessary to make resource use more efficient. This judgment was echoed by others, for example Owen and Pamuk (1998, 137), who remarked that "once the regime found itself in possession of huge new funds towards the end of the 1970s, all pressure for public sector reform evaporated."

Some commentators contended that the sudden growth in foreign-exchange availability created an Egyptian variant of the "Dutch disease" phenomenon. This "disease" is an appreciation of the exchange rate that undermines the country's international competitiveness. It is most commonly caused by a sharp increase in earnings from primary product or natural resource exports. Revenues from workers' remittances, foreign aid, and oil can produce a similar effect, because means of production do not have to be allocated to earning them.

An alternative mechanism with more of a political-economy tint is advanced by Cottenet (2003), who contends that the behavior of the industrial sector during this period can better be explained by an "allocation of talents" mechanism. The boom associated with the infitah created an environment in which rent-seeking activities became much more profitable than productive activities; Egypt's best talents were thus attracted toward the former. These talents, instead of working to improve the productivity of industry, concentrated instead on rent-seeking activities by lobbying for protection against imports for their sectors of industry, fighting to protect subsidies, especially on energy and other activities that would increase rents. The existence of opportunities that offered large financial rewards but were not related to the productivity of the economy distorted the incentive structure and diverted resources into sectors in which profitability was propped up by artificial means.

Distorted incentives led inexorably to socially inefficient outcomes. The combination of an overvalued exchange rate and negative real interest rates provided an encouragement, even an incitement, to invest in capital-intensive activities in manufacturing and agriculture. Bruton (1983, 688–89) compared the composition of gross fixed investment in constant (1975) prices with output and found that it would require $5 of capital to produce an additional $1 of output in manufacturing, and about $4 of capital to produce an additional $1 of output in agriculture. He underlined that these were high by international standards. A World Bank paper confirmed these findings, and pointed out that these capital-output ratios were significantly higher than those in comparable industries in South Korea. It attributed the reasons for the higher efficiency of South Korean manufacturing in these areas to (a) the much larger size of that country's enterprises and the higher economies of scale that they could thereby obtain, and (b) the high import tariffs and other protective devices that enabled Egyptian manufacturers to reap substantial profits in the domestic market without having to push to increase efficiency, as would have been required had they had to compete in the international market.

The bias toward capital intensity in the economy discouraged job creation; a few numbers will illustrate the point. During 1974–78, output growth averaged 9.2 percent annually while employment grew at an average annual rate of only 3.1 percent. Papers by the Ministry of Economy (1981) and Bruton (1983, 690–92) estimated that during this period about LE2.7 billion (in 1975 prices) was invested in agriculture, transportation, public utilities, and housing. This amount, although constituting half of total investment in that period, produced only 21,000 new jobs. Thus, on Bruton's reckoning, an investment of LE10,000 (in 1975 prices) would create only one job in industry; creating 100,000 new jobs would require LE1 billion of investment in the sector, which would amount to about two-thirds of total investment in the entire economy (excluding the petroleum sector). Creating industrial employment would also take a significant amount of time because the plants would have to be set up and the supporting infrastructure created. The Ministry of Planning estimated time lags between the making of the investment decision and the full capacity running of the average industrial project at around four years, and of infrastructure projects at about five years. During the period that these projects were under construction, the labor force would of course continue to increase. It is small wonder that the authorities considered it politically and economically more expedient to simply herd labor into the bureaucracy.

The sudden inflow of resources carried some further unfortunate side effects. Non-oil exports dropped, because the increased purchasing power of Egyptians (facilitated by large inflows of workers' remittances, foreign aid, and an expansionary fiscal stance) enabled them to purchase more of the items that would otherwise have been exported. The drop was particularly noticeable in exports of cotton and cotton products. The value of cotton exports in constant prices fell by 50 percent between 1974 and 1981, textiles by 40 percent, and manufacturing exports as a whole by 46 percent. This increased the export basket's dependence on oil—the Gini index of the concentration of exports increased from 0.442 to 0.483 (a value of 1.0 shows maximum concentration), suggesting an increased exposure of export earnings to external shocks. The vulnerability became all too evident after the fall in oil prices in 1982.

Second, the vast increase in purchasing power of the Arab oil producers created an enormous demand for Egyptian workers in all fields. This eased the unemployment problem in Egypt, and also boosted the country's foreign-exchange earnings, because the expatriate workers sent back a flow of remittances that surged from $189 million in 1974 to $2.855 billion in 1981. However, emigration also imposed costs on Egypt. It constituted a "brain drain" that caused Egypt to lose a large part of the human capital—in all sectors—that was important to its development. Wrote Heikal (1983, 88), "Egypt began to be drained not only of its intellectuals and skilled workers—carpenters, electricians, plumbers and so on—but even of its cultivators. . . . No fewer than one million fellahin migrated to Iraq; 250,000 to Jordan, and hundreds of thousands more to other Arab countries." This large-scale emigration led to complaints of the shortage of a number of skills in the country and a reduction in the quality of the labor force that was left behind.

Serious structural reform did not begin until the 1990s.

Relations with the IMF and the World Bank

Perhaps one should begin with a general word on the background within which the IMF and the World Bank had to operate in Egypt, particularly after 1974 when Egypt radically changed the orientation of its foreign policy and adopted a pro-West stance. Two parameters emerged as particularly strong constraints on the work of the IMF and the World Bank:

- the vital importance of the country in the political calculus of the IMF's and the World Bank's principal shareholders, and
- the fragile legitimacy of the Egyptian regime.

The first provided Egypt with large amounts of concessional resources and thus weakened the IFIs' financial influence. It also induced the major bilateral donors to adopt a flexible attitude on questions of human rights and electoral fair play, and not infrequently to press the IFIs (in particular, the IMF) to ease policy conditions attached to their lending. The second made Egyptian authorities very wary about the degree to which they could impose the austerity that could result from economic reforms.

The combination of these factors meant that—in the absence of unusual pressures—Egypt moved only slowly to implement reforms, and that the IFIs possessed limited leverage to accelerate matters. This outcome was reinforced by the legacy of Egyptian history: a large and centralized bureaucracy, and an aversion to borrowing (as opposed to grant financing) because increased debt and economic dependency might once again expose the country to political subjugation.

The period immediately after the announcement of the "open door" threw up especial difficulties for Egyptian policymakers, who for about two decades had been supervising a socialist economy and thus had little experience in managing a market economy. They had access to analytical and policy support from the IFIs and donor countries, but a degree of wariness on the part of the Egyptian authorities was only natural. They understood that resource transfers from these sources were not purely altruistic, and feared that the policy advice might be seeded with an ideological content not entirely suited to Egypt's circumstances.

Relations between the Egyptian authorities and the IFIs such as the International Monetary Fund and the World Bank ranged at different times from sympathetic to suspicious. With the World Bank, the worst tension resulted from its withdrawal from financing the Aswan High Dam. Thereafter, particularly from 1974 when the World Bank's lending to Egypt was renewed in earnest, relations were more cordial. Two factors helped. First, the Bank's lending mainly comprised credits from its soft-loan affiliate, the International Development Association (IDA). These credits were at highly concessional terms—no interest, an administrative charge of only three-quarters of 1 percent, a repayment period of forty years including a ten-year grace period. This combination provided a grant element of about 88 percent.

Second, about 80 percent of the World Bank's lending was for projects: in agriculture, irrigation, transportation, education, health, and other sectors of the "real" (as opposed to the financial) economy. The conditions put on these loans were intended to ensure the financial viability of the project, and impacted chiefly the project itself or parts of the sector in which the project was located. This could, of course, lead to tough negotiations in particular cases. Thus, when financing the lining of an irrigation canal, the Bank might want a service charge applied to the use of water so that (a) the irrigation department would have sufficient funds for the upkeep of the improved canal, and (b) the farmer would have an incentive to economize on the use of water, which is the main constraint on agriculture in Egypt. However, the Egyptian authorities could have political reasons for not wanting the farmer to pay for water, and some compromise would have to be worked out. The point, however, is that few of the World Bank's conditions would have a serious economy-wide impact. In keeping with its primary focus on the "real" economy, the Bank left the articulation of macroeconomic advice to the International Monetary Fund.

The IMF's mandate dealt with the macroeconomic situation of the country, in particular the balance of payments, the budget, and credit and the money supply. Conditions applied on these elements would immediately ramify throughout the economy. As an example, in the 1970s, Egypt was running a very large deficit on its budget. The expenditures that contributed to this deficit were dominated by defense, government salaries and pensions, interest payments, and consumer subsidies. The first was politically untouchable, while the second and third had legal protection. That effectively left consumer subsidies (at times accounting for 25 percent of budgetary expenditures) as the principal item on which the IMF assumed there could be some flexibility, and largely explains its focus on cutting subsidies in 1977. Similarly, Egypt had consistently run a deficit on its balance of payments, largely because its exports had not kept up with the growth of world trade. If this were to be corrected, it would, among other measures, require devaluing the exchange rate to reduce the foreign price of export commodities and make them internationally attractive.

These actions, however, had broad social and economy-wide effects. The effect on the people of cutting subsidies, and thereby raising the prices of important items of consumption, hardly needs elaboration—the 1977 bread riots provide a brutal comment on this measure. The devaluation of the currency also carried important collateral effects: it would make imported wheat and other foodstuffs more expensive in terms of Egyptian pounds, and thus subsidies on bread and other items would have to be increased in order to hold down the price to consumers. The government would also require more resources in Egyptian currency to service the external debt, with the result that taxes might have to be increased. The point is that most of the Fund's conditions had serious economy-wide effects and had to be implemented within a short time frame. It therefore is not surprising that negotiations between Egypt and the IMF could at times be tense.

In attempting to blunt the effect of the Fund's conditions, Egyptian authorities generally fell back on a couple of standard defenses. The first was on the lines of: "This is not feasible in Egypt's social and political situation." Owing to the political support that Egypt had from the principal shareholders in the IMF, the outcome of the negotiations often reflected a fudge, with the conditions being softened. The economy's underlying problems continued.

The second favored line of defense was: "We agree that Egypt should do such and such, but the time is not quite ripe for this measure." Members of the Fund's negotiating teams said that they were never able to ascertain when the time would in fact be ripe. This defense was a perennial. Thus, at a meeting toward the end of the 1990s to discuss a proposed law to increase domestic competition, the two dozen or so prominent businessmen attending were unanimous that the proposed law was exactly what Egypt needed, but also in complete accord that the present was not quite the right time to implement it. The Australian ambassador, Victoria Owen, who had convened the meeting, whispered to me, "I didn't know there were so many St. Augustines in Egypt." She was referring to the prayer that, in his *Confessions*, St. Augustine reports he used to offer: "O, God! Make me chaste, but not just yet."

Egyptian ministers, on the other hand, often charged donor agencies with insensitivity; as one minister said, "They are too eager to announce the crime and to pronounce the sentence." These remarks were directed more at the IFIs; the USAID and other bilateral donors were more circumspect in pressing for economic reforms because their assistance was principally for strategic reasons, and thus their business was to provide financial support in exchange for political support. To the IFIs, it appeared that the Egyptian authorities accepted their analyses of the problems, but recoiled from applying the required policies. "They [the Egyptians] wanted us simply to waive the penalty, not to rescind the judgment," an IFI negotiator noted in his minutes.

The political economy of decision-making during this period is the story of a complex interaction between the views of the Egyptian government, bilateral donors, and the multilateral agencies. World Bank and IMF reports of this time highlighted different shortcomings in Egypt's economic management at different times, but three principal weaknesses were identified.

First, the years of running a centrally directed socialist economy had required the development of a different set of tools for economic management than would be effective in dealing with a private-sector-led economy. Those years had also left few officials in senior positions who were comfortable supervising a market economy that required management through indirect measures, such as incentives and disincentives, rather than fiats. Back-to-office reports and memoranda from World Bank missions, for example, describe being asked questions such as: If the economy is increasingly run by the market, then if things start to go bad, how can the government control matters? What tools or institutions, short of reversing the entire process and taking direct charge, will be needed to control the economy? How can Egypt ensure that the market works along socially desirable lines? How much direct control should particular ministries exercise over private-sector activity in their areas to ensure that investment is channeled into priority sectors? Thus, for example, should the Ministry of Industry set investment ceilings for the major industrial sectors and issue licenses until the ceilings were reached, or should it just set rather loose barriers to entry and let competition take its course? Would not the latter course of action lead to overinvestment in quick-yielding activities even if these, from a social point of view, are of much lower priority? What should be the role of labor organizations vis-à-vis private enterprises? What can be done to prevent wage costs from rising too quickly? Should the government intervene if the stock market starts to fall? Have other countries successfully managed to reduce consumer subsidies without triggering large-scale social protests, and how have they done it? What, if any, should be the role of government planning in an increasingly privatized economy?

Second, coordination of policies between the different ministries was often weak. Donor opinion vacillated between recommending the appointment of an "economic czar," the creation of a specialized institution, or endowing a ministry with superior powers to rectify this perceived weakness. The idea pushed most frequently was that a unit be set up in the prime minister's or the president's secretariat to harmonize economic policies. A sort of hybrid solution was even officially recommended to President Sadat by a high-level team of advisors from Germany (see the discussion below of the Möller report).

Third, perhaps as a result of the first two shortcomings, Egypt had not managed to articulate a clear economic strategy with strong political backing. In discussions with international agencies, Egyptian teams were reactive rather than proactive. They tended to tinker at the margin with conditions put by, say, the IMF, rather than advance a realistic vision of the country's own goals and the concrete steps that it planned to take to reach the destination. International agencies tended to view this lack of clarity as creating a defensiveness in the Egyptian response to donor recommendations, and possibly making negotiations more contentious than they need have been.

An economic issue with important political overtones cropped up quite early after Egypt's opening to the West, and highlighted the effects of the foregoing weaknesses. This incident—the bread riots of January 1977—traumatized the Egyptian leaders and continues to resonate with policymakers even today. Several decades after the riots, commenting on a series of fruitless discussions on the budget, a participant from one of the IFIs wrote that the memory of the 1977 riots still hovered in the background like King Hamlet's ghost, an intangible presence insisting that there was something rotten in the state of Egypt's income distribution and warning policymakers that they interfered with the subsidy system at their peril. Tignor (2016, 139) describes the riots, without hyperbole, as the "severest popular challenge to the Egyptian government since the 1919 revolution." It is thus worthwhile to look behind the scenes at the political economy of the decisions leading to the incident and the dynamics of the policymaking process that went into creating it.

In 1975, Egypt was afflicted by two macroeconomic gaps: between foreign-exchange earnings and payments for imports, and between revenues and expenditures in the domestic budget. The government sought to fill these gaps by obtaining resources from abroad. It understood that a substantial amount of these funds could be obtained from the IMF and the World Bank on terms more favorable than those from commercial markets.

Loans from the IMF and the World Bank are accompanied by policy conditions. The World Bank's conditions are applied principally to projects and are intended to secure the financial sustainability of the project, and to enable the price system to perform its signaling function to equilibrate supply and demand. The IMF's remit deals principally with the wider economy and macroeconomic stability. The reasoning behind its conditionality is that in the absence of some unavoidable shock, a country's macroeconomic difficulties largely result from defects in the policy framework. The IMF recommends adjustments to these policies, and imposes conditions on its resource transfer in order to monitor the country's move toward the revised policy framework.

Apart from the differences in the composition of the lending, one must note that there are differences in the approach to a country's development by the two institutions. While the World Bank's concern is largely with projects (which accounted for around 75 to 80 percent of its loans in the 1970s and 1980s), it does have views on a country's macroeconomic performance, because 20–25 percent of its lending impacts on macroeconomic variables. The Bank's and the Fund's views on these issues may differ.

This is not to suggest that the World Bank advice frequently cuts against the grain of the IMF's typical narratives concerning the budget, the exchange rate, the interest rate, the money supply, inflation, and so on. The Bank remains alive to the importance of the areas treated by the Fund and respects the expertise of its staff. But the Bank's focus is on the "real" economy—agriculture, irrigation, industry, energy, transportation, education, health, questions of poverty, social safety nets, the environment, the empowerment of women, and so on. Where their concerns overlap, the differences in the approach of the two organizations are more often than not of balance, nuance, and timing. In general, the World Bank's instincts incline toward growth, while the IMF's priority is macroeconomic balance. There is room for disagreement on the precedence of the approaches—it depends upon the particular circumstances of the country and of the international environment at that time.

Since both budget and the balance-of-payments deficits reflect that a country is living beyond its means, the IMF's proposals to move the economy back into balance are likely to create some austerity before, so the thinking goes, the policies begin to improve matters. However, no politician is thanked for imposing austerity, even if it is intended only for the short run. This fact was particularly important in Egypt in view of the abbreviated tenure of ministers in the Sadat era. The tug of war between the government and the IMF therefore centered on efforts by the former to eliminate some of the conditions that Egypt considered particularly onerous, or to water them down and to stretch out the period over which they had to be implemented.

The principal policy defect identified by the IMF in the case of Egypt was the deficit on the budget, of which the chief cause was the expenditure on cost-of-living subsidies; hence, for most of 1975 and 1976 the IMF's attention focused on this issue. Its principal condition for agreeing to provide resources was that Egypt substantially cut consumer subsidies. This prescription, especially in so far as it affected the subsidy on bread, carried sizable political risks—the price of bread had not been changed since 1945—and was resisted by the Egyptians. However, by July 1976 the budgetary situation had greatly deteriorated and it appeared impossible for the country to put off approaching the IMF for financial support. The word in Cairo was that Egypt was ready to sign an agreement with the Fund. It also was known that the cabinet was divided on the question whether to agree to the Fund program. The Ministry of Economy was said to be leaning, albeit reluctantly, toward an agreement, while the Ministry of Finance categorically opposed the measure.

The minister of economy (Zaki Shafei) explained that his ministry's position was based on three principal considerations. First, filling the gap in the budget required a substantial amount of resources, and the IMF was the best source for providing liquid resources in a hurry. Second, with the discipline imposed by the Fund's policy package, the ministry reckoned that Egypt might be able to make quicker progress in reducing its reliance on external funds and thereby lessen its vulnerability to external donors. Third, the Fund's "Good Housekeeping seal of approval" would reassure foreign investors; in view of Egypt's history with external debt, the minister preferred foreign direct investment to borrowing from abroad. The minister was not enthusiastic about the Fund's package; indeed, it was well-nigh impossible to find any Egyptian official who was. However, his criticism was muted and he merely pointed out that subsidy cuts were not the only means of reducing the budget deficit; tax increases could have much the same effect.

In response to my question as to which of the alternatives—subsidy cuts or tax increases—would act more quickly and meet the IMF's timetable on the budget, the minister accepted that savings from subsidy cuts could be immediate; producing the same result through tax increases could take longer. The tax administration would have to be improved, and moreover the taxes that could raise revenue most quickly would be indirect taxes with a regressive effect; therefore increases in their rates might have to be kept down, and thus their effect would take place more gradually. However, the advantage of relying on taxes rather than subsidy cuts was that the government could target the richer classes to be taxed, while leaving the subsidies untouched would protect the less well-off. I asked him why, if he thought the government would actually tax the richer classes appropriately, it had not done so until the present time. His answer seemed to imply that the chances of doing so were now stronger, because Egypt's economy was in a very tight corner. He judged that the coalition of the richer classes had been weakened by circumstances and thus economic sense might prevail over political instincts.

I left the meeting with the sense that although Zaki Shafei was not happy with the Fund's program, he regarded it as a necessary evil, and in the cabinet discussions he might maintain a somewhat equivocal position. Indeed, while the negotiations were going on, the IMF's mission told me that Zaki Shafei, while certainly not enthusiastic about the program, was the minister who had been the least negative about it in the deliberations. The minister who adamantly and stridently opposed the Fund package was Ahmed Abou Ismail, the minister of finance. Zaki Shafei thought the IMF proposals, while repugnant, might be necessary; Abou Ismail thought they were repugnant, *tout court*.

I was then called by the minister of finance for an urgent meeting. He emphasized a different set of concerns. He objected to both the content and the time frame of the IMF agreement. He regarded the terms of the agreement as inimical to growth, harshly affecting the poorer sections of society, and certain to sink the government in a political quagmire. He argued that attaining the Fund's targets required a longer time frame, during which the budget deficit could be brought down gradually by eliminating the more egregious subsidies, reducing some of the others by better targeting them, and increasing revenues by improving tax administration. He had already begun the process by making cuts that reduced the subsidy bill by about $185 million. He was as keen as Zaki Shafei to see a lessening of Egypt's vulnerability to external pressure; it was, however, even more important not to risk the country's social and political stability. The internal reaction would be more immediate and more unsettling, and would derail investors' plans and badly damage Egypt's growth prospects.

Abou Ismail said that after 1973, Egypt had made a deliberate political choice to orient its foreign policy away from the Soviet Union and toward Western countries. These countries did not want to see a major political upset in the region, and they were economically strong enough to support a measured restructuring of Egypt's policies and institutions. Egypt needed more time to fully implement reforms. He described it as "irresponsible" for an Egyptian policymaker not to call on these countries for assistance so that policy changes could be introduced at a pace that would not impose an intolerable burden on Egyptian society. This would also provide tangible proof of the success of President Sadat's policies. Abou Ismail was very skeptical whether the Fund's policy package would actually encourage foreign investment; such investors would be unlikely to derive much comfort from the "revolution" (his word) that he was certain would follow on the heels of a cutback in food subsidies. He was certain that Egypt's current situation and long-term prospects would be damaged by accepting the Fund's conditions, and he would vehemently oppose an agreement on the terms being discussed.

Some twenty-five years later[5] Abou Ismail reconfirmed that in 1976 he had told representatives of the Fund that there would be a "revolution" in Egypt if they pressured the government to accept their proposals on subsidies. He expressed pride that the cabinet in which he had served had not accepted the Fund's terms. He pointed to the bread riots of 1977 as a clear vindication of the position he had adopted in 1976 and of the political warnings he had given at that time. He added that if the Fund had shown some "political maturity" and understanding about the pace at which deeply entrenched institutions, such as the bread subsidy, could be restructured, they would have discovered that reforms could indeed take place and that these changes would be permanent. Blindly charging full speed ahead had only resulted in a disaster and set back necessary reforms for decades.

Neither minister was happy with the Fund's conditions. In cabinet, however, they were likely to take different positions, because they approached the matter from dissimilar perspectives, one emphasizing the economic aspect and the other the political. The difference in the stance of the two ministries is likely to have reflected differences in the backgrounds of the respective ministers. The minister of economy was a well-known academic economist, while the minister of finance was a member of the National Assembly and had to answer to constituents every day. It soon became clear that the cabinet debate on these issues would not be conducted in an exclusively economic vocabulary.

Ahmed Abou Ismail and his undersecretary, Hamed Rizk, showed me the letter of policy drafted by the Fund that laid out the conditions. They asked whether Egypt should press the Fund for adjustments, especially to the credit ceilings, the interest rate, and the actions on subsidies. The minister also raised an issue concerning the structure of exchange rates. His ministry was interested in discussing whether a dual exchange rate would serve Egypt better than an across-the-board devaluation. The ministry's thinking was that a dual exchange rate—the more depreciated one applying to exports that were considered more price-responsive (such as manufactures and tourism) and the other to exports that were less price-elastic (such as agricultural products)—would be the more suitable in Egypt's circumstances. What had been the international experience?

I replied that, first, the agreement was between Egypt and the Fund, and thus the World Bank could not properly take a position on it. I also tried to dislodge the ministry team from the view (to which they adhered with some tenacity) that a policy proposed by the Fund must axiomatically be silly or necessarily damaging to Egypt's interests. Second, a dual exchange-rate structure did not seem a particularly good idea. The experience of countries—I gave an example of Pakistan's Bonus Voucher Scheme—that had experimented with dual exchange rates had shown that interest groups would pressure the government to move items to the more favorable rate and to create intermediate rates, and the dual rates would soon become hopelessly multiple. Moreover, which rates applied to which exports would depend on the political strength of the various factions rather than on any economic rationale. In such circumstances, economic signals would become terribly muddled.

I offered the World Bank's services for a study of the price elasticity of foreign demand for Egypt's exports to ascertain whether devaluation was likely to improve the current account of the balance of payments. However, the cabinet's schedule for responding to the Fund had been advanced to that very afternoon, and there was no time for any investigation. Subsequent studies by the World Bank and by Nathan Associates showed that the Marshall-Lerner-Robinson conditions for a devaluation to improve the trade balance were comfortably met; for a more detailed discussion see Ikram (2006, 135–41).

Third, there was little point in dissecting the draft policy letter prepared by the IMF; the most effective negotiating strategy was to be proactive and not reactive. Egypt would be better off putting forward its own priorities, such as reducing poverty and increasing employment, and working out what this implied for GDP growth, investment, and the time and the policies required to create a suitable investment climate. Moreover, the effects of some key elements of the Fund's proposals, such as those relating to subsidy cuts, appeared not to have been examined carefully either by the Egyptians or by the Fund itself. The World Bank's consumption and poverty studies suggested that for the poorest groups the subsidies increased a family's income by an average of 15 percent. Cuts of the size implied by the Fund's letter of intent could have a devastating effect on families at the lower end of the income distribution. The burden would be especially heavy in Upper Egypt, and particularly in the rural areas of that region, where poverty was disproportionately located. The intensification of regional disparities in disposable incomes would cause additional political headaches for the government. Given a little more time, Egypt should be able to develop a more targeted and efficient subsidy system. After Egypt had developed its own plan to attain its investment and other goals, it could engage the Fund in a more fruitful discussion on the merits of their respective approaches. Preparing such an approach to the negotiations would obviously take a bit of time, and Egypt might have to ask the Fund mission to return in a few months to finalize the negotiations. However, the stakes were high, and it was more important to get the right agreement than an immediate agreement.

The minister responded that much of the cabinet considered that the state of the economy did not allow Egypt time to develop a counterproposal; the cabinet was under pressure to reach a decision on the Fund's proposals that very afternoon. Moreover, members of the cabinet were aware of the differences between the ministries of Finance and Economy and wanted them to be settled. The agenda for the cabinet meeting therefore called for the two ministries to debate their contrasting evaluations of the Fund's proposals, and the cabinet would adjudicate any disjunction between the two readings. Abou Ismail was adamant that a debate focusing exclusively on economic costs and benefits would miss the really crucial point, namely, that accepting the Fund's proposals would expose the country to serious political danger. In Abou Ismail's view, the Ministry of Economy appeared not to grasp that the political salience of the issue was far greater than the economic. Since the economic content of the Fund proposals was heavily freighted with political implications, Abou Ismail said that at the cabinet meeting he would center his arguments on the political impact of the Fund's economic proposals.

He would ask the prime minister three questions.

1. He had had the Ministry of Planning calculate the effects of the IMF package on consumer prices; this showed a likely increase of at least 30 percent. At the cabinet meeting, the minister of planning would stand behind his calculation. (I had these estimates examined by Professor Lance Taylor of the Massachusetts Institute of Technology and by the World Bank's economic mission, who were both in Cairo; they broadly accepted the Ministry of Planning's methodology and estimates.) Abou Ismail would ask: Was the prime minister prepared to take the government into an election in three months' time with the public hit by a 30 percent increase in the price level?

2. President Sadat's major foreign policy achievement was to change Egypt's alliances from the Communist Bloc to the West. The president had argued in favor of the change not only on political grounds, but also that Western countries would provide much greater support for Egypt's economy, and permit the country to institute economic reforms at a pace that society could tolerate. Now here was the Fund demanding that sizeable subsidy cuts (effectively, reductions in poor families' incomes) be delivered immediately. The Fund was seen as a Western institution, and thus Western countries would be blamed for the consequences of the Fund's policies. If the public viewed these policies as crushing the common Egyptian man, support for the president's Western-pivot would face widespread hostility. Was the prime minister ready to face the president after undercutting his global strategy?

3. In view of the probable level of public antagonism, would the cabinet and the president have the stomach to pursue further economic reforms? The attempt to appease the IMF in the short term would almost certainly trigger a violent response that would set back reform for a very long time. Did the prime minister consider that to be in Egypt's best interests?

    Given the caution of Egyptian policymakers, it would take a very unusual prime minister to answer "yes" to the foregoing questions. It was obvious that once the economic argument was opposed by a political one, the likelihood of an immediate agreement with the Fund would evaporate. Indeed, after the cabinet meeting, the IMF representative in Cairo was informed (ironically, Zaki Shafei was designated to convey the news) that several lengthy studies—a list of seventeen or so issues was provided—would have to be completed before the cabinet could reach a decision on the subsidy question. The IMF representative, Paul Dickie, of course understood this as a polite bureaucratic way of rejecting the conditions. This terminated the negotiations with the Fund.

Subsequent events conformed more closely to the Ministry of Finance's reading of the situation than that of the Ministry of Economy. The dénouement arrived in January 1977 after a new cabinet had taken office in November 1976. The state of the economy had not improved, and early in January 1977, Cairo was flooded with rumors of major price increases in the forthcoming budget. Discussion with different sources and the World Bank's research made it apparent that an abrupt reduction in cost-of-living subsidies could carry severe consequences. I telephoned Vinod Dubey, the chief economist of the World Bank's Middle East region, and presented an analysis of the economic and political situation. I was concerned that the Bank could be complicit in doing Egypt great harm if, without further analysis, it allied itself with the Fund to pressure the country into imposing severe cuts in cost-of-living subsidies. The Bank's position, rather, should be that if Egypt continued on the path of reform, the Bank would remain open to discussions regarding its pace, and that it would be prepared to offer technical advice and information on how some countries had successfully navigated the reform of subsidies.

While I had serious questions about the subsidy cuts, there were other features in the proposed IMF package that also gave rise to disquiet. There appeared to have been insufficient attention to analyzing the effects of some important elements of the program that could make for inconsistency between the program's goals. Thus, an important goal of the draft program was a substantial cut in the budget deficit through higher tax collections, increased utility rates, and major subsidy cuts; the program also envisaged sharply higher interest rates and a significant currency devaluation. The latter two actions would directly swell the government's domestic and foreign debt service obligations and thus make it more difficult to meet the target for the budget deficit mandated in the agreement, while a possible recession triggered by the sharp reduction in demand effected by the total package could cut domestic tax and trade-dependent revenues, and intensify the difficulty of reaching the targeted budget deficit. Perhaps the circle could be squared, but the assumptions and the figures that were being discussed left considerable room for skepticism. More homework had to be done by all sides.

Dubey agreed with me and said he would take up the issue with the region's management in the Bank. The next day he telephoned to say that the regional management and the World Bank's president, Robert McNamara, both had accepted my assessment of the situation and recommendations on the Bank's response. I was authorized to inform the government that the Bank's views on the cost-of-living subsidies and on the budget deficit were not identical with those of the Fund.

In brief, the Bank regarded the subsidies issue as having two crucial facets: (a) the size of the subsidies, and hence their contribution to the budget deficit; and (b) the question of who were the major beneficiaries from the subsidies. The Bank considered that the subsidy issue would be better approached through the latter facet. The available evidence showed that the cost-of-living subsidies were not well targeted—better-off groups captured a disproportionate amount of the benefits. Thus a restructuring of the system could both make the system more efficient and also reduce the size of the bill. The Fund appeared to be approaching the problem via the first facet, namely, to reduce the budget deficit by cutting down the size of the subsidy bill, without considering the impact of this measure on different income groups. In the Bank's view, the Fund had got the development issue backward—the essential goal of development was to improve the prospects of the less well-off elements in society, and not primarily to attain a more or less arbitrary number for the budget deficit. Of course the World Bank was not arguing that a large budget deficit could or should be sustained indefinitely. The argument was that the Fund was mandating a policy without examining its consequences or investigating alternatives, such as improving the subsidy system's targeting, that could both protect the vulnerable and reduce the deficit.

I was authorized to inform the government that the Bank would separate its approach from that of the Fund if the latter persisted in demanding an immediate and major reduction of cost-of-living subsidies. I was to assure the cabinet that, as evidence of this separation, the Bank was prepared to hold the first meeting of the Consultative Group of aid donors if Egypt moved on reform, regardless of whether or not the country concluded an agreement with the Fund. I was also asked to inform the cabinet that McNamara would convey his intentions to the secretary of the U.S. Treasury and the managing director of the International Monetary Fund.

McNamara's decision represented a major breach of Bank–Fund understandings on relationships and procedures, and could not have been easy. The convention was that in order to receive the Bank's policy-based loans, the country had to have an IMF program in place, or that the IMF had to provide the World Bank with a "letter of comfort" confirming that it did not object to the World Bank's policy loan. McNamara's decision broke with this convention. On a visit to Egypt in 1978, McNamara told me he had taken the decision to separate the Bank's approach from that of the Fund on his own; he had subsequently informed the secretary of the U.S. Treasury and received "total support." The IMF's managing director was, understandably, less effusive in his welcome of the decision, but accepted that the distribution of the different policy responsibilities between the World Bank and the IMF was a convention that was not set in stone, and could permit some flexibility.

I briefed Hamed al-Sayeh on my discussions with Washington and on the World Bank's position regarding the meeting of the Consultative Group. In return, he gave me a detailed account of where negotiations with the Fund stood, and the current cabinet position on them. It appeared that the cabinet was not happy with the pace at which reforms were expected to be implemented, and was still pondering how much leeway the state of the economy gave them to prolong the negotiations. The other complication was that Egypt wanted the first meeting of the Consultative Group of donors to be held as soon as possible, because such a meeting would be likely to produce a large commitment of assistance in one go, and Egypt would not have to live hand to mouth while going from donor to donor to scrape together its financial requirements for the year. In order for this meeting to be successful, the cabinet's view was that it was important to get a supportive statement from the IMF.

Sayeh arranged for me to meet Kaissouni and members of the economic group in the cabinet. We had a lively discussion, in which I was asked to present the World Bank's views, and also to lay out the pros and cons of the Fund's policy package. This was somewhat awkward. I was authorized to speak on the World Bank's behalf, but I had no such approval from the Fund. However, I presented the pros as best I could, and let the ministers argue the cons; there was no shortage of volunteers for this task. The next day Sayeh told me that, after much disputation and with considerable reluctance, the ministers had accepted that they had to go some distance with the Fund's proposals in order to ensure a "good statement" from it at the Consultative Group meeting.

The areas of major concern to ministers were the equity effects of the subsidy cuts and the danger of an economic slowdown triggered by a sharp drop in aggregate demand that might result from the steep cuts in budgetary expenditures. On the first issue, Sayeh said that they would try to negotiate a package of items on which the reduction of subsidies would impose the least burden on the poor. On the second issue, he said that the only outcome of the IMF package on which the ministers agreed was that it might be successful in curbing inflation. The ministers were clearly unhappy. Sayeh quoted Kaissouni as saying at the ministerial meeting that the Fund's "strategy" consisted of little more than pushing the economy into a recession in order to reduce inflation; this was like cutting off a patient's head in order to cure his headache. However, since the forthcoming Consultative Group would be the first of a series, the ministers felt that they had to start the sequence on an upbeat tone by getting strong endorsements from the key participants.

The budget announced on January 17, 1977 cut subsidies and increased the prices of several widely consumed commodities: rice 16 percent, gasoline 31 percent, cigarettes 12 percent, household cooking gas 46 percent, and sugar 3.3 percent. Cooper (1982, 236) reports estimates that the subsidy cuts would increase the cost of living for someone with an average income by at least 15 percent; this was in line with the World Bank's own findings. The public's reaction was immediate and ferocious. Riots erupted on January 18 and 19, the first that Cairo had witnessed since 1952. Official sources put the death toll at 73, with about 800 injured, and 1,270 arrested. Unofficial sources derided these figures and put the numbers two or three times higher. The army was called in, but it appeared on the scene only after the commander, General Gamasi, had been assured by the president that the price increases would be rolled back. A curfew was imposed, but the violence did not abate until the afternoon of January 20, after an official announcement that the price increases had been rescinded.

The United States ambassador, Hermann Eilts, a diplomat with outstanding experience in the Middle East and with exceptionally well-informed sources, told me that an acrimonious dispute had flared up in the cabinet over which individual or group should be held liable for the fiasco. His view was that the president would pin the blame on the ministers responsible for internal security. However, ministers in the economic group would be under close scrutiny, and it was unlikely that they would propose, or the president support, any major economic reform for at least the next twelve months.

He was correct—about three weeks later the minister of interior was replaced and economic policymaking became much more circumspect. I have described my discussion with Ambassador Eilts in more detail earlier in the book, and that account should be read in conjunction with the present remarks (see pages 59–60). The information he gave me was authoritative—some years after his retirement, when I met him at a conference in Washington, he told me that it was President Sadat who had informed him about his planned cabinet changes.

There is little doubt that the cutting of subsidies and other expenditures was mishandled. Given the economic and social circumstances of the country, too much was attempted too quickly. Some in the Fund attempted to deflect criticism by arguing that the *Letter of Intent* had been prepared by Egypt and represented a domestically-birthed reform program, not one imposed on the country. This idea was angrily brushed aside by Egyptian economists, journalists, and politicians. Ismail Sabri Abdallah (a former minister of planning), for example, derided the *Letter of Intent* as a government's suicide note, and said that one should question any government's grip on reason if it voluntarily poured itself a cup of hemlock and cheerfully quaffed it without extreme pressure from the Fund.

The outcome of this episode shocked the Fund; it certainly had not expected to see blood on the streets of Cairo as a result of its advice. It became properly contrite. In subsequent talks between the IMF and the Egyptian authorities, the question of subsidies was left unmentioned, the Fund displayed a more emollient attitude, and the first meeting of the Consultative Group duly took place in May 1977 with the IMF making a statement supportive of Egypt's development efforts.

After the riots, the economic group of ministers was roundly criticized in political circles. Members of the budget and planning committee of the People's Assembly said that the government had not considered the impact of the price increase on family budgets. Moreover, outside the main urban areas, sources of subsidized commodities were much fewer and sellers generally used their oligopolistic position to charge a premium over the official price. The entire pricing structure would now move sharply upwards and rural families, which accounted for the majority of the poor in Egypt, would be hit especially hard. The subsidy cuts would also have an adverse regional effect, because poor households were disproportionately located in Upper Egypt. Finally, in the view of committee members, the subsidy cuts showed that the government was poorly connected to the realities of Egyptian life, and the budget's actions had resulted not from "so-called economic rationality" but from political naiveté. Other commentators complained that the country had been made to pay a high price merely to teach the government an already well-known political lesson, namely, that people get very upset when their lunch is put at risk.

This was too severe a judgment. Salah Hamed (minister of finance in 1977) listed the steps that the economic ministers had taken to ascertain the views of different factions within the cabinet.

- They had conferred with individual ministers to ascertain their views on the subsidy cuts.
- There had also been a comprehensive discussion in cabinet concerning the number of commodities whose prices would be raised. The problem was that the Fund had specified a target for the overall budget deficit, and acting on a smaller number of items meant that the price increases for such items would have to be much steeper.[6] He further maintained that no minister at these discussions had disagreed with the decision.
- On the night before the budget announcement, the ruling party's caucus in the National Assembly had been consulted and had authorized the course adopted.
- The prime minister had informed President Sadat of the budget proposals, and the president had orally given his approval.

Salah Hamed said that no cabinet member had raised any serious objections or offered any practical suggestions at the time on how to tackle the budgetary problem; their cavils came strictly from hindsight. The budget problem essentially resulted from sharply rising expenditures on consumer subsidies and government salaries. The cabinet had proposed cutting some administrative expenditures and deferring salary increases, but Sadat had vetoed these proposals. The president possibly took this into account when deciding whom to blame for the fiasco. The economic ministers tendered their resignations, but the president did not accept them. He put the blame squarely on the Ministry of Interior, accusing it of having failed to first see that Nasserists, communists, and other anti-government elements were preparing to create instability in the country, and then of not being able to control the disturbances.

In a meeting that I had with the economic team, Kaissouni elaborated their thinking. He said that a political decision had been taken not to directly increase the burden on the people by raising taxes; hence the budget deficit would have to be reduced by cutting expenditures. The contractual expenditures, such as on salaries and debt servicing, were legally protected and could not be cut. The choices that the team was left with were to: (a) cut defense expenditure; (b) cut investment; (c) cut subsidies. The first was politically impossible; the second would compromise Egypt's growth prospects and, anyway, much of it was on projects that were already under way, and stretching out their timeframes would only increase the total cost and delay the benefits for the country; only the third option was available.

The cabinet thought that subsidies could be cut in a manner that did not impinge on the poorest elements of society and thus would not provoke a backlash. Therefore, the cuts left the subsidy on *baladi* bread (Egyptian flatbread, a national staple) untouched but fell on items such as French bread, fine flour, macaroni, beer, granulated sugar, and so on. He said that the cabinet had not fully realized the extent to which the consumption patterns of parts of the middle class had changed; for example, French bread was now commonly used by elements of the middle class to make lunch sandwiches. Indeed, Baker (1978, 167) reports one cabinet minister admitting that the strategy of cutting consumer subsidies in order to mollify the IMF had been faulty, but had been pushed through because "We are not trained politicians. We did not anticipate trouble." The 1977 riots were not predominantly an uprising of the poorest parts of Egyptian society (that part was not a huge consumer of French bread), although parts of the marginalized classes joined in once the disturbances had started. The primary protagonists were public-sector workers and students; in the words of Soliman (2011, 59), "the uprising was primarily the work of current and prospective civil servants."

Sadowski (1991) also points out that the rioters were, for the most part, industrial workers, students, and public sector employees protesting against the unfairness of the subsidy cuts, who were then joined by lower income groups. Gutner (1999, 18) comments that "Although the riots are commonly termed 'food riots,' they were in fact 'equity riots' since the underlying issues had more to do with the perception that the policy change was unfair, rather than the actual policy change itself."

The rescission of price increases had serious consequences for the budget. The initial budget for 1977 had incorporated a number of policies to bring down the deficit by some LE280 million. After the riots and the suppression of expenditure-cutting measures, the budget forecast an improvement of only LE45 million. As a result, Egypt would have to accept that the share of foreign financing in the budget would increase.

A much more important consequence of the riots was their durable effect on economic policymaking. For many years the fear of a repetition was almost inscribed onto the DNA of Egyptian policymakers. "It has become a given of Egyptian politics that the bread subsidy cannot be touched except at the peril of the regime. Bread has become the staff of life and the staff of regime survival," sums up Waterbury (1983, 230). Several other commentators concur; for example, Gutner (1999, 19) writes that "The infamous 1977 riots deeply unnerved Egyptian policymakers and left a legacy of government caution not only toward food policy reform, but economic reform more broadly." From 1977 until at least 2016, policymakers remained wary of directly touching the bread subsidy.

The 1977 riots further strained the already tense relationship between Egypt and the International Monetary Fund. For some time the two sides had appeared to be talking past each other—conducting bilateral monologues rather than a dialogue. The IMF argument, as was to be expected, had focused on technical matters—cut subsidies, increase revenues, decrease the budget deficit, rein in public-sector salaries, raise interest rates, depreciate the exchange rate, and so on—"eat your spinach," drily summed up a World Bank review of the Fund's proposals in a briefing for McNamara's 1978 visit to Egypt. All of it very standard, and most of it very unpalatable to the Egyptians. The Egyptian response was strategic rather than technical. The IMF's measures would produce social unrest, could fell the government, destabilize the largest Arab country and thus unsettle the region, and open the doors to extremists of all persuasions. There was little attempt to rebut the Fund's analysis; the retort was to hint at the dire consequences that might follow from acting on its recommendations. The government drove home its message by exerting pressure on the Fund through the U.S. State Department and the Treasury. Several examples have been given in this book to illustrate the point.

After the 1977 riots, both the IMF and the government became more circumspect on the question of subsidies. The draft letter of intent dated May 13, 1976, which was drawn up when an agreement between Egypt and the Fund appeared to be on the cards, was explicit about the government's intention to remove subsidies on a number of items and even specified a target of reducing food subsidies by LE100 million annually. The riots of January 18–19, 1977 put an end to prospects of an agreement, and the letter of intent remained unsigned. In March 1977, Egypt approached the Fund for a one-year standby arrangement. The request for this arrangement evaded commitment to any fiscal policy, contenting itself with a vague intent "to introduce further measures during the year," and skirted the question of subsidies; the wisdom of not committing to a date and a number had evidently been absorbed. A revised letter of intent (dated June 10, 1978) was signed the following year. In this letter the government offered no pledge to shrink the absolute amount of subsidies, but merely stated an intention to reduce their rate of growth (it did not say to what rate the growth would be reduced).

I have dealt at some length with the cabinet discussions and the negotiations between Egypt and the IFIs and the U.S. embassy, because of the important consequences that flowed from the bread riots of January 1977, and because of some confusing descriptions that have appeared of these events. Thus, for example, Tignor (2016, 140–41) describes Heikal as claiming that both Zaki Shafei, the minister of economy, and Abdel Aziz [sic] Kaissouni, the deputy prime minister in charge of economic affairs, opposed the recommendations of the IMF that led to the riots.

This requires some clarification. First, Zaki Shafei and Abdel Moneim el-Kaissouni were not in the same cabinet. The former was in the cabinets that took office on April 16, 1975 and March 19, 1976; the latter was appointed to the cabinet formed on November 9, 1976, from which Zaki Shafei had been excluded. Heikal may be conflating two separate sets of negotiations: one early in the second half of 1976 in which Zaki Shafei was involved, and the other in January 1977 when he was no longer in the cabinet, and in which Kaissouni was the deputy prime minister.

Second, the positions of both Zaki Shafei and Kaissouni when they were (separately) engaged in negotiations with the Fund were more nuanced. I have described my discussions with both ministers earlier in this chapter. My conclusion was that Zaki Shafei and Kaissouni were both unenthusiastic about the Fund's proposals that were presented to them (in July 1976 and January 1977 respectively), but neither was implacable in his opposition; indeed, the cabinet in which Kaissouni served accepted the Fund's conditions on subsidies.

Third, even though Kaissouni did have reservations about the Fund's proposals, unlike Abou Ismail, he did not make the political effect of the economic package the centerpiece of his argument. Keeping to economics weakened the force of his narrative and had the effect of diluting his opposition. By the time of the critical cabinet meeting, I had relayed McNamara's message to both Hamed al-Sayeh and Kaissouni that the World Bank would hold the first meeting of the Consultative Group for Egypt, whether or not the country had reached an agreement with the Fund. Hamed al-Sayeh told me later that although this had strengthened their hand and despite their misgivings about the effects of the IMF package, the ministers had decided to go along with the proposals in order to secure a supportive statement from the Fund at the forthcoming Consultative Group meeting.

Fourth, while the IMF, the World Bank, and USAID all wanted a reform of the subsidy system, their methods of trying to bring this about differed significantly. The IMF exerted direct pressure by making their resource transfer conditional on cuts to subsidies. The USAID, for political reasons, could not press directly and preferred to shelter behind the IFIs (see my discussion with Hermann Eilts, the U.S. ambassador, on pages 59–60). The World Bank, however, refrained from pressing Egypt on the question of subsidies and approached the matter indirectly, on the grounds that the division of responsibilities between the Bank and the Fund assigned fiscal matters to the remit of the latter institution. Perhaps, also, the World Bank's wounds from the Aswan High Dam fiasco were still raw, and it did not want to see itself cast as a villain in a repeat imbroglio with Egypt. Indeed, after the 1977 riots, the chairman of the National Assembly's Budget and Plan Committee stated categorically in newspaper interviews that there had been a clear difference between the attitudes of the IMF and the World Bank, with the latter favoring a more selective and gradual approach.

The Bank recognized that there was no magic bullet that would significantly reduce the subsidy bill and yet be painless in its effects. A memorandum noted that "one had to eat the elephant a bite at a time," and that one had to look for specific items on which subsidies could be cut while minimizing the pain for the most vulnerable elements in society. This meant working closely with the Egyptian authorities and examining the budget in detail to identify such items.

In meetings with the minister of finance and other relevant ministers, the Bank was able to persuade them that items such as *halawa* (a dessert), first-class travel on railways and airlines, and a number of special perks for higher bureaucrats did not merit subsidies and that the savings from eliminating them could be better used elsewhere. Cuts in these and some other items were effected, with savings from the preliminary exercise amounting to about $185 million. This initial step was not a huge figure (about 8 percent) compared with the total subsidy bill of $2.3 billion. However, it was only a first step; moreover, it procured $185 million more in savings than any other method had done, and it did not result in the burning down of large parts of Cairo or the killing and wounding of hundreds of protesters.

It is regrettable that the Egyptian authorities let themselves be hustled into enforcing a large cut to subsidies so as to "solve" the problem in one big stroke, rather than going through the unglamorous process of painstakingly identifying a number of smaller items that could have added up to the required amount. Many years later, Salah Hamed (the minister of finance in 1977) agreed that there was no "glorious road to the stars" so far as the subsidy issue was concerned, and his ministry should have followed the more pedestrian path.

Mobilizing Donor Support
The United States soon realized that since Egypt had been cut off for many years from major sources of funding, the scale of financing that the country required could not be met exclusively from the United States' aid budget. On the Egyptian side, some of President Sadat's advisers were uneasy that the degree of economic and military dependence on the United States could severely constrict Egypt's room for maneuver in the area of foreign policy. Thus, for different reasons, both the United States and Egypt were anxious to enlarge the circle of support. The expansion of donor efforts occurred in a number of ways.

The Möller mission
Together with the attempts to expand the group of donors for financial support, the Egyptian government also sought to widen the sources of economic advice. It reached out to agencies such as USAID, UNDP (the United Nations Development Program), and others. Some of the specialist international agencies—for example, the United Nations' Food and Agriculture Organization (FAO), the World Health Organization (WHO), or the United Nations Children's Fund (UNICEF)—provided valuable assistance on problems in their specialized areas. However, the government also wanted a more comprehensive survey of economic issues and recommendations for dealing with them.

Thus, in 1976 President Sadat turned to Germany's chancellor, Helmut Schmidt, for high-ranking advice on economic and financial policy. In response the chancellor sent a team of German experts led by former finance minister Alex Möller. The report was completed in June 1977 and submitted to President Sadat in September.

The Möller report ranged over many issues confronting the economy. Its underlying philosophy was: "Egypt needs a flexible mixed economy in which production would be largely steered by market-economy instruments." It thus largely endorsed the open-door policy, but noted that securing Egypt's economic future required "a departure from some deeply rooted traditions of the country." The most important of these were described as:

- a population policy and family planning program;
- a regional diversification program to counteract the concentration of industrial and commercial activity in the Greater Cairo and the Greater Alexandria areas;
- a willingness to delegate decision-making powers from the center to regional bodies, subordinate authorities, and self-governing institutions;
- a "streamlining" of the administration with the aim of making it contribute more to economic development.

The report identified raising the domestic savings rate as "the basic precondition required to put Egypt's economy on its feet and to reduce the share of external investment financing." This would require reducing the inflation rate to less than 10 percent and strengthening the confidence of investors.

It acknowledged that Egypt might never be able to forgo the subsidization of the most important food items, but described mechanisms (such as a "foodgrain compensation fund") whereby the impact on the budget over the long term could be moderated. The report also provided one of the earliest public recommendations for the project that was commenced in the late 1990s and has come to be known as the "Toshka" project. The report recommended that "all possibilities to create development regions outside the Nile Valley and the Nile delta should be exploited right now," and went on to specify as one of these regions "the New Valley, whose agricultural potential can be used if a canal link to the Lake is established" (Möller et al. 1977, 57, 124–25).

The Möller report and the reform of the economic decision-making structure

It does not take long for discussions on Egyptian development to turn to the question of government administration and coordination between the different arms of the administration. A weakness that many observers consider particularly detrimental to the country's development is the lack of integration between the plans of different ministries. This problem is a hardy survivor. Even in 2013, a study by the Japan International Cooperation Agency (JICA) complained about the "dispersal of plans and knowledge." Sakamoto (2013, 8) reported having found that "41 plans existed in various forms: 14 'plans,' three 'visions,' seven 'strategies,' and three 'programs,' among others. These 41 plans were individually drafted by ministries and other organizations, supported by international donors. The problem here was the absence of interrelation among them and linkage to the five-year plans, which should have acted as the guiding vision for each of the individual plans." He dismissed the national plan as "simply a concept paper that did not call for execution." And his summing up resonates with many other studies: "the problem with the (*sic*) planning in Egypt was the lack of its execution" (Sakamoto 2013, 9).

The issues highlight the fragmented nature of the decision-making process, the slowness and over-organization of the bureaucracy, and what Hansen and Marzouk (1965, 286) describe as "a destructive dependence on officialdom." The writers further avow that "if far-reaching reforms, nay revolutions, and improvements are needed anywhere in Egypt, it is precisely in the Government administration." To this, most observers of the Egyptian scene would respond with a fervent "Amen!"

The area in which the focus of the Möller report differed most from those of the World Bank, the International Monetary Fund, USAID, and similar organizations was its emphasis on reforms to Egypt's administrative structure. It is therefore worthwhile to examine the main recommendations and to see what became of them and why. This examination should highlight a lesson for (especially foreign) advisers: The content of a report is not by itself sufficient to ensure its acceptance. It must also be couched in a manner that is alive to bureaucratic sensitivities if it is to successfully negotiate its passage through a maze of often conflicting administrative interests. The medium can be as important as the message.

The Möller committee recognized that improving the formulation and implementation of plans and policies would require changes in Egypt's administrative structures and procedures. An important part of the Möller report and, as it turned out, one of the most contentious, consisted of a supplement that addressed this issue. The supplement (dated June 1977) was issued separately and treated as a confidential document because it was felt that its recommendations for reorganization would necessarily require the realignment of existing power relationships between ministries and thus might prove to be a touchy subject.

The core message of this part of the report was that Egypt was an "over-organized" country and it was necessary to simplify the administration. The report argued:

Care should be taken to see that the mistakes which have repeatedly been made in the course of numerous administrative reforms in the

last 25 years are avoided, namely, the creation of additional administrative units, committees, etc. which, in the last resort, only resulted
in an extension of the administrative apparatus. (Möller et al. 1977,
Supplement, 1)

The unwittingly ironical solution that the report proposed was more
administrative units: "the creation of an integral 'presidential' decision
and performance control structure which would enable a clear delinea-
tion of competences in the fields of planning, implementation control
and coordination within the huge administrative set-up." The report
recommended that "a competent Advisory and Planning Unit with administrative, political and international experience should be established with
the president; it would prepare the general planning framework and
the guide-lines for the development of the economy by formulating the
medium and long-term goal system and the basic policies required to
achieve these goals."

The report further suggested that the presidential economic and
developmental decision-making center should not confine its activities to
planning tasks alone, but should also control implementation. Much more
controversially, the recommendation was made that "the Advisory and
Planning Unit proposed here should help the President to control the performance of the government, that is, the performance of the Prime Minister
and the ministers in the achievement of the goals set by the President."

However sensible may have been the recommendations to restructure
the administration to harmonize the formulation and implementation of
development policies, the manner in which the recommendations were
put forward was, to say the least, inept. The prime minister was offended
because he felt that his actions were to be overseen by a committee of
bureaucrats and/or technocrats who had no political standing or experience. Ministers in the economic group were affronted and lost no time
in telling the World Bank that the recommendations were unacceptable,
because they would empower an unidentified committee, with unknown
expertise, of anonymous political standing, and under nebulous terms of
reference, to second-guess the workings of constitutionally established
ministries. These and other ministries vented their ire principally on the
Ministry of Administrative Development that was believed to be the chief
beneficiary of the restructuring, and hence suspected to be the main culprit pushing for the reorganization. The opposition of the economic and

other affronted ministries ensured that the report sank without the cabinet reaching a decision on its proposals.

"Well-intentioned but naive" was Kaissouni's dismissive verdict on the report when I met him in London after his retirement from the cabinet. He confirmed that he had told Sadat that there was nothing in the Möller report that the Egyptians had not already considered, and also that the report's recommendations for restructuring the administration were impractical. The president rarely bothered with administrative details and showed no interest in pursuing the issue. His only concern was that the matter should be handled in a manner that did not ruffle the Germans' feathers.

I asked Kaissouni if the attempt to improve the functioning of economic decision-making in Egypt and the implementation of these decisions was an inevitably doomed enterprise. He responded at length; in his view it boiled down to settling the clash of interests between different factions—in this case, ministries.

A significant change in the responsibilities of different ministries would alter the balance of power between ministers and hence affect their status in the cabinet. Those ministers who perceived themselves as being "demoted" would fight hard against such a change, using all their influence and that of their allies to resist it. Therefore, any major changes in the boundaries of ministerial responsibilities should be settled by the president at the time of appointing a new cabinet. Ministers would then know in advance what would be their real influence in the cabinet and they could decide whether or not to accept the office. This, Kaissouni said, was to some extent already the practice and its extension would not pose an insurmountable difficulty. The problem was likely to arise when the same incumbents were retained, but "the boundaries of their empires" shuffled around.

Ministers, however, were not the most important part of the problem. Much of the resistance came from the bureaucracy. The merging of ministries or the transfer of some of the responsibilities to others inevitably meant that the authority of senior bureaucrats in one ministry was enlarged while in others it was abridged. These measures had at times occasioned considerable resistance, foot-dragging, and reduced cooperation on the part of bureaucrats who felt they had lost out because of the change.

What was the answer? He thought that it would require a strong president who was informed about the details of the working of the administrative apparatus and who could thus settle the basic lines of authority and maintain them more or less unchanged (although some flexibility would always be necessary). However, most presidents did not have the interest or the time to immerse themselves in the minutiae of administration, so in practice much of the problem manifested itself in a struggle or negotiations between the prime minister and other ministers. President Sadat, in particular, had shown very little appetite for details of management.

Kaissouni said that as deputy prime minister for economic affairs he had adopted a more pragmatic attitude. He realized that the "economic ministries" should comprise more than just the ministries of finance, planning, economy, and economic cooperation over which he had formal authority. He had therefore adopted the practice of inviting to meetings of the economic group the ministers of petroleum, agriculture, industry, trade, and others whose portfolios had a direct impact on the economy. He had paid special attention to their concerns, with the result that an informal coalition of economic ministries had started to come together to collectively support policies and thus increase their chances of acceptance by the cabinet.

This, however, was a personal initiative. He could neither compel the other ministers to attend meetings of the economic group, nor could he be certain that ministries over which he did not have formal authority would carry out decisions that had been reached even at meetings in which these ministries had participated. In Kaissouni's view, the lines of authority would have to be made formal before these things could happen. All the ministers concerned with economic affairs should meet under the chairmanship of the deputy prime minister because the rules of business said that they had to, and not simply because they personally wanted to.

He said that by the end of his term in office the ministers of petroleum and agriculture consistently attended his meetings, and the minister of industry had also become a fairly regular attendee. These individual ministers had come to recognize that influence within the cabinet in support of a policy, particularly one that would be beneficial in the medium term but was not immediately popular, was multiplied if it came from a group rather than from an individual.

He regretted that the difficulties of coordinating the policies of different economic ministries had been made worse because some cabinet members were wont to give rein to populist over economically practical ideas. This, of course, could be because they had particular agendas to pursue. However, he took the more charitable view that it was because they did not have a proper grasp of economic matters.

Kaissouni provided an example of a problem that tended to recur. He said that people were particularly focused on the nominal exchange rate and considered that a devaluation of that rate was somehow a terrible thing. There was no understanding that what importers in other countries reacted to when deciding whether to purchase goods from Egypt was the effective exchange rate (the nominal rate adjusted for differences in inflation between Egypt and competing countries). There were periods when Egypt's inflation rate had far outstripped that of its competitors, but Egypt had kept the nominal rate unchanged. The result was that the effective exchange rate had been *appreciating*. It had proved difficult to convince fellow ministers (and the president) that the nominal rate had to be depreciated in line with the inflation differentials if Egyptian exports were to remain competitive. The result was that policymakers continued to talk of export-propelled growth, while ignoring the fact that the appreciating effective exchange rate was actually making exports more expensive! He wondered how many of his fellow ministers would buy something from a shop if they knew that they could purchase the same item next door at a markedly lower price.

Herr Möller was awarded the Grand Collar of the Nile by President Sadat for services to Egyptian economic development, but the president was totally uninterested in ascertaining the fate of the report's proposals. It seems clear that the president's motive for soliciting a report from Germany was to send a political message that Egypt did not depend for economic advice exclusively on the United States or on U.S.-dominated international organizations. A laundered version of the Möller Report, in particular excising the discussion of reforms to the administrative process, was published in Berlin in 1980 by the German Development Institute see (Möller et al., 1980). I have used the version of the Report given to President Sadat, rather than the published version, for two reasons. First, it was the presidential version of the Report on which policy action was expected; and second, the presidential version contains the Supplement on reforming the decision-making process, which has been expunged from the published document.

Several years later, Atef Ebeid (Prime Minister 1999–2004) offered a further comment on why the Möller Report's recommendation of the special unit would not have made any difference to the functioning of Egypt's administration or to the country's development. He pointed out that an elite unit, as recommended in the Report, would be too small to handle the nuts and bolts of administrative work and could only have been able to play an advisory role The principal weakness of Egypt's administration lay in implementation. This required daily interaction with the public of large numbers of civil servants, and unless their motivation was increased and they were provided with more and better training, there would be no increase in their efficiency. An elite unit overseeing the work of ministers might inflate the egos of the unit's members, but it would do nothing to improve Egypt's administration. In order to make a real difference, there really was no way of avoiding reforms that took in the bulk of the civil bureaucracy.

The Consultative Group

Egypt and its principal advocates also understood that it was imperative not only to increase the circle of financial support, but it to coordinate their efforts. The World Bank was thus asked to set up a consultative group of aid donors. The first meeting of this group was held in Paris in May 1977 and was attended by about twenty-five donor countries and institutions. The donors collectively had four interests: (a) increasing the quantum of assistance to Egypt; (b) easing the burden on individual donors by enlarging their number; (c) minimizing the duplication of donor projects and programs; and (d) setting conditions that would prevent Western assistance from being recycled by Egypt to repay its debt to the Soviet Union.

The Egyptian government's instructions to its delegation emphasized five strategic objectives for the Consultative Group meeting. The first was political. The participation of so many countries and institutions in the meeting would demonstrate to potential investors the wide range of support that Egypt was able to attract, and would confirm to the Egyptian public the success of the president's foreign policy. Second, it was to get at a single meeting an estimate of the external resources available to Egypt, and in what form (for example, for projects or programs) they would be committed. This would greatly cut down the uncertainty and reduce the delays in bilateral aid negotiation, a process that otherwise might occupy several months. Third, it was to try to obtain as large a portion of the assistance as possible in a quick-disbursing form. The delegation was to emphasize that project aid could remain unutilized if the domestic component of the financing requirement was not met, and program assistance provided Egypt a means of generating the domestic resources. Fourth, in order to avoid the country's sinking deep into debt, it was to make a case for assistance in the form of grants rather than loans. Kaissouni, the leader of the Egyptian delegation, said that his principal directive from Sadat was to obtain the required resources, but also to "ensure that Egypt's past does not become its future." Fifth, it was to "tell the story of the new Egyptian economic policies" to private-sector investors in developed countries, and to encourage them to invest in Egypt. Indeed, reaching out to the private sector gathered pace—the following year's gathering of the Consultative Group included special meetings and a lunch for private-sector participants.

The first meeting was extremely successful. Donors heard a detailed presentation from the Egyptian side on the principal economic issues that the country confronted and what it was doing to overcome the difficulties. This "getting to know you" part of the meeting was important. Egypt had been politically distant from Western countries and institutions for many years, and consequently most of the donors had little reliable knowledge of the country's economic situation. The Egyptian presentation and a comprehensive six-volume report by the World Bank helped in informing them.[7] Egypt was heartened by the amount of support that it received, with donors pledging $3.4 billion for the country's development for the coming year. Egypt was further encouraged that it received substantial support from countries other than the United States, principally from some of the European countries and Japan, and from institutions such as the OPEC Fund. The donors also agreed that the group should meet annually, so that Egypt would be assured of the continuity of support.

The G-7

Another attempt to spread the burden of providing economic assistance to Egypt was made by the United States in 1979. It put this item on the agenda for the meeting of the G-7 (the seven most industrialized countries in the free world) in Tokyo. Egypt was required to provide an estimate of amounts that it would need, together with a rationale to support the figures.

Meetings at the ministerial level do not call for overly technical submissions. At that level, policymakers from donor countries want, above all, a clear and persuasive storyline that resonates with their values. A credible document would have to contain: (a) an enunciation of a goal by the recipient country that would be politically appealing to the donors; (b) an assurance, buttressed by some evidence, that the recipient was doing its best to solve its own problems; and (c) an assessment of what the recipient could not accomplish despite its best efforts, and was thus calling upon the donors to provide in the shape of financial, technical, and other assistance, such as food aid, debt relief, cash, and so on.

The foregoing was a straightforward bread-and-butter exercise for a policymaking body. It was only a matter of formulating the overall goal and coordinating inputs from the ministries of Economy, Planning, Finance, and Trade, and the Central Bank of Egypt. This group would already have all the required information.

The outcome, to put it mildly, was disappointing. Representatives of the various agencies were more concerned with protecting turf than with coordinating the work with their colleagues. Other observers were also confounded by the result. McDermott (1988, 138–39) describes the submission—entitled "Statement of Policy and Requirements for External Assistance"—as "a travesty, full of inconsistent statistics (dollars and Egyptian pound signs were confused in places) and doubtful economic conclusions." The U.S. ambassador had advised that the apocalyptic strain in the narrative be toned down, but the ultimate content of the document was, of course, decided by the Egyptian authorities.

Needless to say, the donors were not impressed and nothing came of Egypt's aid request. The ministries of Economy and Foreign Affairs (who were managing the Egyptian submission) were embarrassed that a straightforward task had been bungled. It appeared that the officials in charge of the exercise had taken the assignment much too lightly; perhaps Ambassador Eilts's remark (quoted earlier) about some Egyptian officials regarding foreign aid as an entitlement might be relevant in this case. Another request at a summit meeting in Tokyo in 1986, at which Egypt appealed for the establishment of a Middle East development fund of $30 billion, also came to naught, possibly for similar reasons.

Toward a Strategy to Address Underlying Grievances

Hardly had the dust of the 1977 riots settled when the cabinet went into a huddle to work out an explanation of why the disturbances had occurred. These discussions were acrimonious, unfocused, and inconclusive. The flurry of finger-pointing between ministries to ensure that the blame for the disaster fell on anyone but themselves made it all but impossible to reach a consensus. Any explanation would have to be imposed ex cathedra.

President Sadat decided to pin the blame on communists and Nasserists (a move that was also likely to play well with the United States) and assigned responsibility for the law and order breakdown to failures by the Ministry of Interior and the security services. However, the absolution given to the economic ministries was not total—they understood that they would be held culpable should a similar outcome recur. The 1977 riots and the desire to avoid even the hint of a possibility of their repetition has made Egyptian policymakers extremely risk-averse to this day.

The 1978–82 Five-Year Plan

The economic ministries realized that although they had been reprieved on this occasion, they were unlikely to escape conviction if a comparable failure recurred. More than one minister said that a serious problem facing the cabinet was that the public did not believe the government's soothing pronouncements on the economy. The public's skepticism was warranted. McDermott (1988, 120) quotes Abdel Meguid, the deputy prime minister for economic affairs, reporting that Sadat had instructed him to "keep the picture rosy." Ironically, it was Abdel Meguid who, in the 1978–82 Five-Year Plan, offered the most candid assessment of the economy in an official document.

After the 1977 riots, the government recognized that it had to face up to the deep-seated public discontent and to assure people that the most serious causes of it would be resolved. The first order of business was to restore the government's credibility. It was therefore necessary to discuss more openly the economic problems that Egypt faced and to put forward an agenda for tackling them.

The People's Assembly at this time also held extensive discussions on the economic situation, and settled on the following as the principal aspects of the problem:

- inflation;
- the large deficit in the balance of payments;
- the inability of investment in national saving to meet the requirements of social and economic development;
- the difficulty of changing traditional habits of thinking that were detrimental to development;
- a decrease in manpower productivity;
- the increase in population;
- a shortage of administrative leadership in areas related to development.

As part of the response, it was decided that the 1978–82 Five-Year Plan should seek to restore the government's credibility by presenting a frank analysis of Egypt's economic predicament, point to the long-term nature of the solution, and suggest that the government, having correctly analyzed the problems, was moving to resolve them. The detailed plan (Ministry of Planning 1977) comprised fourteen volumes, with the first, entitled *The General Strategy for Economic and Social Development*, issued in August 1977.

The main author for the strategy volumes of the plan was Abdel Razzaq Abdel Meguid, who in May 1978 was appointed minister of planning and in May 1980 was promoted to deputy prime minister in charge of economic matters. For a government document, the 1978–82 Plan was refreshingly frank in its dissection of some of the major political and social issues, even if the analysis was at times colored with a tinge of special pleading and affected by a touch of amnesia. The reason for the schizophrenia evidently came from the desire to acquit the economic ministries of any responsibility for the events of January 1977.

"The unfortunate events of January, 1977 were precipitated by the irresponsibility of certain individuals, and aggravated by the enmity of others," was the opening sentence of the 1978–82 Plan. The document went on to argue that "the vast increase in the value of imports was the main cause of the economic problem" (Ministry of Planning 1977a, 10). It assigned the principal reason for the surge in the value of imports to increases in international prices. Having thus implicitly deflected the principal responsibility for the problem onto external agents, the document slurred over the economic issues that almost all observers held to be the chief culprits—the visible and growing income disparities, the grotesque conspicuous consumption by certain classes, the steep rise in the costs of housing that played havoc with family structures,[8] the obvious economic favors accorded to groups close to the presidency, the building up of Egypt's external debt and the foreign-exchange costs of servicing it, the contribution of huge budget deficits (28.4 and 21.3 percent of GDP in 1975 and 1976 respectively), and the monetization of these deficits to the rapidly rising inflation rate (the official Consumer Price Index in 1977 was about 50 percent higher than in 1974, and even this was a rather poor measure of the actual situation because of the large weight assigned within the index to commodities whose prices were fixed but were generally not available at those prices).

However, if one disregards these attempts at self-justification by the economic ministries, some of the broader economic and the political and social comments made in the document reflected a candor infrequently seen in government publications. In large measure they echoed the views of Abdel Meguid, the minister of planning, who succinctly defined as the essence of Egypt's economic problems that "her social and political responsibilities far exceed those domestic and foreign resources available to her" (Ministry of Planning 1977a, 2).

The authorities recognized that they had to mobilize a much larger amount of resources. In discussions with the World Bank, Abdel Meguid acknowledged the necessity, but was frank about the authorities' quandary: two crucial elements of the political-economy strategy—not antagonizing the domestic political base and avoiding external pressures—were in conflict. The former requirement meant that the authorities could not raise appreciable amounts of resources domestically; the latter that they could not *not* raise the necessary resources domestically. The authorities had to choose from two unthinkables. The choice generally tilted in favor of maintaining the support of the base, and trying to minimize the conditions on the resources obtained externally.

The document recognized some of the areas in which the results of the open-door policy had been very different from those intended.

> It was not intended that the private sector use the Open Door policy as a means to import luxury consumption goods, but this is in fact what has happened. Nor did the Open Door policy encourage the private sector to bid on land and buildings, but it did so, with huge support from foreign capital. Finally, the Open Door policy was not intended to promote class divisions, but this has happened. (Ministry of Planning 1977a, 13)

> Hundreds of thousands of wealthy Arabs come to Egypt, and around them has grown the parasitic class who enjoy increased incomes with little effort and no regulation. (Ministry of Planning 1977a, 14)

The document even questioned the merits of the subsidy system: "The question is whether the subsidies represent the best way to achieve social justice, to fulfill the social contract between the government and the people." The document pointed out that the subsidies were in fact the least effective method of fulfilling the social contract, "since the rich benefit equally with the poor," and that the benefits from subsidies were concentrated in urban areas (Ministry of Planning 1977a, 26–27). The plan criticized the "hidden subsidies," that is, providing items at less than their market price. It pointed out that even though these did not appear as subsidies in the national budget or in the accounts of the public sector, they nevertheless represented an increase in people's real incomes paid for by a loss in the government's potential revenue, and therefore were genuine subsidies. The document referred in particular to the domestic price of gasoline that was set far below its international level,[9] and to the difference between the cotton price paid to farmers by the government and the export price; this difference benefited the textile mills even though it did not show up in any account (Ministry of Planning 1977a, 25).

The analysis of social issues was particularly sharp. The plan did not consider the subsidies problem primarily as a financial issue; it looked at it "as substantially a social problem, basically that of redistribution of income" (Ministry of Planning 1977a, 29). It also suggested that the government should "treat the Egyptian people as mature adults and not as ineffectual dependents in need of a guardian" (Ministry of Planning 1977a, 30). It therefore recommended a new social contract by which subsidies on necessary commodities "could be redirected in favor of the low income groups, whose interests are the principal concern of the government's economic policies." It pointed out that

> Political wisdom recognizes the inherent danger in allowing the standard of living of the majority to continue to deteriorate, when they can see around them luxurious consumption and special privileges. It is only human that they should feel discontent, ambition and envy. (Ministry of Planning 1977a, 16)

Perhaps the best summing up of the plan's view on what was happening in Egyptian society is expressed in the following:

> More and more young people and workers perceive the contradictions of a socialist society which thinks with a capitalist mind, which takes from socialism and communism the concepts of public ownership, dominance of the public sector, guaranteed employment, education, services and social security, but neglects to take firm enforcement of civil authority or condemnation of the carelessness which decreases productivity. Similarly, the government has taken from capitalism the features of consumption and interclass mobility, the concept of the importance of the individual and of historical

tradition. But it has not adopted from the capitalist system the stringency of market competition or the responsibility of the firm for quality control, upon which depends the success or failure of the firm.

The end result is a society lacking in discipline or supervision: distribution without production, promises without obligations, freedom without responsibility. (Ministry of Planning 1977a, 19)

Abdel Meguid said that there had been considerable discussion in the cabinet about the stance to take regarding the 1977 disturbances. There was a group that wanted to simply blame everything on communists, Nasserists, and *agents provocateurs* and to write off the whole episode as a failure of security. President Sadat seemingly leaned toward this view, as evidenced by his actions in dropping the minister of interior in the cabinet reshuffle. However, the withdrawal of the price increases and the caution with which the cabinet reacted to subsequent proposals from the IMF suggested that the president also recognized that people really had grievances and that these had to be resolved. Abdel Meguid thought that if he could put some forthright analyses of the social dissatisfaction into the plan and get Sadat to sign off on it, some of the government's credibility would be restored, and policies to address the underlying issues could progressively be introduced. He did manage to include in the document a certain amount of candor on how several elements of society had been hurt and had become disillusioned, and where the infitah had been misused. However, diagnosing the illness was one thing; applying the remedy quite another. The president may have signed off on the plan, but he made no effort to implement policies that would have addressed the social and distributional issues, or to rein in the excesses of the private sector. It was, once again, a case of wanting the ends, but not providing the means.

The actual implementation of the "open-door" strategy proceeded in fits and starts. A new economic order replacing Nasser's étatist economy had not been established even by the end of the Sadat era. Implementation of the strategy was in part watered down because key ministers remained opposed to the new direction or were only half-hearted converts. And in large part it arose from contradictions between the politics and economics of the regime.

There was general agreement in the regime in favor of a more open economy, but none on which groups would bear the burden of moving toward it. As Hinnebusch (1988, 257–58) noted, the regime could not go back to authoritarian means of reform, "equally and strictly disciplining the appetites of all social forces and carefully tailoring *Infitah* to serve planned development objectives." The degree of authoritarian control required would have antagonized the very constituency from which infitah drew its support. It also could not undertake a totally free-market strategy, because (among other things) the enforced competition on a level playing field and the elimination of economic rents would have alienated the vested interests that supported the regime, while the impact on prices and employment would have created a tidal wave of popular anger. The regime, therefore, resorted to the easier option of relying on foreign aid to fund the country's development.

For a number of years after the announcement of the infitah Sadat walked a tightrope—liberalizing parts of the economy and encouraging foreign private investment while denying that the new policy was either a return to the pre-revolutionary brand of capitalism or that it represented a move away from social control of the basic means of production. Hinnebusch (1988, 257) provides a reason for the muddle: "aside from agreement on the desirability of a more mixed and open economy, the elite possessed no coherent shared conception of the goals or means of reform." The lack of clarity within the cabinet concerning the vigor with which the new route ought to be followed is reflected in the manner in which for several years the policy was portrayed in official pronouncements as being compatible with socialism. The discussion in Ministry of Planning (1977b, 7–13) offers a good example, and Dessouki (1982, 75) writes that it was only in 1979 that President Sadat felt able to tell representatives of industry and commerce that capitalism was no longer a crime in Egypt.

The thinking that informed the strategy proposed in the plan reflects an important facet of political economy. Nelson (1990, 29) points out that "responses to economic crises . . . are strongly influenced by the intellectual lenses through which economic advisers and political leaders perceive the crisis and the available options." Egypt's economic managers perceived the ills of the economy to be short-term and not structural, and such as could be cured fairly quickly by an infusion of financial resources. This also explains the emphasis on aiming for Arab funds. These funds were likely to be mobilized more quickly than those from other sources, and would not impose distasteful policy conditions on Egypt. The 1978–82 Plan confirms such an interpretation, pointing out that policymakers thought

in early 1975 that the crisis of the Egyptian economy was temporary, resulting from insufficient liquidity and a temporary deficit
in the balance of payments because of international developments.
From this point of view, it was logical that efforts should be concentrated on seeking liquid resources from abroad without changes in
domestic economic structure and general policy. (Ministry of Planning 1977a, 5)

Thus, in the years immediately following the *October Paper* the authorities viewed the economic problem principally as a stabilization issue to be
addressed through conventional demand-management instruments, with
funds from Arab countries used to insulate the population from some of
the pressures of adjustment. The economy's difficulties were regarded as
resulting primarily from liquidity shortages, and not from structural distortions. As the *Five-Year Plan for 1978–82* put it, "Until recently, economic
policies have emphasized foreign aid and the reduction of spending instead
of regulating and reorganizing the economic structure of the society"
(Ministry of Planning 1977a, 5–6).

The plan thus identified several of the most important problems confronting Egypt. However, it did not, indeed perhaps could not, articulate the
ultimate problem. The ultimate problem was that the country's trio of fundamental objectives—political, social, and economic—were irreconcilable.

The political aims included maintaining a military confrontation
with Israel; prosecuting a war in Yemen (in effect against Saudi Arabia);
acting as a leader of the "nonaligned" group of countries; championing the anti-colonial movement in Africa; and confronting the Western
countries which then cut Egypt off from their concessional resources
and modern technology. The social objectives were to set up a welfare
state with a wide range of consumer and other subsidies, together with
guaranteed employment and free education and health care. The economic objectives were to accelerate economic growth, which required
a high level of investment and therefore of savings. However, the economic objective clashed with the simultaneous pursuit of another goal,
namely, to increase the consumption level of the population. The latter
goal could not be compromised because the regime's very existence was
founded on a social compact with the populace whereby the latter surrendered political rights in exchange for a certain level of living sustained by
government subsidies. Waterbury (1985, 69) offers the same conclusion:

"Egypt's social contract . . . is centered on the commitment of the state to provide goods and services to the public in exchange for political docility and quiescence."[10]

Egypt may have been able to attain a limited number of the social, political, and economic goals without overstraining its economy; achieving the totality of the objectives was well beyond the capacity of its resource envelope. However, there was never any serious discussion in the cabinet about possible trade-offs—how much one set of objectives should be curtailed in order to achieve some more of another. The simultaneous pursuit of all the objectives only drove Egypt into further external borrowing and domestic inflation. The various contradictions became especially critical when resources became tightened because of decreasing foreign inflows (for example, with the collapse of oil prices in 1986) and rapidly increasing military expenditures. Egypt's goals far exceeded its means, and it is no wonder that the quest made the economic system crack at the seams.

The explanations for the political-economy behavior of successive Egyptian regimes provided by Baker (1978, 167), Cooper (1979, 482–84), Roy (1980, 3–9), McDermott (1988), Springborg (1989), Waterbury (1983, 1985), Hansen (1991, 116–17; 1993, 250–54), Wahba (1994), Soliman (2011), Kandil (2012), and others all essentially boil down to the following paraphrase.

Egypt's regimes have lacked the legitimacy conferred by a free election. They therefore have had to placate—(Kandil [2012, 64] says "bribe," and Baker [1978, 167] bluntly describes the subsidy program "as a form of material incentive to secure mass loyalty to the regime") the population to refrain from overturning the regime. These inducements drove continuing increases in public consumption expenditure, because they required providing a rapidly expanding population with subsidized bread, flour, cooking oils, sugar, and other consumption items (at times even cigarettes and dessert were subsidized); free health care; free education at all levels; subsidized fuel and transport; subsidized electricity; guaranteed government employment for graduates, thus creating a hugely overstaffed bureaucracy with all its attendant ills; and the list goes on.

Regimes also had to be careful not to risk unpopularity by burdening the population with taxes. They therefore relied heavily on economic rents, especially those that impacted most strongly on foreigners. Such rents included Suez Canal dues; higher prices for travel, hotel stays, and access to tourist sites for foreigners than for Egyptians; foreign aid (that is, taxes on foreigners); and the pricing of oil exports.

The political-economy bias that favored the interests of consumers over those of savers was reflected in continuing budget deficits and the maintenance of an overvalued exchange rate. These resulted in an investment rate that was too low to propel the GDP at a rate that would create the number of jobs required by an ever-expanding labor force, discouraged exports, and compelled Egypt to continually resort to borrowing resources from abroad. Problems of servicing the external debt led to a succession of crises on the external accounts, and kept the country subject to outside pressures.

Egypt's rulers may have found the political-economy strategy satisfactory in supporting regime survival—the country was ruled by only three presidents for almost sixty years from 1952 to 2011—but the economic cost, inflicted by the economy performing well short of its potential, was high.

6

Political Economy in the
Mubarak Period, 1981–2011

After the assassination of President Sadat on October 6, 1981, the vice-president, Hosni Mubarak, was sworn in as president on October 14, 1981. Mubarak's incumbency was the longest of any Egyptian ruler since the revolution of 1952; he resigned on February 11, 2011 in the face of a popular revolt.

This period of almost thirty years saw several developments in the economy, which responded to different political and economic stimuli. Because of the length of Mubarak's rule, and in order not to become too absorbed with the trees and thus lose sight of the forest, it might be useful to begin with a brief overview of the economy's performance during the three decades, before focusing on the major durable political-economy initiatives.

Overall Performance

Over the three decades of the Mubarak era, GDP growth averaged about 4.8 percent a year, which was in line with the average for the entire 1965–2015 period. The growth rate, however, fluctuated a good deal. Over the period as a whole, the coefficient of variation (a measure of the fluctuation compared with the average) was about 135 percent. There were two relatively brief episodes in which GDP growth would have been sufficiently brisk to employ all the additions to the labor force—in 1982–85, when it exceeded 6 percent a year, and in 2006–2008, when it was around 7 percent a year. (Most estimates of the GDP growth required to provide jobs for all the additions to Egypt's growing labor force and to reduce the backlog of existing unemployment put the figure at about 7 percent a year.)

The ratio of investment to GDP averaged 21.7 percent, higher than the average for 1965–2016, but still insufficient to sustain GDP growth at rates that would create jobs for the expanding labor force. There was a major change in the sources of investment. With the private sector assigned a progressively larger role, the share of public investment in the total began to fall and the share of private investment reached a level roughly equal to that of public investment in 1989. It dropped quite sharply after that, partly because of unsettled political conditions in the region and partly because of uncertainties over Egypt's macroeconomic situation. The public and private investment series more or less converged in 1999 and remained within one percentage point of GDP of each other until 2005; thereafter, private-sector investment outpaced that of the public sector, and until the end of the Mubarak era in 2011 it accounted annually for around two-thirds of total gross fixed capital formation.

The change in the fortunes of the two sectors did not result from private-sector investment increasing rapidly and swamping public investment. The changeover came about because while private investment, despite fluctuations, exhibited a slow but fairly steady upward trend, public investment tailed off sharply. In 2011 public investment was only about one-quarter of the share of GDP that it had been in 1982, while the share of private investment had risen by about one-third. However, from 1993, when the Economic Reform and Structural Adjustment Program (ERSAP, discussed later in the chapter) began to change the roles of the public and private sectors, total investment continued to hover around 20 percent of GDP. In short, private investment appears to have expanded by occupying the space vacated by the public sector; for virtually the entire period it did not exceed 15 percent of GDP. Thus the private sector responded, but not spectacularly, to the incentives offered (see figure 17). Some of the reasons for the behavior of private investment, such as the state of the business environment and crony capitalism, are discussed in the final chapter of the book.

The savings rate, at 14.3 percent of GDP, was a little higher than the 13.5 percent average for the fifty years 1965–2016, but still much less than the investment rate, and Egypt had to borrow substantial sums from abroad to finance the deficit in the external accounts that averaged 7.6 percent of GDP over the Mubarak period. As a consequence, external debt, disbursed and outstanding, increased from $19 billion in 1980 to $36.5 billion in 2010, even though Egypt received packages of debt forgiveness and rescheduling amounting to $5.7 billion in 1987–88 and close to $20 billion in 1991–93.

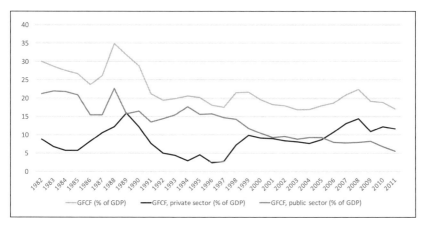

Figure 17. Public and private gross fixed capital formation, 1982–2011 (percent GDP)

The biggest weakness in the macroeconomic situation resulted from the budget deficit. Virtually every IMF report, even when it commended policy actions taken by the government, continued to point to the necessity of greater "fiscal consolidation" and the reduction of the budget deficit. The Fund's recommendations and technical assistance were not overly successful; during the Mubarak period the deficit remained very high, averaging more than 8 percent of GDP. This contributed to the rise in inflation, particularly after 2004. The reader should be reminded that the official Consumer Price Index understates the true inflation rate because of the weight of subsidized items in the index, which in fact are not always available at the subsidized price.

Fiscal and balance-of-payments performances reflected the old political problem. Revenues continued to depend to a large extent on "exogenous sources" and thus fluctuated according to developments in the international economy and to decisions taken outside Egypt. Public expenditures, on the other hand, moved in line with domestic inflation and thus could only go up. This was almost the only way in which the implicit political compact between the rulers and the ruled could be maintained.

The external accounts were a source of concern, to which the mounting external debt bore vivid testimony. The problems on the balance of payments resulted in large part from Egypt's maintaining, through exchange-rate and trade-protectionist measures, an anti-export environment. The politically dominant business faction continued to be that of importers and consumers, not of exporters and savers. A serious effort to change this environment began in 2004, but was short-lived, since the international financial crisis supervened in 2008.

Sectoral performance was lackluster. Value-added in agriculture increased at 3 percent a year, only a little more than population growth. Value-added in industry grew at an annual rate of 4.8 percent, thus gradually changing the structure of the economy. Between 1981 and 2011, the share of agriculture in GDP fell from about 20 percent to 14.5 percent, while that of industry (including petroleum) increased from about 32 to 37 percent.

Mubarak's Philosophy of Political Economy of Reform

The conduct of economic policymaking in the Mubarak period might be understood better if set in the context of the president's approach to policy reform.

President Hosni Mubarak was known for his cautious approach to change. Let me summarize my minutes of a lengthy meeting in 1996 between President Mubarak and James Wolfensohn, the president of the World Bank. At this meeting, the Egyptian president provided a clear account of his view of the dynamics of policymaking and the pace of reform, and explained why he favored a gradualist approach.

> President Mubarak said that the imperatives of Egypt's situation mandated irreversible reforms in the direction of a market-oriented economy. One of the key characteristics of the twenty-first century would be the lowering of trade barriers and the greater integration of countries into a global economic system. His responsibility was to prepare Egypt to be successful in this fiercely competitive environment, and for that he would require resources for investment in new technology, in education and training, in financial restructuring, and in upgrading management. These resources would not be available if the public sector continued to act as a drain on the budget. Its role would therefore have to be restrained and the private sector would have to play the preeminent part in the economy.
>
> However, the president stressed that progress toward this goal was likely to be slower than Mr. Wolfensohn might like to see. This was because, for the reforms to be irreversible, public opinion had to be carefully prepared so that it would accept them. It was especially important that the government not announce a package of reforms from which it might have to back down. Retreat would erode people's

confidence in the government's seriousness about subsequent efforts, and each sequential failure would exponentially increase the damage. If the government climbed down from its announced measures, it would be seen to be weak ("opponents would smell blood") and this would be certain to incite demands for further concessions.

On the other hand, the successful implementation of one set of reforms made it easier to convince the public that the government was serious, and this facilitated the acceptance of subsequent steps. President Mubarak cited as a case in point the successful acceptance of the reforms conducted by his government in 1991–93, although they had been far more demanding than those attempted by President Sadat in 1977. Because the ground for the 1977 proposals was not carefully laid, even those less burdensome measures had to be rescinded, and serious reforms could not be ventured for many years. But because in the early 1990s his (President Mubarak's) government invested a good deal of effort in convincing the public of the necessity of reform, the measures of 1991 and subsequent years had found acceptance. Reforms could only "stick" if public opinion remained persuaded of their benefits.

The president pointed to another benefit of his step-by-step methods. One could add reforms gradually, and if they were opposed, one had the ability to selectively withdraw only those that had given rise to the opposition. The rest of the reforms could remain in place. On the other hand, if all the reforms were proposed as a single suite (as in the Big Bang approach), in case of unrest one would not know which elements the public had found the most distasteful, and the entire package would have to be withdrawn. This had happened with Sadat's 1977 measures. As was the case in 1977, the country would be pushed back to square one, and the public would be confirmed in the view that it could at one stroke compel the repeal of a whole package of policies.

President Mubarak said that Egypt's experience with the two approaches convinced him that reforms must be conducted at a deliberate pace and supported by measures to moderate the harshest effects on society. Therefore, donor countries and institutions wishing to see sustained economic reform in Egypt should not simply pontificate about what should be done, but should also be ready to help finance the "cushion" that would inevitably be required. He was grateful to the World Bank and other donors for financing the Social Fund for Development, which served as a shock absorber for his government's reforms. He summed up by expressing his faith in (the Arabic equivalent of) the saying: "More haste, less speed."

It is difficult to say whether, in part at least, the content and tenor of the president's remarks were constructed for the benefit of an international audience. However, President Mubarak's cautious approach to reform can actually be seen in several policies, for example, the handling of the bread subsidy. The price of the basic loaf of bread had remained at one piaster per loaf for almost twenty years, even though the cost of making it had steadily increased and now exceeded the sale price. The chief trigger for the 1977 riots was the increase in the price of bread. Egyptian policymakers were unwilling to risk a repetition of those events, and yet something had to be done because the bread subsidy formed the chief element of the total subsidy bill (which, in turn, was a major contributor to the budget deficit).

The policy response was, as Sadowski (1991, 165) put it, "reform by stealth." A foreign diplomat termed it more bluntly as "the frog in hot water" strategy. He referred to the observation that if a frog is put in a bucket of water that is heated slowly, the animal will not try to escape for some considerable time because it becomes accustomed to the gradually increasing temperatures. However, if the frog is dropped into water that is already quite hot, it will show its displeasure and react immediately.

The quality of the one-piaster loaf was made to gradually deteriorate and the loaf itself was made smaller and increasingly hard to obtain. In 1981 the government introduced a new loaf of better quality that cost two piasters. The public began switching to the new loaf and in 1985 the government could stop the production of the one-piaster loaf without provoking an adverse reaction from the public, most of which had by now transferred to the two-piaster version. This strategy was continued. Sadowski (1991, 165) lists some of the changes. In 1986, the two-piaster loaf that had weighed 169 grams was reduced to 135 grams, and in 1988 the wheat content of the two-piaster bread was further cut by 20 percent. The stealth strategy—reducing the quality, in some cases the quantity, and offering a better-quality but more expensive substitute—was also applied to other subsidized goods, such as gasoline and cigarettes.

The slow and hesitant approach to policy adjustment was much in evidence in 1987–91 even though the economy faced a financial crisis.

The minutes of meetings and the memoranda of the discussions between Egypt and the IFIs during this period often reflected exasperation on the part of the latter, who did not understand why Egypt was delaying necessary reforms. Asked one note: "Is there a strategy, other than that of just buying time? And if time is being bought, what is it for?" Another memorandum said that the only "strategy" that could be discerned from discussions with the Egyptian authorities was that of the Charles Dickens character Mr. Micawber, namely, "Something will turn up." And, by chance, at times something does turn up—for example, the Gulf War of 1990–91 in which Egypt sided with the Western powers and Saudi Arabia against Iraq, and consequently was granted an extremely generous package of aid and debt relief. This development resolved the debt crisis that had become very serious from 1987 (see later in this chapter.) Fortuitous episodes such as this only hardened Egyptian policymakers' conviction in the correctness of their attitude and created a belief that history had endorsed their rectitude.

The drawn-out negotiations in 1987–91 led critics to doubt Egypt's commitment to reform. Richards, for example, was particularly scathing on Egypt's "dilatory reform" and the country's negotiating tactics with international agencies. He wrote:

> One tactic was to promise much and to deliver little: The GOE [government of Egypt] constantly promised "bold new reforms" throughout the economy; it actually did little in comparison with the IMF's recommendations and even less in comparison with the magnitude of the economic problems facing the country in the 1990s. Negotiating tactics included "numbers games," "smoke-screens," and "musical ministers." . . . The government created interministerial committees with overlapping jurisdictions to confuse outsiders—no one knew who was really in charge (if, indeed, anyone was). . . . World Bank and IMF teams often met with the GOE negotiating team composed of four or five ministers, all of whom disagreed with each other; the composition of the team changed from day-to-day, as "important business" took one member away, leading to his temporary replacement with someone else. Such tactics helped to postpone a break with the IMF, buying time for Mr Mubarak to persuade Mr Bush to call Mr Camdessus [the managing director of the IMF]. (Richards 1991, 1727)

Sentiments recorded in memoranda of the IFIs ricocheted between exhortation and despair. One paper advised that when contemplating a potentially unpopular policy, it was best to do it quickly and get it over with. Hesitation would allow the issue to fester, while the inevitable leaks to the press would allow opposition to build up and possibly compel the policy to be aborted. At one point, when it appeared that the Egyptians were teetering on the verge of agreement, one of these notes urged Egypt to recognize its "Macbeth moment" and went on to quote the Bard, "If it were done when 'tis done, then 'twere well/It were done quickly." On the other hand, when it became clear that the Egyptians would not move in a hurry, a back-to-office memorandum by an IFI official engaged in some marathon negotiations wailed that his tombstone would bear an epitaph from Rudyard Kipling's *The Naulahka*, "A fool lies here who tried to hustle the East."

Nevertheless, the gradualist approach brought Egypt a number of dividends in the stabilization process of the 1990s. The IMF, for example, commended the privatization measures of the 1990s reforms as a successful example of a deliberate and inclusive approach. The IMF's seal of approval was displayed in a major report (1998, 54–55): "Labor participation in and endorsement of the program of privatization was seen as essential to its success, as evidenced by the lack of social discontent in the face of employment reductions." Labor participation took a variety of forms, initially that of selling minority stakes to Employee Shareholder Associations (ESAs). The IMF offered several reasons for believing that sales to ESAs were an efficient mode of privatization. It also noted that the financial performance of the companies sold to ESAs improved substantially after privatization, which supported the view that ESA sales led to the efficiency gains that were a central object of the privatization program. Egyptian officials maintained that the success of these reforms derived from the careful preparation that had gone into them, and regarded the IMF's remarks as an endorsement of the government's measured approach.

In the course of Mubarak's three decades, it is to be expected that the authorities had to enact several short-term policies. The period, however, was dominated by three big issues—external debt pressures, economic stabilization, and the privatization of state-owned enterprises—which elicited reforms that had major and durable effects, and a fourth—crony capitalism—that was not touched. I must again remind the reader that while it may be convenient to discuss these three topics separately, many of their elements were intertwined with, and fed off, each other. Thus, for example, the debt forgiveness and rescheduling that alleviated external debt pressures also reduced the domestic financing requirements, thus lowering the budget deficit and forming a key element of the stabilization effort.

External Debt Issues

The Mubarak period saw two phases of growth in external debt. Between 1981 and 1990, external debt grew at a rapid pace, averaging 9.6 percent a year; for most of the period the removal of restraints on consumption by the infitah continued to take its toll. In the second period, 1991–2015, the growth was barely 1.5 percent a year because of the effects of the rescheduling agreements and Egypt's policy of holding down fresh borrowings.

The rising stock of debt was a source of disquiet to policymakers, but of even more concern was the rise in the debt service requirements. The debt service ratio (the annual debt service due as a proportion of foreign-exchange earnings) rose steadily and quickly. There are no universal formulae to define at what point these ratios become critical; the World Bank uses a guideline of 25 percent as a point beyond which the alarm bells are readied to sound.

External Debt Problems, 1981–90

After the assistance from GODE in 1977 had rescued Egypt from its immediate financial crisis, the country continued to borrow heavily—between 1982 and 1987 external indebtedness increased by about 50 percent, and debt service obligations tripled. By 1988, total external debt exceeded $45 billion, and the debt-to-GDP ratio reached 175 percent. While payment requirements increased, resources to make these payments fell. Egypt's export earnings relied excessively on a single commodity, namely, oil, and the average price that Egypt received for its oil (weighted according to the prices received and the shares contributed by each oilfield in exports) dropped by 20 percent from $33.6 per barrel in 1981 to $26.4 per barrel in 1985, and collapsed further to $13.5 in 1986—halving from the price of the preceding year. To add to the policymakers' difficulties, tourism receipts in 1986 dropped by 23 percent compared with a year earlier, because riots that took place in February and involved members of the security forces raised questions about the security situation in the country. The uncertain oil-price situation also discouraged the flow of remittances from Egyptians working in the Gulf countries—the pressure on the Egyptian balance of payments raised the prospect of a devaluation of the Egyptian currency, and created an incentive to defer remitting until after the probable currency adjustment. Combined receipts from oil, tourism, and remittances in 1986 and 1987 were respectively 19 and 30 percent lower than in 1985, and total foreign-exchange earnings fell 15 percent between 1985 and 1987.

Servicing the debt became impossible. Total debt service (including arrears) due in 1986 exceeded 100 percent of current-account receipts— Egypt would have had to set up a Ponzi scheme whereby new debt would have to be incurred in order to pay off old debt.

After a series of intense negotiations with creditors, Egypt reached an agreement with the Paris Club in May 1987. Under this agreement, outstanding arrears of $6.9 billion were rescheduled, together with $4.4 billion of interest and amortization payments on public medium- and long-term loans falling due until June 30, 1988. The creditors also agreed, in principle, to meet the Egyptian authorities to consider debt service payments falling due after June 1988. However, this latter part of the agreement was contingent on Egypt's fulfilling a number of conditions, such as maintaining an arrangement with the IMF (which was expected to provide discipline on the budget, credit expansion, and the exchange rate), securing comparable treatment from non–Paris Club creditors, and so on. It suggests that even the official creditors were running out of patience and were determined to keep Egypt on a short leash.

Egypt could not be expected to embrace such conditions with any eagerness, and whatever synthetic enthusiasm it was able to manufacture soon fizzled out. With oil exports and tourism recovering in the second half of 1987, and having obtained some immediate relief from the debt agreement, Egypt did not fulfill many of the conditions, and a meeting with the creditors in the following year did not come about.

The next round of negotiations on Egypt's debt did not take place until four years later, and was driven by a vastly changed political dynamic. Egypt and the creditors approached these negotiations with a much heightened degree of seriousness. The outcome of these negotiations and of Egypt's much more disciplined approach to managing its external accounts slowed down the growth of external indebtedness to less than 1.5 percent a year between 1990 and 2015, compared with 9.6 percent annually between 1981 and 1989 (and 22.0 percent a year between 1970 and 1989). The next section describes these events.

External Debt Travails, 1991–93

The incentive system continued its anti-export bias. Between 1982 and 1987, the real effective exchange rate appreciated by 32 percent; this was in addition to the 28 percent that it had appreciated between 1970 and 1982. The World Bank reported several other impediments to export: exporting firms had to navigate their way through numerous administrative encumbrances, complicated and time-consuming duty drawback schemes, bank guarantees, travel allowances, export credit insurance, and procedures for the transfer of export proceeds. All these matters impacted with particular severity the country's non-oil exports.

By 1990, Egypt's foreign-exchange earnings had still not picked up sufficiently and the country had continued to borrow on hard terms. The external debt situation once again began to edge toward the unmanageable. Once again, a political event intervened to rescue the country from its financial predicament. In August 1990, Iraq invaded and occupied neighboring Kuwait, and rejected United Nations demands to withdraw. In response, a number of Western and Arab countries formed a coalition to eject the Iraqi forces. The Gulf War, as this conflict came to be known, lasted from August 2, 1990 until the coalition declared a cease-fire on February 28, 1991, after comprehensively defeating the Iraqi army.

President Mubarak took the decision to have Egypt join the Western-led coalition. The decision was more political than military. The fighting was done mainly by Western troops, but Egypt's participation was politically important in showing that the conflict was not simply a case of the West versus Arabs.

After the 1991 Gulf War, there was a meeting of minds between the principal donors and Egypt. The donors were prepared to reward Egypt for participating in the war on their side, and offered very generous terms for writing off and rescheduling Egypt's external debt. They were also ready to help restructure Egypt's economy to make it more efficient. The principal drag on the economy was identified as the public-sector enterprises, in which about one-third of the labor force was judged to be redundant. The high labor costs squeezed the resources available for investing in new technology, training labor, and implementing other measures to enhance productivity.

Restructuring these enterprises or privatizing them would inevitably involve a reduction of the labor employed. The donors offered to help finance the Social Fund for Development, which would pay for the retraining of workers who would lose their jobs as a result of privatizing public enterprises, and for helping them to set up small and micro enterprises. A large package of resource transfer in the form of debt write-off, rescheduling, and fresh assistance was put together to be provided on condition that Egypt completed the Economic Reform and Structural Adjustment Program (ERSAP).[1]

There were two important differences in Egypt's attitude toward the ERSAP as compared with earlier reform programs. First, Egypt showed a determination to exit the recurring cycle of external indebtedness and vulnerability to foreign pressures. Youssef Boutros-Ghali, who was responsible for much of the technical work on the Egyptian side, said President Mubarak's overriding instruction to the economic team was to negotiate an agreement that would quickly trigger the debt relief arrangements offered by the Paris Club, but also in which the reform conditions would not impose excessive hardship on the country. Second, in addition to having the firm backing of the president and clear terms of reference, the Egyptian team (Kamal al-Ganzoury, Atef Ebeid, Mohammed Ahmed al-Razaz, Salah Hamed, and Youssef Boutros-Ghali)[2] was experienced, technically strong, and politically adept, and more than able to hold its own in the negotiations.

The terms of the arrangements that were arrived at would make it possible for Egypt to get out from under the debt problem for several years; the donors thought that this could buy time to restructure the economy and make it more competitive. The debt relief package (described below) had major influence on the balance of payments, the fiscal balance, and recovery from the debt hangover.

Egypt followed up the debt agreement by imposing much greater discipline on its external borrowing. It restricted new loans to those that carried a grant element of at least 40 percent, and it worked hard to secure external funds in the form of grants and soft loans. As a result, the share of concessional debt in the total increased from 37 percent in 1990 to nearly 60 percent in 2014.

Economic Reform and Structural Adjustment Program (ERSAP)

President Mubarak's reward for joining the Western-led coalition against Iraq comprised not only large-scale debt relief, but also support for a program of economic stabilization and structural reform. Egypt concluded a standby agreement with the IMF in May 1991 and a program with the

World Bank in November 1991. This arrangement, the Economic Reform and Structural Adjustment Program (ERSAP), aimed at stabilizing the economy and starting structural reform.[3]

The stabilization part of the program required action by Egypt on: (1) fiscal policies, for example, widening the coverage of the sales tax and reducing government investment expenditures; (2) monetary policies, such as making interest rates positive in real terms (they had to be raised to over 20 percent to do this); and (3) exchange rate policy, such as devaluing and unifying the foreign-exchange rate. Full unification of the exchange rate was accomplished in October 1991, and the Egyptian pound was pegged to the U.S. dollar. The structural adjustment part of the program concentrated on the privatization of public enterprises, in order to use their assets more efficiently and, more importantly, to give a clear signal that the idea of a socialist economy had been consigned to history, and that henceforth the private sector would function as the engine of growth for the Egyptian economy.

The donors' contribution to the stabilization effort was a massive write-off and rescheduling of Egypt's external debt, plus additional financial aid. On May 25, 1991, Egypt entered into an agreement with members of the Paris Club to restructure its debt. The restructuring comprised several measures, such as forgiving principal, reducing interest rates, and rescheduling payments. The reduction or restructuring was to take place in three phases[4] and the arrangements were subject to three main conditions: Egypt was required to: (1) have an agreed program with the IMF; (2) keep current during 1991–94 with payments due under the terms of the agreement; and (3) obtain comparable terms of debt relief from non–Paris Club creditors.

The Paris Club debt relief package amounted to a total of $19.6 billion (Egypt's sovereign foreign debt was about $48 billion) and saved Egypt an average of more than two percent of GDP a year in debt service payments from 1992 to 1997 on debt owed to Paris Club members. Arab countries and institutions wrote off an additional $6.6 billion, and the United States canceled military debt of $7 billion. From all the relief measures, Egypt is estimated to have reduced its external debt servicing by at least 4 percent of GDP from 1992 to 1997. The debt relief package was vital to easing both external and internal balances by reducing the foreign-exchange requirements as well as the budgetary appropriations for servicing the debt. Subramanian (1997) estimated that the debt relief improved the balance of payments by $2.2 billion, and that in order to obtain an equivalent benefit Egypt would have had to depreciate the real exchange rate by 17 percent.

Although the details of the 1991 agreement varied somewhat from those of 1987, the general thrust was similar. This time, however, the Egyptian government had taken the decision to act unequivocally on the debt problem. The president appeared to have reached the end of his tether with the continuing recurrence of this problem and the political vulnerability to which it exposed Egypt.

A discussion some time later with the economic ministers might highlight President Mubarak's attitude. At the discussion, it was pointed out that the ratio of debt to GDP had fallen sharply, Egypt's standing in international capital markets had risen commensurately, and the country could borrow on very favorable terms. A time might be approaching when Egypt should consider the opportunity cost—in the shape of investment forgone and lower GDP growth and job creation—that *not* borrowing was likely to imply. It was also necessary to examine the economics of borrowing for the social sectors, such as health and education. Egypt's budgetary allocations for projects and programs in these areas had dropped off significantly, and these sectors were vital for meaningful economic growth, even though returns to investment in them might take longer than, say, from investment in industry. The ministers replied that the president was looking to decrease the *absolute* amount of external debt because he was determined to reduce Egypt's vulnerability to political pressure from foreigners; a discussion of ratios would obtain no traction with him. The political considerations outweighed the economic.

The chief intent of the structural adjustment part of the program was to increase the productivity of the Egyptian economy. The principal element in achieving this aim was to give the private sector the leading role in economic activities while reducing the ambit of the public sector. The Economic Authorities (such as the Suez Canal Authority) would continue to play a key part but, generally speaking, in matters of industry and services the public sector would no longer occupy a privileged position. (The structure of the public sector is briefly described on page 369.)

The consequence of this strategy was a decision to privatize most of the public-sector enterprises engaged in industry and services, including financial services. This part of the program could also help in achieving a balance between domestic revenues and expenditures: the sale of the enterprises augmented the government's resources, and the government no longer had to incur expenditure on the enterprises once they were sold off the government's books. The principal aim of the privatization program, however, was not the mobilization of additional financial resources (although these, no doubt, would be very welcome). The principal aim was to transfer assets to the private sector where they were likely to be used more efficiently, and to signal unambiguously that Egypt's future lay in a competitive, market economy that was integrated into the global economic system. Only this would dissipate the ambiguity of what the 1978–82 Plan had termed "a socialist society that thinks with a capitalist mind."

However, it was clear to many observers that the salience of the technical issues that dominated the discussions between Egypt and the IFIs—such as the sequencing of the reforms, the speed of the transition, the manner and extent of the exchange rate adjustment, the reforms to the financial sector, the size and role of the public enterprises, and so on—was secondary to the social impact that the collectivity of the changes would produce. The program would make important changes in the distribution of winners and losers in the country and thus it could not be regarded simply as a technical exercise. It carried social and political-economy consequences that would endure well beyond the term of the program; indeed, the change would signal a rejection of the economic and social model on which a generation of Egyptians had been brought up. A back-to-office memorandum by a staff member of one of the IFIs reported that some Egyptian economists described ERSAP as "a surreptitious agenda of social restructuring."

Experience under the ERSAP

The heart of the adjustment was a sharp reduction of the budget deficit, which dropped from 15.3 percent of GDP in 1991 to 0.9 percent in 1997.[5] The increase in revenues accounted for about one-third of the adjustment, while the decrease in expenditures contributed about two-thirds. The main reductions in expenditure impacted public investment, subsidies, and interest on foreign loans. Expenditures on employee compensation (wages, salaries, and pensions) and interest on domestic borrowing continued to increase.

From a political-economy viewpoint, three items in the policy package—(1) government investment, (2) subsidies, and (3) privatization of public enterprises—raised special sensitivities.

1. Government investment bore the biggest brunt of the reduction in expenditure, halving from 11.5 percent to 5.4 percent of GDP. This was in keeping with the strategy of relying increasingly on the private sector to drive investment. The strategic reasoning was that if public

investment were cut but at the same time the private sector were permitted to invest in areas, such as infrastructure, from which it had hitherto been excluded, the overall investment rate could be sustained and moreover the investment would be used more efficiently. Indeed, the government's thinking was that with the totality of incentives offered to the private sector under the ERSAP, the increase in private investment might even more than offset the fall in public investment, so that the investment rate might actually rise.

The authorities recognized that this approach offered hostages to fortune—they could certainly cut public-sector investment, because this decision was under their control, but there was no assurance that the private sector would respond commensurately, so that the total investment rate might actually fall. This, in fact, is what happened. The private sector took up some opportunities in infrastructure, such as Build-Own-Operate-Transfer (BOOT) projects in power generation, but as the discussion of figure 17 showed, its response fell short of expectations.

The essence of the private sector's justification for its lukewarm reaction was that the unsatisfactory functioning of key institutions increased the cost of doing business and greatly reduced the real profitability of investment. In several discussions with, and in replies to questionnaires from the World Bank, businessmen expressed many complaints. The chief of these concerned the glacial working of the commercial judicial system, the lackadaisical performance of a cumbersome and intrusive bureaucracy (and which also expected "gifts" simply in order to do its job), the lack of transparency and frequent arbitrariness of the taxation system, and the unpredictability of macroeconomic policies.[6] Perhaps business did protest too much, but regular surveys by the World Bank and other organizations of the investment climate and of impediments to doing business tended to validate the substance of the charge.[7]

The outcome also reflected a weakness in the IMF/World Bank program. Two principal assumptions underlay the strategy of shrinking the space for the public sector and enlarging it for the private. The first was that the private sector was *able* to fill the gap caused by the withdrawal of the public sector—that is, that the private sector possessed the necessary resources. The second was that the private sector was *willing* to fill the gap—that the private sector would consider it profitable to step up its investment. The outcome also demonstrated an important political-economy conundrum. In dealing with the private sector, the authorities face an important asymmetry. They can always *prevent* the private sector from engaging in an activity (by, say, passing a law or denying it access to some crucial input), but it cannot *make* the private sector undertake an economic activity. The private sector's decision to enter into an economic activity rests on its own determination of risks and rewards. In a market economy, the government can offer incentives, but the private sector decides whether these incentives are sufficient. In the case of Egypt, for a considerable period the private sector evidently did not consider the risk–reward balance to be sufficiently attractive to step up its investment in a major way. Indeed, as figure 17 shows, it was nearly fifteen years before private-sector investment exceeded even a much reduced public investment.

Atef Ebeid (prime minister 1999–2004; previously minister of the public enterprise sector) suggested two reasons for the private sector's hesitation. First, Egypt lacked an adequate number of institutional investors and financial institutions, with the result that the equity market, especially for new investors, remained thin. Second, most of Egypt's leading businessmen had been bred in trading companies (because thirty years of socialism had prevented the growth of a substantial entrepreneurial class) who tended to be cautious about taking on the risks associated with manufacturing in a liberalized market.

Another reason was that financial policies had drastically raised the opportunity cost of productive investment. The structural adjustment program had required the real interest rate to be made positive, and this required substantial increases in the nominal rate. With inflation at times running close to 20 percent, nominal interest rates had been pushed up to 22 percent. The inflation rate in due course fell, but declines in nominal interest rates followed only with sizable time lags. As a consequence, for significant periods, the real interest rate on financial assets (including bank deposits and government paper) remained in excess of 10 percent, the income from which was not taxed. Private investors therefore had the option of obtaining returns of this amount without making any effort or incurring any risk.

It would be rational on their part to want the real net return on the capital that they invested in entrepreneurial activities to be much higher, because not only would they be exposing their capital to the risk and uncertainty in the market, but they would also have to struggle daily with labor, the bureaucracy, and the tax authorities. Indeed, during this period businessmen indicated to the World Bank that they were looking for a net real return on capital of at least 25 percent. Such expectations could imply nominal profit rates of around 35–40 percent and perhaps even higher, because in order not to appear too greedy the businessmen were likely to have moderated their responses in the questionnaire. Not many activities readily offered such returns, and it was thus not surprising that private investors chose to avoid the vexations of dealing with the bureaucracy and the risk involved in committing their resources to new capital formation.

2. Another important item of expenditure reduction was consumer subsidies, which were cut from 5.2 to 1.6 percent of GDP, and were limited to four items (compared with eighteen items in 1980): bread, wheat flour, sugar, and cooking oil. These cuts were more carefully prepared than the subsidy reductions of January 1977 that had led to widespread riots and forced the restoration of the subsidies. The four items preserved the essential elements in a poor consumer's budget. Some studies—for example, Ali and Adams (1996)—judged that subsidies on these items functioned effectively, in that they were "self-targeted" toward the poor, and that eliminating them would significantly worsen income distribution, especially in urban but also in rural areas. Eliminating subsidies on some of the other items also offered a measure of balm to aid donors, who in earlier years had wondered why their taxpayers should be expected to subsidize Egyptians' consumption of dessert (halawa) and cigarettes, items that one would be hard put to describe as "essential." However, even after the stabilization reforms a number of major subsidies remained on items (such as fuel and higher education) that primarily benefited the better-off classes.

3. The third item, the privatization of public enterprises, was particularly contentious. The financial and production efficiency of the public-enterprise sector was the subject of several inquiries—for example, Mabro (1974), Hansen and Nashashibi (1975), Waterbury (1983)—and in studies by multilateral and bilateral donors.[8] An examination by the World Bank (1987) of a sample of 366 public companies and 37 Economic Authorities in the nonfinancial sector from 1973 to 1984 turned up some depressing results. The study

found that while some of the Economic Authorities (such as the Suez Canal Authority and the Egyptian General Petroleum Company) made a surplus, the performance of the public-enterprise sector as a whole was dismal.

The overall deficit for the sector had increased from 3.9 percent of GDP in 1973 to 8.4 percent in 1984. The net rate of return on book values had halved, dropping from 9 percent to 4.8 percent. Capital invested in the industrial public sector earned a negative rate of return on assets—in 1984 it was *minus* 5.7 percent. The aggregate deficit of the public companies and Economic Authorities was substantial and persistent. Thus, in eleven out of the twelve years covered by the study, the aggregate deficit of these entities accounted for 17 to 37 percent of the total government budgetary deficit, and was a much higher percentage than the public sector accounted for in a sample of twenty countries at Egypt's level of development. The study cautioned that even the foregoing figures might understate the actual gravity of the situation, because the accounting procedures of public enterprises were far removed from international practices.

Further work only strengthened these findings. A World Bank (1983) report showed that calculations of the domestic resource costs of earning foreign exchange using market prices indicated that, for several industries, it would be more economical for Egypt to import their products than to produce them domestically. The disappointing performance continued—World Bank (1991) reported that out of 397 state-owned enterprises, 197 showed returns on assets of less than 5 percent in 1989, including 35 that repeatedly earned zero or negative percentages and which remained alive only because the government continued to pump liquidity into them. Moreover, policies did not withhold resources from uncompetitive industries in order to redirect them toward those that were competitive. Public sector investment resources thus continued to flow toward noncompetitive sectors; World Bank (1983, 226); Ott (1993, 208).

Numerous reports and policy papers arguing for a restriction of the government's role in production were prepared by the IFIs and think tanks, and seminars and conferences were held in Cairo, Washington, and Abu Dhabi. Many ingenious arguments from different sources were marshaled—even the fourteenth-century historian Ibn Khaldun was dragooned into the debate to highlight the perils of government participation in commerce and production. Kanaan (1989, 232–33) quoted Ibn Khaldun's statement in Chapter 40 of the *Muqaddimah* that "Commercial Activity on the Part of Government Is Harmful to the Subjects and Ruinous to Tax Revenue." Ibn Khaldun's argument was that if the government moved into the productive sectors of the economy, the private sector would be unable to compete with it because the government could deploy more resources. Merchants and producers would therefore cut back on their investment, thereby reducing their production and income, "and everybody will become worried and unhappy." The government's tax base and revenues would thus also decrease. Ibn Khaldun therefore reached the dire conclusion that "measures taken by the government in the way of engaging in commerce or [production] soon turn out to be harmful to the subjects, ruinous to the revenues, and destructive of civilization."

The IFIs and the Egyptian authorities considered that the best way of dealing with the problems inflicted on the economy by a domineering public sector, consistent with the new direction of the Egyptian economy, would be to privatize most of the public-sector enterprises. The structural changes in the economy that such a move required would, of course, raise important political-economy issues.

The memoranda and the minutes of meetings between the World Bank and Egyptian officials on the subject show that four items occupied most of the attention: the financial gains to the government from selling off the enterprises; the reduced pressure on the budget because the government would not have to inject public funds into loss-making enterprises; the more efficient use of the privatized assets because these enterprises would have to face increased competition; and the greater agility provided to management by freeing it from incessant government intrusion.

But the most fundamental issue was intangible. Egypt's economic and social landscape would be drastically altered, and the changes would produce many unforeseeable outcomes. The change in strategy could not be viewed as simply a more efficient means of attaining a universally agreed-upon result, namely, faster economic growth. The most important impact would result from abandoning a model of development that had shaped Egyptian society for a generation. Moreover, the changes were not restricted to privatizing 314 public enterprises. Privatization was to proceed concurrently with the relaxation of controls in several areas of industry and trade. Controls generated rents—barriers to market entry produced monopoly profits, high import tariffs enabled domestic producers to charge higher than international prices and made it possible for inefficient firms to survive, and bureaucrats with even some access to the levers of control were able to parlay that situation to their financial advantage. The upheavals in the economic environment were bound to throw up a different set of winners and losers from those produced by the existing system. The recipients of rents had a powerful interest in the survival of the status quo. They regarded privatization as a Trojan horse that would not simply enable alterations to the working of public enterprises, but would insinuate far-reaching social and political changes that would be to the rent seekers' detriment. It is no wonder, therefore, that the debate on an apparently straightforward technical exercise of privatizing 314 public enterprises should have become so acrimonious.

The changes would also have a major impact on labor. The common estimate—as in IMF (1998, 55), Khattab (1999, 12–13)—was that one-third of the approximately 900,000-strong labor force in public enterprises was surplus to requirements. Much of this excess would have to be eliminated before a private investor could be expected to show any interest.

Given the wide range of political views that were affected, not everyone would embrace the changes with much gusto. The idea of privatization was indeed hotly contested in some quarters; as a sample, see Bush (1999), Farah (2009), el-Naggar (2009), and Kandil (2012). Opponents of the change argued that many public-sector enterprises were in fact profitable, and that a part of the profits of these enterprises could be used to improve the efficiency of many of the remainder. There was no economic need to throw out the baby with the bath water.

Proponents of public-enterprise reform held no truck with such opinions and could be caustic in their rebuttals. Let me convey a flavor of the exchanges by quoting an extract from one such response.

"Profitability" of Public Enterprises
Many of the public enterprises were said to be profitable. Some of them indeed are. However, if "profitability" requires high protection from competing imports; the massive benefits of a monopoly position

in a captive domestic market; subsidized capital via the National Investment Bank; exclusive access to government contracts; negative real interest rates; a soft budget constraint; unlimited availability of government-guaranteed bank credit; subsidized electricity and fuel; wages that can be kept low because incomes are supplemented by budgetary subsidies; and a labor force that is kept docile by the government repressing trade unions, outlawing strikes, and co-opting trade union leaders into the ruling political party, then we are looking at an Alice in Wonderland economy with a Through the Looking Glass system of accounting, and "profitable" must be understood in a Humpty Dumpty sense.[9]

"Profitability" in such circumstances has no congruence with "efficiency." The ever-continuing loss of international market share of Egypt's exports is powerful testimony to this fact. In 1950, out of every $100 of world exports, Egypt accounted for one dollar. In 1965, out of every $100 of world exports, Egypt accounted for 37 cents; in [2015] even this derisory share had plummeted to [14] cents.[10]

The foregoing does not, of course, mean that the Egyptian public sector is genetically programmed for inefficiency. A glimpse of the sector's possibilities has been seen, for example, in managing the operations of the Suez Canal, the construction of the High Dam, and the functioning of the Egyptian General Petroleum Organization.

But these isolated oases in the vast desert that is the Egyptian public sector only highlight the exceptional conditions under which the public sector *can* function efficiently. The heads of these organizations were chosen to be men of outstanding ability, qualifications, and commitment. They were given preferred access to scarce resources, such as foreign exchange. Recruitment of staff emphasized merit. The management of the enterprise was given wide autonomy and not hemmed in with a plethora of bureaucratic interferences. Egypt is not short of able and dynamic persons, but even such individuals are rendered impotent by the system in which they are trapped.

The outstanding example of an efficient Egyptian public-sector organization is the Suez Canal Authority. Baker (1978, 75–76) quotes from an article by Heikal describing the degree of independence given to Mahmoud Yunes [who was appointed in 1956 to head the Suez Canal Authority]. "One refrained from submerging him with instructions and orders [from Cairo] . . . Gamal Abdel Nasser ordered

Cairo not to communicate too frequently with Yunes. . . . [T]he traditional government apparatus was prevented from invading the domain which had just been conquered."

Most importantly, they were given a single, clearly-defined purpose. They were not required to pursue several mutually-inconsistent objectives—act as social-welfare organizations by selling products below cost; function as reservoirs in which to dump the unqualified and unemployed of the country; make do with minimal new investment or upgrading of existing equipment; forgo most funds for training; but at the same time be called upon to generate savings, improve quality, and remain competitive in international markets. If conditions under which, say, the Suez Canal Authority operates can be replicated widely in the public sector, there is no reason why public enterprises should not perform efficiently. However, merely to catalog the conditions that are required highlights the near-impossibility of applying them universally.

Egyptian critics could be equally acidic. Waterbury (1983, 101) quotes a member of parliament (and leader of the liberal opposition) as writing, "All the profits of industrial companies are fictitious. Every industrial enterprise in Egypt runs at a loss. Take for example the Egyptian Spinning and Weaving Company. It buys Giza 68 cotton at LE16.75 while the world price is LE31.65. After that they pull out their accounts and say we're making profits."[11]

In the early years of the program, privatization proceeded rapidly. Of the original portfolio of 314 public enterprises slated for privatization under Law 203 of 1991, by the year 2000 the government had sold the controlling interest in 118 of them. The number of workers employed by public enterprises had also been reduced—some by normal attrition of leaving at full retirement age or death (and not being replaced), while about 110,000 employees had chosen to take early retirement packages. These packages in general provided benefits equal to three years' compensation, and cost about LE25,000 each. The IMF (1998, 55) pointed out that what made the retirement packages affordable from the government's point of view was the low wages and benefits paid in the public sector. It calculated that cutting the labor force in the public enterprise sector by about 300,000 workers (the number judged to be redundant) would require only a one-time payment of 2.5 percent of the GDP.

However, there is an obverse to this issue. While the authorities welcomed having to pay only relatively small amounts to retire labor, the necessary corollary was that the workers received only relatively small amounts with which to secure their future. The retirement packages were unlikely to do this, especially given the rates of inflation that Egypt had experienced and which formed workers' expectations for coming years. The government made an attempt to assist workers who had taken early retirement to find new avenues by setting up the Social Fund for Development, which provided retraining and financial assistance to set up small and micro enterprises. The Social Fund appears to have performed reasonably well in its earlier years, but its later performance was rated "unsatisfactory" by the World Bank (2014a). Moreover, it is moot how useful the "retraining" part of the Social Fund's remit was, seeing that during most of that institution's existence the economy's growth rarely reached a rate that would create the number of jobs required by the expanding labor force. Where, people asked, were the jobs for which these workers approaching retirement age were being "retrained"?

Workers' disquiet developed into unrest in the years after 2000 and exploded into major strikes from 2006. The workers' demands centered on the inadequacy of their wages in a time of inflation, the danger of losing jobs if their enterprises were privatized, and the insufficiency of the early retirement packages; see, for example, Beinin (2009). The strikes, demonstrations, and other manifestations of labor unrest persuaded the government to consider whether the privatization program might have run its course. Slackman (2010) quoted the chairman of al-Ahram (a large state-owned media group and research organization) as saying that "the value became less than the headache, and the whole cabinet decided to forget it."

By 2008 some influential ministers had become convinced that the economic benefits of the privatization program were swamped by the political dangers that it created. They began to examine alternatives to the standard privatization methods that had hitherto been used— namely, selling shares on the stock market, sales to Employee Shareholders' Associations, liquidating enterprises and selling their assets, sales to anchor investors. These measures had created a perception among the public that Egypt's patrimony was being sold at knockdown prices to a favored few— see, for example, Farah (2009), Kandil (2012), and the papers in el-Mahdi and Marfleet (2009). The government's response, announced in November 2008, was to propose a method of widening the shareholding. Under this plan, Egyptians aged twenty-one years and above would receive shares in 86 public companies out of the 153 that remained to be privatized, and would thus participate in the profits of these enterprises. The existing privatization program would be suspended until parliament passed the law that would put the participation measure into effect. As matters turned out, parliament took no action and the privatization program was effectively frozen from 2009.

Assessment of the ERSAP

When Chinese prime minister Zhou Enlai was asked in the 1970s whether the French Revolution of 1789 had been a success, he famously replied, "It is too early to tell." That judgment might not apply literally to an assessment of the ERSAP, but a definitive conclusion will have to be preceded by a fair amount of research. Moreover, since the central intent of the structural reforms was to change the economic model that had shaped Egyptian society for a generation, value judgments about the kind of society in which one wants to live will play a very large part in any verdict. These value judgments are likely to differ sharply between persons and to be strongly held, so one should not expect a commonly agreed narrative to hold sway soon. All that can be done here is to offer a brief note on how far the program attained its ends and where it fell short.

The program obtained the reduction of a very substantial part of Egypt's external debt, eased the pressure on the balance of payments by lowering the requirements for servicing the debt, and reduced the budget deficit. The GDP growth accelerated markedly, the inflation rate fell, and people's confidence in the future of the Egyptian economy improved, as shown by the sharp decrease in the rate of dollarization (the proportion of money and quasi-money held in foreign currency) from 50 percent in 1990 to 20 percent in 1997. These are significant pluses.

On the other hand, the program remained over-optimistic concerning the speed and the extent to which private investment would step in to fill the gap created by the withdrawal of public investment. The outcomes on the labor shed by the privatized enterprises remain ambiguous. The workers that were "let go" were provided a separation package of three years' wages. The intent was to provide some sort of a shield for this labor by setting up the Social Fund for Development, which would provide resources for retraining and setting up small and micro enterprises. Unfortunately, because of the low wages in the public sector, it is debatable how long this package could have shielded the redundant labor, and the performance of the Social Fund, especially in the period after 2000, has often received less than laudatory ratings from the World Bank.

The program also put too much emphasis on the privatization of public-sector enterprises; indeed, at times it appeared to give the impression that structural reform consisted only of privatizing public enterprises. The Bank appeared not to appreciate that privatization by itself could not guarantee a more efficient use of resources. Unless the institutional environment is strengthened, for example, by enforcing more competition, there is an ever-present danger that privatization might only result in replacing public monopolies by private monopolies. The most important lesson from the privatization experience of many countries is that it is not the public or private ownership of a firm that determines its efficiency, but the competitive environment in which it operates. Privatization by itself does not necessarily create competitive efficiency. The discussion of crony capitalism in this chapter underscores the results of this failure of understanding.

Soon after the stabilization was completed, the Egyptian economy was hit by two serious blows. First, a banking crisis erupted in Thailand and spread through the fast-growing economies of East Asia, especially South Korea, Indonesia, Malaysia, and the Philippines. These countries moved quickly to protect their balances of payments by rapidly depreciating their currencies or, as in Malaysia, by imposing capital controls. Egypt's currency remained tied to the U.S. dollar, and thus continued appreciating against the East Asian currencies in tandem with the dollar. By 1998, a year after the start of the crisis, the average devaluations against the Egyptian pound were: the Malaysian ringgit by 36 percent, the South Korean won by 42 percent, the Thai baht by 46 percent, and the Indonesian rupiah by 73 percent.

The devaluations gave exports from the East Asian countries a price edge in third markets, and made them especially competitive against Egypt's nontraditional exports. The effective appreciation of the Egyptian pound against these currencies also made East Asian imports into Egypt cheaper. The resulting flood of imports coupled with the failure of nontraditional exports to grow commensurately intensified the pressure on Egypt's balance of payments.

Second, on November 18, 1997 extremists attacked a tourist bus in Luxor, killing fifty-eight foreign tourists and four Egyptians. The consequence was an immediate and sharp drop in tourism, substantially reducing the earnings from a key source of foreign exchange. Concerns with security kept most tourists from Western countries away for some time after the incident. Egypt attempted to compensate for this fall by encouraging more tourism from Eastern Europe, a region that tended to give especially heavy priority to price incentives. However, the attempts were made difficult by the slowness with which the exchange peg was adjusted; it was not changed until 2000. The interests of importers, and the government's concern that devaluation would require it to extract additional domestic resources to pay for external debt servicing and for the import of wheat and other subsidized commodities, were chiefly responsible for the tardiness of the response. The result, however, gave an unfortunate signal to exporters concerning their position in the hierarchy of Egypt's economic priorities.

Crony Capitalism

A feature of the Mubarak era from the 1990s was the greater participation of businessmen in the political arena as members of the ruling National Democratic Party. They had evidently absorbed the lesson that economic affluence was not unrelated to political influence. Reporting on this, a World Bank memorandum noted that before the parliamentary elections of 2000, only about 8 percent of all deputies in the National Assembly came from the business sector, but after the elections of that year their share more than doubled to nearly 17 percent.

An unfortunate characteristic of Egypt's foray into a market economy was the growth of what is popularly termed "crony capitalism." This refers to favored treatment in the economic field accorded to persons who are in or close to the power centers. As Mitchell (2007, 13) describes it, "The reform program did not remove the state from the market or eliminate profligate public subsidies. Its main impact was to concentrate public funds into different and fewer hands." The government's special treatment of its favored businessmen took many forms. The minimum loan size from the public–private commercial banks was typically set at over LE1 million, which effectively ruled out participation by the SMEs that accounted for 95 percent of Egypt's enterprises. The size of the loan also required large collateral, and the relative scarcity of funds for lending to the private sector meant that good personal connections between bankers and businessmen were important.

Other forms that the favors took included privileged regulatory treatment, access to scarce resources, protection against imports, tax concessions, and the like, and generally had the effect of providing the recipient with large economic rents. The matter did not stop there. Favored individuals were appointed to the boards of agencies that regulated the very activities in which the person had an interest—the fox put in charge of the henhouse. Moreover, the large increases in wealth resulting from the favors enabled the individual to purchase political influence, and the merry-go-round of privileges leading to wealth, leading to the purchase of political influence and thus leading to more privileges, was continually supplied the fuel with which to keep revolving.

This phenomenon has been noted by several writers—for example, Amin (1995), Rutherford (2008), Farah (2009), Soliman (2011), Kandil (2012)—and even in World Bank documents, for example, World Bank (2014b). The overall political-economy conclusion they reach is that this phenomenon brings the market economy into disrepute and has damaged the liberalization strategy in the eyes of many Egyptians. Income and wealth are seen to result not from merit but from relationship—"they depend not on *what* you know, but *who* you know," is a recurring comment.

Some interesting work by Diwan, Keefer, and Schiffbauer (2015) puts quantitative flesh on the bones of a discussion that has often leaned toward the merely descriptive and/or polemical. Diwan, Keefer, and Schiffbauer identified 32 politically connected (PC) businessmen and 469 firms that these businessmen directly or indirectly controlled. Diwan and his coauthors then constructed a database of PC firms under the Mubarak regime, combining it with additional sources of firm-level information, data from the World Bank on non-tariff barriers to trade, and energy intensities of manufacturing industries from the United Nations.

The writers addressed the question whether politically connected firms in Egypt received policy advantages from government that permitted them to earn higher rents at the expense of other firms. These rents could reduce the competitive pressure to increase productivity and, therefore, could contribute to lowering the country's growth and employment.

Diwan, Keefer, and Schiffbauer's principal findings regarding the 469 firms were as follows.

1. Politically connected firms had average net profits that were thirteen times higher than the profits of the remaining firms in the sample.

2. The difference between the profits of politically connected firms and the unconnected was systematically related to the survival of the regime. The differential in profits was more than two times larger between 2005 and 2010, but after the fall of the Mubarak regime on February 11, 2011, this large differential suddenly disappeared.

3. Egypt's import tariffs were reduced at the end of the 1990s and protection against imports was increasingly provided through the use of non-tariff measures (NTMs) such as exclusive license requirements, rules of origin, or quality and sanitary controls, which left much scope for bureaucratic discretion. The researchers found that:

    - most of these NTMs were introduced when prominent businessmen started to head directorates for economics and business in the policy committee of the ruling party;
    - politically connected firms were significantly more likely to operate in sectors protected by NTMs than unconnected firms;
    - products of politically connected firms were significantly more likely to be granted NTM protection than those manufactured by other firms; and
    - the larger the number of NTMs imposed on a product, the higher the probability that the product was sold by a politically connected firm.

4. Politically connected firms operated disproportionately (45 percent compared with 8 percent of all firms) in energy-intensive sectors, which were the beneficiaries of very large government subsidies.

5. Politically connected firms were more likely to have obtained government land (at less than market prices), to be located in an industrial zone (with tax concessions and better infrastructure), and to have access to bank credit (for example, firms in sectors with five politically connected CEOs were 60 percentage points more likely to have obtained a bank loan than firms in sectors without such CEOs).

6. Politically connected firms could reduce their own regulatory burden and speed up the acquisition of licenses and permits; for example, firms in connected sectors obtained their construction permits, on average, eighty-six days quicker than those without such connections.

7. The higher profitability of politically connected firms could be entirely explained by their access to NTMs and energy subsidies;

absent (especially) import protection, they were not more profitable than unconnected firms.

8. The entry of politically connected firms into previously unconnected sectors had a large negative effect on employment growth in those sectors, by reducing competition and thus the growth opportunities of the large majority of unconnected firms. Diwan, Keefer, and Schiffbauer estimated that it could imply as much as a 25 percent reduction in employment growth between 1996 and 2006, and would more than wipe out any positive growth impact of the entry of connected firms. It also skewed the distribution of employment toward micro and small firms, where productivity was lower. In short, the artificial cost advantages provided to connected firms led to a misallocation of a major resource, labor, in ways that would reduce productivity growth.

Diwan, Keefer, and Schiffbauer (2015, 33) offer an important political-economy lesson: "Tepid job creation has shown the limits of apparently significant market reforms . . . adopted over the past 10 years. One hypothesis that explains slow job creation, despite the relaxation of many formal, de jure regulatory and legal obstacles to private-sector activity, is that close state–business relations have circumvented market reforms and continue to stifle competition, innovation, and job creation." Their valuable study provides abundant support for this hypothesis.

Ghanem (2014, 30) highlights a possible structural reason for the strength and continuation of crony capitalism in Egypt. He points out that when the private sector consists of a small number of large firms, it is profitable for them to build special links to authoritarian governments which are constrained by fewer checks than are democratic governments on doling out special favors. It is then in the interests of these "connected firms" to support such autocratic regimes, because that would continue their access to protection, financing, government contracts, and location in the best parts of the infrastructure. The large businessmen have no interest in supporting democracy, because that would overturn their special relationship with autocratic regimes.

Developments, 2000–2011

The following section departs from the earlier format in that it highlights key political-economic developments chronologically from 2000 to 2011, when the Mubarak period ended. This provides a closer tracking of developments in the economic situation leading to the revolution of January 2011.

At the beginning of the new millennium, Egypt's economy was hit by a series of crises. The economic performance between 2000 and 2003 was affected by the outcomes of the attack in New York on September 11, 2001 and the Iraq war; uncertainties about the direction of macroeconomic policies (especially exchange-rate policy); and the slowing of structural reform. GDP growth during the three years averaged only about 3 percent annually, and was well below the minimum required to absorb labor-force growth and reduce poverty. Both unemployment and poverty could be expected to increase. Matters began to change by mid-2003 when global economic growth started to improve. Exports participated in the international expansions, benefiting from the nearly 40 percent depreciation of the real effective exchange rate since 2000 and becoming more competitive (during 2000 Egypt had departed from the de facto peg to the U.S. dollar adopted in early 1991, and in January 2003 the pound had been allowed to float).[12] This helped to maintain foreign-exchange reserves at close to nine months of imports of goods and services, and held down the service of external debt to less than 12.5 percent of exports of goods and services.

In July 2004 a new cabinet was appointed with a strong mandate to pursue economic reforms. This cabinet had an unusual composition, in that the prime minister and nearly one-third of the ministers were businessmen. While this may have had some advantage in that ministers would better understand the problems confronting the private sector in an economy led by that sector, what raised public concern was that several cabinet members were put in charge of the very ministries that supervised the private enterprises that they continued to own. Would these businessmen-turned-ministers employ policies that were determined exclusively by the interests of the country, or would policy choices be swayed by the interests of their own private businesses and those of their friends and clients?

Reflecting on this matter, Loewe poses a series of questions that can only be rhetorical.

> Would the entrepreneurs in government favor themselves and their friends? Could the owner of a large hotel company who also ran the Tourism Ministry resist the temptation? What about the owner of an automobile import and assembling company who serves as minister

for transportation? The owner of a food-processing company, which exports large shares of its products to Europe, who doubles as minister for trade and energy? The minister of housing who also owns a construction company? The minister of health who works in the medical business? (Loewe 2013, 29)

In view of the earlier discussion of crony capitalism, finding answers to these questions should not detain one for long.

Ministers in this cabinet said they were concerned with three immediate problems. First, there was the usual pressure on the balance of payments, because foreign-exchange earnings had not kept pace with imports. Second, the financial system was fragile and the banks were loaded with a substantial amount of nonperforming loans. Third, the state-owned enterprises were making large losses, and required subventions from the budget. There were also more deep-seated structural problems, such as unemployment, the official rate of which was in excess of 12 percent; a budget deficit exceeding 8 percent of GDP; and an inflation rate that even official estimates put at more than 10 percent a year.

The cabinet had to deal quickly with the immediate problems. The exchange rate was devalued, thereby making imports more expensive and providing an incentive for exporters. The foreign-exchange market was also reformed, with a start being made toward eliminating the dual exchange rate. A financial reform program was instituted, under which both taxes and subsidies were cut. The idea behind the tax cuts was to provide businesses and individuals with an incentive to increase their efforts and to produce more, and thus was expected to generate more revenues than the tax cuts would have lost. This, incidentally, was the same strategy that was successfully adopted by President John F. Kennedy in 1960 on the advice of Professor Walter W. Heller, the chairman of his Council of Economic Advisers. Wage increases and the regular annual bonus for workers were held to the minimum that was politically feasible. Taken together, these measures freed resources with which to capitalize the banks and to provide a cushion against their nonperforming loans.

The government's thinking was that if the business environment could be improved, both foreign and domestic investment would be encouraged and the resulting more rapid growth of GDP would provide the jobs that the expanding labor force required. Discussions with cabinet members showed that some ministers understood that the low investment levels were largely a consequence of the poor functioning of key institutions. They adopted a concrete approach to correct the situation. The World Bank's *Doing Business* indicators were scrutinized to see what the ten best-performing countries of the most important indicators were doing, and to try to replicate their policies in Egypt. The financial-sector and exchange-rate strategies amounted to following an IMF-type program without taking any money from or being supervised by that institution. (The president was still adamantly opposed to having the IMF back in Egypt.)

The cabinet focused on the exchange-rate system, the trade regime, the budget, the financial sector, and the privatization of state enterprises. Several other reforms were instituted (see IMF reports from 2005 through 2009 cited in References).

1. Egypt made the transition to a unified, effective exchange rate regime during 2004, an interbank market was launched, and flexibility was restored to rate-setting. Exports surged, although the policy changes were not the only propellants; external factors, such as higher oil prices and greater Suez Canal traffic, also played an important role.
2. The average import tariff rate was cut from 14.6 percent to 9.1 percent in order to enforce more competition.
3. The prices of subsidized fuel and electricity were raised, thereby easing some pressure on the budget.
4. A comprehensive restructuring plan was announced for the financial sector. This included a five-year horizon comprising mergers, sale of stakes in joint venture banks, resolution of nonperforming loans from public and private enterprises, privatization of a state bank, and reforms to the non-bank financial sector.
5. In the fiscal year 2005, a total of twenty-two companies were privatized, yielding approximately LE3.3 billion in proceeds. Total employment in state-owned enterprises had been reduced from around one million workers in 1991 (when the privatization process began) to 400,000 workers in 2005. An ambitious plan was announced to further privatize most state-owned firms, including those in sectors that previously had been off-limits.
6. An important initiative from 2004 was a renewed emphasis on industrial policy;[13] Loewe (2013) provides a comprehensive discussion of the policy and its outcomes from 2004 to 2011. He concludes that the strategy was more efficient and transparent than earlier such

strategies, but the policies addressed only a small fraction of the structural problems that debilitated the private sector in Egypt, and that therefore the business environment continued to be plagued by many serious constraints. He lists in particular: low-quality education and training, corruption, market distortion and lack of competition, deficits in the rule of law, a lack of transparency in decisions taken by the government, the public administration, and the judiciary, "and the private sector's lack of voice and political participation" (Loewe 2013, 46–50). The last constraint presumably refers to the lack of participation by small and medium enterprises, because the larger businessmen had seen the wisdom of forging political connections, including by financing and/or joining the ruling political party and by getting elected to the National Assembly.

The policy did not resolve the fundamental weaknesses; rather, it papered over them by providing subsidies and other benefits. Constraints on financial resources imposed selectivity on which enterprises could be assisted in this manner, and it is not unlikely that the rhetorical questions posed earlier could provide a hint as to the identity of the probable beneficiaries. The overwhelming number of beneficiaries were the large businesses; funds to assist SMEs were only a small fraction of those earmarked for the large firms, even though SMEs constituted over 95 percent of Egyptian enterprises.

After parliamentary elections, the same cabinet was reappointed in December 2005 and pressed ahead with its program, concentrating on public finance management, privatization, and financial-sector restructuring. The IMF (2006) remarked that the privatization of public assets had been particularly successful and had yielded almost $2.5 billion in sales. While offering accolades to the government for undertaking these reforms, the IMF pointed out that major structural impediments to higher growth and job creation continued, listing these as large fiscal deficits, unproductive public expenditure, red tape, deficiencies in financial intermediation, and labor market rigidities. The IMF (2006, 4) cautioned that "these reforms pose difficult socio-political challenges, and will require broad political consensus to implement." The country was clearly moving into a phase when "second-generation" reforms had become essential. The IMF also pointed out that, despite the economic improvements, employment growth in 2005 fell short of labor force growth, and for a time the official unemployment rate reached 12 percent; taking account of the "discouraged labor" would have further increased the rate.

The economy continued to respond to policy changes, with real GDP growth in 2006 reaching 7 percent. Capital formation, national savings, and official reserves increased and total external debt fell as percentages of GDP. While lauding this performance, the IMF (2007a) pointed to continuing problems in the labor market, noting that "skill mismatches remain a hindrance to job growth, and formal sector employment is hindered by high nonwage labor costs and expensive firing rules." The IMF (2007b) also pointed to inefficiencies in Egypt's spending on education, health, and social welfare, noting that the provision of services was frequently cost-ineffective.

More ominously, the IMF (2007a) drew attention to some darkening of the political horizon, observing that "opposition to the reform has become more vocal, fueled in part by high food-price inflation and some frustration about the lag in the 'trickle-down' of the benefits of growth." Such comments should have raised warning flags among Egypt's policymakers. The IFIs almost invariably refrain from making political comments, and on the rare occasions that they do make them, do so in discreet and guarded terms. The reader is expected to understand that such remarks are understated, and that the actual situation could well be more extreme. To the discerning, it would be apparent that the IMF's comments signaled that the pursuit of GDP growth had not been accompanied by sufficient attention to questions of distribution.

With a financial crisis hitting world markets in 2008, it was almost inevitable that economic activity in Egypt would also slow down. The growth of real GDP in 2009 dropped to 4.7 percent (well below that required to create jobs for all the additions to the labor force) from an average of 7 percent in the three previous years. Investment and savings also fell below their levels in 2008. The current account of the balance of payments showed a deficit of 2.5 percent of GDP, a noticeable swing from the modest surpluses in each of the previous three years. Gross external financing requirements increased to $7 billion, compared with $1.4 billion in 2008. The fiscal situation continued to be delicate, and the general government balance fell into a deficit of 7 percent of GDP. Inflation increased, with the Consumer Price Index averaging 16 percent more than in the previous year. Although the IMF (2010) commented that "core inflation" remained within the Central Bank's informal comfort zone, this would provide little joy to a housewife who would not face the "core" inflation rate—which strips out volatile items, such as energy and food prices, from the "headline" inflation rate—but in the market would have to cope with the headline rate. A metric that may be appropriate for an economist preparing a medium-term plan can be irrelevant for a consumer struggling daily to survive within her budget. A political-economy axiom is that political opposition results from a householder's discontent; a statistician's concern to adhere to some theoretical orthodoxy counts for naught. It would be well to remember that the devastating 1977 riots took place because of an increase in the price of food items.

The global financial crisis was largely responsible for the decline in Egypt's output in 2009 by decreasing export demand, remittances, and capital inflows. The IMF was concerned about "spillover" effects (such as increased financial stress in advanced economies and the slowdown in economic activity in Egypt's trade partners) from the collapse of the Lehman Brothers investment firm and their impact on the Egyptian economy. However, the Egyptian authorities reacted quickly by drawing down international reserves to meet the financial outflow, providing a sizable fiscal stimulus that accelerated investment in the public sector and in public–private partnerships amounting to a combined total of 2 percent of GDP, and postponing some fiscal reforms. These measures helped to limit the spillover effects of the crisis.

The economy recovered in 2010, with GDP increasing by 5.1 percent over the previous year. Gross fixed capital formation rose by 7.6 percent, led by private-sector capital formation of 9.2 percent; total investment was aided by a rapid buildup of inventories of more than 20 percent. After all the privatization measures that successive governments had taken, it is not surprising that fixed capital formation in the public sector increased by only 2.3 percent. The biggest sectoral increase, of 13.2 percent, was in construction. Private national savings reached 21.3 percent, but the savings performance was diluted by the public sector's dissaving of 3.8 percent. The current account of the balance of payments was again in deficit, this time 2 percent of GDP. The IMF continued to be concerned by fiscal weaknesses; the overall budget balance, excluding grants, was a deficit of 8.5 percent of GDP.

To sum up briefly: During 2004–10 economic growth was buoyant (averaging about 5.5 percent a year), but apart from 2005–2008 still insufficient to create jobs for all the additions to the labor force. The investment rate was inadequate and the external sector's contribution negative. The main driver of growth was consumption. An important weakness was the slow growth of productivity—the IMF (2015) estimated that total factor productivity in this period was growing by a mere 0.8 percent per year. It identified the most binding constraints to growth and job creation as macroeconomic risks, microeconomic distortions, low productivity, low access to finance, and poor external competitiveness.

The chief macroeconomic risks arose from the weak fiscal performance and the vulnerabilities in the external sector. The principal microeconomic distortions stemmed from high subsidies, inefficient labor markets, weak governance, and constraints to doing business. Most of these weaknesses were deep-rooted and continued to persist—Egypt ranked 131st out of 189 countries in the World Bank's 2016 *Doing Business* survey, and 119th out of 144 countries in the World Economic Forum 2014–15 *Global Competitiveness Index*. The private sector's low access to finance was reflected in a declining trend of credit to the sector as a share of GDP (in fact, that trend had been going on for a decade). Of particular concern was that credit to SMEs, which accounted for 95 percent of Egypt's enterprises, was extremely low. The negative contribution of the external sector to growth reflected its poor competitiveness, which the IMF attributed to the unfavorable business environment, real exchange-rate appreciation, and limited linkages with external firms and markets.

Thus, although Egypt's macroeconomic performance was improving in a number of areas, serious structural problems persisted, especially those relating to unemployment, poverty, and income distribution. The economy was thus still emerging from a fragile state in January 2011 when the country was hit by a political cataclysm. Huge public demonstrations erupted against President Mubarak. Even the use of force could not control them, and the president was compelled to resign on February 11, 2011, ending a rule of three decades.

An upheaval of this magnitude could not fail to have a drastic impact on the economy. This impact was of two kinds: disruptions to production, which began almost immediately; and an intangible, but possibly more pernicious, impact in the shape of increased uncertainty that raised questions about the future of the economy, and which persisted for several years. Real GDP growth dropped to 1.8 percent in 2011, and hovered around 2 percent (about the rate of population growth) in each of the next three years.

The growth rate recovered to about 4.0 and 3.8 percent in 2015 and 2016 respectively, but these rates were nevertheless well below the sustained 6–7 percent that the IMF (2006, 10; Ikram 2006, 279) estimated was required to create jobs for the expanding labor force. The official unemployment rate in 2015 was 13.2 percent of the labor force, compared with 10.4 percent in 2011. Both estimates of unemployment are likely to be understated, because the method of measurement does not take account of "discouraged labor," and does not address the issue of *under*employment. Unemployment (officially measured) was particularly severe among the age group of 15 to 29 years.

7
After Mubarak, 2011–2016

Several analyses of the background and especially of the political circumstances leading to the overthrow of the Mubarak regime are available—for example, Bradley (2008), Rutherford (2008), el-Mahdi and Marfleet (2009), Osman (2011), Amin (2011), Soliman (2011), Cook (2012), Kandil (2012), Roccu (2014), Bassiouni (2017), and others. There is thus no need to cover the same ground in detail here. Only a brief review of the timeline of key political events is provided in order to put the economic discussion in context.

A Brief Review of the Political Timeline

In December 2010, a Tunisian street vendor set himself on fire as a protest against his harassment by the police. This incident set off a wave of protests that culminated in the president's fleeing the country. The success of the demonstrations in ridding Tunisia of a "strongman" president set off similar demonstrations in other Arab countries, and the movement as a whole came to be called the "Arab Spring."

Egypt was not immune to this movement. Starting with the national Police Day—which commemorated the memory of an attack by British forces on a police station in Ismailiya on January 25, 1952—Cairo witnessed massive demonstrations, centered on the city's Tahrir Square, calling for President Mubarak and his government to step down and be replaced by a democratic government. They were also protesting against poverty, unemployment, government corruption, police brutality, and the absence of the rule of law. Similar demonstrations were held in other Egyptian cities, with noticeably large turnouts in Alexandria and Suez. It was clear that the people's frustration and anger had boiled over, and the day has appropriately been named "the Day of Rage."

The president's resignation was announced on February 11 and power was handed over to the Supreme Council of the Armed Forces (SCAF), which dissolved parliament and suspended the constitution. The military vowed that it would cede power to a civilian government, and announced a six-month timetable to prepare a new constitution and hold new parliamentary and presidential elections.

Elections for parliament were held between November 28, 2011 and February 15, 2012, and provided a sweeping victory for Islamist parties. In the lower house, the Muslim Brotherhood-led Freedom and Justice Party (FJP) won nearly half the seats, and the conservative Salafis another quarter. In the upper house, Islamists captured nearly 90 percent of the seats. Elections for president took place on June 16 and 17, 2012; Mohammed Morsi of the FJP won 51.7 percent of the vote and took the presidential oath of office on June 30, 2012.

Mohammed Morsi: June 30, 2012–July 3, 2013

Mohammed Morsi's presidency lasted for only one year. The period saw a series of politically insensitive steps that showed the president to be following an exclusionary strategy, building up the influence of his Islamist allies and alienating the liberal elements who had carried the main burden of the revolution. Islamists, for example were overwhelmingly appointed on the committee to draft the constitution.

The measure that aroused the greatest dismay was a decree Morsi issued in November 2012 that stripped the judiciary of the right to challenge his decisions, effectively putting himself above the law. The decree was rescinded in the face of popular protests, but the political damage was deep and lasting.

The exclusionary policy continued. In December the constituent assembly dominated by the Muslim Brotherhood and its allies approved a draft constitution that restricted freedom of speech and assembly, and seemingly marginalized the role of religions other than Islam. The draft was approved in a public referendum (with low turnout), but prompted extensive protests by the secular opposition, Christians, and women's groups. Large-scale demonstrations continued, during which many people were killed (more than fifty in January 2013 alone). The army warned the president that political strife and continuing divisions were tearing apart the fabric of society and pushing the state to the brink of collapse, and urged him to adopt a more conciliatory attitude.

The advice was ignored. Further consolidation of Islamist power continued; for example, in June Morsi appointed Islamists as governors in thirteen of Egypt's twenty-seven governorates. The contempt of political sensitivities was highlighted by appointing as governor of Luxor a member of a former Islamist armed group linked to the 1997 massacre of sixty-two tourists (including fifty-eight foreigners) in that very governorate. It again took the eruption of massive protests to reverse the appointment.

On July 3, 2013, amid massive popular opposition to the FJP government, the army ousted Morsi, suspended the constitution, and imposed an interim government consisting of technocrats. The chief justice of the Supreme Constitutional Court, Adly Mansour, was appointed the interim president. New elections for president were announced.

Abd al-Fattah al-Sisi

A new constitution was adopted in January 2014. The election for president took place between May 26 and 28, 2014, and resulted in an overwhelming victory for Field Marshal Abd al-Fattah al-Sisi, the head of the armed forces and former minister of defense. He took the oath of office as president of Egypt on June 8, 2014. A newly elected parliament was convened in January 2016.

This is not to say that it was all smooth sailing. Supporters of the Muslim Brotherhood staged angry demonstrations against the dismissal of Morsi, an elected president. The demonstrations were forcibly countered by the army, with many protesters losing their lives and others being imprisoned.

Political Instability and Economic Growth

Political upheavals of this frequency and magnitude could not but have serious consequences for the economy. The connection between political instability and economic growth has been much examined. This is not the place to catalog the studies, but it is worth referring, even if briefly, to some whose findings have a particular bearing on the Egyptian experience.

The theoretical arguments underlying the relationship vary between different studies. Thus, for example, Rodrik (1989) focuses on the damaging effects of policy uncertainty on private investment: if investors are uncertain about the policies of a potentially new government (for example, on the taxation of capital and income, or tariff policy, or toward private property), they are likely to hold back on new commitments or may even switch to investing abroad. Such actions are likely to impact the growth rate negatively. Kim (2010) found that in a large sample of developing countries, foreign direct investment, in particular, was discouraged by a high degree of political instability. This echoed earlier findings by Lucas (1990).

Barro (1991) studied a large sample of countries and found that variables such as the number of assassinations and the incidence of revolutions and military coups significantly affected the average growth level. Alesina et al. (1996) examined the relationship between political instability and per capita GDP growth in a sample of 113 countries for the period 1950–82. They defined "political instability" as the "propensity of a change in the executive, either by 'constitutional' or 'unconstitutional' means." Their focus was on whether a high propensity of an executive collapse led to a reduction of growth. They found that countries and time periods showing a high propensity of government collapse also showed significantly lower growth than otherwise. A sensitivity analysis of the model showed that the effect remained strong even under a more restricted definition of "government change" as cases in which there were substantial changes of the government.

Another large sample was analyzed by Aisen and Veiga (2011), who looked at outcomes in 169 countries between 1960 and 2004. They, too, found that higher degrees of political instability were associated with lower growth rates of GDP per capita. Political instability adversely affected growth principally by lowering the rate of productivity growth and, to a smaller degree, the accumulation of physical and human capital.

There is no need to labor the point. Even though the studies highlight different mechanisms, the overwhelming amount of theoretical analysis and empirical evidence supports the finding that political instability disrupts economic growth.

From 2011 to 2016, Egypt demonstrated a very high degree of instability, principally caused by four factors. First, there were rapid changes of regime. Between 1952 and 2011, that is, for almost sixty years, Egypt had known only three regimes. On the other hand, in the three years 2011 to 2014, the country came under five different governments. Some of these governments were purely technocratic, others political. Economic agents remained uncertain about the content of policies that new governments would bring in and for how long they would remain in force. Such an environment could hardly be conducive to investments, especially those that would be durable and would be expected to bring their returns over at least the medium term.

Second, the objectives of the 2011 revolution were unclear. The movement had brought together parties from the political right wing and the left, religious and secular. They were all united in the aim of removing Mubarak, but there was no consensus on what came after. The different factions projected very different visions for Egyptian economy and society, and there was no telling which of them would triumph.

Third, while the different factions may have been united against the autocrat, they had little or no experience in dealing with each other. Their differences therefore tended to be settled in the street. This did not augur well for a peaceful and stable political future, and would be another disincentive for an economic actor to commit resources for even a medium-term activity.

Fourth, the first political government, that of Morsi, labored under a further disadvantage—it did not control the state apparatus, which had both reason and ability to protect its own long-standing interests. The Morsi government attempted to bring Mubarak, his sons, and his associates to account. Mubarak had ruled for thirty years; thus virtually every soldier, policeman, civil servant, and judge had been appointed by him, and most of the successful businessmen owed their prosperity to favors bestowed by his regime. It would require a high degree of political naiveté and ignorance of human behavior to expect all these persons to suddenly abandon their own long-standing interests and benefactor, and turn against Mubarak and the economic and institutional structures he had built up and from which they had profited. As it turned out, the Morsi regime proceeded to demonstrate just this naiveté.

An explanation for Morsi's erratic policies, political and economic, might be that his candidacy was essentially Plan B for the Muslim Brotherhood. The original candidate was Khaled al-Shater, the deputy head of the party, who outranked Morsi. However, on April 14, 2012 he was barred by the Supreme Council of the Armed Forces from the presidential race on the grounds that he had been released from prison only in March 2011, and the election rules required that a candidate had to be released from prison for at least six years before he could be eligible. Nonetheless, he was said to be continuing to play a very influential role from behind the scenes, especially in issues of economic policy. Teams from the IFIs held several discussions with him on these matters. In view of the tight discipline of the Muslim Brotherhood, it is not clear which of Morsi's policies were his own, and which were the results of instructions from above. Morsi's position appears to have been weak vis-à-vis both the state apparatus and his own party. It is, thus, perhaps not surprising that his policies aimed more at appeasing the apparatus than at reforming it.

Economic Performance, 2011–2016

Egypt's experience between 2011 and 2016 reflected the widespread findings that political instability disrupted economic growth. The steep drop in 2011 (the year of the first Tahrir Square demonstrations and Mubarak's ouster) is striking; see figure 18.

In the five years (2006–2010) leading to Mubarak's ouster, the GDP growth rate corrected for price changes averaged 5.9 percent a year; in the next five (2011–2015) it averaged 2.7 percent. The latter rate was also well below the forty-five-year trend growth rate of 4.9 percent between 1965 and 2010. A measure of the income loss may be gauged from considering that a dollar growing at 2.7 percent a year becomes $1.14 (that is, increases by 14 percent) at the end of five years, while a dollar growing at 4.9 percent a year becomes $1.27 (that is, increases by 27 percent) at the end of the same period.

However, as pointed out in the introduction, regimes had a strong incentive to buy popularity, and could not afford to antagonize the population by cutting down benefits provided by public consumption. This

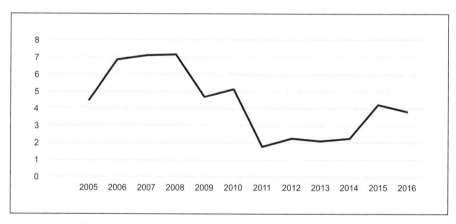

Figure 18. Real GDP growth, 2000–2015 (percent)

finding continued to hold. Thus, between 2010 and 2015, that is, for most of the period during which widespread political demonstrations were taking place, public consumption increased at an annual growth rate of 5 percent a year, well above the GDP and population growth rates and also much higher than the 3.2 percent average of 2006–2010.

Other economic indicators showed similar deterioration. The investment rate remained flat at about 14.8 percent of GDP in both 2010 and 2016 (about half the rate required to propel GDP growth to a level that would create sufficient jobs for the additions to the labor force). Between the same years (as percentages of GDP), gross domestic savings fell from 11 percent to 5.7 percent, and exports of goods and services from 17 percent to 12 percent; foreign exchange reserves halved from $35 billion to $17 billion; revenue from tourism dropped by two-thirds from $12.5 billion to $3.8 billion; by 2015 the poverty rate had risen to 27.8 percent of the population (the highest rate since 2000)[1], putting 25 million persons below the poverty line, with another 20 percent estimated to be close to the poverty line; and in 2014 the unemployment rate reached 13.4 percent of the labor force (3.3 million persons unemployed), from about 10 percent in 2010. Fiscal deficits remained above 10 percent of GDP from 2011, reaching 12.3 percent in 2016, pushing up the inflation rate (it spiked to 15.5 percent in August 2016). Gross public debt had risen from about 70 percent of GDP to nearly 95 percent (of which about 87 percentage points represented domestic debt and 8 percentage points debts to foreign sources).

The external accounts continued to weaken: imports of goods and services increased from 20.7 percent to 22.3 percent of GDP. The stagnating investment rate, the falling savings rate, the shift in the use of resources from savings to consumption, the increase in the import ratio, and the halving of foreign-exchange reserves weakened Egypt's growth prospects and intensified the country's vulnerability to potential external pressures.

The less than stellar results owed much to structural weaknesses that had not been addressed for a long time, and were even less likely to be comprehensively tackled in a period of political instability and rapid government change. The key issue was that the Egyptian economy was not growing at a rate that would provide jobs for the estimated 700,000 persons entering the labor force each year, and especially for its youth component. The chief structural matters, which are interlinked, underlying the state of affairs were:

1. persistent macroeconomic imbalances:

    - a significantly overvalued exchange rate that undermined export competitiveness, encouraged imports, and thus depleted foreign-exchange reserves
    - a high budgetary deficit caused principally by weak revenue collection combined with high and poorly targeted subsidies (especially for energy) and a growing public-sector wage bill

2. persistent high cost of doing business that discouraged investment, competition, and innovation. These factors were largely due to the poor functioning of what is sometimes referred to as the "software" of growth—institutions such as the commercial judicial system, the bureaucracy, the taxation system, the education and training system, the structure of incentives, and so on.[2] Not surprisingly, Egypt's rank was 131 out of 189 countries in the World Bank's *Doing Business 2016* that measured the effects of regulations impacting on 11 areas in the life cycle of a business. (World Bank 2016, 4.)

To make matters more difficult, the structural issues had to be tackled in an environment in which regional instability was increasing and the security situation becoming more fraught. These matters had a serious impact on the Egyptian economy, especially on foreign investment and tourism earnings.

This is not to say that nothing had been attempted. Energy subsidies were reduced by 30 percent in 2014 (a saving of about 2 percent of GDP), and the Egyptian pound devalued by 13 percent in March 2016 in an effort to close the gap between the official and unofficial currency rates. The effort did not succeed. Market equilibrium was not restored, and by the end of September, the parallel market premium over the official exchange rate had risen to more than 30 percent. Severe dollar shortages continued.

It was clear that another effort had to be made. The government bit the bullet and on November 3, 2016 the Central Bank of Egypt devalued the Egyptian pound by 32.5 percent against the U.S. dollar and allowed the exchange rate to float. The official exchange rate was devalued to LE13/$1. The Central Bank also removed restrictions on setting own buy and sell rates by banks, and allowed the exchange rate to be market-determined.

However, structural problems are not solved by piecemeal reforms. Egypt entered into a three-year program with the IMF under the Fund's Extended Fund Facility for a loan of $12 billion. The program was comprehensive and attempted to tackle the macroeconomic imbalances identified above, and also the structural problems that discourage investment and competition, while at the same time strengthening social protection nets.

The program design emphasized four pillars (IMF 2016).

1. Major policy adjustments, such as (a) liberalizing the foreign-exchange system to encourage investment and exports; (b) directing monetary policy to contain inflation; and (c) strong fiscal consolidation (increasing revenues through the introduction of a value-added tax, phasing out energy subsidies, and holding down increases in the public wage bill) to ensure that public debt becomes and remains sustainable.
2. Strengthening social safety nets by directing about 1 percent of GDP in fiscal savings to additional food subsidies, cash transfers to the elderly and poor families, and other targeted social programs. This pillar aims to replace poorly targeted subsidies with programs that directly support poor households.
3. Structural reforms to reduce the cost of doing business in order to promote higher and inclusive growth, and increase employment opportunities for youth and women.
4. Fresh external financing to close the financing gaps.

Sustainable Development Strategy: Vision 2030

The IMF's program claimed to be supporting Egypt's "home-grown" strategy. This strategy was put forward in documents entitled Strat_EGY (Government of Egypt 2015a) issued in March 2015 for the Egypt Economic Development Conference in Sharm al-Sheikh, designed to inform potential investors of Egypt's development strategy and targets for the period up to 2030, and in a more detailed document—*Sustainable Development Strategy: Egypt's Vision 2030*—published by the Ministry of Planning.

The document described the strategic vision as follows:

"By 2030, Egypt will be a country with a competitive, balanced, and diversified economy, depending on knowledge and creativity, and based on justice, social integration, and participation, with a balanced and varied ecosystem, a country that uses the genius of the place and the citizens in order to achieve sustainable development and improve the quality of the life for all. Moreover, the government looks forward to lifting Egypt, through this strategy, to a position among the top 30 countries in the world, in terms of economic development indicators, fighting corruption, human development, market competitiveness, and the quality of life." [Government of Egypt, 2015b, 3.]

The strategy rests on a number of "pillars," such as economic development, energy, education, health, urban development, environment, social justice, and others that are the staples of vision statements of virtually all countries. These are also components of the United Nations Millennium Development Goals.

The economic development pillar visualizes the GDP growth rate tripling from 4 percent in 2015 to 12 percent in 2030, generating real GDP per capita of $10,000 in the latter year, compared with $3,436 in 2015 (Government of Egypt 2015b, 16); the average annual growth rate of per capita income over the period as a whole thus works out to 7.4 percent a year, which implies an average annual real GDP growth rate of between 9 and 10 percent. Other targets are to reduce extreme poverty from 4.4 percent of the population in 2015 to zero percent of a much larger population in 2030; quadruple per capita health expenditure from $152 per year to $600 in 2030 while reducing out-of-pocket spending by half; increasing spending on pre-university education from 3 percent of GDP to 8 percent; reducing class sizes at all educational levels, and increasing enrollment in higher education from 31 percent to 45 percent in 2030. The budget deficit is to be brought down from 12 percent of GDP to 2.28 percent in 2030; the current balance on the external accounts will swing from a deficit of almost 4 percent of GDP to a surplus of 1 percent (Government of Egypt 2015a, 2015b).

The goals have attracted comment on three grounds. First, of course, is the question of feasibility. Few countries have sustained an average real GDP growth rate in excess of 9 percent a year for a period of fifteen years; in Egypt's case, reaching this average is even more difficult because it is starting from a (2016) rate of only 4 percent. Egypt's best effort was a 9 percent growth rate between 1975 and 1985, when it received a fortuitous flood of foreign exchange resources from the return of oil fields following the peace agreement with Israel, massive amounts of United States aid (amounting to nearly 10 percent of Egypt's GDP), a surge in tourism and in worker remittances because of more secure conditions in the region (expected from the cessation of hostilities between Egypt and Israel), and the access to international capital markets after the reorientation of Egypt's foreign policies toward the West.

However, by 2016 United States aid had steadily declined and accounted for less than one-half of one percent of Egypt's GDP; oil prices had collapsed and, anyway, rising domestic consumption had severely decreased the exportable surplus of oil; and tourism has fluctuated widely with changes in the perception of the security situation following a number of incidents of terrorism. Debt (domestic and external) had risen to 95 percent of GDP, severely limiting the government's ability to provide a fiscal stimulus for growth. Rates of investment and saving were both well below the 1965–2015 average which, in any case, was insufficient to propel GDP growth at the rate required to meet the Vision's targets.

Achieving the growth rates implied by Egypt's Vision would require an unprecedented effort. They would also require a fair amount of good luck, because much of the performance—such as export growth, Suez Canal revenues, foreign investment, workers' remittances—depends on factors that are not under Egypt's control, but on favorable developments in the international economy. Moreover, as some commentators, such as Esterman (2016), have pointed out, a further difficulty is that "virtually every other goal listed in Vision 2030 appears to rely on maintaining this extraordinary level of growth." The implication is that if the growth rate is not attained, all the other aims of the vision are also likely to be frustrated. The fact that there is no systematic discussion of how the productivity of the Egyptian economy will be increased adds to the difficulty of assessing the realism of the targets.

Second, the discussion of some crucial areas, such as the finance of the program, is opaque or puzzling. The review in chapter 2 showed that for the entire fifty-year period 1965–2016, Egypt's investment rate fell substantially short of that required to generate a GDP growth at a level that would provide jobs for the labor force, and that the savings rate fell well below even the inadequate investment rate; indeed, the fifty-year average of 13.5 percent was barely half the 25–30 percent that will be needed to finance the required investment rate without incurring excessive foreign debt. There is little discussion of how the savings rate will be increased. Moreover, a goal of the vision is not to raise the tax rate, while at the same time cutting the budget deficit and reducing public debt from about 95 percent of GDP in 2015 to 75 percent in 2030. This would imply severe cuts to public expenditure and raises questions about the ability to deliver key services, such as security, public education, and health. The Vision expects energy and food subsidies to be eliminated; whether this will be adequate, or indeed whether it even turns out to be politically acceptable, is a matter of conjecture.

Third, questions of income distribution and the impact of economic growth on the environment receive at best a cursory mention.

From Vision to Realization

"No battle plan survives first contact with the enemy," Marshall Helmuth von Moltke is famously reported to have said. The outcomes of separate tactical engagements so quickly change the situation that a commander is unable to see beyond the first battle; plans must continually be revised. Perhaps one might similarly say that no long-term economic and social plan survives contact with reality. A great many unforeseen events can intrude that destroy the premises on which the plan was constructed.

Egypt is no stranger to such disruptions: the war in Yemen eroded resources for the second five-year part of the "comprehensive plan" for 1960–70; the war with Israel in 1967 delivered the coup de grâce to that plan; Sadat's assassination, the international financial crisis of 2008, the massive demonstrations leading to the overthrow of the Mubarak regime, similar disruptions during Morsi's rule, the deterioration in the regional security situation causing Egypt's tourism revenues and foreign direct investment to plummet, may be cited as other unforeseen (and largely unforeseeable) events that would make mockery of a rigid long-term plan. "Unlikely" events, while still rare, can occur much more frequently than one might expect.[3]

A vision, like a long-term plan, should therefore not be regarded as immutable. It is useful for examining the path toward alternative objectives and providing the country with a sense of where a representative government aims to take it. If a vision document is to be credible and not written off by investors and the public as merely a political public-relations exercise, it must concern itself with the path as well as the destination. An example of a document that not only identified a goal that inspired the country but also provided direction for strategy was Prime Minister Mahathir's "20-20 vision" for Malaysia. This created guidelines for two twenty-year plans that were directed toward eliminating income disparities between the *Bumiputeras* (local-born Malays) on the one hand and the Chinese and Indian communities on the other.

Vision documents have also been prepared by many other countries, and policymakers have worked hard to formulate plans and policies that would help the country attain the vision's objectives. A brief review of the views and the experience of these policymakers may be helpful for their Egyptian counterparts.

The chief weakness with most vision statements is that they are prone to turning into lists of the ideal with little connection to the feasible or to the path that would lead from the existing situation to the envisioned ends. Egypt's vision document, in fact, ranks as one of the better ones that I have read. It provides a clear statement of the goals; it was formulated following a participatory process; it is alive to many of the challenges—internal and external—that lie in the path of attaining the vision; it accepts that legal, institutional, and regulatory reforms will have to be undertaken; and it is candid about several of the shortcomings in the country's economic performance. However, some important parts of the document need elaboration.

By and large, a vision statement primarily focuses on the goals that a country would like to attain; it focuses on the *what*. In order to be useful, one needs also to think of the *how*. The comments that follow are gleaned from discussions with policymakers in many countries who wrestled with the problems of constructing an inspiring but realistically attainable vision and the plans and policies that would lead to the goal. These policymakers were confronted by the following major questions.

- Why *this* particular vision and not any other? Instead of the proverbial "chicken in every pot," one may ask, why not two chickens? Indeed, why not two chickens plus a duck and a partridge in a pear tree? Why a GDP growth rate of 12 percent (the Egyptian target for 2030), and not, say, 20 percent? Unless one examines what it would cost (in terms of financial and human resources and/or alternatives forgone) to attain the vision, one can stuff any number of desirable outcomes in the vision. Crafting a vision without considering the constraints on the means of attaining it will not help to move from the vision to a realistic plan—the essence of planning is to formulate a way of optimizing under constraints. If a vision document is not to end up merely as a wish list, then what are the most important trade-offs?

- What is the strategy for realizing the vision? What prevented such a strategy from being pursued in the past? How has the political and economic environment changed so that the strategy is now feasible? (Have resources increased dramatically, or is there now a broad consensus on what goals must be dropped or deferred in order to attain others?)
- If the vision is realized, which groups will be the losers and which the winners? Or is the vision that of a win–win situation? If it is the latter—that is, everyone benefits—then why has the country not made more progress toward it already? Indeed, if trade-offs are involved, then it is difficult to see a win–win situation; almost by definition, some groups will have to give up something, or get less, relative to other groups, of something.
- What difficulties (political and other) will be created if some of the present winners become losers? One cannot expect smooth sailing— the present winners are winners because they wield significant power and influence. Why would they give up this position? How will the losers be handled? Will they be compensated in some way? Or will they be cajoled, or will there be the political will and strength to compel them to accept a diminution in their position?
- What political compromises will be needed for all groups to work together? Why did they not cooperate in the past?

Of course these questions cannot all be explicitly discussed in a public document, and I understand that a vision document is intended more to sketch a theme than to resolve intricate details of policy. However, some balance between the visionary and the realistic must be maintained; otherwise the policymaker will be offered no guidance on the path to be taken to realize the vision, and the vision document will degenerate simply into a collection of promises of "jam tomorrow." Several policymakers from East Asia, South Asia, and Latin America have told me that they had to find answers to the questions listed above to be able to proceed from an idealized vision to a realized outcome. Egypt's policymakers might also find it helpful to mull over these questions..

8

The Task Ahead

Some tension between dream and reality is unavoidable if policy is not to be managed by a completely short-term view; as Edgard Pisani emphasizes, a policymaker must listen to the silent long-term, even when being assailed by the insistently screaming short-term.[1] What are some approaches that could help Egypt's policymakers chart a path for the country's future?

The literature indicates that so far as economic outcomes are concerned, the results under democracy and authoritarianism are indistinguishable; see for example Alesina et al. (1996). Since Egyptians have demonstrated their preference for a democratic form of government, it is assumed that Egypt will have such a political system with a generally market-oriented economy, where the government plays the key role of an umpire to guarantee a level field for all players, provides essential public services, protects the most vulnerable members of society, and restricts income inequalities. The last function is particularly important for policymakers, and is dictated by considerations of both humanity and common sense. The Commission on Growth and Development headed by the Nobel laureate Michael Spence (el-Erian and Spence 2008, 7) points out, "Otherwise, the economy's progress may be jeopardized by divisive politics, protest, and even violent conflict. . . . If the ethical case does not persuade, the pragmatic one should."

This chapter examines two broad development strategies that at different times have been regarded as effective. A discussion of their pros and cons, and especially of the conditions under which they have proved practicable, could be useful in thinking how Egypt might go about formulating an approach that would be most helpful in the country's particular situation. But first, one must define the task for Egypt's policymakers.

What Is the General Challenge for Egypt's Policymakers?

In broad terms and in view of Egypt's history, one may say that the task confronting any Egyptian government is to provide a better life for the country's citizens and to make it less vulnerable to outside pressures. The operational policy goals could be defined as providing an adequate income for all citizens, and achieving at least a rough balance on the country's external accounts. The first would permit Egyptians to obtain the goods and services that enable them to lead lives that they value; the second could avert the external political pressures arising from economic weakness that have been a recurrent feature in the country's modern history.

In a modern economy, the bulk of the population earns its income through employment. On the income side, therefore, as a first approximation one might say that the task for the Egyptian government is to create a sufficient number of productive jobs for all the additions to the labor force and to progressively reduce the numbers of the existing unemployed. On the external side, the task is to follow a growth strategy that emphasizes exports much more than has been done in the past. Of course, the economy functions as an integrated whole, and policies to attain the two goals interact continuously—for example, export growth helps to balance the external accounts, and it also raises incomes; higher income growth creates demand for additional imports, and thus requires more vigorous export growth if the external accounts are to be balanced.

Since much of the focus of an appropriate development strategy for Egypt would be on employment, one should begin by looking at the principal challenges that the labor market poses for policymakers. The following paragraphs offer a brief review.

- *The unemployment challenge is serious.* In 2015, the labor force was about 28 million, of which 13 percent (3.65 million) was defined as "unemployed." The actual unemployment rate is likely to be higher, because the definition effectively excludes the "discouraged" workers, that is, those who would have looked for a job had they had the means to do so, and those who got so fed up with looking unsuccessfully for a job that they did not "actively search" for one in the reference period covered by the labor force surveys. Egypt and other countries (including the United States) have found that when the "discouraged" workers are included in the reckoning, the unemployment rate can rise quite significantly.

- *The challenge is likely to be prolonged.* The present "youth bulge" was created by a period of low child mortality and high fertility that was followed by a period of low child mortality and low fertility (World Bank 2014a, 40). The bulge is now reaching reproductive age and, because of its size, would in any case have produced another large generation. However, fertility among women of the bulge generation has sharply increased, creating an extraordinarily large second youth bulge. This means that the economy will not only have to create jobs for large numbers, but also that it will have to keep doing so for an extended period.
- *Changes in Egypt's GDP growth have tended to be reflected in changes in job* quality *rather than job* quantity (World Bank 2014a, 2). Sharp decreases in the GDP growth rate tend not to result in sharp increases in unemployment, but rather in a shift of the employment pattern toward informal jobs that are lower paid and in which workers' rights are offered minimal protection.
- *Changes in the labor market are shifting the structure toward informal jobs and will require markedly different policies from the past to deal with the employment problem.* Three structural changes are particularly important: contraction in public-sector employment (dropping from 34 percent in 1998 to 27 percent in 2013); stagnation in formal private-sector employment (fluctuating between 13.0 and 13.5 percent); and expansion in informal private-sector employment (from 31 to 40 percent).[2]
- *An important reason for the slow growth of employment is that young and small Egyptian firms do not grow over time.* International experience shows a close association between job creation and the growth of firms: see, for example, Mansfield (1962); Hall (1987); Hart and Oulton (1996); Davidsson, Delmar, and Wiklund (2006); Ayyagari et al. (2011); Hsieh and Klenow (2012); and Haltiwanger, Jarmin, and Miranda (2013). However, the effect on employment differs between the growth of small and large firms. The growth of the small firms (and consequently their job creation) results from competition, efficiency, and innovation; employment expansion in the larger and older firms mainly results from the acquisition of other firms. Thus, a substantial part of employment growth by older firms may not actually add much net employment, but may simply represent a shuffling around of existing jobs.

- In Egyptian manufacturing, however, two unfortunate factors are at play. First, there is only a small probability that micro or small firms will become medium-sized or large. In fact, the World Bank (2014, 110) calculated that the probability of an establishment with six to ten workers in 2007 growing to employ more than twenty employees in 2011 was only 3.3 percent. Small Egyptian firms typically do not grow and thus they do little to increase aggregate employment. The lack of firm growth also means that industry leaders are not challenged, and competition and thus productivity growth are much weaker.

- Second, even most of the large enterprises in Egypt did not become large as a result of their own dynamism, but achieved their size through mergers and nationalizations in the socialistic period of Egypt's development; they were "born" large.[3]

- *The labor market is marked by very large gender differences.* In 2013, nearly 80 percent of men aged between fifteen and sixty-four were employed or actively seeking work, compared with only 23 percent of women. The much lower participation rate of women in the labor force is a matter of constraints and not choice. Indeed, the World Bank (2014a, 80) reported that the unemployment rate among women was so high that in 2014 women made up the majority of jobseekers despite their low levels of participation in the labor force.

- *The labor market suffers from substantial regional disparities.* Labor market outcomes in terms of wages, job formality, and unemployment are generally best for the metropolitan regions (Cairo, Alexandria, Port Said, and Suez) and worst for rural Upper Egypt.

- *Education does not guarantee a formal job.* In 2012, illiterate men and men with below-secondary education had unemployment rates of only about 2 percent, but men with secondary education and those with post-secondary education had unemployment rates of 5 and 7 percent respectively. A World Bank report (2014a, 30–31) commented drily that "it is uncommon for educational attainment to be associated with higher unemployment rates." Another World Bank report (2015, ix–x) deplored the fact that "the current generation of young men and women are the most educated in history, but they cannot find secure and stable jobs and women are increasingly shut out of the labor market entirely."

What Strategies Would Help to Meet
Egypt's Development Challenges?

For our purposes, the bulk of the political-economy strategies can be divided into two stylized groups. One of them has acquired the title of the "Washington Consensus," and is a broadly market-oriented strategy that until the early 2000s was much favored by the IFIs. The other, which may be labeled the "East Asia Approach," relies on substantial government intervention, and proved very successful in the development of some fast-growing economies in East Asia, such as China, South Korea, Taiwan, Hong Kong, Singapore, and Malaysia.

The disjunction between the two approaches is not absolute. The strategies are neither "pristine market" nor "pristine government." Kanbur describes the issue well. Development strategies can be put on a continuum of policy emphases. One end would be occupied by strategies that emphasize less reliance on the market, a greater role for government regulation of economic activity, redistribution, and the provision of social services; the opposite emphasis would be at the other end. "It is not a case of one or the other, but rather one of having a combination of policies whose center of gravity is closer to one end rather than the other" (Kanbur 2009, 37).

What are the main features of these two political-economy strategies?

The Washington Consensus

The Washington Consensus was an approach that emphasized three keys to success in development: macroeconomic stability (especially price stability), liberalization of trade and markets (including labor markets), and privatization (that is, removing the entrepreneurial functions of government). It was put forward in 1989 by John Williamson at a conference organized by the Institute for International Economics in Washington, DC entitled *Latin American Adjustment: How Much Has Happened?* and was elaborated in the conference volume with the same title. The main points were amplified in Williamson (1990) and Williamson (2003) and are summarized in table 2.

These ideas quickly ran into controversy.[4] Much of the ensuing controversy rested on ideological differences, where the Washington Consensus was seen as favoring market fundamentalism and extolling the virtues of a minimalist state. Later commentators recognize that Williamson was not advocating anything as radical as a withering away of the state and, indeed, questioned "how many people know that 'reordering public expenditure priorities to

Table 2. The "Ten Commandments" of the Washington Consensus

1. Fiscal discipline	Set budget deficits at levels that can be financed without recourse to the inflation tax.
2. Public expenditure priorities	Move public expenditure away from nonmerit subsidies toward areas with high economic returns, such as infrastructure, and to basic health care and education.
3. Tax reform	Broaden the tax base and make marginal tax rates moderate.
4. Positive real interest rates	Let the market ultimately determine interest rates. In the transition, abolish preferential interest rates and aim at achieving a moderately positive real interest rate.
5. Competitive exchange rates	Adopt a unified exchange rate that is set at a level sufficiently competitive to induce rapid growth in nontraditional exports.
6. Trade liberalization	Replace quantitative trade restrictions by tariffs, and progressively reduce these until a uniform low tariff (around 10 percent) is attained.
7. Foreign direct investment	Abolish barriers impeding foreign direct investment and the entry of foreign firms. Allow foreign and domestic firms to compete on equal terms.
8. Privatization	Privatize state enterprises.
9. Deregulation	Abolish regulations restricting competition, except those that are justified on grounds of safety, environmental protection, or prudential supervision of financial institutions.
10. Property rights	Strengthen the legal system to provide secure property rights without excessive costs, and ensure that these rights are easily available to the informal sector.

Source: Based on Williamson (1990) and Williamson (2003).

switch towards basic health care and education was number 2 in the original list of 10'" Kanbur (2009, 4). Critics have highlighted rather different shortcomings of the Consensus; principal among them are the following.

- The Consensus relied exclusively on the experience of Latin America, and thus tended to ignore issues raised in other regions and the solutions to the problems offered by them.
- It drew its principal lessons from the success of a small sample of countries in a limited subperiod of their experience, and generalized these as nostrums for the rest of the world. It thus proposed a "one size fits all" approach to development policy, regardless of geographical location, historical context, political structure, or institutional capability.
- It ignored questions of poverty, income distribution, and sustainable development. The reform policies that the Consensus recommended, therefore, seldom gained the political support that was necessary to implement them.
- It was silent on the sequencing of reforms. Birdsall, Torre, and Caicedo (2010, 7) accused it of leaving "open the question whether the outcomes would be similar, independently of whether reforms were implemented simultaneously or separately and, in the latter case, regardless of the order of implementation." Particularly important was the Consensus's emphasis on liberalization without taking due notice of its risks; critics with as disparate political-economy views as Bhagwati (1998) and Stiglitz (2002) pointed out that premature financial-market liberalization could lead to financial crises, which could rapidly wipe out gains that had been painstakingly achieved over many decades.
- Subsequent experience has not demonstrated the efficacy of some of the key doctrines of the Consensus. For example, a crucial principle of the Consensus is "make labor markets more flexible," that is, permit wages to be lowered. This was supposed to lead to greater hiring and thus to lower unemployment. As a former chief economist of the World Bank, the Nobel laureate Stiglitz (2000), pointed out, the evidence on wage flexibility, even in Latin America, did not support this conclusion—wage flexibility was not associated with lower unemployment, nor was there more job creation in general. Stiglitz commented caustically that "labor market flexibility was designed to move people from low productivity jobs to high productivity jobs. But too often it moved people from low productivity jobs to unemployment, which is even lower productivity." He concluded that the Consensus's precepts, while important, were neither necessary nor sufficient for successful development.[5]

- Economic growth and poverty reduction in the 1990s, even in Latin America (with the exception of Chile), fell significantly short of reformers' expectations. Birdsall, Torre, and Caicedo (2010, 16) comment on the "sense of disenchantment with the Washington Consensus" deepening dramatically in the late 1990s and early 2000s. They report that policymakers consequently found it virtually impossible to mobilize the political coalitions required for additional reforms, and that major public opinion polls documented Latin Americans' resentment of market-oriented reforms, especially privatization, and people's weariness with high unemployment and stagnant wages. The region was said to have entered into a period of "structural reform fatigue." The outcomes led Naím (2002, 3) to declare that "the [Washington Consensus] brand is irreparably damaged." He considered this to be unfortunate, because although the Consensus as a whole might be an impaired brand, some of its ideas were sound.

- Even the theoretical underpinnings of the Washington Consensus were fragile. Stiglitz (2004) pointed out that the conditions under which Adam Smith's "invisible hand" would lead to efficient outcomes required that there be no externalities (such as air or water pollution), no public goods, no issues of learning, perfect capital markets, no imperfections of information, no changes in the information structure, and no asymmetries of information. This hardly described the real world of developing economies. Stiglitz therefore underlined that *"there is no theoretical underpinning to believe that in early stages of development, markets by themselves will lead to efficient outcomes."* (Italics in the original.) Stiglitz (2004, 3).

A series of follow-up conferences between 2000 and 2002, again under the auspices of the Institute for International Economics, produced a volume entitled *After the Washington Consensus: Restarting Growth and Reform in Latin America* (Kuczynski and Williamson [2003]). In this, Williamson (2003, 323–31) attempted to clear away the ideological baggage that had become attached to the original formulation of the strategy, and to rebut some of the criticism that it had attracted. He accepted, however, that "even my version of the Washington Consensus fell short as a manifesto for guiding economic policy in the 1990s. It failed to warn countries about some of the risks that they encountered. It neglected institutional reforms. And it was too narrowly focused on growth." Williamson offered a successor agenda that sought to remedy these weaknesses.

For our purposes, it would suffice to say that if in the spectrum of economic policies described by Kanbur (2009) the original formulation of the Washington Consensus was regarded as well to the right of center, Williamson's revisions would move the policy package closer toward the center.

The East Asia Approach

The patchy economic performance of Egypt compared with the spectacular success of a number of East Asian countries (such as China, South Korea, Taiwan, Malaysia, Hong Kong, and Singapore) during the last four decades has interested many developing countries, not least Egypt, to consider whether they too could follow the same path. This raises a number of crucial questions.

How and why did the growth experience of Egypt diverge from that of the East Asian "tigers"? What were the essentials of the East Asian model? How did policies and performance in the key areas of investment, savings, exports, industry, education, and so forth differ between Egypt and the East Asian countries? What was the approach to industrial policy, productivity, and competitiveness? What policies propelled the unremitting surge in exports by the East Asian countries? How did these countries view the role of external assistance? Did the East Asian countries sacrifice equity in the pursuit of rapid GDP growth? How important was economic planning? What was the contribution of governance? What lessons could Egypt learn from the experience of these economies (and what perhaps would be better left unlearned)? Such questions keep recurring in Egyptian discussions on development strategy.

Since the East Asian model appears particularly attractive to many policymakers, it would be useful to examine its key areas to see how far Egypt could replicate the experience. The analysis in this chapter draws both on the extensive literature and on numerous discussions with key stakeholders—including policymakers, academics, business leaders, members of think tanks, journalists, and participants from civil society—over a decade-long period when I was responsible for the World Bank's economic program in some of the "tiger" countries.

Although Egypt can learn from the experience of all the high-performing East Asian economies—and this chapter examines Taiwan's experience in a number of areas—South Korea is taken as the exemplar that offers the most lessons for Egypt. This is so on three grounds. First, South Korea has a significant population (in 2015 it was about 50 million) and thus falls between the extremes of, say, the People's Republic of China (1.3 billion, and with a very different political structure from that of Egypt) and Singapore (5 million). Second, South Korea (like Egypt) has had to devote a considerable portion of its GNP (between 7 and 8 percent on average during 1953–70) to defense. Third, South Korea (like Egypt) has been ruled by military autocrats for long periods.

The East Asian Model

The fast-growing East Asian countries had differences of history, geography, culture, and natural resources, but they possessed some key factors in common that were major contributors to the success of their economies. What are the essentials of the East Asian development model? Chalmers Johnson characterizes it as having four elements.

1. Stable rule by a political-bureaucratic elite not acceding to political demands that would undermine economic growth.
2. Cooperation between public and private sectors under the overall guidance of a pilot planning agency.
3. Heavy and continuing investment in education for everyone, combined with policies to ensure the equitable distribution of the wealth.
4. A government that understands the need to use . . . methods of economic intervention based on the price mechanism. (Johnson 1987, 145–46)

To the foregoing, a fifth element should be added. Every writer on the success of the East Asian countries emphasizes that they placed economic growth and more equitable distribution of its fruits at the top of their priorities; indeed, South Korea and Taiwan are frequently cited as exemplars of combining rapid growth with equity. The successful pursuit of this goal provided a way of legitimizing regimes that had not come to power through a democratic process.

The East Asia achievement

A few figures will demonstrate the scale of the East Asia achievement. In 1950, expressed in 1974 U.S. dollars, South Korea had a per capita income of $146, compared with $203 for Egypt, Nigeria with $150, or Mexico with

$562. By 1980, South Korea's per capita income (again in 1974 U.S. dollars) had shot up to $1,553 (an annual growth of 8.2 percent); Egypt's was $480 (annual growth of 2.9 percent), Nigeria's $670 (5.1 percent), and Mexico's $1,640 (3.6 percent). Note that the last three are important oil producers. In the two decades 1962–80, South Korea's GNP grew at an annual rate of 8.4 percent in real terms (Johnson 1987, 136). In particular sectors, the growth was even more impressive: for example, between 1962 and 1980, value-added in manufacturing increased at an average annual rate of 18 percent. South Korea's exports grew from $55 million to $22 billion, giving an annual growth rate of nearly 40 percent; in 2016, exports exceeded $600 billion (more than twice Egypt's entire GDP in that year). The composition of exports changed: manufactures accounted for less than 10 percent in 1962 but 90 percent as early as 1980. And the economic growth was achieved while maintaining one of the most equitable income distributions in the developing world.

International comparisons of income can be beset with uncertainties, but the contrasts between the outcomes of the East Asian countries and Egypt are so staggering that the story remains unambiguous. It would help to put the South Korean record in perspective for Egypt by considering the following. In 1960, Egypt's per capita income was about $200, while that of South Korea was roughly $130. In 1990, Egypt's per capita income was $765, compared with about $4,200 for South Korea (by 2016, Egypt's GDP per head was about $3,400, South Korea's about $26,300).

The performance of international exports can give some idea of a country's productivity and competitive ability. Egypt's exports in 1960 were about $725 million, South Korea's about $50 million. In 1990 Egypt's exports were $8.6 billion, South Korea's $65 billion. In other words, starting thirty years (say, a single generation) ago from a per capita income that was about two-thirds the Egyptian level and exports that were only about 7 percent of Egypt's, by 1990 South Korea's per capita income was about five-and-a-half times and exports were almost eight times those of Egypt. To make the picture even starker, consider that South Korea's exports in 1990 were one-third higher than Egypt's entire GDP. Egypt's falling competitiveness is reflected in its continual loss of share of the international market—in 1950, of every $100 of international exports, Egypt's share was $1; by 1965 it had dropped to 37 cents, and by 2016 was down to 14 cents (South Korea's was $3, more than twenty times that of Egypt).

Over the fifty-year period 1960–2010, Taiwan's GDP increased at an annual average rate of about 8.6 percent in real terms and South Korea's at

8.4 percent. Both these rates were much higher than Egypt's, where GDP growth was of the order of 5.0 percent. Moreover, since the population in the East Asian countries increased at a significantly slower rate than that in Egypt, the disparity in per capita income growth was much greater. The difference compounded over a fifty-year period can be staggering: During this fifty-year period, per capita income in Egypt increased at best at a rate of 2.8 percent a year, but in South Korea and Taiwan at nearly 6.5 percent a year. One dollar increasing at 2.8 percent a year over fifty years would become about $4; a dollar growing at a rate of 6.5 percent a year in the same time would become more than $23—almost six times as much.

There is little point in pushing detailed contrasts beyond 1990, because by that time the size and structures of the East Asian and Egyptian economies had become so different that comparisons would provide no meaningful lessons.

GDP Growth and Its Drivers

What were the drivers of the East Asian countries' spectacular growth? Broadly speaking, the growth impulses came from five main areas.

Investment rates

The dramatic growth of the GDP in South Korea and Taiwan was driven by very high rates of investment and savings, and by steady increases in productivity. Between 1960 and 2010, South Korea and Taiwan invested 35 percent of their GDP on average; during the same period Egypt averaged an investment rate of barely 20 percent.

Increases in Factor Productivity

In the standard growth accounting model developed by Solow (1956, 65–94), the sources of GDP growth are apportioned among the contributions of capital, labor, and a residual factor which is frequently associated with "technical progress," but is more neutrally referred to as total factor productivity (TFP), or the efficiency with which the factors were used. How much of the growth in South Korea, Taiwan, and Egypt resulted from increases in the quantities of factor inputs, and how much resulted from increases in the efficiency with which they were used?

Estimates of the contributions of these inputs differ between various studies, but the broad conclusion appears to be that for South Korea in the period 1960–2010, increases in physical capital accounted for about

40 percent of the GDP growth, and increases in labor about 30 percent, while increases in total factor productivity contributed about 30 percent. Over roughly the same period, the contribution of capital to the growth of output in Taiwan was about 46 percent, that of labor about 18 percent, and TFP growth contributed nearly 36 percent.[6]

The outcomes for Egypt were discussed in the introduction. The conclusion was that GDP growth in Egypt was driven primarily by increases in inputs, with a relatively small contribution from productivity improvements (in fact, there were periods when total factor productivity was negative). South Korea and Taiwan not only invested much more of their GDP than Egypt, but also used their inputs much more productively.

Industrial Policy

"If IPs [industrial policies] are defined as interventions which alter the way resources are allocated in the industrial sector, then South Korea surely has had an active industrial policy" (Leipziger 1988, 121). Moreover, South Korea's industrial policy remained intimately linked with its trade policies. This strategy arose from the requirement of a resource-poor country that had to export in order to buy capital goods and intermediate products, as well as defense matériel, from abroad. Since only about 20 percent of the country's land was suitable for cultivation, South Korean policymakers had little choice but to turn to manufacturing to provide the goods for export. As a result of intensive intervention—including tax concessions, export subsidies, a favorable exchange rate, wage restraint imposed on trade unions, the outlawing of strikes, and, most importantly, preferential access to credit—the manufacturing sector increased its share from 12 percent of GDP in 1960 to nearly 34 percent (of a very much bigger GDP) in 1990.

Export Policies

The word "miracle" has become something of a cliché when describing the growth and structural changes of South Korea's exports. In 1962 the value of South Korea's exports was only $55 million; then came the export drive. In 1964 exports passed the $100 million mark; in 1968 the $500 million level; twenty years later exports exceeded $60 *billion*. In 1960 South Korea ranked 101st among the world's exporters; in 2015 it was the tenth biggest. The structural change is no less impressive: in 1960 primary products accounted for 86 percent of merchandise exports and manufactures for 14 percent; by 1980 the shares had been completely reversed—primary products accounted for 10 percent and manufactured goods for 90 percent of exports (Balassa 1984, 145–46, and especially table 3.2.) The export surge enabled South Korea to run large surpluses on its current account from 1986 and to retire much of its substantial external debt. In 1985, South Korea was the fourth most highly-indebted developing country (after Mexico, Brazil, and Argentina), with an external debt amounting to $47 billion; by 1990 that figure had dropped to about $30 billion, as surpluses on the current account were used to retire debt.

The remarkable story of South Korea's export growth has been told by numerous writers, and this chapter has neither the space nor the necessity to repeat the details.[7] In any case, for our present purpose, what is important is not a rehearsal of the chronological ups and downs of export policy, but rather a broad view of the factors that propelled and sustained South Korea's exports on its extraordinary trajectory.

The South Korean government's commitment to boosting exports

The effectiveness of the government's decision and implementation procedures must begin with the government's commitment to the export drive. A thoroughgoing commitment to boosting exports began with President Park, whose strategy called for priority in economic development but with less economic reliance on the United States. The paucity of South Korea's own resource base meant that this development had to be based on import-intensive industrialization, and reducing dependence on the United States meant that South Korea would have to finance this industrialization through its own efforts, that is, by increasing its savings and exports. Song (2003, 90) reports that President Park's favorite maxims were "nation-building through exports" and "exports first."

The export surge was achieved through policies that combined incentives with punishments. The incentives included subsidies (especially bank credit at below-market interest rates); rapid rebates of import duties on the imported component of exports; and preferential access to scarce inputs. Perhaps the extreme case of punishment was the withholding of all bank credit to underperforming *chaebol*s (business conglomerates), which would then be likely to find it impossible to meet their wage, utility, and tax bills. They would thus become technically bankrupt, and be compelled to sell off some components of the conglomerate, even at knock-down prices, in order to avoid that fate.[8]

Industrial and trade policies are more than "picking winners"

A question that invariably comes up when discussing the performance of the East Asian countries concerns their aggressive industrial and foreign-trade policies of "picking winners." Under this approach, the government judges which industries have the potential to grow, and provides them with all the support that they need, in the shape of subsidies, tax breaks, access to foreign exchange, flexibility of labor laws for them to hire whatever specialties they require, and so on. The most active practitioner of such policies was South Korea.

Egypt can learn from South Korea's successes and failures with trade and industrial policies, and how these were carried out. In analyzing these policies, the World Bank (1987, 1:100–101) distinguished between the impact of government interventions on three types of incentives: (1) the overall incentive regime, created by fiscal, financial, exchange-rate, and trade policies; (2) functional incentives, that is, interventions to offset some systematic pattern of market failure or distortion (such as imperfections in the markets for technology and human capital, or deficiencies in physical infrastructure); and (3) selective incentives, which seek to identify and support "sunrise" industries, and manage the orderly elimination of "sunset" activities.

Since the last of these incentives appears to have acquired an inordinate importance in the minds of some Egyptian policymakers, it might be as well to put it in perspective. A policy of "picking winners" and supporting them and, because of the limitations on government resources, its necessary corollary of "recognizing losers" and terminating support to them, was only one of an array of strategic measures and was used within a framework of policies that emphasized economic efficiency. A respected authority on the economic development of East Asian countries, Robert Wade, wrote,

> Given that selective promotion [in East Asian countries] has been successful, overall, it does not follow that it has been *the* major element in superior economic performance. One of the dangers of focusing on a narrowly defined industrial strategy is that the wider policy context gets left out of the calculation. The experience of East Asia confirms that successful industrialization is critically dependent on effective macroeconomic management. . . . Low inflation rates and the maintenance of a stable and realistic exchange rate are essential in providing domestic industry with competitive access to international

markets as well as ensuring an appropriate balance of incentives between tradable goods and non-tradables. (Wade 1987, 18)

The most important factor in South Korea's export drive was an overall incentive regime that did not penalize exports and, for manufactures, was modestly pro-export. This consisted of a competitive exchange rate, together with the ability of exporters to obtain their necessary imports basically tariff-free. Some other subsidies (such as for bank credit) were also significant in making exporting relatively more attractive than producing for the domestic market. Moreover, as Rhee, Ross-Larson, and Pursell (1984, 11–14) stress, the authorities took pains to create an institutional structure that would ensure that the incentives legislated were, as far as possible, automatically and immediately made available to the exporter—an important lesson is that in a private-sector economy "an incentive delayed is an incentive denied" (see also Wade 1990).

The role of functional incentives has been less intensively documented, but in order to get the export drive going, the effects of overcoming market imperfections and infrastructure deficiencies could only have been helpful. The verdict on selective interventions is mixed, and has attracted a good deal of negative comment, especially concerning its use in the period of the Heavy and Chemical Industry (HCI) drive (1973–79). The reason appears to be that, while governments might have an advantage in gathering information needed for long-term decisions in the earlier phases of industrialization, at later stages entrepreneurs and markets become keenly concerned with dynamic factors and are more likely to show flexibility in moving into profitable markets and out of losing ventures than do governments.[9] During the HCI drive, the South Korean government continued to support its chosen industries even when the costs—both the direct financial costs and the opportunity costs (in terms of what the country was losing by depriving the more efficient smaller industries of bank credit and other resources)—had become clear.

For most of the period since the early 1960s, the South Korean government used international prices and export sales (that is, competitiveness in the international market) as a set of performance indicators. South Korea's experience was that the most efficient results with industrial and trade policy were obtained when the authorities provided, on the average, almost equal incentives for domestic sale and for export, and within manufacturing did not markedly discriminate between different items of export.

This "level playing field" left it to the market to channel factors of production into areas of South Korea's greatest comparative advantage. And the market responded to the outward-looking strategy by channeling resources into labor-intensive activities that rapidly increased exports and employment, and improved the income distribution.[10] This factor, namely, that government interventions generally worked to strengthen the allocative actions of the market—and thus remained pro-efficiency—distinguishes East Asian policy actions from those of Eastern Europe, and is perhaps the most useful lesson for Egypt.

The question arises whether Egypt should adopt an active policy of picking winners. There indeed are a number of products and activities that involve moving up the value chain from the existing industrial structure, and which appear to be clear examples of winners. For example: the textile sector could be supported in restructuring its production toward higher-value items, such as garments, that would make better use of the wonderful Egyptian cotton; more stringent quality control and better packing of fruits and vegetables would secure higher prices in the European market, and so on. These are obvious examples, and government support is likely to bring substantial dividends for the country.

However, an across-the-board policy of picking winners as Egypt's industrial strategy requires careful deliberation. Let me offer some points to consider.

First, even the South Korean experience had a significant downside, in that it discriminated against SMEs, especially in the allocation of credit; it created substantial excess capacity in certain industries, where the policymakers misjudged the required scale of enterprises; and it created inflation at various times because of a mismatch between what was demanded by consumers and what was supplied by the country's industries.

Second, the ultimate success of the strategy depended on the country's possessing an efficient, well-informed, and hard-working civil service. The necessity of a good educational degree for a South Korean civil servant is a given, while competitive examinations ensure that entry is merit-based. On the work ethic of the South Koreans, I need only say a few words. As recently as the mid-1980s (when South Korea had been enjoying rapid economic growth for more than twenty years), government officials "enjoyed" (that was indeed the term used) five days of leave in the year (plus a couple of days for Christmas and the New Year and one or two other holidays). By adding a weekend on each end of the five days they were able to get nine consecutive days of leave, and thus able to go to their home towns or villages. Although most outsiders would regard five days of annual leave as rather austere, the South Korean officials shrugged it off as something that had to be accepted in the interests of the country's development.

Laying great store by hard work continues. *The Economist*, in its issue of November 12, 2011, reported that South Koreans put in 2,200 hours of work a year, which was about 50 percent more than that worked by the Dutch or the Germans. This work ethic is not confined to South Koreans—the same issue of the *Economist* reported that in the international economic recovery of 2009–10, Taiwan and South Korea (in that order) had the largest increase in hours worked in manufacturing.

Is there something in the Koreans' genes that predisposes them toward hard work, and which is missing from the Egyptians' genetic makeup? Hardly. For many years, Koreans were considered indolent. Tudor (2012, 170) quotes several writers to this effect: "Legendary traveler and writer Isabella Bird Bishop visited Korea in 1897 and wrote, 'Seoul is a boring, dirty, and dead city. The people are lazy and slothful.' *Call of the Wild* author Jack London, who spent four months in the country, also wrote in 1904 that Koreans were 'weak and lazy.' The Japanese colonizers appear to have taken the same view: Okita Kinjo, in an unpleasant book named *Korea, Behind the Mask* (1905), called Koreans 'the world's laziest people,' adding that the country's only 'products' were 'shit, tobacco, lice, *kisaeng* [roughly, a Korean geisha equivalent], tigers, pigs, and flies.'"

Compare that with the present-day image of the diligence and reliability of the Korean worker.

A president of the Daewoo Heavy Industry Corporation told me that Koreans had a reputation until the 1960s for being addicted to drink, gambling, and women. He said that the key to learning from Korea's experience was to ask what incentives and disincentives had in one generation changed a people with this reputation into the fanatically hard-working and reliable workforce that one saw today. There is no reason why Egypt cannot absorb the lessons, the most important of which are discussed here.

Third, the East Asian tigers placed great emphasis on education. In 1945, the adult literacy rate in South Korea was about 22 percent; by 1970 this had risen to 88 percent (McGinn et al. 1980, 47; see also Kim 1980, 234–75). Currently it is 100 percent. The earlier imbalance between male and female literacy has also been eliminated: in 1970 male literacy was 95 percent compared with 82 percent for females; by 1988 both sexes had essentially attained the same rate. School enrollments increased at all levels: in 1953 less than 60 percent of the corresponding age group was enrolled in primary schools; by 1970 the figure had reached 100 percent; the enrollment for middle schools rose from 21 percent in 1953 to over 90 percent (of the appropriate age group) in 1980, while that in high schools went up from 12 percent to around 50 percent. The speed of the change in South Korea's educational attainment was dramatic. Thus, for example, in 1970, less than half of South Koreans attended secondary school; by 2016 they were more likely to graduate from university than people in any other country.[11] Literacy in Taiwan also followed a steep trajectory—rising from about 55 percent of the population over six years of age in 1952, to 95 percent in 1993. It should be borne in mind that attaining literacy in Taiwan and South Korea takes much more work than in other countries because of the large number of characters in their scripts.[12]

The structure of the school system and the finance of education in South Korea show an interesting direction of government intervention. The government has concentrated on providing basic and compulsory (that is, primary-level) education, leaving a large proportion of the higher levels to be supplied privately. Thus, by the mid-1980s practically all primary schools were public, but over 40 percent of middle and nearly 60 percent of high schools were private. The financial contributions of families mirrored this division: at the primary level, the government provided almost 97 percent of the expenses of schooling (all fees for tuition and textbooks were abolished in 1978); at both the middle- and high-school levels, families provided over 75 percent of expenses. Overall, private households paid about two-thirds of the direct costs of education (Bunge 1982, 96; see also Mason et al. 1980, 355). Government budgets reflect this: on the one hand, the share of education has generally been from 16 to 20 percent of the budget since 1964; on the other, about 70 percent of this spending has been for primary education (McGinn et al. 1980, 45–47). These figures underline the importance of the private contribution to spending on education: although the country devotes about 6–8 percent of its GNP to education, the government's share averages just over half that figure, and is targeted chiefly toward primary education.

Much of the spending that makes South Korean education so good therefore comes from private, not public, sources. In 2014, for example, the government spent a little less than 5 percent of GDP on education, which was slightly below the OECD average. Families added an extra 2.8 percent of GDP on top of that, which made it easily the highest rate among the OECD countries. Moreover, families spent an estimated 8 percent of their household budgets on after-hours programs for each child. This last figure gives some measure of the sacrifices that families make for education—if a family has three children, for example, their after-school activities alone could swallow up a quarter of the household budget. The ratio of private to public spending on education increases as one goes up the education ladder—at universities, family spending is three times that of the state. The result is that South Korea spends a larger share of its GDP on tertiary education than any rich country other than America.

Fourth, economic policy is strongly knowledge-based. The economic ministries conduct a certain amount of in-house research and analysis, but they also receive outstanding support from the Korean Development Institute (KDI). This impressive institution is home to a large number of economists, statisticians, sociologists, political scientists, and researchers from other disciplines, and maintains close links with government ministries.

Even after a forty-year association with the Egyptian economy, I remain surprised by how little interaction there is between the economic ministries and the universities and think tanks. Egypt is fortunate in the number of gifted and trained economists it possesses; indeed, many of them have performed brilliantly in the ministries, central banks, and universities of virtually all the Arab countries. However, their input into policymaking in Egypt has seldom been commensurate with their abilities. If the Egyptian economy is to be managed on the basis of evidence-based policies, ways must be found of bringing together the country's economic talents, regardless of whether they are located in the public sector or the private.

Fifth, the importance of implementation cannot be overstated. A development strategy delivers benefits only to the extent that it is actually put into effect. A vital lesson that Egypt can learn from South Korea's experience is the importance of implementing announced policies. It has now been reduced to a truism that South Korea's success owed more to its capacity to implement policies than to formulate plans; in fact, a background paper for the Sixth Five-Year Plan carried the motto, "An implemented second-best plan is better than a first-best that sits on the shelf."

South Korea has never lacked for plans. The Office of Planning was established under the government of President Syngman Rhee as far back as 1948; this office duly prepared a five-year plan (never implemented), and revised it later (also not implemented). There were numerous missions by foreign experts to advise on policies and to prepare plans (for example, the "Nathan Plan" submitted in 1953, but never adopted). A three-year plan was prepared in 1960, but was first postponed for a year and then came into effect only for a few months before the Rhee regime fell. The succeeding government of Chang Myon abandoned that plan and directed the preparation of another five-year plan in 1960; this was made irrelevant by the military coup of May 16, 1961 by which President Chung Hee Park came to power.

It was the Park regime (1961–79) that put economic development unambiguously at the top of its priorities, with the president proclaiming that "in human life, economics precedes politics or culture" (Park 1963, 26). President Park, in addition to strengthening the planning process, laid great emphasis on carrying out announced policies. Policy implementation was accomplished through a rigorous structure of rewards and punishments, including compulsion and administrative discretion. I have earlier described the findings of the Jones and SaKong Il (1980) study which quantified the sharp increase in the public's perception that the Park government meant what it said, and how this eased the government's task of implementing policies.

The foregoing insights from the East Asian experience suggests some crucial issues that must be thought through before deciding whether conditions are appropriate for Egypt to consider a wide-scale policy of "picking winners."

The feasibility of following the East Asian model by Middle East countries has also been studied by, for example, Campos and Root (1996) and Noland and Pack (2008). The latter conclude that "the East Asian experience reflected exceptional circumstances that are not likely to be reproduced" (Noland and Pack 2008, 93). They provide three reasons for this judgment: (1) the high level of human capital in the East Asian workforce relative to the contemporaneous level of income; (2) the very high rates of savings and investment attained by East Asian countries for several decades; and (3) the comprehensive land reforms in Japan, South Korea, and Taiwan after the Second World War that gave these countries a starting position with a much better distribution of income and assets and on which a process of "growth with equity" could be based. Moreover, they argue that "the benefits [of a policy of picking winners] may be sufficiently small, and the long-term risks sufficiently large, that nations may be well advised to avoid the extraordinarily difficult task of the *ex ante* identification of likely successful sectors" (Noland and Pack 2008, 97).

The necessity for thinking carefully before employing such a strategy in a sweeping manner is reinforced by some sober findings of Egyptian experience. Galal and el-Megharbel (2008) examined the Egyptian government's industrial policy over the period 1980 to 2000, during which the authorities employed several tools (such as tariffs, subsidies, and price controls) to encourage various elements of the industrial sector. The study found that these measures: (1) did not raise productivity; (2) did not significantly increase the diversification of firms or products (in fact, the manufacturing sector and exports both appeared to have become more concentrated over time); and (3) industries that did not receive favored treatment (through effective rates of protection, subsidies, and barriers to entry) performed better than those that did. Possible reasons for the inefficacy of support measures was that they were not linked explicitly to measurable outcomes, and that Egyptian industrial policy was effectively open-ended, with no "sunset" provisions, or clear criteria for identifying inefficient industries, and a credible process for withdrawing support and letting them wither away. The subsidy mentality, rather than a proactive investment one, created a parasitic public–private ecosystem that bred inertia on both sides.

External Assistance
South Korea and Taiwan were major recipients of external assistance (especially from the United States) at the start of their development drive. However, from an early period these countries recognized the political importance of reducing their dependence on concessionary foreign savings in order to minimize external pressures. They therefore explicitly planned to reduce their dependence on foreign aid and succeeded in doing just that.

South Korea's experience
In the case of South Korea, as bilateral aid from the United States was being phased down (it was virtually eliminated in 1974), the World Bank set up a Consultative Group to mobilize and coordinate assistance from other donors; the group's first meeting was held in 1966. South Korea received its first credit from IDA (International Development Association, the World Bank's concessional lending affiliate) in 1962; in 1973 (that is, after only eleven years), the country graduated from IDA. The Consultative Group for Korea was terminated in 1984 because, as the official communiqué put

it, "its role as a forum for aid coordination and enhanced mobilization of external capital for (South) Korea's development is now being fulfilled by the (South) Korean Government."

Taiwan's experience

Foreign aid in Taiwan followed a largely similar pattern. The country was the recipient of substantial amounts of U.S. assistance from the early 1950s; however, the acceptance of this assistance was gradually phased out in the 1960s and ended in 1965. A Taiwanese policymaker and analyst commented:

> The lesson that can be learned from Taiwan is that—with the exception of an emergency, such as a destructive earthquake, flood, or drought— foreign aid in the sense of an open-ended, long-range commitment of resource transfer is not needed after a time. Such commitments violate the sound principle of self-help, which is, after all, a cardinal moral principle of the market-oriented economy. Moreover, the habit of dependence on hand-outs from foreigners violates the principle of self-respect just as much as the habitual dependence of manufacturers on protected markets and government subsidies. (Li 1995, 231)

Economic Governance

The role of the state in economic development has never been far from discussions of economic strategy, and is central to a study of Egyptian development. How far, and in what areas, should the state intervene directly, and to what extent should the questions of what to produce and how to allocate the items produced be left to private markets? For many economists, the fall of communism in Eastern Europe appeared to have provided a clear-cut answer—economies developed most quickly when their functioning was left to market forces. However, the earlier questions have resurfaced with a vengeance, triggered by the financial crisis of 2008 in which several of the biggest financial houses and major industries of the United States and Europe ran to the government, pleading to be rescued from the consequences of their own improvidence.

Keynes would assign the state a nuanced role.

> The most important *Agenda* of the State relate not to those activities which private individuals are already fulfilling, but to those functions which fall outside the sphere of the individual, to those decisions which

are made by *no one* if the State does not make them. The important thing for Government is not to do things which individuals are already doing, and to do it a little better or a little worse, but to do those things which at present are not being done at all. (Keynes [1926] 1972, 291)

Economic theory provides some guidance, but rather more on the nature of activities that the state could concentrate on than to what extent it should pursue these activities.[13] According to economic theory, there are two closely connected justifications for state intervention in the production and distribution of goods and services: (1) the existence of "pure" public goods; and (2) the existence of externalities in the production and/or consumption of certain items. A public good is one whose consumption is non-exclusive; when A has it, so does B. National defense, the police force, and the judicial system are classical examples of public goods, in that if these items exist, they protect not only individual A but also every other resident of the country. The benefits from public goods are indivisibly spread among the entire community; therefore these goods and services cannot be commercially marketed.

An externality arises if there are substantial benefits (or detriments) to society other than those received directly by the consumer, and are thus not reflected by market prices. In such cases the market will not give the proper signals, and the production/consumption of the item in question will not reach the optimal point. A frequently quoted example of a beneficial externality is primary education. There is substantial evidence that universal primary education provides general benefits to society, such as a reduction in population or the crime rate,[14] but if this education were to be provided exclusively through the private sector (and hence only to those who could afford to pay for it), it would stop short of the socially optimal level.

Government actions in the real world do not, of course, conform to this pristine view of things. All governments intervene in numerous economic decisions and they intervene for a myriad of reasons, many of which—such as to protect the interests of a particular group or region—have nothing to do with economic efficiency. However, even disregarding such intentions, most governments intervene in economic decisions because they are suspicious of the efficacy or timeliness of the "invisible hand." As Jones and SaKong (1980, 8) comment, "Market failures being ubiquitous in the real world, a rigorous presentation of the beauties of the invisible hand ultimately provides a brief for the visible."

The lesson that seems to emerge is that the command economy, with government micro-management of all production and allocation decisions, has been unsuccessful and has been abandoned even by most countries that profess a communist ideology. On the other hand, in view of all the institutional constraints and market imperfections that exist in any economy, and particularly in a developing economy, reliance on untrammeled market forces is hardly a realistic option for Egypt. This lesson is underscored by the recent collapse in the developed world's financial and housing markets, and even in its industrial structures. Given the striking success of the East Asian economies, whose experience combined a strong dose of state direction with an unremitting pressure for market efficiency, the question has been raised as to what extent their modalities and behavior could serve as a paradigm for Egypt.

Most studies conclude that state intervention in the East Asian economies succeeded because it chiefly concentrated on creating positive externalities (such as expanding primary education) or in encouraging an environment in which market signals could play the chief role in allocating resources (primarily through adopting an outward-looking development strategy, in which export sales and the ability to produce at international prices became the main performance indicators). At the same time, the state strictly held the private sector accountable for living up to the targets that were considered socially crucial. These targets were few and carefully selected, generally relating to export performance and the modernization of technology, but were rigorously enforced through a combination of incentives and punishments.

Government Intervention in the East Asian Economies
The interplay of politics and economic policy in the East Asian "tiger" countries requires some elaboration in order to judge what made this model succeed in the those countries and how useful it could be in Egypt's circumstances.

Domestic Politics and the Prioritization of Development
Most explanations for the failure of development come back to the ineffectiveness of policymaking in the developing country. The literature therefore shows an interest in the focus of the country's political leaders on the development effort, the priority it gets, the strength of the country's institutions, and the vigor with which development programs are implemented. These matters have attracted considerable interest in discussions about Egypt.

The question has often been raised of why East Asian countries, such as China, South Korea, Taiwan, Hong Kong, Singapore, Malaysia, and now Indonesia and Vietnam, have succeeded in developing their economies so rapidly, while Egypt has not. The short answer is that Egypt has neither assigned economic development the priority that the fast-growing East Asian countries gave, nor pursued it by taking the ancillary actions, however difficult, that attaining the goal would require.

A number of factors were at work in the East Asian countries, especially the emphasis on education and the outward-looking economic strategy that forced their industries to emphasize efficiency and to become competitive internationally. However, the primary factor was the government's focus on a single objective, namely, economic development. It was striking, for example, that after 1953 there had been no hot war in South Korea, despite the continuous tension between North and South Korea. The South had not reacted to any number of provocations, including an attack on the South Korean president's residence by the North. South Korean ambassadors told me that their principal terms of reference on being assigned overseas were simple: (1) prevent their host country from recognizing North Korea, and (2) boost South Korean exports to their host country. A South Korean deputy prime minister had also told me that his country's philosophy was that it could not have political independence without first achieving economic independence. The government had therefore taken the political decision that until South Korea was firmly on its feet economically, it would forgo the luxury of an unfettered foreign policy, and would keep itself aligned with the United States, which was its main market, source of finance and technology, and shield against North Korea.

Egypt, on the other hand, had been involved in four full-scale wars and a "war of attrition" with Israel, and a proxy war against Saudi Arabia in Yemen that had lasted for five years and, in addition to the human losses, had drained the treasury of about one-third of its revenues annually. This stance made enormous inroads into Egypt's economic and human capital. Moreover, Egypt's foreign policy included assuming a leading role among the Arab countries, among the nonaligned nations, in the Islamic countries, and in Africa, opposing the United States and the United Kingdom for setting up the Baghdad Pact (and also over the Suez Canal with the United Kingdom and France), championing the cause of the Palestinians, supporting the Algerian revolutionaries (and thereby antagonizing France), and generally acting as the point man for the Third World against the West.

This stance made enormous inroads into Egypt's political capital with Western countries and mostly cut it off from the principal sources of capital and technology in the world.

No one could deny Egypt the right, as a sovereign nation, to pursue any policy that it regarded to be in its interests or to which it felt morally committed. However, actions have consequences, and Egypt had to accept the results. One clear result was to underline that a country in Egypt's situation could not engage in multiple wars, physical and/or diplomatic, with the United States, the United Kingdom, France, Israel, and Saudi Arabia without paying a heavy price.

The Politics of Economic Decision-making

Several analysts have commented on the politics of economic decision-making in Egypt, generally blaming tardy policy response and lack of an effective champion (whether individual or group) for the weaknesses of the economy. The structure and dynamics of economic decision-making have thus elicited a considerable amount of discussion. Let me quote a few.[15]

Some writers—for example, Cooper (1982), Richards (1984)—blamed features embedded in Egypt's political and economic system for standing in the way of major policy changes. Richards argued that

> It is increasingly clear why the state persists with its current set of inefficient and inequitable policies, and why it can get away with it: The class structure engenders policy stasis, while international rents permit the state to avoid the balance of payments crises and other pressures for change which would otherwise result from such inaction. (Richards 1984, 325)

Richards's analysis thus relies on the concept of a clash between different coalitions, as was discussed in chapter 1. He identified the class that most stood in the way of change as being composed of the old elites who had melded with the upper layers of the technocracy. This was a powerful combination of interests that could direct not only policies, but also their implementation. The rents that had rescued Egypt from even worse economic outcomes, especially on the external accounts, were: (1) oil rents, directly in the form of petroleum exports, or indirectly as workers' remittances and Suez Canal revenues; and (2) locational rents, in the form of tourist receipts or as international aid provided to Egypt because of its strategic location and political influence.

Similar views were advanced by Soliman (2011), Marcou (2008, 53–55), and others. Marcou went on to argue that the availability of these rents permitted Egypt to take the soft option and in particular encouraged the country not to take risks, such as those associated with exporting.

Other commentators elaborated this basic argument, adding additional nuances. Weiss and Wurzel (1998, 169–70) charged the ruling elite with not supporting economic reform, because basic changes in the economy would require greater political liberalization than those in power were prepared to concede. Therefore, "there [was] no broad political coalition in favor of reform and international competitiveness," and Egypt's political and administrative culture remained subject to a "neo-pharaonic control."

McDermott took this a step further, saying,

> Above all, there has been a sense—which the government has been willing to exploit in both domestic and international negotiations— that the Egyptian government and populace are miraculously owed a living from outside. The former has become accustomed to external sources of income, ranging from oil-related wealth to aid; and the latter has taken it for granted that subsidies will not come to an end. (McDermott 1988, 148–49)

He also criticized what he saw as "a lack of determination in executing policies. The *announcement* of a new direction has been confused with its implementation" (McDermott 1988, 149). [16]

Indeed, weaknesses in the implementation of policies and projects feature as recurring themes in the reports of IFIs and bilateral donors. An internal memorandum by one of the IFIs echoed McDermott's point about announcement being accepted as action by quoting from Gilbert and Sullivan's *The Mikado*. The Lord High Executioner says that when the Mikado orders something to be done, it is as good as done. It is *inconceivable* that the thing is not done. In fact, "*practically*, it is done" (italics in original); and implies that therefore there may be no need to actually do it. I have already quoted the comment in a Korean plan's background paper that a conceptually second-best plan that did get implemented was preferable to a first-best plan that remained unimplemented. An attempt by donors to help Egypt address problems of economic decision-making and implementing economic policies was put forward in the Möller Report, discussed in chapter 5.

Mason (1984, 10–11) argued that the most important factor affecting the economic growth of Egypt was that development did not occupy the same priority in policymakers' preferences as it did in the fast-growing East Asian countries. He pointed to several resemblances between South Korea and Egypt in 1979: both countries had similarly sized populations; severely restricted endowments of arable land; comparable structures of production, and an authoritarian government. However, the experience of economic growth since the 1960s had been very different.

For Mason, the principal reason for the differences lay in the objectives pursued by the two governments. The South Korean government focused almost entirely on facilitating economic growth. Mason referred to the insistence of President Park, who initiated South Korea's development drive, in affirming the precedence in human life of economics over politics or culture. Park's strategic thinking was that rapid improvement in people's living standards would legitimize his regime, which had come to power through a military coup. In Mason's view, Nasser did, in his early years, use distributional policies to create a political constituency that would support his revolution. However, he was equally intent on playing a leading role in the Arab, African, Islamic, and nonaligned countries, and this led him to divert resources into supporting external adventures instead of using them for economic growth at home. Moreover, the pursuit of economic development would have required policies to increase savings and therefore to restrict consumption, and the latter policy would have got in the way of building a domestic constituency. Therefore much of Nasser's foreign policy was devoted to efforts at obtaining resources from abroad. Sadat's survival strategy suffered from the same contradictions, and he, too, was loath to extract savings from domestic sources, directing many of his foreign-policy activities to the pursuit of obtaining financial resources from abroad.

Hansen (1991, 250–54) argued that Egyptian regimes had entered into an implicit contract with their citizens whereby "the latter [offered] acquiescence and surrender of political rights in return for *la dolce vita*." He went on to say that it was the country's own policies that were responsible for its inadequate economic performance, and not exogenous factors. His conclusion was that "Egypt's main enemy has been Egypt."

Holt and Roe (1993, 216–21) argued that Egyptian regimes were structurally prone to short-termism. They had not been democratically elected, and therefore did not in general enjoy popular support. This made them reluctant to adopt policies that might require immediate sacrifices from the people, even though these policies might bring large benefits to the country over the medium and long terms. Short-term popularity for the regime invariably outweighed longer-term benefits to the country at large. Regimes were also not eager to take on the large, deeply entrenched bureaucracy. Although for the efficient implementation of economic projects and policies Egypt needed to reform the bureaucracy, any general reform was almost certain to damage some important part of the bureaucracy's interests, and would thus run into strong opposition from powerful ministries. This not only would frustrate the implementation of the policies, but was also likely to weaken the bureaucracy's support for the regime.

The East Asian tiger economies, particularly during the period in which they commenced their rapid growth, were characterized by a political structure in which discretion and command by the ruling authority played a strategic role—what Myrdal (1968, 66) termed a "hard" state.[17] The essence of this form of intervention is the use of compulsion, subtle or overt, at the discretion of the ruling authority and the discriminatory targeting of this compulsion (positive and negative) toward particular sectors, enterprises, associations (such as trade unions), or even individuals.[18]

The South Korean government's ability to employ these tools gave it formidable power over the economy. Especially potent was its ability to instruct commercial banks on whether and how much they could lend to specific borrowers, particularly in the large-scale sector, where enterprises had high ratios of debt to equity and thus depended on bank credit for their very survival.[19] Steinberg's assessment of this aspect of the government's actions concludes:

> Because the government had a complete monopoly on all institutional credit, firms that failed to fulfill government-set objectives could lose access to bank credit, forcing them to seek credit on the curb, or informal, market at double or more the interest rates and, thus, making them uncompetitive.... It could force firms to fire or hire key executives, require companies to merge or to move from family to public ownership, and stress critical industries. (Steinberg 1989, 134–35)

And Mason et al. comment:

> If incentive procedures do not work, government agencies show
> no hesitation in resorting to command backed by compulsion. In
> general, it does not take a Korean firm long to learn that it will "get
> along" best by "going along." (Mason et al. 1980, 265)

And again:

> All Korean businessmen, including the most powerful, have been
> aware of the need to stay on good terms with the government to
> assure continuing access to credit and to avoid harassment from the
> tax officials. (Mason et al. 1980, 337)

A crucial question

In view of the degree of government intrusion in their economies, the crucial question is: How were the East Asian governments able to avoid the
rent-seeking activities that in other countries accompanied microeconomic
interventions? Rodrik (1996, 19) responds candidly that "we do not really
know." However, he suggests that the East Asian countries shared a number
of special initial conditions that might have helped.

First, education policies in these countries had produced a labor force
that was much better educated than would have been expected on the basis
of their income levels. They would thus be able to establish competent
bureaucracies. Second, at the time that they commenced their period of
rapid growth, the distribution of income and wealth in the East Asian countries was much more equal than in most other developing countries. Many
of the earlier elites had already been replaced.

In South Korea and Taiwan, for example, the Japanese occupation had given much of the land to Japanese or to their collaborators.
After the defeat of Japan in the Second World War, it became easy and
politically popular for the South Korean and Taiwanese governments to
confiscate these landholdings. This meant that generally, governments
did not have to battle against factions comprising powerful industrial or
landed interests, and thus policymaking was largely insulated from pressure groups. Moreover, since the governments did not have to spend too
much time on questions of redistribution, they could focus on enlarging
the economic pie, that is, on economic growth. Third, since the political

leadership could give priority to and focus on economic goals, it had the incentive to "supervise the bureaucracy closely and make sure that the bureaucrats assisted rather than hindered private entrepreneurship." Rodrik (1996, 34)

The third issue may be especially important. When I was responsible for the World Bank's economic policy dialogue with a number of East Asian "tiger" countries, I discussed the question of corruption with a senior South Korean official. His response was that corruption did in fact exist in the South Korean bureaucracy, as it did elsewhere (indeed, a number of ministers and senior officials had been jailed for this offense [as was the incumbent president in 2017]), but the system of incentives and oversight generally ensured that corrupt practices did not run counter to the country's policy priorities. He provided the following example.

> Suppose that a bureaucrat was offered, say, $100,000 by Businessman X to use discretionary powers to circumvent some administrative processes to approve the sale of a piece of government land for a project that was essentially import-competing, while Businessman Y offered him, say, $50,000 for the same favor to set up a largely export-oriented project. In all probability, the bureaucrat would go for the smaller bribe. If he chose the import-competing project, Businessman Y could create a massive hue and cry and accuse the bureaucrat of sabotaging the country's economy. This would trigger a speedy investigation and result in condign punishment for the bureaucrat. If, however, the bureaucrat ruled in favor of the export project, Businessman X would have to bite his tongue and remain silent, because otherwise he could be charged with trying to damage the country's vital interests. Thus, corruption would indeed have taken place, but the country's economic priorities would not have been disrupted.

Campos and Root (1996) suggest another reason why corruption in the East Asian countries did not derail the growth process. They argue that corruption in these countries was concentrated at the top of the political system, and that the decisions taken at the top were implemented by a bureaucracy that was tightly controlled. This enabled these countries to limit the total amount of dishonesty by preventing what Schleifer and Vishny (1993) term "cascading" corruption.

Institutional, political, and international factors make it impractical for Egypt to follow the East Asian route in an undiluted form

Three broad reasons suggest that Egypt is likely to find it impractical to follow the East Asian route in its undiluted form. First, the successful application of a policy in which the government intervenes directly to identify "winners," and works closely with such industries and enterprises to support them through their presumed periods of "infancy," requires strong government institutions, considerable bureaucratic skills, and a firm commitment to economic growth as a national objective. If some or all of these conditions are absent, there is a strong likelihood that selective interventions will be captured by the intended beneficiaries simply to generate economic rents (that is, unearned profits) for as long as possible.

The second reason is political. This has two major facets: (1) the government's commitment to development; and (2) the methods by which the government pursues this aim. Can Egypt, as South Korea did, elevate economic development to the top of its agenda?

The pursuit of economic development requires critical trade-offs between the requirements of development and of other policies. A key element is a resolution to refrain from wars and strife. I have already mentioned the absence of a "hot" war on the Korean Peninsula since 1953, and that there has been no such war between Taiwan and the Republic of China, while Egypt, on the other hand, was involved in a series of wars with Israel, with Saudi Arabia in Yemen, and with Libya. These matters are costly and major disrupters of economic development.

The second important political element relates to the methods by which economic development is pursued. The most dubious aspect of the East Asian, and particularly South Korean, experience was the trade-off between political liberties and economic gain. In both South Korea and Taiwan, unrepresentative and authoritarian regimes were the rule during the period of their most rapid economic growth. In both countries, the regimes sought to legitimize their rule through the provision of economic gains for their subjects. But the surrendering of political rights for the possibility of economic benefits is a chancy proposition. The rulers might not put economic development at the top of their agendas, or they might put it but not succeed in achieving it.

Moreover, the Egyptian people have only recently been engaged in a long struggle against authoritarianism. After this long struggle, I doubt that the electorate would view with much favor the widespread employment of tax inspectors as instruments of harassment, discriminatory directions to commercial banks, discretionary interest rates, concessional effective foreign-exchange rates targeted toward particular enterprises, legal injunctions against trade unions, the outlawing of strikes, or a generalized use of "command backed by compulsion." Nor would an attitude as embodied in such statements as this one from President Chung-Hee Park sit well with the contemporary Egyptian citizen:

> In order to ensure efforts to improve the living conditions of the people in Asia, even undemocratic emergency measures may be necessary. . . . The gem without luster called democracy is a meaningless route for people suffering from starvation and despair. (Park 1970, 39–40)

Ultimately, of course, it is a question of choice—how much democratic freedom one is prepared to give up to (perhaps) get some more economic growth. The South Koreans were not given the choice. I suspect that the average Egyptian, who has seen that "undemocratic emergency measures" do not necessarily bring economic affluence in their wake, might well look askance at an invitation to accept such trade-offs. It means that many of the key measures adopted by South Korea to make it, in Myrdal's terms, a "hard state" are unlikely to appeal to the Egyptian people.

The third reason is the change in the international environment since the time that the East Asian tigers began their charge. The international climate in the two or three decades starting from the 1960s was more permissive than it is today. The East Asian countries were able to pursue an export-oriented strategy that could draw, initially at least, on subsidies and special concessions for the exporting industries, and a significant degree of protection against imports; in effect, these countries followed a neo-mercantilist regime. That train has left the station. Today, the many requirements of the World Trade Organization make it difficult to brazenly follow such a strategy without inviting retaliation or attracting penalties of various kinds.

What Would be a Practical Approach for Egypt to Follow?

Perhaps the clearest result of the discussion of the pros and cons of the Washington Consensus and of the East Asian model, and of the impossibility of adopting the latter in the form used by the "tiger" economies in the heyday of their growth spurt, is that there is no universal development formula that would guarantee the success of all countries at all times. As Rodrik (2008) succinctly sums it up, "each country must devise its own mix of remedies. Foreign economists and aid agencies can supply some of the ingredients, but only the country itself can provide the recipe. . . . If there is a new Washington consensus, it is that the rulebook must be written at home, not in Washington." This is also the message emphasized by the Commission on Growth and Development (el-Erian and Spence 2008).

But it would not be very helpful to leave matters there; as Rodrik (2006) says, such advice would amount to little more than "different strokes for different folks." Fortunately, we do not have to leave matters there. Attempts have been made to provide guides to help developing countries to select a strategy that would at least start off the process of rapid growth.

An important such initiative is Hausmann, Rodrik, and Velasco (2005), which outlines a framework for undertaking "growth diagnostics," that is, ascertaining the most binding constraints on economic growth and targeting them with reform. The authors avoid sweeping recommendations such as, for example, "You must fix the institutional structure," because (1) institutions commonly reflect deeply held beliefs and values, and thus their reform could take a very long time; and (2) there are major examples of countries that have accelerated their growth rate without initially doing very much to reform their institutions. Of course, sustaining a high growth rate over a long period is very likely to require strengthening of institutions, but a country might not find it necessary to do much of this simply in order to start the process of more rapid growth; an example would be India from the 1990s.

The approach suggested by Hausmann, Rodrik, and Velasco (2005, 2006)—and reinforced in Rodrik (2005, 2006)—is for the government to focus on the most binding constraints. A binding constraint is a distortion, the removal of which would produce the largest economic gains (compared with other economic policies). A binding constraint could be identified by direct evidence, for example, that removing the constraint would result in a large increase in the growth rate; or by indirect means, for example, that the economy contained many activities that it was worthwhile pursuing to get around the constraint. The removal of the most binding constraints should set off a period of rapid growth, and the authorities could use the tailwinds from this process to convince the country to undertake further and more deep-seated reforms, such as those of the institutional system.

Hausmann, Rodrik, and Velasco (2005) proposed a taxonomy to help identify the most basic constraints. Their point of departure was that in a low-income country, economic activity would be constrained by (1) the cost of finance being too high, or (2) the private returns to investment being too low. In the former case, one must examine whether the constraint results from low domestic savings, insufficient access to foreign savings, or distortions in the financial system and consequent inefficiencies in financial intermediation. In case (2), the problem must either be due to (a) the absence of supporting factors such as public infrastructure or institutional infrastructure (such as the predictable enforcement of property rights), or inadequate supply of labor skills; or to (b) low private "appropriability" (that is, businesses could not retain a sufficient share of the results of their efforts, because factors such as high taxes, bureaucratic corruption, or a dysfunctional legal system intercepted and siphoned off a substantial part of the profits and prevented it from reaching businesses). In their articles, the authors applied the methodology to countries such as Brazil, El Salvador, and the Dominican Republic.

The recommendation from Hausmann, Rodrik, and Velasco (2005) is that countries design reform priorities according to the magnitude of the direct effects of alleviating the constraint. Their pragmatic advice is that "the best approach is to focus on the reforms where the direct effects can be reasonably guessed to be large. . . . The principle to follow is simple: go for the reforms that alleviate the most binding constraints, and hence produce the biggest bang for the reform buck." They recommend that policymakers start by focusing on the immediate drivers of economic growth, such as saving, investment, productivity, infrastructure, and the like, and then look for economic distortions associated with the factors whose removal would have the biggest effect on easing the constraints on growth.

Hausmann, Rodrik, and Velasco worked with World Bank economists and with Barry Eichengreen (of the University of California, Berkeley) serving as an independent umpire to further develop the framework of growth diagnostics and to clarify its strengths and limitations. Bank economists applied the growth diagnostics method to twelve pilot studies (including Egypt, described below) and subjected the results to review and discussion.

In a brief review of the experiment, Leipziger and Zagha (2006: 16–17) report that it was not possible to apply the framework with the same rigor in all the pilot studies, and therefore a definitive assessment cannot be made. They quote the Nobel laureate Michael Spence to describe the identification of binding constraints on growth in our present state of knowledge as more "disciplined art" than science. More and better data, and more widespread experience with the use of the growth diagnostics framework will be required to arrive at secure conclusions. The principal lesson from applying the framework to the twelve countries was that in order to be effective, policy advice has to be "customized"; it is particularly important to pay special attention to the country's key institutions and figure out ways to move dysfunctional institutions and policies in the direction of the best practice.

In our present state of knowledge, the growth diagnostics framework does not provide a universal formula for easily identifying growth triggers that would work in all countries at all times; that Holy Grail, if it exists, has yet to be found. In the meantime, a bespoke approach, requiring in-depth knowledge of the economy being analyzed, is our best bet. The benefits of the growth diagnostics framework are that it helps policymakers to focus on the basic foundations of sustained growth, enables them to rank reforms according to their impact on growth (thus distinguishing between the critically necessary and the merely desirable), and provides a disciplined structure for identifying areas in which more research is needed.

To the foregoing growth-centric approach, one may usefully add a political-economy counsel from el-Erian and Spence (2008, 3), "Early and continuing attention to the importance of the social compact(s), including distributional ones, appears to be a critically important feature of successful and sustainable growth strategies."

This is an important rider that should be inserted into the discussion. The growth diagnostics approach can be helpful for identifying the most binding constraints on growth, but it does not have much to say about how growth translates into benefits for the population at large and a safety net for the most vulnerable elements in society. Piketty (2013) has argued that over the long term, the returns to owners of capital have exceeded the growth rate of the economy; hence, the gap between incomes of owners of capital and of wage earners has increased, and is likely to keep increasing unless remedial policies are deliberately adopted. The "trickle down" model of distribution has not worked. Its persistent failure led Galbraith (1992, 23) to dismiss it as "the less than elegant metaphor that if one feeds the horse enough oats, some will pass through to the road for the sparrows."

Efforts have been made to preempt the worsening of income inequalities by advocating policies of "inclusive growth," for example, providing subsidies for education. In this case, there need be no conflict between increasing equity and boosting growth; distribution and efficiency would complement each other. This could be an attractive proposition, but one must be aware, as Lindbeck (1998, 304) points out, that (a) the effects on factor-income distribution take considerable time; and (b) large-scale, tax-financed training programs for adults have turned out to be quite expensive and generally require higher taxes. Society has to be prepared to take the long view that such a strategy requires.

Identifying and removing the most binding constraints on growth is essential, but the strategy must also pay close attention to the distributional aspects of the growth, including *perceptions* of equity. A pioneering study by Verme et al. (2014) examined data on income, consumption, and responses to extensive questionnaires on (among many other subjects) happiness, life satisfaction, social status, income classes, and subjective perceptions of inequality between 2000 and 2008 to analyze facts and perceptions about inequality in Egypt.

They examined estimates of equity using different indexes: Gini, Atkinson, Coefficient of Variation, Top and Bottom Deciles, and General Entropy. All the inequality indexes showed declines in inequality between 2000 and 2009; the finding that inequality had not increased in this decade appeared robust. However, there was an apparent mismatch between income inequality measured by household surveys, such as the House-hold Income, Expenditure and Consumption Surveys (HIECS 2000, 2005, 2009) conducted by CAPMAS, and the perception of income inequality measured by values surveys, such as the World Values Surveys (WVS 2000, 2008). Although measured inequality had not increased between 2000 and 2008, *perceptions* of inequality were not congruent with the facts, and people had grown more inequality-averse. Why?

The paper offered no definitive conclusion—it said that "the final culprits of our puzzle may not have been found yet" (Verme et al. 2014, 9)—but suggested some leads. Perhaps the most telling finding was that while GDP per capita had grown steadily, household consumption had not increased, which suggested that GDP growth had not trickled down to households. According to the study, most of the GDP growth had accrued to private enterprises and nongovernment organizations, which grew by more than 40 percent in cumulated terms over the period. Moreover, it appeared that private enterprises had retained the bulk of their earnings or transferred them abroad, rather than distribute them as wages and dividends or invest them domestically. The study observed that "while households may well have observed wealth growing in the public and private sectors, they have seen little accruing to their own pockets" (Verme et al. 2014, 80).

The WVS (2008) threw up another finding that was important from a political-economy viewpoint. The two themes that respondents ranked highest among what should be the government's concerns were economic growth and price stability. If this was the case in 2008 (the year of the survey), the fact that Egypt's growth slowed markedly from that year could only have contributed to heightening discontent. Verme et al. (2014, 90) say that "the revolution in perceptions [concerning welfare and inequality] was already occurring throughout the decade that preceded the 2011 revolution and an attentive look into these data might have provided a different picture from the one portrayed by GDP growth alone." Discontent with and opposition to a regime can be shaped as much by perception as by fact. The Mubarak regime ignored this at its peril.

Attempts have been made to apply the Hausmann, Rodrik, and Velasco (2005) framework to Egypt, for example by Dobronogov and Iqbal (2004) and Enders (2007). The former study found that the most important constraint, especially since 1999, was the relatively high price of financing, and that growth in Egypt had been constrained by the inefficiency of financial intermediation rather than the lack of financial resources. They attributed much of this inefficiency to distortions in access to finance. They pointed out that in the public-sector-dominated banking system, access to finance was not merely a matter of being able to afford the interest rate, but also of connections and relationships with key banking-sector and finance ministry officials. This created wide discrepancies in the availability of finance to different firms, with the problem being especially acute for small firms.

A later study by Enders (2007) arrived at somewhat different conclusions, arguing that "while the evidence strongly supports the view that financial intermediation in Egypt is weak, there is less evidence that this has recently constituted a critical constraint on growth." It pointed out that growth picked up sharply during 2004–2006 (the earlier study had examined the situation only up to 2003), that this was unrelated to any efficiency improvements in the financial sector, and that the access to finance indicators in the World Bank's *Doing Business* reports remained broadly unchanged. Enders therefore remained agnostic on the question of access to finance as the main recent or current obstacle to growth, but accepted that it might become binding soon, even if it was not so already.

The Enders study put its main weight behind the appropriability of returns as a critical constraint, because complex regulations and an inefficient bureaucracy imposed high costs and thus reduced private returns. It also pointed to shortcomings in the education system and the consequent dearth of skills that businesses required, saying that over the longer run Egypt would need to bolster its human capital if the economy were to continue growing at an acceptable pace.

The intention of this chapter is not to adjudicate the merits of the different findings; it is to point to a pragmatic approach that Egypt's policymakers could adopt and develop in deciding upon their interventions. It should also be emphasized, as Hausmann, Rodrik, and Velasco (2006) explicitly do, that the proposed approach is "concerned mainly with *short-run* constraints" (italics in the original). For growth to be sustained over several decades, there is no getting away from strengthening the institutions that underpin the economy's performance. Drawing on the experience of fast-growing countries, Ikram (2006, 283–315) discusses issues bearing on the bureaucracy; the commercial judicial system; the taxation system; the education and training system; social safety nets; and policies to promote equity, including regional equity, such as those that would enable economic outcomes in Upper Egypt to catch up with the rest of the country. For an elaboration of these and other institutional issues, see World Bank (1992), Galal (1995), Giugale and Mubarak (1996), el-Mikawy and Handoussa (2002), Rutherford (2008), Ikram (2006), and World Bank (2012).

The "binding constraints" approach represents only one possible strategy. Others, even more fruitful, will no doubt be developed and in that endeavor one can expect Egypt's gifted economists to play a prominent role. The only comment I would offer is that in constructing a strategy they do not lose sight of the political realities that underlie the economic situation, remembering always that the original name of economics was "political economy."

Economic Management in a Mixed Economy

An important issue that policymakers face in managing a mixed economy concerns the role of planning in the new environment. The increased globalization and privatization of formerly controlled economies have vastly reduced the space for planning by previous methods, whereby the government set targets and used direct controls and instructions to realize them. Increasing globalization also means that the private sector's view of economic prospects will depend not only on the vision of the plan and the impact of its forecasts, but also on factors that are extrinsic to the plan.

Thus, a credit crisis in the United States, a slowdown in the Japanese economy, sharp changes in oil prices, a decision by China to move aggressively into the manufacture of textiles, or other external events could condition businessmen's investment intentions far more than the picture painted by the government's plan.

Privatization raises another set of problems. The government's ability to influence the private sector suffers from the basic asymmetry pointed out earlier—the government can stop the private sector from doing something, but it cannot make the private sector do something. Increasing privatization, therefore, means that the government's control over an ever-growing part of the national economy becomes progressively more diluted.

The difficulties that the planning process runs into when the economy contains a large private sector can be illustrated by an examination in Ikram (2006, 310–12) of the precision of Egypt's plan forecasts for four five-year plans between 1983 and 2002. The estimates used the method employed by the Centraal Planbureau of the Netherlands, namely, a variant of Theil's "U-statistic,"[20] which is based on the root mean squared error (RMSE).[21] Table 3 shows that the forecasts of most variables were less precise than a simple "no-change" extrapolation; the only exceptions were the GDP growth rate in the Third Plan, and employment in the Third and Fourth plans. The performance of the employment forecasts is not surprising: aggregate employment is much less volatile than GDP growth or investment.

And yet, it is often felt that a country cannot abandon its fate to the untrammeled working of a free market. Private markets, even when supposedly efficient and with a generally sound regulatory framework, can fail to deliver

Table 3. Precision of plan forecasts, 1983–2002 (Theil's U-Statistics)

	First Plan (1983–87)	Second Plan (1988–92)	Third Plan (1993–97)	Fourth Plan (1998–2002)
GDP growth rate	1.13	1.65	0.91	1.57
Public investment	2.02	2.11	3.59	1.97
Private investment	4.65	2.33	1.21	2.34
Employment	1.09	1.10	0.35	0.68

Source: Ikram (2006, 311, table 10.2)

the best, even to the people who can pay; just compare the costs and outcomes of the United States' healthcare system with those of the "socialized" systems of the Scandinavian countries or France or the United Kingdom. Moreover, surrounded today by the detritus of the international financial system occasioned in very large measure by the unregulated working of the free market, one recalls Keynes's comment on Hayek (who was the prime proponent of leaving matters to free markets): "It is an extraordinary example of how, starting with a mistake, a remorseless logician can end in Bedlam."[22]

In a situation of ever-increasing space for the private sector, what can policymakers do to ensure that its activities remain in line with social priorities? Is there a role for planning in such a situation and, if so, what might be the nature of the role?

Perhaps the question to ask should really be: why plan? Britain's Industrial Revolution did not arise out of a plan, nor did the rapid early development of France, Germany, the United States, and of virtually every Western country originate from an explicit government-sponsored plan. What is the rationale for such planning in developing countries, for example, China, South Korea, Taiwan, Malaysia, Vietnam, India, , and several others in our day, and with even developed countries, such as France and the Netherlands, taking enthusiastically to planning after the Second World War?

Different answers have been offered, but perhaps the most common goes along the following lines (Dobb 1960; Waterston 1965; Lewis 1966, 1969; Griffin and Enos 1970). A country may have set itself some economic goals, for example, attaining a minimum standard of living for its citizens and warding off external pressures. In operational terms, this would mean increasing the country's production of goods and services (its GDP), paying attention to the distribution of the GDP, and ensuring that it does not pile up unmanageable debts to foreigners, that is, its foreign exchange earnings and expenditures do not get too far out of line. The country's economic actors—citizens, government agencies, farmers, business enterprises, educational bodies, legal and other institutions, and so on—must work toward these ends.

Relying exclusively on market forces to attain these ends faces two crucial difficulties. First, markets are prone to failures of various kinds—such as absence of competition, positive and negative externalities, and incomplete information—that distort economic signals and result in outcomes that may deliver handsome private profits, but are suboptimal from society's point of view.

Second, the strategy can take an inordinately long time to produce results. The country may have millions of independent decision-makers with a host of different preferences and priorities, and market incentives are likely to only slowly align their preferences, and thus their efforts, in the furtherance of society's goals. Thus, for example, two-thirds of Egypt's 2016 population of 90 million was over the age of fifteen years; there might be as much as 50–60 million decision-makers regarding individual consumption. The three million or so nonagricultural private enterprises would provide at least that number of decision-makers for production and distribution activities; while a good part of the 20 percent of Egypt's labor force in agriculture would add a sizable number to the production decision-makers. Marshaling these tens of millions of independent decision-makers to march in a united manner toward the country's goals can be a difficult and time-consuming exercise, especially if coercive measures are ruled out.

Some countries, therefore, decided that the quickest path toward attaining the goals would be to reduce the number of independent decision-makers. The communist countries went furthest in this direction by reducing the decision-makers to a single one—the state. The implementation of their plans could also require a considerable degree of compulsion to make people's actions conform to the plans' priorities.

Democratic countries obviously could not follow this extreme path, and adopted other means of reducing the number of independent decision-makers or aligning the efforts of economic actors with the government's priorities. France, for example, began planning in 1947 and drastically reduced the number of decision-makers in production by offering substantial fiscal incentives that would encourage smaller firms to merge and form oligopolies in their sectors.[23] Schonfield (1965, 128–29) writes that French planners believed in the "80–20 ratio," namely, that around 80 percent of production ought to come from about 20 percent of the firms, and that a diluted ratio of even 60–40 would be unmanageable in the long run. The government also set up state-owned enterprises in key sectors, such as steel production.

The Netherlands, another country with a sophisticated planning apparatus, adopted a somewhat different mechanism. The country had implemented a system of price controls after the Second World War, and the government was prepared to be "understanding" regarding price increases requested by firms that went along with the priorities of the plan.

The economies of Japan and South Korea were dominated by the *zaibatsu* and the *chaebol* respectively (very large conglomerates)[24] and the governments of these countries were able to concentrate the offer of incentives and the imposition of disincentives on the holding companies of these conglomerates. The governments of Japan and South Korea were thus able to control the commanding heights of their economies by influencing only a few dozens, instead of millions, of decision-makers.

Moreover, different types of coercion were employed. Tudor (2012, 67) records that immediately following his successful coup on May 16, 1961, President Park Chung-Hee of Korea arrested several leading businessmen "and subjected them to public humiliations, such as being forced to march through the streets carrying placards proclaiming, 'I am a corrupt swine.'" Businessmen were offered the choice of following the country's development plans or going to jail. It did not take them long to decide, especially as following the government's aims not only avoided the stick, but also delivered several carrots.

The *chaebol* were provided preferential access to scarce resources— such as land (in South Korea usable land is in extremely short supply), foreign exchange, bank credit, tax exemptions on imported intermediate inputs, and other incentives—provided they met the targets (especially for exports) mandated by the government. This encouraged the conglomerates to grow rapidly and reap the benefits of economies of scale, thus maintaining the spectacular growth of the South Korean economy.

Especially after the Second World War, a number of democratic countries that wanted to rebuild their economies rapidly also adopted economic planning. However, they could not appoint the state as the sole arbiter of economic decisions, and nor could they employ intimidation as a tool to compel millions of small enterprises to align their production with the plans' targets. Countries adopted solutions that differed in details, but the general approach was to develop a form of planning that was not "controlling," but was "indicative."

As described by Arthur Lewis (1966, 19–21), a "controlling" plan is of the type that was prepared by communist countries and was a document of authorization; it instructed economic units on what they had to produce, how much to invest, how much labor they could hire, and so on. On the other hand, an "indicative" plan for the private sector does not attempt to define binding commitments, but only reflects expectations and intentions. An indicative plan can lay out targets, but there is no way of making them compulsory for the private sector. The desired outcomes are attained by policies that provide the appropriate mix of incentives and disincentives for the private sector.

The basic theory behind indicative planning has been articulated by Meade (1970), Estrin and Holmes (1983), Crémer and Crémer (1994, 57–73), and others, but perhaps most succinctly by Brada and Estrin (1990, 523–30). The latter argue that since forward markets[25] do not exist for many commodities and services, economic agents are forced to make decisions based on incomplete or incorrect information. This lack of coordination is likely to produce a suboptimal allocation of resources, which will impact adversely on saving, investment, and future growth. On the other hand, if credible forecasts of future production, exports, imports, labor market trends, and so on were available, they would provide much the same information as would prices generated by a complete system of forward markets. The provision of missing information about the future by means of indicative plans would enable economic actors to share a coherent view of the future. This should lead to better coordination, more efficient decisions, and a more optimal allocation of resources. The government would reinforce the informational and exhortative effects by measures such as taxes, subsidies, and interest rates, to push private decisions in directions that were judged to be socially desirable.

While dyed-in-the-wool planners might feel uncomfortable with the degree of looseness and uncertainty implicit in such an approach to planning, there is no way around it. Making plans for an economy with a large and growing private sector is intrinsically more precarious and less definite than doing it for a command economy. As the Egyptian economy becomes more complex and privatized, the Ministry of Planning will have to fashion the tools and develop the skills for indicative planning.[26] The planners will have to focus on devising effective policies and on ensuring that public and private projects work in congruence; they will also have to obtain regular feedback from the private sector and establish systematic ways of interacting with it.

In the early 2000s, the Ministry of Planning started background work on indicative planning that included setting up public–private advisory committees on economic policies and targets. This broadly emulated the approach adopted by South Korea for its Sixth Five-Year Plan (1987–91), which was prepared by thirty-two committees, each of whose membership comprised equal numbers of government and private sector representatives.

The chairmen of these committees, following South Korean law, were appointed by the public sector, but the private sector was empowered to provide the co-chairmen. If the government wishes to use planning as one of its tools for managing the Egyptian economy in its new environment, work on a type of indicative planning will have to be revived and built upon, and successful examples from other countries will have to be studied.

In today's circumstances, ministries of planning in many countries increasingly see their work as chiefly comprising (1) evaluating and monitoring public sector projects; (2) helping formulate policies in cooperation with other ministries that would provide incentives to the private sector for acting in accordance with society's priorities (and disincentives for acting against them); (3) maintaining a continuing dialogue (including formal surveys) with the private sector to determine the main factors that increase the cost of doing business in the country, and to ascertain how these elements have been tackled in the more successful countries; and (4) keeping an eye on income equity in the country, including regional differences. Obviously, Egypt's policymakers may have to modify this list to suit the particular circumstances of the country.

Egyptian policymakers face multiple challenges. They have to deal with serious economic problems, and must do so in an environment of political uncertainty, incipient terrorism, and an international economy that has yet to recover much of its dynamism and in which for many countries the appeal of protectionist impediments to trade is not far from the surface. They will also lack some of the important tools of economic management and control that were available to their predecessors. It will require all of the government's political-economy skills, and a certain amount of luck, to successfully navigate Egypt through the difficulties that confront the country. The Egyptian people, however, have shown their fortitude and their resilience in previous crises, and this gives one the confidence in their ability to overcome any that lie ahead. To which sentiment one must, of course, add the traditional Egyptian *"insha' Allah."*

Annex: The Economic Activities of the Public Sector

Four major types of public institutions (in addition to the government) are involved in economic activities: (1) local government productive enterprises; (2) service authorities; (3) Economic Authorities; and (4) public enterprises. The last two are the main public-sector economic agents in Egypt.

There are somewhat more than sixty Economic Authorities, which cover the most important sectors of the economy: the utilities, the Suez Canal Company, the Petroleum Company, the General Authority for Supply (which controls the import and distribution of the basic subsidized commodities), social and health insurance, and so on. They are organized as semi-autonomous corporations, and in the beginning of the 1990s employed about 3 percent of the labor force and produced about 20 percent of the GDP. In the early 1990s, the public enterprises produced around 10 percent of GDP and employed about 6 percent of the labor force. They also dominated the banking and insurance sectors.

As part of its structural reform program, the government committed itself to privatizing 314 public enterprises, but not the Economic Authorities.

Notes

Introduction

1 Ikram (2010) provides an accessible introduction to ancient Egypt.

2 According to Eisenhower (1965, 92n10) the United Kingdom's gold and dollar reserves fell by $57 million in September 1956, $84 million in October, and $279 million in November—an amount equal to 15 percent of the British reserves' total.

3 Cameron Cobbold, the governor of the Bank of England, quoted in Subramanian (2011, 14).

4 See Rivkin (2009, 1–35, 95–105) for a discussion of the relationship between demography and economics in Arab countries generally as well as specifically in Egypt.

5 Indeed, Abramovitz (1956, 1) referred to it as "a measure of our ignorance."

6 Human capital-adjusted labor incorporates the contribution of education and size of the labor force to labor input.

7 In a similar survey for 2016, Egypt ranked 131st out of 189 countries.

8 The same lesson has been pointed out for other countries; see, for example, Ikram (2011) for Pakistan, and Panagariya (2008, 110–25) for India.

1: The Political Economy of Reform

1 See especially Drazen (2000) for a comprehensive discussion.

2 Kandil 2012, 8–9. He also notes that eight of the eleven ringleaders of the Free Officers Movement came from landless families. See Abdel-Fadil (1975, 7–17) for details of the land distribution program.

3 These owned plots larger than fifty *feddan*s.

4 A *feddan* is equal to 1.038 acres or 0.42 hectares.

5 However, it did nothing to improve the situation of the poorest section of the population, namely, the landless rural laborers.

6 The situation had analogies with that in Korea and Taiwan after the Second World War. Much of the best agricultural land had been owned by the colonial power (that is, Japan) and its collaborators. After Japan's defeat in the war, the governments of Korea and Taiwan faced little opposition in redistributing this land to their own (non-collaborating) citizens, with very little compensation paid to the original owners.

7 See also Bhagwati (1988, 72–73) and Ray (1998, 718–21). The latter also provides an interesting speculation on why the most successful trade lobbies have historically been protectionist rather than export-oriented. He suggests that potential exporters may be just as diffuse a group as consumers, and that exporters may unite in a coalition only after a market is opened or an export subsidy has been offered.

8 Emphasis in the original.

9 More strictly, economic rents are payments to factors of production greater than what is required to put the factor into use. They generally arise because of the scarcity of that factor or because the government restricts other factors or agents from coming into use.

10 The ideological and political range in the views of the Free Officers is commented on in chapter 5. Springborg (1989, 61) even asserts that the Egyptian government "is not united either organizationally or ideologically."

11 Interview March 27, 2000.

12 Paul Dickie was the IMF representative in Cairo. It is, in fact, unfair to blame him for the content of the IMF program, which reflected standard IMF thinking and was authorized by his superiors in Washington.

13 The average cost as a percentage of GDP was: Tunisia, 2.1; Syria, 3.3; Lebanon, 3.4; Algeria, 3.6; and Morocco, 3.7.

14 See, for example, Magee 1972; Bale 1976; Mutti 1978; Baldwin, Mutti, and Richardson 1980; Morkre and Tarr 1980; Dixon, Parmenter, and Powell 1984; Tarr and Morkre 1984; de Melo and Tarr 1990; Takacs and Winters 1991; de Melo and Roland-Holst 1994; Harrison and Revenga 1995; and Matusz and Tarr 2000.

15 Baldwin, Mutti, and Richardson (1980) examined 367 sectors.

16 For names and periods of incumbency see Guwwadi (1997).

17 Dr. Higazi figured in cabinets from 1972, rising successively from minister of the treasury, to deputy prime minister for economic affairs, to prime minister in 1974.

18 They estimated that in 1964 prices, the 1999 salary worked out to a mere LE73.51.

19   The question of low government salaries and damaged incentives regularly came up in meetings of donors in Cairo. Few new ideas were offered—all the solutions appeared to involve more financial resources. The government was reluctant to raise more by way of taxation, and the donors felt that in their aid budgets Egypt was already an outlier and could not reasonably expect more. Donors for the most part fell back on offering advice in the shape of aphorisms. Two such aphorisms that were repeated so frequently as to become virtual clichés were: (i) a statement by the first prime minister of Singapore, Lee Kuan Yew, to the effect that "if you pay peanuts, you get monkeys." (ii) a frequently repeated remark by the shipbuilders in Poland that "they [the government] pretend to pay us and we pretend to work."

20   He was the Russian minister of finance for fifteen years and prime minister for a year, and was responsible for establishing the Russian banking system as well as for a large part of the industrialization of the country, and for the development of the railway system. See also von Laue (1963).

21   He had previously been the U.S. ambassador to Saudi Arabia, Iran, Iraq, and the United Arab Emirates, and had managed the Middle East desk at the U.S. embassy in London.

22   We continued to meet regularly, both in Cairo and in Washington, and I must acknowledge how much I benefited from his experience and sagacity.

23   For example, March 28, 1987 and May 23, 1987.

24   Signed on September 17, 1978. The 1978 Consultative Group meeting took place in June.

25   Peter Kemp, "Egypt: A Very Soft Deal," *Middle East International* 29 (May 1987). Quoted in Springborg (1989, 288 fn36). The senior IMF official headed the strategic Exchange and Trade Relations Department.

26   See Sharp (2010).

27   Quoted in Nelson and Sharp 2013, 15.

28   As an example, Egypt might receive wheat, or meat, or tallow in the form of a grant under the aid program (as it did under the Public Law 480 program), which is then sells in the domestic market and thereby earns domestic currency for the budget.

29   Boone (1996) provides a useful overview of the politics of aid, while good discussions of strategic aid and aid effectiveness include McKinley and Little (1979), Maizels and Nissanke (1984), Burnside and Dollar (1997), World Bank (1998a), Dollar and Kray (2001), and Ludborg (1998). A comprehensive review of issues bearing on the effectiveness of

aid is provided in the volume edited by Mavrotas (2010), especially the paper by Tarp (2010).

30 *Grant element* measures the concessionality of a loan. It is defined as the difference between the face value of a loan and the discounted present value of the stream of repayments (including interest) to which it will give rise, expressed as a percentage of the face value. By combining the effects of the various elements of the terms into a single measure, the grant element enables loans with differing terms to be compared. For example, if a set of terms (interest, maturity, and grace period) produces a grant element of, say, 30 percent, it essentially means that the recipient of the funds should be indifferent between receiving a grant of 30 percent of the face value, or a loan of 100 percent of the face value on the terms that gave rise to the 30 percent grant element. See Schmidt (1964), Pincus (1965), and Ohlin (1966, especially 102–105 for derivation of the relevant formulae).

31 Bossuat 2008, 13; Gardner 2001, 120.

32 Note that Tarp (2010, 46) points out that cross-country econometric studies also have faced methodological criticisms; see also Solow (2001) and Acemoglu and Robinson (2010).

33 U.S. ambassador Hermann Eilts told me he was embarrassed that the Mercedes buses assembled in Iran had proved more durable on Cairo's potholed streets than the U.S.-supplied buses.

2: Challenges and Performance, 1952–2016

1 *National savings* represent savings by Egyptian nationals, no matter in which country they are generated; *domestic savings* represent savings generated within Egypt. Of course *national* savings must be compared with Gross *National* Product, which for Egypt tends to be higher than Gross *Domestic* Product.

2 The "discouraged worker" problem affects the unemployment data of many countries, including the United States (see Ikram, 2006, 322 fn 29).

3 A qualification must be entered at this point. The activities of the National Investment Bank and the social security and pension funds have not been treated consistently in budgets; correcting for this could significantly change the details for certain years.

4 This refers only to the defense expenditures shown in the budget. It is believed that a significant amount of defense spending is off-budget.

5 For example: World Bank 1974; IMF 1976; Roy 1980; Abdel-Fadil 1983; Richards 1984; Waterbury 1983; World Bank 1983; Beblawi 1987;

Springborg 1989; Hansen 1991; Sadowski 1991; Roussillon 1998; Marcou 2008; Farah 2009; Soliman 2011; and Kandil 2012.

6 A VAT is a percentage tax on value added, applied at each stage of production. It is essentially an alternative method for collecting a retail sales tax.

7 Namely, the real revenue obtained by the government when inflation erodes the real value of its nominal liabilities, that is, the money base (the Central Bank of Egypt's liability) and the domestic public debt (the Ministry of Finance's liability). In real terms, the seigniorage, R_s, is given by $R_s = \sigma M/P$ where σ is the money growth rate, M the money balances, and P the price level. The inflation tax, R_i, on the other hand, is given by $R_i = \pi M/P$ where π is the rate of inflation. This is not a revenue directly received by the government in the period in question, but is a capital loss sustained by the holders of money. Seigniorage is identical with the inflation tax only when $\sigma = \pi$, that is, if households maintain a constant value of real money balances. Since the inflation tax is the product of the inflation rate and the demand for real high-powered money (the demand for which falls as inflation rises), the inflation tax has a theoretical maximum, depending upon the interest elasticity of demand for high-powered money (that is, the monetary base, consisting of currency and banks' deposits with the Central Bank of Egypt). See the discussion in Burgess and Stern (1993, 768–70). The use and behavior of the inflation tax in Egypt are discussed in more detail in Ikram (2006, 168–71).

8 For example, if inflation increased by, say, 10 percent, current budgetary expenditure would increase by more than 10 percent.

9 The principal accounts include Radwan and Lee 1977; Ikram 1980; Ibrahim 1982; Abdel-Khalek and Tignor 1982; World Bank 1991; Korayem 1994; UNDP 1996; el-Leithy and Osman 1996; Cardiff 1997; el-Leithy, el-Khawaga, and Riad 1999; Datt, Joliffe, and Sharma 1999; Haddad and Ahmed 1999; World Bank 2002b; MOP/World Bank 2004; Ikram 2006; World Bank 2007; World Bank 2011; and CAPMAS 2015.

10 As an illustration, World Bank (2011, 4) estimated the food poverty line (extreme poverty) for 2009 at LE1,656 of food consumed per person per year; the lower (main) poverty line at about LE2,216; and the upper poverty line at LE2,806. These criteria defined 21.6 percent of Egyptians as "absolute poor," of which 6.7 percent were classified as "extreme poor," while another 19.2 percent were defined as "near poor."

11 The 1982 estimate (el-Leithy, el-Khawaga, and Riad 1999) is based on an income poverty line while the others are derived from household expenditures.

12 Defined for 2015 as LE482 per month (compared with LE326 in 2013).
13 van der Weide, Lakner, and Ianchovichina (2017, 2).
14 Say the international price of a widget is $100, and the government imposes a tax of 10 percent on the import of widgets; the price to an Egyptian consumer would therefore be $110. An Egyptian producer of widgets or its substitute could thus sell his product in the domestic market for $110, and would have no incentive to export them to the international market where he would get only $100.
15 The effective rate of protection measures the protection given to value-added in an activity.
16 Formally, the condition states that if trade is initially balanced and the elasticities of supply of exports and imports are infinite, devaluation will improve the trade balance if the absolute sum of the foreign elasticity of demand for exports and the home elasticity of demand for imports (measured in the same currency) exceeds unity. That is, devaluation will improve the current account of the balance of payments if: $|E_m| + |E_x| > 1$, where E_m is the price elasticity of demand for imports, and E_x is the price elasticity of demand for exports. The condition is named after Marshall (1924, Appendix J), Lerner (1944, 377–79), and Robinson (1937, 138–46).
17 The Real Exchange Rate is the nominal exchange rate adjusted for the difference in inflation between the home country and its competitors.
18 Namely, 3.5 against 4.7 percent.
19 The average maturity on Egyptian loans during the 1980s was over twenty-five years, more than double those of the main Latin American borrowers; the grace periods averaged almost ten years; the average interest rate charged on Egyptian loans was substantially lower than that charged on loans to other countries at comparable levels of per capita income.

3: The Population and Related Issues

1 By depositing silt, the Nile has also over centuries added to the land in the Delta and thereby increased the area of the country. It was because of this that Herodotus in his *Histories*, Book 2, Chapter 5, referred to Egypt as "the gift of the river."
2 The Egyptian definition counts as "urban" the governorates of Cairo, Alexandria, Port Said, Ismailiya, Suez, frontier governorates, and capitals of other governorates, as well as district capitals (*marakiz*, sing. *markaz*).
3 Quoted in Kunzing (2012).

4 At that time, Egypt's population was 18 million.

5 Egypt's population was then 21 million.

6 Egypt's population at that time was 26 million.

4: Political Economy in the Nasser Period, 1952–70

1 Quoted in Baker (1978, 102).

2 Little (1965, 25) estimated the flow in 1878–79 as providing 130 billion cubic yards in excess of Egypt's requirements.

3 The coefficient of variation, which measures the fluctuations with respect to the mean, works out at 21.5 percent between 1870 and 1959.

4 For a discussion of some of these issues see Waterbury (1979).

5 Until June 1972 the Egyptian fiscal year ran from July 1 to June 30 of the following year, and was frequently written as a split year; for example, the fiscal year ending in June 1972 would be written as 1971/72. From 1973 to 1979 the fiscal year was changed to a calendar-year basis, but from July 1980 it reverted to a July–June basis. In this book, a simpler transcription has been adopted; thus the fiscal year ending in June 1972 simply appears as 1972. The text will make clear if a calendar year is meant.

6 Quoted in O'Brien (1966, 68).

7 Mead 1967, 272–73; O'Brien 1966, 100, 107; and Mansfield 1965, 136; see also Wahba (1994, 73, table 4), who gives the private-sector share of GDP in 1961 as 76 percent. The figures probably understate the share of government in GDP, but even after correcting for this, O'Brien (1966, 107–108) concludes that at least two-thirds of GDP took place outside the government's contribution.

8 Availability of resources = GDP (market prices) + Indirect Taxes + Imports. Resource use = Consumption + Investment + Exports.

9 See, for example, Hansen and Marzouk 1965, 72; O'Brien 1966, 214–15; Amin 1968, 41–42; Hottinger 1968, 118–19; and Baker 1978, 63–65.

10 United Arab Republic, Information Department, *The Charter* (n.d., 49–74). For a summary of the economic sections, see O'Brien (1966, 132–36) and Mansfield 1965, 130–32).

11 This asymmetry is common to all attempts at private-sector planning.

12 The budget year ran from July 1 to June 30 of the following year; thus the budget years should properly be written 1959/60 and 1964/65. However, the convention followed in this book is to write, for example, the budget year 1959/60 simply as 1960. The context will make it clear whether the date refers to a fiscal or a calendar year.

13 As matters turned out, however, the nationalizations of 1960 and 1961 dramatically accelerated government control over the country's productive apparatus.

14 "Industrial" at this time basically connoted "manufacturing," as oil production was negligible.

15 Baker (1978, 63), quoting UAR Information Department.

16 The foregoing estimates are from Hansen (1968, 31, table 8).

17 *Akhbar al-Youm*, September 7, 1974 quoted in Waterbury (1983, 94).

18 Interview with Kaissouni.

19 That is, what it could earn in an alternative use, for example, simply being sold as raw cotton.

20 Reliance on inefficient or outdated technology work persisted for quite some time. A visit to Egypt's second-largest textile complex even in the mid-1970s showed it to be employing Swiss technology from the 1930s. The manager explained that the mill had been provided with Eastern Bloc machines which worked faster, but they repeatedly broke the threads, and machines had continually to be stopped in order to repair the threads. The result, as the manager bitterly complained, was that the "beautiful Egyptian cotton" was producing cloth that was full of knots and could only be sold internationally at low prices. He had consequently packed up the Eastern machinery and restored the old Swiss machines, even though these worked much more slowly. The use of the old machinery created its own problems, in that spare parts for the obsolete Swiss machines were no longer available, but he made do with semi-satisfactory replacements fabricated in his own machine shop.

21 A vice-president.

22 This appears to overlook the agrarian reforms.

23 Say that producing a meter of cotton cloth cost an Egyptian businessman LE10 in labor and LE20 in raw cotton, and that he earned $10 from exporting the cloth. The returns to the businessman, that is, the private cost of earning a dollar, would be LE3. Let us assume that the foreign exchange rate ($1= LE3) reflected free market conditions and that at that rate the transaction was just profitable for the businessman. However, if the domestic businessman had received the raw cotton at an administratively controlled price, and in the international free market the cotton could have been sold for, say, LE40 (that is, $13.3) then the real resource cost to society of earning a dollar was LE5 [(LE40 + LE10)/$10]. The export of the cloth would produce a social loss—the country would have given up $13.3 in resources in order to earn $10.

24 Social profit is the difference between costs and revenues measured at their scarcity or opportunity cost [the latter is the maximum benefit that could be obtained in an alternative use of the resource] rather than at administered values.

25 See, for example, Nutting (1972), Mabro (1974), Waterbury (1983), and Hansen (1991).

5: Political Economy in the Sadat Period, 1970–81

1 The Central Agency for Public Mobilization and Statistics (CAPMAS) uses a Laspeyres-type estimator as the Consumer Price Index. This type of index number assumes that quantities remain fixed from time period to time period, until the weights are revised; at the time under discussion, the index was based on weights estimated in 1965, about ten years earlier. There were also questions concerning the coverage of the index, and other technical problems in its construction that were pointed out by World Bank, IMF, and USAID statisticians. These technical considerations would be apart from any political "massaging" of the figures.

2 The conflict also marked the first use of the "oil weapon" by the Arab countries, by which they reduced their oil production and differentiated between consumers according to their stand on the Arab issue and Israel.

3 I interviewed Dr. Higazi on December 28, 1999; July 11, 2000; July 4, 2001; September 5, 2006; and May 14 and 15, 2008.

4 The absence of properly conducted household income and expenditure surveys meant that indirect measures had to be used for estimating levels of income. The indirect measures were essentially the per capita consumption of the most widely used commodities and services.

5 On July 5, 2001.

6 Interviews, April 10 and August 27, 2000.

7 Although the USAID director (Don Brown) was heard to mutter under his breath the old saying, "If you think you understand the Egyptian economy, it has not been explained to you properly."

8 Heikal (1983, 88) reports that in the late 1970s the smallest flat in Cairo would cost a family at least LE30,000, while to rent one would require a deposit of at least LE5000. To put that in perspective, note that the per capita income in 1978 was LE217.

9 Parenthetically, one may note that the World Bank estimated that the implicit subsidy in 1979 to users of petroleum products was as large as

the combined subsidy bill arising out of all explicit consumer subsidies and public authority deficits.

10 This also led to a variety of initiatives proposed by international organizations, such as a "basic needs" approach, the idea of which was to meet the essential needs of the poor while avoiding the waste of untargeted subsidization; see for example, Ikram (1980).

6: Political Economy in the Mubarak Period, 1981–2011

1 The performance of the economy leading to the ERSAP is discussed in more detail in Subramanian (1997), Abdel-Khalek (1998, 2001), and Ikram (2006).

2 Respectively deputy prime minister for economic affairs, minister of public enterprises, minister of finance, governor of the Central Bank of Egypt, and minister of international cooperation.

3 This is discussed in much more detail in Ikram (2006, 60–84).

4 The first two stages each provided debt relief of 15 percent of the net present value (NPV) and were completed in July 1991 and October 1993, respectively. The third stage provided relief of 20 percent of NPV and was completed in 1996.

5 The pre-stabilization period has been taken to be from the 1987 debt rearrangement to 1992; the stabilization period from 1992 until 1997, that is, after the completion of the 1991–96 debt rearrangements.

6 For an overview of these issues see Ikram (2006, 287–315).

7 See World Bank (1994) and World Bank (1995a).

8 For a more detailed discussion see Ikram (2006, 76–84).

9 "When *I* use a word," Humpty Dumpty said, "it means just what I choose it to mean." Lewis Carroll, *Through the Looking Glass*.

10 Figures in square brackets represent updates from World Trade Organization, *Trade Profiles 2015*.

11 World Bank (1978, 3) confirmed that by 1975 Egypt's public-sector spinners were being sold cotton at one-third the international price but, despite the subsidy, production costs remained high owing to overstaffing and inefficiency.

12 Prior to January 29, 2003 the Egyptian pound was pegged to the dollar with all foreign-exchange transactions taking place within a +/- 3 percent range around the central rate, which was announced by the Central Bank of Egypt. Effective January 29, 2003, the Egyptian pound was allowed to float.

13 Government interventions that encourage or decide how resources are allocated in the industrial sector.

7: After Mubarak, 2011–2016

1 Thus in 2015, more than 25 million persons would be classified as "poor."

2 The role of growth "software" is gaining increasing attention in discussions of development strategy; see for example, Ikram et al. (2011); Pakistan Planning Commission (2011); and Lam, Rodlauer, and Schipke (2017).

3 See, for example, Nassim Taleb's *The Black Swan*.

8: The Task Ahead

1 Quoted in Bianco (2015).

2 The International Labor Office definition for formal employment covers workers in government or public enterprises, or whose jobs provide either social insurance or a formal written work contract. Workers whose employment arrangements do not meet these conditions and who are not in the farm sector are defined as being in the informal sector.

3 World Bank (2014, 106).

4 For example, Williamson himself reported that at the 1989 conference it was argued by some participants that "consensus" was too strong a term, and that "convergence" would better capture the degree of agreement. Similarly, others preferred a more nuanced approach to the time horizon of the policies considered; for example, one participant argued that there was a certain amount of consensus on short-term policy issues, less on medium-term issues, and still less on the long-term issues.

5 By the late 1990s, the World Bank had joined the critics on many elements of the Washington Consensus; the U.S. Treasury, the IMF, and some other institutions continued to favor it. See Stiglitz (2004).

6 See World Bank (1993a, 60–70); Thorbecke and Wan (1999, 3–20); Kim and Hong (1997, 183, table 8-5); Stiglitz and Yusuf (2001, 16, tables 1.3 and 1.4); World Bank (2006, 13, tables 2.2 and 2.3).

7 See, for example, the references cited in Frank, Kim, and Westphal (1975), Mason et al.(1980), Westphal and Kim (1982), and Song (2003).

8 The government continued to use the carrot and the stick on recalcitrant businesses. In the mid-1990s I was told by the president of a large conglomerate that he had been compelled by the government to sell the very profitable shoe-making company from his group for having fallen foul of the government's policies. He was particularly upset because the shoe-making enterprise was so profitable that it could comfortably subsidize the rest of the conglomerate.

9 World Bank (1987, 1:102, and 2:85–92). See also 2:131–214 for three useful case studies.

10 A detailed study by Westphal and Kim (1982, 271) concluded that over the 1960s, "manufactured exports were more labor-intensive than manufactured imports, and they became increasingly more labor intensive over time even as shifts in the composition of output caused manufacturing production for the domestic market to become somewhat more capital intensive. The aggregate labor-capital ratio in the manufacturing sector actually increased between 1960 and 1973; at the same time, total factor productivity about doubled."

11 *The Economist*, "Moon Mission?" May 6–12, 2017, p. 12.

12 The Korean language, Hangul, has a phonetic script, but about two thousand Chinese characters are still widely used and are taught in schools. They must be learned in order to be sufficiently literate to read newspapers, books, and so on. Taiwan, of course, uses only the Chinese script.

13 See William J. Baumol (1965).

14 See Cohn (1979, 53) for a summary of the findings of some of these studies.

15 This should be read in conjunction with the discussion in chapter 1 above.

16 Egypt is not alone in confusing announcement with implementation. Krueger (1992, 3) notes that Argentina announced eleven reform programs in the three years 1989–91.

17 For the Korean case see Jones and SaKong (1981, 241–42); Johnson (1987, 143–44); Cole and Lyman (1971, especially chapters 3 and 5). For the Taiwanese case, see Johnson (1981, 9–18).

18 For examples, see Jones and SaKong (1980, 127–35 and appendix B); Amsden (1989, 15).

19 For example: Mason et al. (1980, 267–68) put debt–equity ratios in manufacturing in the range of three or four to one in the first half of the 1970s; Scitovsky (1986, 153) notes that from 1972 to 1981, the current plus fixed liabilities of Korean manufacturing enterprises were 364 percent of their net worth—more than four times as high as in the United States. Moreover, almost two-thirds of that debt was short-term (current liabilities), making the firms even more vulnerable to movements in interest rates and to the continued availability of bank credit. Kim (1990, 344) estimates that during 1977–86 the ratio of equity to total value (equity plus debt) for all nonfinancial firms listed on the Korean stock exchange was about 16 percent, compared with around 45 percent for Japan and the United States. The *chaebol* (large conglomerates) were in debt to government-sponsored or approved institutions for more than

four times the value of their equity assets (Steinberg 1989, 135). See also Harvie and Lee (2003).

20 The U-statistic has a number of properties that make it attractive for assessing the precision of forecasts. The most important are that U = 0 if and only if the forecasts are all perfect (the projected outcome is equal to the realized outcome); and that U = 1 when the projection procedure leads to the same RMSE as the naive projection. The U-statistic has no upper bound, which means that it is possible to do considerably worse than by extrapolating on a naive, no-change basis. Thus, the higher the value of U, the less precise is the projection, and if U > 1, then the projections are on average worse than the naive forecasts. Theil (1966, 27–28) provides an interpretation of the U statistic—a value of, say, U = 1.25 means that the RMSE is 125 per cent of the RMSE that would have been observed if the forecaster had confined himself to a no-change extrapolation.

21 The root mean squared error: $RMSE = \sqrt{\frac{\Sigma(P_i - A_i)}{N}}$, where P_i and A_i are, respectively, the projected and actual values, and N is the number of observations.

22 Quoted in Skidelsky (1992, 457).

23 A commentator on these activities described a French official announcing that he had that day created "un véritable holocaust" of small firms by merging them together to form a larger entity.

24 The Korean *chaebol* are modeled on the Japanese *zaibatsu*; indeed, both words are spelled the same in Chinese characters. The *chaebol* are family-controlled; the *zaibatsu* control is held more widely.

25 Forward markets are contracts between buyers and sellers for future delivery of currency or commodities at prices agreed-upon at the date of making the contract. They provide a hedge against fluctuations in prices.

26 For a detailed discussion of this issue in the case of Pakistan, see Ikram (2009).

References

Abdel-Fadil, M. 1975. *Development, Income Distribution and Social Change in Rural Egypt (1952–1970): A Study in the Political Economy of Agricultural Transition*. Cambridge, UK: Cambridge University Press.

———. 1980. *The Political Economy of Nasserism*. Cambridge, UK: Cambridge University Press.

———. 1983. *Speculations on the Question of the Egyptian Economy*. Cairo: Dar al-Mustaqbal al-'Arabi.

Abdel-Khalek, G. 1998. "Egypt's Economic Reform and the Challenges of Globalization." In *The Middle East and Development in a Changing World*, edited by D. Heisel. *Cairo Papers in Social Science* 20 (2): 35–54.

———. 2001. *Stabilization and Adjustment in Egypt*. Cheltenham, UK: Edward Elgar.

Abdel-Khalek, G., and R. Tignor, eds. 1982. *The Political Economy of Income Distribution in Egypt*. New York: Holmes and Meier.

Abdel Rahman, S.H. 1959. "A Survey of the Foreign Trade of Egypt in the Post-war Period, with Special Reference to Its Impact on the National Economy." PhD diss., Faculty of Commerce, Cairo University.

——— 1962. *Comprehensive Economic Planning in the UAR*. Memo 238. Cairo: Institute of National Planning.

Abramovitz, M. 1956. "Resource and Output Trends in the United States since 1870." *American Economic Review* 46 (May): 5–23.

Acemoglu, D., and J. Robinson. 2010. "The Role of Institutions in Growth and Development." Commission on Growth and Development, Working Paper 10. Washington, DC: World Bank on behalf of the Commission on Growth and Development.

Adam, C., and S. Dercon. 2009. "The Political Economy of Development: An Assessment." *Oxford Review of Economic Policy* 25 (2): 173–89.

Ahmed, S. 1984. "Public Finance in Egypt." Staff Working Paper 639. Washington, DC: World Bank.

Aisen, A., and F.J. Veiga. 2011. "How Does Political Instability Affect Economic Growth?" IMF Working Paper. Washington DC: IMF.

Alderman, H., J. von Braun, and S.A. Sakr. 1982. *Egypt's Food Subsidy and Rationing System: A Description*. Washington, DC: International Food Policy Research Institute.

Alesina, A. 1992. "Political Models of Macroeconomic Policy and Fiscal Reform." Policy Research Working Paper 970. Washington DC: World Bank.

Alesina, A., S. Özler, N. Roubini, and P. Swagel. 1996. "Political Instability and Economic Growth." *Journal of Economic Growth* 1 (2): 189–211.

Ali, S., and R.H. Adams. 1996. "The Egyptian Food Subsidy System: Operation and Effects on Income Distribution." *World Development* 24 (11): 1777–91.

Amin, G. 1968. "The Egyptian Economy and the Revolution." In Vatikiotis 1968, 40–49. London: Allen and Unwin.

——. 1995. *Egypt's Economic Predicament*. Leiden: E.J. Brill.

——. 2011. *Egypt in the Era of Hosni Mubarak, 1981–2011*. Cairo: American University in Cairo Press.

Amsden, A. 1989. *Asia's Next Giant: South Korea and Late Industrialization*. New York: Oxford University Press.

Anis, M.A. 1950. "A Study of the National Income of Egypt." *L'Égypte contemporaine* 261–262 (November–December): 651–924.

Atkinson, A.B., T. Piketty, and E. Saez. 2011. "Top Incomes in the Long Run of History." *Journal of Economic Literature* 49 (1): 3–71.

Ayubi, N. 1980. *Bureaucracy and Politics in Contemporary Egypt*. London: Ithaca Press.

Ayyagari, M., A. Demirguc-Kunt, and V. Maksimovic. 2011. "Small vs. Young Firms across the World: Contribution to Employment, Job Creation, and Growth." Policy Research Working Paper 5631. Washington DC: World Bank.

Baer, G. 1962. *A History of Landownership in Modern Egypt, 1800–1950*. London: Oxford University Press for the Royal Institute of International Affairs.

Baker, R.W. 1978. *Egypt's Uncertain Revolution under Nasser and Sadat*. Cambridge, MA: Harvard University Press.

Balassa, B. 1984. "Foreign Trade and the Economic Development of Korea." Washington, DC: World Bank.

Baldwin, R.E., J.H. Mutti, and J.D. Richardson. 1980. "Welfare Effects on the United States of a Significant Multilateral Tariff Reduction." *Journal of International Economics* 10:405–23.

Bale, M.D. 1976. "Estimates of Trade Replacement Costs for US Workers." *Journal of International Economics* 6:245–50.

Banerjee, A. V. 2000. "Comment on the Paper by Stephan Haggard," In Krueger 2000: 57–59.

Barro, R. 1991. "Economic Growth in a Cross-section of Countries." *Quarterly Journal of* Economics 106 (2): 407–43.

Bassiouni, M.C. 2017. *Chronicles of the Egyptian Revolution and Its Aftermath, 2011–2016*. Cambridge: Cambridge University Press.

Battesti, V., and F. Ireton, eds. 2011. *L'Égypte au présent: inventaire d'une société avant révolution*. Paris: Sindbad.

Bauer, P. 1971. *Dissent on Development*. Cambridge, MA: Harvard University Press.

Baumol, W.J. 1965. *Welfare Economics and the Theory of the State*. 2nd ed. London: G. Bell and Sons.

Baxter, J. 1923. "Notes on the Estimate of the National Income of Egypt, 1921–22." *L'Égypte Contemporaine* 73 (May): 405–69. (Includes "Reply" by M.I.G. Lévi).

el-Beblawi, H. 1987. "The Rentier State in the Arab World." *Arab Studies Quarterly* 9(4): 11–23.

———. 2008. "Economic Growth in Egypt: Impediments and Constraints (1974–2004)." Commission on Growth and Development, Working Paper 14. Washington DC: World Bank.

Beinin, J. 2009. "Workers' Struggles under 'Socialism' and Neoliberalism." In El-Mahdi and Marfleet 2009, 68–86.

Bhagwati, J.N. 1967. "The Tying of Aid." UNCTAD Secretariat, TD/7/Suppl. 4; United Nations; reprinted in J. Bhagwati and R.S. Eckhaus, eds., *Foreign Aid*. London: Penguin Books, 1970.

———. 1988. *Protectionism*. Cambridge, MA: MIT Press.

———. 1998. "The Capital Myth." *Foreign Affairs* 77 (3): 7–12.

Bianco, J.-L. 2015. *Mes années avec Mitterrand*. Paris: Fayard.

Birdsall, N., A. Torre, and F.V. Caicedo. 2010. "The Washington Consensus: Assessing a 'Damaged Brand.'" Policy Research Working Paper 5316, Office of the Chief Economist, Latin America and the Caribbean Region & Center for Global Development. Washington, DC: World Bank.

Bloom, D., and D. Canning. 1999. "From Demographic Lift to Economic Lift-off: The Case of Egypt." Paper presented at a conference on Growth beyond Stabilization: Prospects for Egypt. Cairo: Egypt Center for Economic Studies.

Bloom, D., D. Canning, and P. Malaney. 2000. "Demographic Change and Economic Growth in Asia." *Population and Development Review* 26 (Supplement): 257–90.

Bloom, D., and J. Williamson. 1998. "Demographic Transitions and Economic Miracles in Emerging Asia." *World Bank Economic Review* 12:419–56.

Boone, P. 1996. "Politics and the Effectiveness of Foreign Aid." *European Economic Review* 40:289–329.

———. 2006. "Effective Intervention, Making Aid Work." Center for Economic Performance, Winter 2005–2006. London: London School of Economics.

Boopen, S., R. Sawkut, and S. Ramessur. 2009. "Using Growth Accounting to Explain Sources of Growth: The Case of COMESA." *International Journal of Business Research* 9 (3): 12–25.

Bossuat, G. 2008. "The Marshall Plan: History and Legacy." In *The Marshall Plan: Lessons Learned for the 21st Century*, edited by E. Sorel and P. C. Padoan, 1–29. Paris: OECD.

Bowman, A.K., and E. Rogan, eds. 1999a. *Agriculture in Egypt: From Pharaonic to Modern Times*. Oxford and New York: Oxford University Press for the British Academy.

———. 1999b. "Agriculture in Egypt from Pharaonic to Modern Times." In Bowman and Rogan 1999, 1–32.

Brada, J., and S. Estrin. 1990. "Advances in the Theory and Practice of Indicative Planning." *Journal of Comparative Economics* 14 (December 1990): 523–30.

Bradley, J.R. 2008. *Inside Egypt: The Land of the Pharaohs on the Brink of a Revolution*. New York: Palgrave Macmillan.

Bruno, M., and W. Easterly. 1996. "Inflation's Children: Tales of Crises That Beget Reforms." *American Economic Review Papers and Proceedings* 86:213–17.

Bruton, H.J. 1983. "Egypt's Development in the Seventies." *Economic Development and Cultural Change* 31 (July): 679–704.

Bunge, F.M., ed. 1982. *South Korea: A Country Study*. Washington, DC: American University Press.

Burgess, R. and N. Stern. 1993. "Taxation and Development." *Journal of Economic Literature* 31 (2): 762–830.

Burns, W. J. 1985. *Economic Aid and American Policy toward Egypt, 1955–1981.* Albany, NY: State University of New York Press.

Burnside, C., and D. Dollar. 1997. "Aid, Policies and Growth." Policy Research Working Paper 1777. Washington, DC: World Bank.

———. 2000. "Aid, Policies, and Growth." *American Economic Review* 90:847–68.

Bush, R. 1999. *Economic Crisis and the Politics of Reform in Egypt.* Boulder, CO: Westview.

Campos, E.J., and H. Root. 1996. *The Key to the Asian Miracle: Making Shared Growth Credible.* Washington, DC: Brookings Institution.

CAPMAS. [Central Agency for Public Mobilization and Statistics] 2000, 2005, 2009, 2015. *Household Income and Expenditure Survey 2013.* Cairo: CAPMAS.

———. 2016. *Population and Housing Census, 1882–2016.* Cairo: CAPMAS.

Cardiff, P. W. 1997. "Poverty and Income Distribution in Egypt." In *Research in Middle East Economics 2*, edited by K. Pfeifer, 1–38. Greenwich CT: JAI Press.

Cassen, R. 1994. *Does Aid Work?* 2nd ed. Oxford: Clarendon Press.

Cohn, E. 1979. *The Economics of Education.* Cambridge, MA: Ballinger.

Cole, D.C., and P.N. Lyman. 1971. *Korean Development: The Interplay of Politics and Economics.* Cambridge, MA: Harvard University Press.

Collier, P. 1997. "The Failure of Conditionality." In *Perspectives on Aid and Development*, edited by C. Gwin and J. Nelson, 20–32. Washington, DC: Overseas Development Council.

Commander, S. 1987. *The State and Agricultural Development in Egypt since 1973.* London: Ithaca Press.

Conference Board. 2015. *Total Economy Database.* www.conference-board.org/retrievefile.cfm?filename=The-Conference-Board-2015-Productivity-Brief-Summary-Tables-1999-2015.pdf&type=subsite. Accessed March 27, 2016.

Cook, S.A. 2012. *The Struggle for Egypt: From Nasser to Tahrir Square.* New York: Oxford University Press.

Cooper, M. 1979. "Egyptian State Capitalism in Crisis: Economic Policies and Political Interests, 1967–1971." *International Journal of Middle East Studies* 10 (4): 481–516.

———. 1982. *The Transformation of Egypt.* Baltimore, MD: Johns Hopkins University Press.

Cooper, R.N. 1971. *Currency Devaluation in Developing Countries.* Essays in International Finance 86. Princeton NJ: Princeton University Press.

Corbo, V., S. Fischer, and S. Webb. 1992. *Adjustment Lending Revisited: Policies to Restore Growth*. Washington, DC: World Bank.

Cornia, G., R. Jolly, and F. Stewart. 1987, 1988. *Adjustment with a Human Face*. 2 vols. Oxford: Oxford University Press.

Cottenet, H. 2003. "Booms de ressources exogènes et développement manufacturier en Égypte: L'illusion du syndrome hollandais." PhD diss., Université d'Auvergne Clermont-Ferrand I.

Craig, J.I. 1924. "Notes on the National Income of Egypt." *L'Égypte Contemporaine* 76 (January): 1–9.

Crémer, H., and J. Crémer. 1994. "L'apport des théories économiques récentes à la planification indicative." *Revue Économique* 44 (Special issue): 57–73.

Crouchley, A.E. 1938. *The Economic Development of Modern Egypt*. London: Longmans, Green and Co.

Datt, G., D. Jolliffe, and M. Sharma. 1999. "A Profile of Poverty in Egypt: 1997." Washington, DC: International Food Policy Research Institute.

Davidsson, P., F. Delmar, and J. Wiklund. 2006. *Entrepreneurship and the Growth of Firms*. Cheltenham, UK: Edward Elgar.

Deaton, A., and C. Paxson. 1997. "The Effects of Economic and Population Growth on National Savings and Inequality." *Demography* 34:97–114.

de Melo, J., and D. Roland-Holst. 1994. "Economy-wide Costs of Protection and Labor Market Rigidities." In *The Effects of Protectionism on a Small Country: The Case of Uruguay*, edited by M. Connolly and J. de Melo, 26–38. Washington, DC: World Bank.

de Melo, J., and D. Tarr. 1990. "Welfare Costs of US Quarters in Textiles, Steel and Autos." *Review of Economics and Statistics* 72:489–97.

Denis, E. 1999. "Le Caire à l'orée du XXIe siècle: Une métropole stabilisée dans un contexte de déploiement de la croissance urbaine." In *Lettre d'information de l'Observatoire Urbain du Caire Contemporain* 48, 24–42. Cairo: CEDEJ [Centre de Recherches et de Documentation Économique, Juridique, et Social].

Denison, E.F. 1962. *The Sources of Economic Growth in the United States and the Alternatives before Us*. New York: Committee for Economic Growth.

———. 1985. *Trends in American Economic Growth, 1929–82*. Washington, DC: The Brookings Institution.

De Soto, H. 1997. *Dead Capital and the Poor in Egypt*. Distinguished Lecture Series 11. Cairo: Egyptian Center for Economic Studies.

———. 2000. *The Mystery of Capital*. New York: Basic Books.

Dessouki, A.E.H. 1982. "The Politics of Income Distribution in Egypt." In Abdel-Khalek and Tignor 1982, 55–87.

Dinh, H.T., and M. Giugale. 1991. "Inflation Tax and Deficit Financing in Egypt." Working Paper No. 668. Washington, DC: World Bank.

Diwan, I., P. Keefer, and M. Schiffbauer. 2015. "Pyramid Capitalism: Political Connections, Regulation, and Firm Productivity in Egypt." Policy Research Working Paper 7354, Macroeconomics and Fiscal Management Global Practice Group. Washington, DC: World Bank.

Dixon, P.B., B.R. Parmenter, and A.A. Powell. 1984. "Trade Liberalization and Labor Market Disruption." *Journal of Policy Modeling* 6:431–54.

Djoufelkit-Cottenet, H. 2011. "L'industrie depuis le début des années 1970: histoire d'un développement contrarié. In Battesti and Ireton 2011.

Dobb, M. 1960. *An Essay on Economic Growth and Planning*. London: Monthly Review Press.

Dobronogov, A. and F. Iqbal. 2004. "Economic Growth in Egypt: Constraints and Determinants." Working Paper 0420. Washington, DC: World Bank, MENA Region.

Dollar, D., and A. Kraay. 2001. "Trade, Growth, and Poverty." Policy Research Working Paper 2615. Washington, DC: World Bank.

Dollar, D., and J. Svensson. 1998. "What Explains the Success or Failure of Structural Adjustment Programs?" Policy Research Working Paper 1938. Washington, DC: World Bank.

Dorfman, R.M., P.A. Samuelson, and R. Solow. 1958. *Linear Programming and Economic Analysis*. New York: McGraw-Hill.

Douglas, R. 1990. "The Politics of Successful Structural Reform." *Policy* (Autumn): 2–6.

Drazen, A. 2000. *Political Economy in Macroeconomics*. Princeton, NJ: Princeton University Press.

Drazen, A., and W. Easterly. 1999. "Do Crises Induce Reform? Simple Empirical Tests of Conventional Wisdom." Working Paper, quoted in Drazen 2000.

Easterly, W. 2003. "Can Foreign Aid Buy Growth?" *Journal of Economic Perspectives* 17:23–48.

———. 2006. *The White Man's Burden: Why the West's Efforts to Aid the Rest Have Done So Much Ill and So Little Good*. New York: Penguin.

Easterly, W., M. Kremer, L. Pritchett, and L.H. Summers. 1993. "Good Policy or Good Luck? Country Growth Performance and Temporary Shocks." *Journal of Monetary Economics* 32 (3): 459–83.

El-Edel, M.R.A. 1982. "Impact of Taxation on Income Distribution: An Exploratory Attempt to Estimate Tax Incidence in Egypt," 132–64. In Abdel-Khalek and Tignor 1982.

Eden, A. 1960. *Full Circle: The Memoirs of Sir Anthony Eden*. London: Cassell & Company.

Eilts, H.F. 1985. "Foreword." In *Economic Aid and American Policy toward Egypt, 1955–81*, edited by W.J. Burns, xi–xviii. Albany: State University of New York Press.

Eisenhower. 1965. *The White House Years: Waging Peace, 1956–61*. New York: Doubleday and Company.

Enders, K. 2007. "Egypt—Searching for Binding Constraints on Growth." IMF Working Paper, Middle East and Central Asia Department. Washington, DC: IMF.

el-Erian, M., and M. Spence. 2008. "Growth Strategies and Dynamics: Insights from Country Experiences." Commission on Growth and Development, Working Paper 6. Washington, DC: World Bank.

Eshag, E., and M.A. Kamal. 1968. "Agrarian Reform in the United Arab Republic (Egypt)." *Bulletin of the Oxford University Institute of Economics and Statistics* 30 (2): 73–104.

Esterman, I. 2016. "Vision 2030: Big Plans, Fuzzy on the Details." www.madamasr.com/en/2016/03/01/feature/economy/vision-2030-big-plans-fuzzy-on-the-details.

Estrin, S., and P. Holmes. 1983. *French Planning in Theory and Practice*. London: Allen and Unwin.

Farah, N.R. 2009. *Egypt's Political Economy*. Cairo: American University in Cairo Press.

Fergany, N. 1999. *An Assessment of the Unemployment Situation in Egypt*. Cairo: al-Mishkat.

Fields, G.S. 2003. *Distribution and Development*. Cambridge, MA: MIT Press.

Fradkin, H., and L. Libby. 2012. "Learning from Sadat: The Dividends of American Resolve." *World Affairs*, September/October 2012, http://www.worldaffairsjournal.org/article/learning-sadat-dividends-american-resolve

Frank, C.R., Jr., K.-S. Kim, and L.E. Westphal. 1975. *Foreign Trade Regimes and Economic Development: South Korea*. New York: National Bureau of Economic Research.

Frey, B. 1985. "The Political Economy of Protection." In *Current Issues in International Trade: Theory and Policy*, edited by D. Greenaway, 139–57. New York: St. Martin's Press.

Friedman, M., and R. Friedman. 1984. *Tyranny of the Status Quo*. New York: Houghton Mifflin Harcourt.

Galal, A. 1995. "Which Institutions Constrain Economic Growth in Egypt the Most?" Egyptian Center for Economic Studies (ECES), Working Paper 1. Cairo: ECES.

———. 2002. "Employment and Unemployment in Egypt." Policy Viewpoint 11 (June). Cairo: ECES.

———, ed. 2008. *Industrial Policy in the Middle East and North Africa*. Cairo: American University in Cairo Press.

Galal, A., and N. el-Megharbel. 2008. "Do Governments Pick Winners or Losers?" In Galal 2008, 11–34.

Galbraith, J.K. 1992. *The Culture of Contentment*. New York: Houghton Miflin.

Ganesh. J. 2015. "Osborne's Budget must end the perversity of the tax system." *Financial Times*, July 6, 2015, p. 9.

Gardner, R. 2001. "The Marshall Plan Fifty Years Later." In *The Marshall Plan: Fifty Years After*, edited by M. Schain, 119–29. New York: Palgrave, 2001.

Ghanem, H. 2014. "Egypt's Difficult Transition: Why the International Community Must Stay Economically Engaged." Global Economy and Development, Working Paper 66. Washington, DC: Brookings Institution.

Giugale, M., and H. Mubarak. 1996. "The Rationale of Private Sector Development in Egypt." In *Private Sector Development in Egypt*, edited by M. Giugale and H. Mubarak, 1–11. Cairo: American University in Cairo Press.

Glaeser, E. 2011. *The Triumph of the City*. New York: Penguin Press.

Gordon, J. 1992. *Nasser's Blessed Movement: Egypt's Free Officers and the July Revolution*. Cairo: American University in Cairo Press.

Gordon, L.D. (Lady). [1863] 1969. *Letters from Egypt 1862–1869*. Edited by G. Waterfield. London: Routledge & Kegan Paul.

Government of Egypt. 2015a. *Strat_EGY: FY14/15–FY18/19*. Egypt Economic Development Conference, Sharm al-Sheikh, March 13–15. Cairo: Government of Egypt.

———. 2015b. *Sustainable Development Strategy: Egypt's Vision 2030*. Cairo: Ministry of Planning, Monitoring and Administrative Reform.

Griffin, K.B. and J. L. Enos. 1970. *Planning Development*. Reading, MA: Addison-Wesley.

Gutner, T. 1999. "The Political Economy of Food Subsidy Reform in Egypt." Washington, DC: International Food Policy Research Institute.

al-Gawwadi, M. 1997. *al-Wuzara': wa ru'asa'uhum wa nuwwab ru'asa'ihim wa nuwwabuhum, tashkilatuhum wa tartibuhum wa mas'uliyatuhum*. 2nd edn. Cairo: Dar El Shorouk.

Haddad, L. and A. Ahmed. 1999. *Poverty Dynamics in Egypt: 1997–1999*. Washington, DC: International Food Policy Research Institute.

Haggard, S. 1994. "Panel Discussion." In Williamson 1994b, 467–71.

———. 2000. "Interests, Institutions, and Policy Reform." In Krueger 2000, 21–57.

Haggard, S., and R. Kaufman. 1992. "Economic Adjustment in New Democracies." In *Fragile Coalitions: The Politics of Economic Adjustment*, edited by S. Haggard and R. Kaufman, 3–26. New Brunswick, NJ: Transaction Books.

Hall, B.H. 1987. "The Relationship between Firm Size and Firm Growth in the US Manufacturing Sector." *Journal of Industrial Economics* 35:583–600.

Haltiwanger, J., R.S. Jarmin, and J. Miranda. 2013. "Who Creates Jobs? Small versus Large versus Young." *Review of Economics and Statistics* 95 (2): 347–61.

Hamza, A.M. 1944. *The Public Debt of Egypt, 1854–1876*. Cairo: Government Press.

Handoussa, H. 1990. "Egypt's Investment Strategy, Policies, and Performance since the Infitah." In *Investment Policies in the Arab Countries*, edited by S. el-Naggar, 16–35. Washington, DC: IMF.

———. 1991. "The Impact of Foreign Aid on Egypt's Economic Development, 1952–86." In *Transitions in Development*, edited by U. Lele and I. Nabi, 31–57. San Francisco: ICS Press.

Handoussa, H., and N. El Oraby. 2004. "Civil Service Wages and Reform: The Case of Egypt." Egyptian Center for Economic Studies (ECES), Working Paper 98. Cairo: ECES.

Hansen, B. 1968. "Planning and Economic Growth in the UAR 1960–5." In Vatikiotis 1968, 19–39.

———. 1975. "Arab Socialism in Egypt." *World Development* 3 (4): 201–11.

———. 1991. *Egypt and Turkey: The Political Economy of Poverty, Equity, and Growth*. New York: Oxford University Press.

Hansen, B., and G. Marzouk. 1965. *Development and Economic Policy in the UAR (Egypt)*. Amsterdam: North-Holland.

Hansen, B., and D. Mead. 1963. "The National Income of the UAR (Egypt), 1939–62." Memo 355. Cairo: Institute of National Planning.

———. 1965. "The National Income of the UAR (Egypt), 1939–62." In *Studies in Short-term National Accounts and Long-term Economic Growth*, edited by S. Goldberg and P. Deane, 233–56. Income and Wealth Series 11. London: Bowes and Bowes.

Hansen, B., and K. Nashashibi. 1975. *Foreign Trade Regimes and Economic Development: Egypt.* New York: National Bureau of Economic Research.

ul-Haq, M. 1967. "Tied Credits: A Quantitative Analysis." In *Capital Movements and Economic Development*, edited by J.H. Adler, 71–92. New York: Macmillan.

Harrigan, J., and P. Mosley. 1991. "Evaluating the Impact of World Bank Structural Adjustment Lending 1980–87." *Journal of Development Studies* 27 (3): 63–94.

Harrison, A., and A. Revenga. 1995. "The Effects of Trade Policy Reform: What Do We Really Know?" Working Paper No. 5225. New York: National Bureau of Economic Research.

Hart, P.E., and N. Oulton. 1996. "The Growth and Size of Firms." *Economic Journal* 106 (3): 1242–52.

Harvie, C., and H.-H. Lee. 2003. *Korea's Economic Miracle.* Basingstoke, Hampshire, UK: Palgrave.

Hausmann, R., D. Rodrik, and A. Velasco. 2005. "Growth Diagnostics." John F. Kennedy School of Government, Harvard University. http://ksghome.harvard.edu/~drodrik/barcelonafinalmarch2005.pdf.

———. 2006. "Getting the Diagnosis Right." *Finance and Development* 43 (1): 11–15.

Heikal, M. 1983. *Autumn of Fury: The Assassination of Sadat.* New York: Random House.

Hellman, J. 1998. "Winners Take All: The Politics of Partial Reform in Postcommunist Transitions." *World Politics* 50 (2): 203–34.

Hevia, C., and N. Loayza. 2011. "Saving and Growth in Egypt." Washington, DC: World Bank, Development Research Group.

Hinnebusch, R.A. 1988. *Egyptian Politics under Sadat.* Updated edition. Boulder, CO and London: Lynne Rienner.

Holt, R., and T. Roe. 1993. "The Political Economy of Reform: Egypt in the 1980s." In *Political and Economic Interactions in Economic Policy Reform*, edited by R.H. Bates and A.O. Krueger, 204–25. Oxford: Blackwell.

Hopwood, D. 1991. *Egypt: Politics and Society, 1945–90.* London: HarperCollins.

Hottinger, A. 1968. "How the Arab Bourgeoisie Lost Power." *Journal of Contemporary History* 3 (3): 111–28.

Hsieh, C.-T., and P.J. Klenow. 2012. "The Life Cycle of Plants in India and Mexico." Working Paper W18133. Cambridge, MA: National Bureau of Economic Research.

Ibrahim, S. E. 1982. "Social Mobility and Income Distribution in Egypt, 1952–77." In Abdel-Khalek and Tignor 1982, 375–434.

Ikram, K. 1980. *Egypt: Economic Management in a Period of Transition*. Baltimore and London: Johns Hopkins University Press.

———. 1981. "Meeting the Social Contract in Egypt." *Finance and Development* 18 (3): 30–33.

———. 2006. *The Egyptian Economy, 1952–2000: Performance, Policies and Issues*. London and New York: Routledge.

———. 2009. "Revitalizing the Planning Commission." Mimeographed. Lahore: International Growth Centre.

———. 2011. *Pakistan and Lessons from East Asia: Growth, Equity, and Governance*. Lahore: Lahore School of Economics.

Ikram, K. Forthcoming. "Structural Transformation in Egypt, 1965–2015." In *The Oxford Handbook of Structural Transformation*, edited by C. Monga and J.Y. Lin. Oxford and New York: Oxford University Press.

Ikram, K., S. Sherani, and S. Ahmed. 2011. "Pakistan: Framework for Economic Growth: Sectoral Strategies for Pakistan's 10th Five-Year Plan." Working Paper. Lahore: International Growth Centre.

Ikram, S. 2010. *Ancient Egypt: An Introduction*. Cambridge, UK: Cambridge University Press.

IMF [International Monetary Fund]. 1976. *Arab Republic of Egypt: Recent Economic Developments*. Washington, DC: IMF.

———. 1998. *Egypt: Beyond Stabilization, toward a Dynamic Economy*. Washington, DC: IMF.

———. 2004. "IMF Concludes 2004 Article IV Consultation with the Arab Republic of Egypt." Public Information Notice 04/69. Washington, DC: IMF.

———. 2005a. "Arab Republic of Egypt: 2005 Article IV Consultation—Staff Report." Washington, DC: IMF.

———. 2005b. "Arab Republic of Egypt: Selected Issues." Washington, DC: IMF.

———. 2006. "Arab Republic of Egypt: 2006 Article IV Consultation—Staff Report." Washington, DC: IMF.

———. 2007a. "Arab Republic of Egypt: Selected Issues." Washington, DC: IMF.

———. 2007b. "Staff Report for the 2007 Article IV Consultation." Washington, DC: IMF.

———. 2009. "Arab Republic of Egypt: 2008 Article IV Consultation—Staff Report." Washington, DC: IMF.

———. 2010. "Arab Republic of Egypt: 2010 Article IV Consultation—Staff Report." Washington, DC: IMF.

———. 2015. "Arab Republic of Egypt: 2014 Article IV Consultation—Staff Report." Washington, DC: IMF.

———. 2016. "Arab Republic of Egypt: Request for Extended Arrangement under the Extended Fund Facility." Washington, DC: IMF.

Issawi, C. 1947. *Egypt: An Economic and Social Analysis*. London: Oxford University Press for the Royal Institute of International Affairs.

———. 1954. *Egypt at Mid-century: An Economic Survey*. London: Oxford University Press for the Royal Institute of International Affairs.

———. 1963. *Egypt in Revolution: An Economic Analysis*. London: Oxford University Press for the Royal Institute of International Affairs.

Johnson, C. 1981. "The Taiwan Model." In *The Taiwan Experience, 1950–80*, edited by J.C. Hsiung, 13–27. New York: Praeger.

———. 1987. "Political Institutions and Economic Performance: The Government–Business Relationship in Japan, South Korea, and Taiwan." In *The Political Economy of the New Asian Industrialism*, edited by F.C. Devo, 43–68. Ithaca, NY: Cornell University Press.

Jones, L., and I. SaKong. 1980. *Government, Business, and Entrepreneurship in Economic Development: The Korean Case*. Cambridge, MA: Harvard University Press.

———. 1981. "Implementation in a 'Hard' State." In *Modernization of Korea and the Impact of the West*, edited by C.S. Lee, 35–64. Los Angeles: University of Southern California, East Asian Studies Center.

Kanaan, T.H. 1989. "Comment." *In Privatization and Structural Adjustment in the Arab Countries*, edited by S. el-Naggar, 230–38. Washington, DC: IMF.

Kanbur, R. 2009. "The Co-evolution of the Washington Consensus and the Economic Development Discourse." *Macalester International* 24 (8): 33–57.

Kandil, H. 2012. *Soldiers, Spies, and Statesmen: Egypt's Road to Revolt*. London: Verso.

Karabell, Z. 2003. *Parting the Desert: The Creation of the Suez Canal*. New York: Knopf.

Kassem, M. 2004. *Egyptian Politics: The Dynamics of Authoritarian Rule*. Boulder, CO: Lynne Rienner Publishers.

Keynes, J.M. [1926] 1972. "The End of Laissez-faire." In *Essays in Persuasion*, 272–94. London: Macmillan.

Khattab, M. 1999. "Constraints to Privatization: The Egyptian Experience." Egyptian Center for Economic Studies (ECES), Working Paper 38. Cairo: ECES.

Kheir el-Din, H., and H. el-Leithy. 2008. "An Assessment of Growth, Distribution, and Poverty in Egypt: 1990/91–2004/05." In *The Egyptian Economy: Current Challenges and Future Prospects*, edited by Hanaa Kheir el-Din, 13–52. Cairo: American University in Cairo Press.

Kheir el-Din, H., and T. Moursi. 2007. "Sources of Economic Growth and Technical Progress in Egypt: An Aggregate Perspective." In *Explaining Growth in the Middle East*, edited by J. Nugent and H. Pesaran, 197–236. Amsterdam: Elsevier.

Kheir el-Din, H., and S. el-Shawarby. 2002. "Trade and Foreign Exchange Regime in Egypt." Paper presented at the Conference on Institutional and Policy Changes facing the Egyptian Economy, Cairo University and USAID, May 26–27, 2002, Cairo.

Kim, E.H. 1990. "Financing Korean Corporations: Evidence and Theory." In *Korean Economic Development*, edited by J.K. Kwon, 341–58. New York: Greenwood Press.

Kim, H. 2010. "Political Stability and Foreign Direct Investment." *International Journal of Economics and Finance* 2 (3): 59–72.

Kim, K.-S., and S.-D. Hong. 1999. *Accounting for Rapid Growth in Korea, 1963–95*. Seoul: Korea Development Institute.

Kim, Y.B. 1980. "Education and Economic Growth." In *Human Resources and Social Development in Korea*, edited by C.K. Park, 111–35. Seoul: Korea Development Institute.

Korayem, K. 1994. *Poverty and Income Distribution in Egypt*. Cairo: Third World Forum.

Kouamé, A. T. 2000. "Egypt: Export Competitiveness Analysis." Washington, DC: World Bank, MENA Region.

Krafft, C., and R. Assaad. 2013a. "The Structure and Evolution of Employment in Egypt: 1998–2012." Working Paper No. 805. Cairo: Economic Research Forum.

———. 2013b. "The Evolution of Labor Supply and Employment in Egypt: 1998–2012." Working Paper No. 806. Cairo: Economic Research Forum.

———. 2014a. "Beware of the Echo: The Impending Return of Demographic

Pressures in Egypt." Policy Perspective No. 12. Cairo: Economic Research Forum.

———. 2014b. "Why the Unemployment Rate is a Misleading Indicator of Labor Market Health in Egypt." Policy Perspective No. 14. Cairo: Economic Research Forum.

Krueger, A. 1992. *Economic Policy Reform in Developing Countries*. Oxford: Blackwell.

———. 1993. *Political Economy of Policy Reform in Developing Countries*. Cambridge, MA: MIT Press.

———, ed. 2000. *Economic Policy Reform: The Second Stage*. Chicago: University of Chicago Press.

Krugman, P. 1997. "Whatever Happened to the Asian Miracle?" *Fortune* 13 (4): 26–27.

Kuczynski, P.-P., and J. Williamson, eds. 2003. *After the Washington Consensus: Restarting Growth and Reform in Latin America*. Washington, DC: Institute for International Economics.

Kunzing, R. 2011. "The City Solution." *National Geographic Magazine*, December. 124–47.

Lacouture, J., and S. Lacouture. 1958. *Egypt in Movement*. London: Methuen.

Lam, W. R., M. Rodlauer, and A. Schipke. 2017. *Modernizing China*, Washington, DC: IMF.

Landes, D.M. 1958. *Bankers and Pashas*. Cambridge, MA: Harvard University Press.

Leipziger, D.M. 1988. "Industrial Restructuring in Korea," *World Development* 16 (1): 121–35.

Leipziger, D.M., and R. Zagha. 2006. "Getting Out of the Rut: Applying growth diagnostics at the World Bank," *Finance and Development* 43 (1): 16–17.

el-Leithy, H. and O.M. Osman. 1996. *Profile and Trend of Poverty and Economic Growth in Egypt*. Cairo: Institute of National Planning and UNDP.

el-Leithy, H., O. El-Khawaga, and N. Riad. 1999. "Poverty Assessment in Egypt: 1991–96." Economic Research Monograph. Cairo: Cairo University.

Lerner, A.P 1944. *The Economics of Control*. London: Macmillan.

Lévi, M.I.G. 1922. "L'augmentation des revenus de l'état: Possibilités et moyens d'y parvenir." *L'Égypte Contemporaine* 68 (December): 596–617.

Lewis, W.A. 1966. *Development Planning: The Essentials of Economic Policy*. London: Allen and Unwin.

————. 1969. *The Principles of Economic Planning*. 3rd ed. London: Unwin University Books.

Li, K.T. 1995. *The Evolution of Policy behind Taiwan's Development Success*. 2nd ed. Singapore: World Scientific.

Lichtheim, M. 1973, 1976, 1980. *Ancient Egyptian Literature*. 3 vols. Berkeley: University of California.

Lindbeck, A. 1998. "How Can Economic Policy Strike a Balance Between Economic Efficiency and Income Equality?" In *Income Equality: Issues and Policy Options* 295–336. Kansas City, MO: Federal Reserve Bank of Kansas City.

Lindbeck, A., and D.J. Snower. 2002. "The Insider–Outsider Theory: A Survey." IZA Discussion Paper series 534.

Little, T. 1965. *High Dam at Aswan: The Subjugation of the Nile*. London: Methuen.

————. 1967. *Modern Egypt*. New York: Praeger.

Lloyd, S. 1978. *Suez 1956*. New York: Mayflower Books.

Loewe, M. 2013. "Industrial Policy in Egypt 2004–2011." Discussion Paper 13/2013. Bonn: Deutsches Institut für Entwicklungspolitik.

Lora, E. 1998. "What Makes Reform Likely? Timing and Sequencing of Structural Reforms in Latin America." Working Paper, Office of the Chief Economist, Inter-American Development Bank. [Quoted in Drazen 2000].

Lora, E., and M. Olivera. 2004. "What Makes Reforms Likely: Political Economy Determinants of Reforms in Latin America," *Journal of Applied Economics* 7 (1): 99–135.

Lucas, R.E. 1990. "Why Doesn't Capital Flow from Rich to Poor Countries?" *American Economic Review* 80:92–96.

Ludborg, P. 1998. "Foreign Aid and International Support as a Gift Exchange." *Economics and Politics* 10:127–41.

Mabro, R. 1974. *The Egyptian Economy, 1952–72*. Oxford: Oxford University Press.

————. 1975. "Egypt's Economic Relations with the Socialist Countries." *World Development*, 3 (5): 299–313.

Mabro, R., and S. Radwan. 1976. *The Industrialization of Egypt, 1939–73*. Oxford: Clarendon Press.

Maddison, A. 1970. *Economic Progress and Policy in Developing Countries*. London: Allen and Unwin.

Magee, S.P. 1972. "The Welfare Effects of Restrictions on US Trade." *Brookings Papers on Economic Activity* 3:645–701.

Mahdavy, H. 1970. "The Patterns of Economic Development in Rentier States: The Case of Iran." In *Studies in the Economic History of the Middle*

East: From the Rise of Islam to the Present Day, edited by M.A. Cook, 428–67. London: Oxford University Press.

el-Mahdi, R., and P. Marfleet, eds. 2009. *Egypt: The Moment of Change*. London and New York: Zed Books.

Maizels, A., and M. Nissanke. 1984. "Motivation for Aid to Developing Countries." *World Development* 12:879–900.

Mansfield, E. 1962. "Entry, Gibrat's Law, Innovation, and the Growth of Firms." *American Economic Review* 52 (5): 1023–51.

Mansfield, P. 1965. *Nasser's Egypt*. London: Penguin Books.

Maraval, J.M. 1997. *Regimes and Markets: Democratization and Economic Change in Southern and Eastern Europe*. New York: Oxford University Press.

Marcou, J. 2008. *L'Égypte contemporaine*. Paris: Le Cavalier Bleu.

Marlowe, J. 1974. *Spoiling the Egyptians*. London: Andre Deutsch.

Marshall, A. 1920. *Principles of Economics*. London: Macmillan.

———. 1924. *Money, Credit and Commerce*. London: Macmillan.

Masera, R. 1974. "The J-Curve: UK Experience after the 1967 Devaluation." *Metroeconomica* 26 (January–December): 40–62.

Mason, A. 1988. "Saving, Economic Growth, and Demographic Change." *Population and Development Review* 14:113–44.

———., ed. 2002. *Population Change and Economic Development in East Asia: Challenges Met, Opportunities Seized*. Palo Alto, CA: Stanford University Press.

Mason, E.S. 1984. "The Chenery Analysis and Some Other Considerations." In *Economic Structure and Performance: Essays in Honor of Hollis B. Chenery*, edited by M. Syrquin, L. Taylor, and L.E. Westphal, 179–203. New York: Academic Press.

Mason, E.S., and R.E. Asher. 1973. *The World Bank since Bretton Woods*. Washington, DC: Brookings Institution.

Mason, E.S., M.J. Kim, D.H. Perkins, K.S. Kim, and D.C. Cole. 1980. *The Economic and Social Modernization of the Republic of Korea*. Cambridge, MA: Harvard University Press.

Matusz, S., and D. Tarr. 2000. "Adjusting to Trade Policy Reform." In Krueger 2000, 365–99.

Mau, V. 1994. "Russia." In Williamson 1994b, 432–38.

Mavrotas, G., ed. 2010. *Foreign Aid for Development: Issues, Challenges, and the New Agenda*. Oxford: Oxford University Press.

McDermott, A. 1988. *Egypt from Nasser to Mubarak: A Flawed Revolution*. London: Croom Helm.

McGinn, N.F., D.R. Snodgrass, Y.B. Kim, and Q.Y. Kim. 1980. *Education and Development in Korea*. Cambridge, MA: Harvard University Press.

McKinlay, R.D., and R. Little. 1979. "The US Aid Relationship: A Test of the Recipient and Donor Interest Models." *Political Studies* 27:236–50.

Mead, D.C. 1967. *Growth and Structural Change in the Egyptian Economy*. Homewood, IL: Richard D. Irwin.

Meade, J. 1970. *The Theory of Indicative Planning*. Manchester, UK: Manchester University Press.

el-Mikawy, N., and H. Handoussa, eds. 2002. *Institutional Reform and Economic Development in Egypt*. Cairo: Economic Research Forum.

Ministry of Economy. 1981. *A Review of Developments in the Egyptian Economy*. Cairo: Ministry of Economy.

Ministry of Planning. 1977a. *The Five-Year Plan: 1978–82*, Vol. 1, *The General Strategy for Economic and Social Development*. Cairo: Ministry of Planning.

———. 1977b. *The Five-Year Plan: 1978–82*, Vol. 3, *Planning the Open Door Policy*. Cairo: Ministry of Planning.

———, and World Bank. 2004. *Arab Republic of Egypt: A Poverty Reduction Strategy for Egypt*. Washington, DC. World Bank.

Mitchell, T. 2007. "Dreamland." In *Evil Paradises: Dreamworlds of Neoliberalism*, edited by M. Davis and D.M. Monk, 1–33. New York and London: The New Press.

Mohammed, N. 2001. "Sources of Economic Growth in Egypt: Past Experience, Experience of Other Countries, and the Way Ahead." Conference paper, Cairo University conference on Growth Strategies for Late Comers, with Special Reference to the Arab Region. Cairo, May 12–14.

Mohi el-Din, K.M. 1995. *Memories of a Revolution: Egypt 1952*. Cairo: American University in Cairo Press.

Möller, A., K. Billerbeck, C. Heimpel, W. Hillebrand, H.-H. Taake, and D. Weiss. 1977. *Proposals for the Solution of the Most Important Structural, Economic and Financial Problems of the Arab Republic of Egypt: Report to the President of the Arab Republic of Egypt Anwar El Sadat*. With a Supplement. "Considerations for the Reform of the Economic and Developmental Decision-Making Process." Published without the Supplement in 1980 as Occasional Paper 63. Berlin: German Development Institute.

MOP/World Bank. 2004. *A Poverty Reduction Strategy for Egypt*. Washington, DC: World Bank.

Morkre, M., and D. Tarr. 1980. *Effects of United States Restrictions on Imports: Five Case Studies and Theory.* Bureau of Economics Report to the Federal Trade Commission. Washington, DC: Government Printing Office.

Mosley, P., J. Harrigan, and J. Toye. 1995. *Aid and Power.* Vol. 1. 2nd ed. London: Routledge.

Mundell, R.A. 1963. "Capital Mobility and Stabilization Policy under Fixed and Flexible Exchange Rates." *Canadian Journal of Economic and Political Science* 29 (4): 475–85.

Musgrave, R.A. 1959. *The Theory of Public Finance: A Study in Public Economy.* New York: McGraw-Hill.

Mutti, J. 1978. "Aspects of Unilateral Trade Policy and Factor Adjustment Costs." *Review of Economics and Statistics* 6 (1): 102–10.

Myrdal, G. 1968. *Asian Drama: An Inquiry into the Poverty of Nations.* New York: Pantheon.

el-Naggar, A. 2009. "Economic Policy: From State Control to Decay and Corruption." In el-Mahdi and Marfleet 2009, 34–50.

Naguib, M. 1955. *Egypt's Destiny: A Personal Statement.* New York: Doubleday.

Naím, M. 1994. "Latin America: The Second Stage of Reform." *Journal of Democracy* 5 (4): 32–48.

———. 2002. "Washington Consensus: A Damaged Brand." http://carnegieendowment.org/2002/10/28/washington-consensus.

Nasser, G.A. 1954. *The Philosophy of the Revolution.* Cairo: Dar al-Ma'arif.

Nathan Associates. 1998. *Enhancing Egypt's Exports.* Cairo: USAID.

National Planning Committee, United Arab Republic. 1958. Memorandum 55. Cairo: Presidency of the Republic.

———. 1960. *General Frame of the Five-Year Plan for Economic and Social Development, July 1960–June 1965.* Cairo: Presidency of the Republic.

Navia, P., and A. Velasco. 2003. "The Politics of Second-generation Reforms." In Kuczynski and Williamson 2003, 265–304.

Nelson, J.M., ed. 1990. *Economic Crisis and Policy Choice.* Princeton, NJ: Princeton University Press.

Nelson, R.M., and J.M. Sharp. 2013. "Egypt and the IMF: Overview and Issues for Congress." CRS Report for Congress. Washington, DC: Congressional Research Service.

Noland, M., and H. Pack. 2008. "The East Asian Industrial Policy Experience: Implications for the Middle East." In Galal 2008, 81–108.

Nutting, A. 1967. *No End of a Lesson: The Story of Suez.* London: Constable.

———. 1972. *Nasser*. London: Constable.

O'Brien, P.K. 1966. *The Revolution in Egypt's Economic System*. Oxford: Oxford University Press.

Ohlin, G. 1966. *Foreign Aid Policies Reconsidered*. Paris: OECD Development Center.

Olson, M. 1965. *The Logic of Collective Action*. Cambridge, MA: Harvard University Press.

———. 1982. *The Rise and Decline of Nations*. New Haven, CT: Yale University Press.

———. 1991. "Autocracy, Democracy, and Prosperity." In *Strategy and Choice*, edited by R. Zeckhauser, 131–57, Cambridge, MA: MIT Press.

Osman, T. 2011. *Egypt on the Brink: From the Rise of Nasser to the Fall of Mubarak*. New Haven, CT: Yale University Press.

Ott, A F. 1993. "Privatization in Egypt: Reassessing the Role and Size of the Public Sector." In *Privatization and Economic* Efficiency, edited by A.F. Ott and K. Hartley, 199–225. Aldershot, UK: Edward Elgar.

Owen, E.R.J., and S. Pamuk. 1998. *A History of Middle East Economies in the Twentieth Century*. London: I.B. Tauris.

Pakistan Planning Commission. 2011. *Pakistan: Framework for Economic Growth*. Islamabad: Government of Pakistan.

Palmer, M., A. Leila, and El S. Yassin. 1988. *The Egyptian Bureaucracy*. New York: Syracuse University Press.

Panagariya, A. 2008. *India: The Emerging Giant*. New York: Oxford University Press.

Papanek, G.F. 1972. "The Effect of Aid and Other Resource Transfers on Savings and Growth in Less Developed Countries." *Economic Journal* 82:934–50.

———. 1973. "Aid, Foreign Private Investment, Savings, and Growth in Less Developed Countries." *Journal of Political Economy* 81:120–30.

Pareto, V. 1927. *Manual of Political Economy*. New York: A.M. Kelley.

Park, C.H. 1963. *The Country, the Revolution and I*. Seoul: Hollym Corporation.

———. 1970. *Our Nation's Path*. Seoul: Hollym Corporation.

Pearson, D.W 1997. "Trade Prospects for Egypt." Research Report No. 38. London: Institute for Middle East Studies.

Phillips, D.A. 2010. *America's Role in a Changing World*. New York: Chelsea House.

Piketty, T. 2013. *Capital in the Twenty-First Century*. Cambridge, MA: Harvard University Press.

Pincus, J. 1965. *Economic Aid and International Cost-Sharing.* Baltimore, MD: Johns Hopkins University Press.

PRIDE [Project in Development and the Environment]. 1994. *Comparing Health Risks in Cairo.* 3 vols. Cairo: USAID.

Przeworski, A., and F. Limongi. 1993. "Political Regimes and Economic Growth." *Journal of Economic Perspectives* 7:51–70.

Radwan, S. 1974. *Capital Formation in Egyptian Industry and Agriculture, 1882–1967.* London: Ithaca Press.

Radwan, S., and E. Lee. 1977. *Job Creation and Poverty Alleviation in Egypt: Strategy and Programmes.* Geneva: International Labor Office.

Ray, D. 1998. *Development Economics.* Princeton, NJ: Princeton University Press.

Rhee, Y-W., B. Ross-Larson, and G. Pursell. 1984. *Korea's Competitive Edge.* Baltimore and London: Johns Hopkins University Press for the World Bank.

Richards, A. 1984. "Ten Years of *infitah*: Class, Rent, and Policy Stasis in Egypt." *Journal of Development Studies* 20 (4): 323–38.

———. 1991. "The Political Economy of Dilatory Reform: Egypt in the 1980s." *World Development* 19 (12): 1721–30.

———. 1993a. "Food, Jobs, and Water: Participation and Governance for a Sustainable Agriculture in Egypt." In *Sustainable Agriculture in Egypt*, edited by M.A. Faris and M.H. Khan, 243–54. Boulder and London: Lynne Rienner.

Rivlin, H.A.B. 1961. *The Agricultural Policy of Muhammad 'Ali in Egypt.* Cambridge, MA: Harvard University Press.

Rivlin, P. 2009. *Arab Economies in the Twenty-first Century.* Cambridge, UK: Cambridge University Press.

Robinson. 1937. *Essays in the Theory of Employment.* Oxford: Blackwell.

Roccu, R. 2014. *The Political Economy of the Egyptian Revolution: Mubarak, Economic Reforms and Failed Hegemony.* Basingstoke, UK: Palgrave Macmillan.

Rodrik, D. 1989. "The Credibility of Trade Reform—A Policy Maker's Guide," *The World Economy* 12 (1): 1–16.

———. 1996. "Understanding Economic Policy Reform." *Journal of Economic Literature* 34 (March 1996): 9–41.

———. 2005. "Growth Strategies." In *Handbook of Economic Growth*, Vol. 1A, edited by P. Aghion and S.N. Durlauf, 967–1014. Amsterdam: Elsevier North-Holland.

———. 2006. "Goodbye Washington Consensus, Hello Washington Confusion?" *Journal of Economic Literature* 44 (4): 973–87.

————. 2008. "Is There a New Washington Consensus?" http://www.project-syndicate.org/commentary/rodrik20

Roháč, D. 2014. "Explorations in Political Economy of Reforms." PhD diss., Kings College, London.

Roussillon, A. 1998. "Republican Egypt: Revolution and Beyond." In *The Cambridge History of Egypt*, Vol. 2, edited by M.E. Daly, 334–93. Cambridge, UK: Cambridge University Press.

Roy, D.A. 1980. "The Egyptian Economy: Conversation on Social Contract, Economic Development, and Policy Alternatives." Mimeographed.

Rutherford, B.K. 2008. *Egypt after Mubarak: Liberalism, Islam, and Democracy in the Arab World.* Princeton, NJ: Princeton University Press.

Sa'ada, I. 1974. *Akhbar al-Youm*, September 7, 1974. Quoted in Waterbury 1983, 94.

Sachs, J.D. 2005. *The End of Poverty: Economic Possibilities for Our Time.* New York: Penguin.

Sadat, A. 1977. *In Search of Identity.* New York: Harper and Row.

Sadowski, Y.M. 1991. *Political Vegetables.* Washington, DC: Brookings Institution.

Sakamoto, K. 2013. "Efforts to Introduce Inclusive Planning in Egypt." Global Economy and Development, Working Paper 58. Washington, DC: Brookings Institution.

Sarraf, M. 2004. "Assessing the Costs of Environmental Degradation in the Middle East and North Africa Region." Environment Strategy Notes 9. Washington, DC: World Bank.

Schleifer, A., and R.W. Vishny. 1993. "Corruption." *Quarterly Journal of Economics* 108 (3): 599–618.

Schmidt, W.E. 1964. "The Economics of Charity." *Journal of Political Economy* 72 (4): 387–95.

Scitovsky, T. 1986. "Economic Development in Taiwan and South Korea." In *Models of Development*, edited by L.J. Lau, 127–82. San Francisco: Institute for Contemporary Studies.

Scobie, G.M. 1981. *Government Policy and Food Imports: The Case of Wheat in Egypt.* Washington, DC: International Food Policy Research Institute.

Sen, A. 2006. "The Man without a Plan." *Foreign Affairs* 85:171.

Sharp, J.M. 2010. "US Foreign Assistance to the Middle East: Historical Background, Recent Trends, and the FY 2011 Request." Washington, DC: Congressional Research Service.

Sherani, S. 2015. "Pakistan's Debt Dynamics." *Dawn*, 16 October 2015.

Shlaim, A. 1997."The Protocol of Sèvres, 1956: Anatomy of a War Plot." *International Affairs* 73 (3): 509–30. Reprinted in *The 1956 War: Collusion and Rivalry in the Middle East*, edited by D. Tal, 119–43. London: Frank Cass.

Sirowy, L., and A. Inkeles. 1990. "The Effects of Democracy on Economic Growth and Inequality: A Review." *Studies in Comparative International Development* 25:126–57.

Skidelsky, R. 1992. *John Maynard Keynes*, Vol. 2, *The Economist as Saviour, 1920–1937*. London: Macmillan.

Slackman, M. 2010. "Egypt Concedes to Resistance on Privatization Push." *The New York Times*, June 27, 2010. http://www.nytimes.com/2010/06/28/world/middleeast/28egypt.html?.

Smith, A. [1776] 1976. *An Inquiry into the Nature and Causes of the Wealth of Nations*. Edited by R.H. Campbell and A.S. Skinner. 2 vols. Oxford: Clarendon Press.

Soliman, S. 2011. *The Autumn of Dictatorship*. Palo Alto, CA: Stanford University Press.

Solow, R.M. 1956. "A Contribution to the Theory of Economic Growth." *Quarterly Journal of Economics* 70 (1): 65–94.

———. 1957. "Technical Change and the Aggregate Production Function." *Review of Economics and Statistics* 39 (3): 312–20.

———. 2001. "Applying Growth Theory across Countries." *World Bank Economic Review* 15:283–88.

Song, B-N. 2003. *The Rise of the Korean Economy*. 3rd edition. Oxford: Oxford University Press.

Spraos, J. 1986. *IMF Conditionality: Ineffectual, Inefficient, Mistargeted*. Essays in International Finance 166. Princeton, NJ: Princeton University Press.

Springborg, R. 1989. *Mubarak's Egypt: Fragmentation of the Political Order*. Boulder, CO: Westview Press.

Steinberg, D.I. 1989. *The Republic of Korea: Economic Transformation and Social Change*. Boulder, CO: Westview.

Stiglitz, J.E. 2000. "Unraveling the Washington Consensus." *Multinational Monitor* 21 (4): 7–14.

———. 2002. *Globalization and Its Discontents*. New York: Norton.

———. 2004. "The Post–Washington Consensus Consensus." Paper presented at the conference sponsored by Foundation CIDOB and the Initiative for Policy Dialogue held in Barcelona in Spain 2004, "From the Washington Consensus towards a new Global Governance."

Stiglitz, J.E., and S. Yusuf, eds. 2001. *Rethinking the East Asia Miracle*. New York: Oxford University Press for the World Bank.

Subramanian, A. 1997. "The Egyptian Stabilization Experience." Working Paper 18, Egyptian Center for Economic Studies (ECES). Cairo: ECES.

————. 2011. *Eclipse: Living in the Shadow of China's Economic Dominance*. Washington, DC: Peterson Institute for International Economics.

Sullivan, D.J. 1990. "The Political Economy of Reform in Egypt." *International Journal of Middle East Studies* 22 (3): 317–34.

Takacs, W.E., and L.A. Winters. 1991. "Labor Adjustment Costs and British Footwear Protection." *Oxford Economic Papers* 43:479–501.

Tarp, F. 2010. "Aid, Growth, and Development." In Mavrotas 2010, 38–56.

Tarr, D., and M. Morkre. 1984. *Aggregate Costs to the United States of Tariffs and Quotas on Imports*. Bureau of Economics Report to the Federal Trade Commission. Washington, DC: Government Printing Office.

Theil, H. 1966. *Applied Economic Forecasting*. Amsterdam: North-Holland.

Thorbecke, E., and H. Wan., eds. 1999. *Taiwan's Development Experience: Lessons on Role of Government and Market*. Boston: Kluwer Academic.

Tignor, R.L. 2010. *Egypt: A Short History*. Princeton, NJ: Princeton University Press.

————. 2016. *Anwar al-Sadat: Transforming the Middle East*. New York: Oxford University Press.

Tinbergen. J. 1952. *On the Theory of Economic Policy*. Amsterdam: North-Holland.

Troen, S.I. 1995. "The Protocol of Sèvres: British/French/Israeli Collusion against Egypt, 1956." *Israel Studies* 1 (2): 122–38.

Tudor, D. 2012. *Korea: The Impossible Country*. Tokyo and Rutland, VT: Tuttle.

UK Department of Overseas Trade. 1931. *Report of the United Kingdom Trade Mission to Egypt, February–March 1931*. London: His Majesty's Stationery Office.

UNDP. 1996. *Egypt: Human Development Report 1996*. Cairo: Institute of National Planning.

United Arab Republic, Information Department. 1962. *The Charter*. Cairo: Government Information Department.

United Arab Republic. n.d. *October Paper*. Cairo. Government Information Office.

United Nations. 2012. *World Population Prospects: The 2012 Revision*. New York: United Nations.

United Nations Food and Agriculture Organization. 1999. *Comparative Advantage and Competitiveness of Crops, Crop Rotations and Livestock Products in Egypt*. Cairo: UN-FAO.

UN Millennium Project Report. 2005. *Investing in Development: A Practical Plan to Achieve the Millennium Development Goals*. New York: United Nations.

van der Weide, R., C. Lakner, and E. Ianchovichina. 2017. "Is Inequality Underestimated in Egypt? Evidence from House Prices." Background paper for report entitled "Inequality, Uprisings and Conflict in the Arab World." Office of the Chief Economist, Middle East and North Africa (MENA) Region. Washington, DC: World Bank.

Vatikiotis, P.J. 1961. *The Egyptian Army in Politics*. Bloomington: Indiana University Press.

———, ed. 1968. *Egypt since the Revolution*. London: George Allen and Unwin.

———. 1978. *Nasser and His Generation*. London: Croom Helm.

Verme, P., B. Milanovic, S. al-Shawarby, S. el-Tawila, M. Gadallah, and E.A.A. el-Majeed. 2014. *Inside Inequality in the Arab Republic of Egypt: Facts and Perceptions across People, Time, and Space*. Washington, DC: World Bank.

von Laue, T.H. 1963. *Sergei Witte and the Industrialization of Russia*. New York: Columbia University Press.

Wade, R. 1987. "The Role of Markets and Governments in the Development Process: Lessons from Some East Asian Market Economies." Background paper for World Bank symposium on The Role of the Market and Planning in the Development Process, Bangkok, Thailand, 18–20 June.

———. 1990. *Governing the Market: Economic Theory and the Role of Government in East Asian Industrialization*. Princeton, NJ: Princeton University Press.

Wahba, M.M. 1994. *The Role of the State in the Egyptian Economy, 1945–1981*. Reading: Ithaca Press.

Warriner, D. 1957. *Land Reform and Development in the Middle East*. Oxford: Oxford University Press.

Waterbury, J. 1977. "An Attempt to Put Patrons and Clients in Place." In *Patrons and Clients in Mediterranean Societies*, edited by E. Gellner and J. Waterbury, 333–60. London: Duckworth.

———. 1979. *Hydropolitics of the Nile Valley*. Syracuse, NY: Syracuse University Press.

———. 1983. *The Egypt of Nasser and Sadat: The Political Economy of Two Regimes*. Princeton, NJ: Princeton University Press.

————. 1985. "The 'Soft State' and the Open Door: Egypt's Experience with Economic Liberalization, 1974–1984." *Comparative Politics* 18 (1): 65–83.

Waterston, A. 1965. *Development Planning: Lessons of Experience*. Baltimore and London: Johns Hopkins University Press.

Weinbaum, M.G. 1986. *Egypt and the Politics of US Economic Aid*. Boulder, CO: Westview.

Weiss, D. 1993. "Institutional Obstacles to Reform Policies: A Case Study of Egypt." *Economics* 47, 66–81.

Weiss, D., and U. Wurzel. 1998. *The Economics and Politics of Transition to an Open Market Economy: Egypt*. Paris: OECD Development Centre.

Westphal, L.E., and K.S. Kim. 1982. "Korea." In *Development Strategies in Semi-industrial Economies*, edited by B. Balassa, 212–79. Baltimore, MD: Johns Hopkins University Press.

Williamson, J. 1983. *The Open Economy and the World Economy*. New York: Basic Books.

————, ed. 1990. *Latin American Adjustment: How Much Has Happened?* Conference volume. Washington, DC: Institute for International Economics.

————. 1994a. "In Search of a Manual for Technopols." In Williamson 1994b, 11–28.

————, ed. 1994b. *The Political Economy of Policy Reform*. Washington, DC: Institute for International Economics.

————. 2003. "Our Agenda and the Washington Consensus." In Kuczynski and Williamson 2003, 323–31.

World Bank. 1974. *Arab Republic of Egypt: Economic Situation and Prospects*. Washington, DC: World Bank.

————. 1978. *Arab Republic of Egypt: Economic Management in a Period of Transition*. 6 vols. Washington, DC: World Bank.

————. 1983. *Egypt: Issues of Trade Strategy and Investment Planning*. Washington, DC: World Bank.

————. 1987. Egypt; *Review of the Finances of the Decentralized Public Sector*. 2 vols. Washington, DC: World Bank.

————. 1990a. *Adjustment Lending: Ten Years of Experience*. Washington, DC: World Bank.

————. 1990b. *World Development Report: Poverty*. New York: Oxford University Press.

————. 1990c. *Arab Republic of Egypt: Country Economic Memorandum, Economic Readjustment with Growth*. Washington, DC: World Bank.

———. 1991. *Egypt: Alleviating Poverty during Structural Adjustment.* Washington, DC: World Bank.

———. 1992. *Arab Republic of Egypt: Private Sector Regulatory Environment Study.* 2 vols. Washington, DC: World Bank.

———. 1993. *The East Asian Miracle.* Washington, DC: World Bank.

———. 1994. *Private Sector Development in Egypt.* Cairo: World Bank.

———. 1995a. *Arab Republic of Egypt: Economic Policies for Private Sector Development.* 2 vols. Washington, DC: World Bank.

———. 1997a. *Arab Republic of Egypt: Egypt—Issues in Sustaining Economic Growth.* 4 vols. Washington, DC: World Bank.

———. 1997b. *China 2020.* Washington, DC: World Bank.

———. 1998a. *Assessing Aid: What Works, What Doesn't, and Why.* New York: Oxford University Press.

———. 1998b. *Egypt in the Global Economy.* Washington, DC: World Bank.

———. 2001. *Egypt: Social and Structural Review.* Washington, DC: World Bank.

———. 2002a. *Cost Assessment of Environmental Degradation in Egypt.* Washington, DC: World Bank.

———. 2002b. *Arab Republic of Egypt: Poverty Reduction in Egypt—Diagnosis & Strategy.* 2 vols. Washington, DC: World Bank.

———. 2006. *Pakistan: Growth and Export Competitiveness.* Washington, DC: World Bank.

———. 2007. *Arab Republic of Egypt: A Poverty Assessment Update.* 2 vols. Washington, DC: World Bank.

———. 2009. *Arab Republic of Egypt: Upper Egypt: Pathways to Shared Growth.* Washington, DC: World Bank.

———. 2011. *Arab Republic of Egypt: Poverty in Egypt 2008–09: Withstanding the Global Economic Crisis.* Washington, DC: World Bank.

———. 2012. *Arab Republic of Egypt: Reshaping Egypt's Economic Geography: Domestic Integration as a Development Platform.* 2 vols. Washington, DC: World Bank.

———. 2014a. *IEG Evaluation of the World Bank's Record on Supporting Poverty Reduction in Country Programs: Egypt Country Case Study.* Washington, DC: World Bank.

———. 2014b. *More Jobs, Better Jobs: A Priority for Egypt.* Washington, DC: World Bank.

———. 2015. *Egypt: Promoting Poverty Reduction and Shared Prosperity: A Systematic Country Diagnostic.* Middle East and North Africa Region. Washington, DC: World Bank.

_____. 2016. *Doing Business 2016: Measuring Regulatory Quality and Efficiency*. Washington, DC: World Bank Group.

World Trade Organization. 2016. *Trade Profiles 2015*. Geneva: World Trade Organization.

World Values Survey [WVS]. 2000, 2008. worldvaluessurvey.org

Yueh, L.Y. 2013. *China's Growth: The Making of an Economic Superpower*. Oxford: Oxford University Press.

Index

In the page numbers, a number following n *is a note number.*

balance of payments: 1952–2016 112–14; foreign aid and 15, 68, 73; in Mubarak period 273, 279–80, 282–83, 295, 296, 302, 305, 306; in Nasser period 87, 177, 180–84, 202–203; policies and 349; in Sadat period 24, 207, 215, 231, 235, 262, 268. *See also* external debt (1952–2016); foreign aid; international financial institutions (IFIs)

Bank Misr 168

banking crisis in East Asia 296

banking sector 210, 224, 302, 361

binding constraints 357–59

al-Bishry, Zaafer 73

Boutros-Ghali, Youssef 282

Britain. *See* United Kingdom

budget deficits: in Mubarak period 273, 285, 295, 302, 305, 306, 380n5; in post-Mubarak period 316; in Sadat period 24, 206, 234, 235–36; targets in post-Mubarak period 318

budget year 377n12

budgets: 1965–2016 93–95, 374n3; influences on 96–98, 103–104, 375n8

building materials industries 191

bureaucracy: and centralized administrations 37–38; difficulties in reforming 7, 256–57, 258–59, 352; employment in 182; as social welfare 52–53. *See also* public-sector organizations

Camp David Accords 61, 65, 94

capital accumulation (1965–2016) 8–9

capital flight 120

capital formation 120–21, 167, 272–73, 288, 305–306

capital markets 80–81, 120, 125, 142, 226, 284, 319

CAPMAS (Central Agency for Public Mobilization and Statistics) 109, 110, 111, 379n1

cement industry 195. *See also* building materials industries

censuses 133. *See also* population

Central Bank of Egypt 100, 119–20, 316

chaebol (conglomerates) 366, 383n24

challenge for future 324–26

challenges and performance (1952–2016) 83–131; economic growth 84–89; external debt 122–30; external sector 112–22; GDP estimates 130–31; income distribution 109–112; population, labor force, and unemployment 89–91; poverty 104–109; public finance 92–104; structure of employment 91

China: economic growth 9; recognition of by Egypt 157, 158

Churchill, Winston 23

class structure 349

coalitions: cabinet as 221–22; economic reforms and 20–21; effects of 349–50; landowners 21–22; organizing abilities of 24–25

command economies 346

commercial borrowing 88–89, 125–26

commercial judicial system 7, 15

commercial sector 224

Communist Bloc: consequences of trade with 155, 157; payments to 125; trade with 153–54, 186, 215

compensations 51–52, 54–55, 285, 293–94, 302. *See also* salaries and wages in public sector

competition: in agriculture sector 48; cronyism and 298–300; discriminatory policies and 47–48; growth and 325–26; labor force and 137–38; not dependent on government type 29; policies and 44, 265–67, 289; reduced 75, 210, 218, 224, 232–33; reform policies for 285, 290–91, 296, 303–304; structural problems and 316–17. *See also* competitiveness in world economy

competitiveness in world economy: achieved by some public sector

organizations 292–93; of agricultural products 48; cronyism and
350; exchange rates and 118–19,
227, 258, 301, 316; exports and 333;
goals of 317–18; inadequate policy
attention to 10, 83, 115–17; product
quality and 75; productivity and 10,
194–95, 307; reform policies for
274–75, 282. *See also* competition;
exchange rates

competitiveness ranking 10

concessional debt: 1965–2016 103; 1970–
2015 127–28; in Mubarak period
74, 282; pros and cons of 80–81; in
Sadat period 229–30

conditionality of economic assistance
71–73

conspicuous consumption 220–21,
223, 263, 265. *See also* income
distribution

Consultative Group for Egypt 59–61,
243, 244–45, 250, 259–60, 373n24

Consumer Price Index 206–207, 263, 273,
305–306, 379n1

cooperatives, agricultural 148, 164

coordination between ministries 233,
253–55, 257–58

cost of doing business 75, 179, 222, 224,
286, 316, 317, 368

cost-plus pricing 192–93

costs and benefits of policy reforms
40–51; differential impact of
reforms 49–50; external trade 40;
perception of equity 50–51; private
versus social profitability 46–49;
time gap between costs and benefits
41–46. *See also* economic decision-
making, politics of

cotton production 48, 183–84, 265,
378n19. *See also* textile industry

cotton trade 169, 228–29

Council for National Production 174–75

credit access in Mubarak period 297, 299,
307, 361

crises, economic: in Mubarak period 73,
127, 276–78, 301; in Nasser period
183–85; in Sadat period 206–208

crises as drivers for reform 10, 20, 25–28,
36

crony capitalism 47–48, 297–300,
301–302, 304, 361. *See also* politically
connected (PC) firms

cross-country studies 78–79, 312, 329, 330,
332–34, 374n32. *See also* East Asian
countries; South Korea; Taiwan

cultivable area. *See* agricultural land

cultivated area. *See* agricultural land

currency of loans 73

debt relief: in 1960s 125, 185; in 1980s
63, 126–27, 280, 373n25; in 1990s
28, 103, 277–78, 281–82, 283–84,
380n4

debt service: in Mubarak period 301;
phasing of payments 73, 207; in
Sadat period 24

debt terms 126–28, 376n19. *See also* concessional debt

decision-makers and market incentives
365–66

democracy: versus authoritarianism 56,
58, 300, 356; and economic reform
28–30

demographics of Egypt 5, 136–38, 325.
See also population

dependency ratio 136

al-Dersh, Ahmed 74

development strategies. *See* political-
economy strategies for future

dictatorships and political economy. *See*
authoritarian systems

dollarization of economy 100, 295

domestic debt 319

domestic resource costs 378n23

donors' views 43, 76–78, 233, 373n19. *See
also* foreign patrons' role

Dubey, Vinod 242

Dulles, John Foster 160

GODE (Gulf Organization for the Development of Egypt) 126, 207
government, local 140
government responsibilities defined 2, 83–84
grant element 74, 374n30
Gross Domestic Product. *See* GDP (Gross Domestic Product); GDP growth
growth diagnostics 356–59
Gulf War (1991) 28, 127, 277, 281

Hamed, Salah 246–47, 251–52
Hawkins-Simon conditions 181
health sector 202, 284, 305
HIECS (Household Income, Expenditure and Consumption Survey) 111
HIES (Household Income and Expenditure Survey) 110–11
Higazi, Abdel Aziz: on building High Dam 164–65; on infitah 43, 211, 213–16, 219–20, 221–22; ministerial posts of 372n17; on Nasser's policies 198; on *30 March Paper* 213; on war in Yemen 178
High Dam. *See* Aswan High Dam
historical roots of political-economy issues: continuity from past 17; infrastructure projects 3–5; policies and problems 1–2; public debt 28, 122–23; public finance 92; relations with Gulf countries 67; water pricing 48
housing costs 263, 379n8
housing sector 152–53, 220

Ibn Khaldun 289–90
IMF (International Monetary Fund): conditions for funding 47, 234–36, 280; debt relief by 63, 373n25; effects of actions by 231–32; mistakes made by 4–5, 36–37, 246, 372n12; on privatization measures 278; reforms in post-Mubarak period 317; stabilization programs (1960s) 184, 187, 198. *See also* IMF and World Bank; IMF and World Bank in Sadat period; international financial institutions (IFIs); riots of 1977; World Bank
IMF and World Bank 286–87
IMF and World Bank databases 131
IMF and World Bank in Sadat period 229–61; cabinet divisions 236–38, 240–41; constraints on 229–32; Consultative Group 259–60; decision to cut subsidies 246–48, 247–48; durable effect on policymaking 248–49; the G-7 260–61; mobilizing donor support 252–59; negotiations with 234–36, 238–42, 250–52; riots of 1977 and consequences 245–49; separation of approach 242–45; U.S. dilemma in 59–60; weaknesses in economic management 232–34. *See also* IMF (International Monetary Fund); IMF and World Bank; international financial institutions (IFIs); riots of 1977; strategy, post-riots; World Bank
implementation of policies and reforms 37–38, 42–43, 350–51. *See also* pace of reform; public perception
implementation pace of projects 76, 77
import protections 116–18. *See also* tariffs
import substitution: defects in strategy of 116–17, 180, 376n14; effects of on external debt 124–25, 128; history of 162, 188, 189; in Nasser period 177
import tariffs. *See* tariffs
imports: 1965–2016 14; change in composition of 218–20; in Mubarak period 297; need for 216–17; in post-Mubarak period 315, 316; restrictions on 203
incentive structure affecting external sector 114–20; exchange rates 118–20; export structure 115–16; import protections 116–18

incentive structure in agriculture sector 148
income distribution 109–112; benefiters
    from debt and 128–29; equity
    effects of subsidy cuts 244–45, 248;
    improved equity 198–200; need
    for equity 14, 359–61; poverty and
    equity 110–12; warnings over 305.
    See also conspicuous consumption
industrial development under Nasser
    188–96; background of 189–90;
    issues of 191–94; performance of
    195–96; planning problems of 191;
    productivity during 194–95; push for
    190–91. *See also* economic planning
    and nationalizations; industrializa-
    tion; nationalization
industrial policy under Mubarak 303–304,
    344
industrial pollution 38–40
industrial sector under Nasser: concen-
    tration of ownership in 170–71;
    connotation of 378n14; nationaliza-
    tion in 169–70; stimulation of capital
    movement to 22, 149
industrial zones 299
industrialization: central planning for
    166–67; First Industrialization Plan
    175; need for 151; priority of 164;
    strategy of 180–81. *See also* import
    substitution
industry sector 86–87, 91, 274. *See also*
    industrial development under
    Nasser; industrial sector under
    Nasser; industrialization
infitah (open-door strategy) 208–226;
    economic background to 205–208;
    essence of 209–211; genesis of 212–
    16; results of 126, 218–26, 264–66;
    system change in 216–18
infitah (open-door strategy) results: con-
    sumption expansion 218–19; failure
    of 224–26; rivalries in cabinet 221–
    22; social consequences of 219–21,
    223–24

inflation: CAPMAS measure of 379n1;
    "core" versus "headline" 305–306;
    effects of 100, 106–107; as form
    of crisis 26, 27; in Mubarak period
    302, 305–306; in Sadat period
    206–207, 263
inflation tax 99–100, 375n7
informal populations 111–12, 140–41. *See*
    also urbanization
infrastructure: public and private sector
    roles in 33–35; refurbishment of
    128; and urbanization 139
insider-outsider conundrum 51–56
instability. *See* political instability and
    economic growth
Institute for International Economics
    327–31, 381n4
institutional weaknesses 14–15, 316, 357
institution-focused models of political
    economy 19–20, 28–38
interest group models of political econ-
    omy 19–20
interest groups: and benefits from debt
    46–49, 128–29; civil servants as
    52–53; as polluters 39–40; resistance
    to reform from 7, 25–26, 47, 54–55
interest groups, crises, and economic
    reform 20–25; Egypt–Israel war
    (1973) 23–24, 207–208, 320; Free
    Officers revolution 20–23; Suez
    Canal crisis 23
interest rates: 1965–2000 8; in Mubarak
    period 73, 100, 283, 287–88, 292; in
    Sadat period 227, 242, 249
internal migration 220
international financial institutions (IFIs):
    meetings with al-Shater 313–14;
    negotiations with 276–78, 280;
    reform policies proposed by 60,
    184, 250–51, 285; U.S. pressures on
    61–63; warnings from 305; weak-
    nesses in policy implementations
    noted by 350–51. *See also* IMF
    (International Monetary Fund);

IMF and World Bank in Sadat
period; World Bank
international markets, Egypt's share in
115–16
International Monetary Fund (IMF). *See*
IMF (International Monetary Fund)
international trade theory 24–25
investment: 1965–2016 80–81, 85, 102–
103, 120–21, 319; in Mubarak period
271–72, 285–88, 302–303; in Nasser
period 152–53, 166–67, 176, 179–80;
in post-Mubarak period 315; in
Sadat period 227–28
investment, foreign 163–64, 209, 211–12,
214–15, 223–24, 260
investment, private 190, 286–88
investment and savings: 1960–2016
95; 1965–2016 14–15, 87–89; in
Mubarak period 305; in Nasser
period 177, 182–83, 197, 203; in
post-Mubarak period 319; in Sadat
period 206
irrigation 48–49, 101, 152. *See also* Nile;
water distribution
Isma'il Pasha (khedive) 92, 124
Israel: in Suez Canal crisis 159–62; U.S.
assistance to 65–66, 69. *See also*
Egypt–Israel war (1973)

Japan, assistance from 73
job creation: foreign aid and 122; in
Mubarak period 47–48, 271–72,
284, 294, 300, 302–305, 306–308;
in Nasser period 172, 174, 187;
population issues and 135; in post-
Mubarak period 107, 315, 319,
324–25, 324–26, 329; in Sadat
period 228, 270

el-Kaissouni, Abdel Moneim: on administrative structure reforms 256–58;
on Consultative Group meeting
259–60; on infitah 219–20; on
Nasser's policies 163–65, 185–87; on

negotiations with IMF 244–45, 250;
proposals for new strategy 212; on
subsidy cuts decision 247–48
Kerry, John 66

labor force: after Second World War
189; dislocation of workers in
49; emigration of 229; expatriate
workers 216; growth in 89; human
capital 75; human-capital-adjusted
labor 8, 371n6; impact of privatization on 291, 293–95; in informal
employment 55–56, 90–91, 108;
misallocation of 300; in public sector 7, 102, 210–11, 303; retraining
of 281–82
labor issues of industrializaton 194
labor laws against dismissals 54–56
labor market: challenges for future 324–
26; gender differences in 326; in
Mubarak period 305; in Sadat period
228; unemployment data and 90–91
labor market reforms 200–201, 329
labor unrest 294
land ownership 21–23, 144–46, 299,
371n3, 371n4. *See also* agricultural
land
land reform 22–23, 144–49, 199. *See also*
agricultural land
land use and urbanization 140–41
landowners 21–22, 101, 144–45
Latin America 329, 330
Leontief input–output system 181
Lloyd, Selwyn 157, 158
Lower Poverty Line (LPL) 105
luxury goods 220–21. *See also* conspicuous
consumption

Mahir, Ali 145
Malaysia 320–21
manufacturing 69, 326. *See also* industrial
development under Nasser; industrialization; industry sector
market economies 345–46

oil exports 13, 228–29
oil prices 24, 279, 319
oil sector 86–87, 219, 318–19, 378n14
oil supply, world 208, 379n2
overpopulation 141–42

pace of project implementation 76, 77
pace of reform 30–38; government type
	and 58; in Mubarak period 35–36,
	274–79; in Nasser period 221–22; in
	Sadat period 237–38, 241, 251–52;
	Washington Consensus on 329
Palestinians, support for 185, 186
Paris Club 280, 283–84
parliament: National Assembly 297, 304;
	People's Assembly 246, 247, 251,
	262–63; pre-1952 21–22
PCDNP (Permanent Council for the
	Development of National Produc-
	tion) 165
People's Assembly 246, 247, 251, 262–63.
	See also parliament
per capita income 86, 332–34
Point Four 22
political economy of reform: costs and
	benefits 40–51; donors' views 76–78;
	environmental impact 38–40; exter-
	nal assistance 67–76; foreign aid:
	benefit or bane? 78–82; insider-
	outsider conundrum 51–56; interest
	groups, crises, and economic reform
	20–25; introduction 1–17; military
	and economic crises 25–28; political
	economy and dictatorships 56–58;
	political institutions and policy
	reform 28–38; role of foreign patron
	58–67; survey (1952–2016) 19–82
political instability and economic growth
	29, 307–308, 311–14
political institutions and policy reform
	28–38; difficulties in generalizing
	32–33; gradual pace of reform 32,
	35–36; rapid pace of reform 30–32;
	type of government 28–30

political legitimacy. See regime survival
	concerns
political-economy strategies for future
	327–34; East Asia approach 331–34;
	growth diagnostics 356–59; Wash-
	ington Consensus 327–31
political-economy strategy: contradictions
	in 5, 13–14, 263, 265–70, 351; external
	debt as 129–30; weaknesses in 63–64
politically connected (PC) firms 298–300.
	See also crony capitalism
pollution 38–40, 372n13
population 133–42; age structure of 5,
	136–38, 325; cultivated area and
	134–36; labor force and 89; over-
	population and 141–42, 377nn4–6
	(ch. 3); size and growth of 16, 133–
	34; urbanization of 136–41. See also
	informal populations; population,
	labor force, and unemployment
population, labor force, and unemploy-
	ment 89–91, 324–26. See also labor
	force; population; unemployment
post-Mubarak period (2011–2016)
	309–322; Abd al-Fattah al-Sisi 311;
	economic performance 314–17;
	Mohammed Morsi 310–11; politi-
	cal instability and economic growth
	311–14; political timeline 309–310;
	sustainable development strategy:
	Vision 2030 317–20; from vision to
	realization 320–22
poverty 104–112; characteristics and
	determinants of 107–109; mea-
	surement of 104–105, 375n10; in
	post-Mubarak period 315; trends in
	105–107, 375n11. See also income
	distribution
pricing issues under Nasser 191–93
private adjustment costs 49–50
private sector: labor problems in 55–56;
	in Nasser period 163–65, 171–72,
	196–97; role of in infrastructure
	building 34. See also privatization

revenue issues 95–101; effectiveness of tax system 98–101; inadequacy of resources 96; unsoundness of system 96–97. *See also* taxation systems; taxes

revolution of 2011 309–310

riots of 1977 226–29; anger at IMF over 37; blame-placing for 261–62, 266; effects of on policymaking 4–5, 234, 248–49; immediate effects of 57; protagonists of 248; toll of 245. *See also* IMF and World Bank in Sadat period; strategy, post-riots

root mean squared error (RMSE) 363, 383n21

rural and urban conglomerations. *See* urban, Egyptian definition of; urbanization

Sadat period (1970-81) 205–270; agriculture plans in Sinai 45; economic pressures and 1977 riots 36, 57, 226–29; IMF and World Bank, relations with 59–60, 229–61; infitah 24, 208–226; infitah background 205–208; strategy to address underlying grievances 261–70; turnover of ministers 42–43

safety net 35, 38, 50, 275–76, 359

Said Pasha (khedive) 92, 123

salaries and wages in public sector 52–53, 102, 372n18, 373n19. *See also* compensations; wages and benefits

Salem, Gamal 163

Salem, Mamduh 222–23

savings: 1952–2016 per capita 136–37; 1965–2016 93, 96, 319; gross national savings 10; in Mubarak period 306; national versus domestic 88, 374n1; in post-Mubarak period 315. *See also* investment and savings

savings, domestic: 1952–74 12; 1952–2016 68; 1960–2016 81; 1965–2016 14–15, 16; in Nasser period 46–47, 173–74, 197, 203

savings, foreign 15, 68, 120–21

al-Sayeh, Hamed 42, 60–61, 244–45

SCAF (Supreme Council of the Armed Forces) 310, 313

Second World War 112–13, 162, 189–90. *See also* war(s)

second-generation reforms 6–7

sectoral composition of growth 85

security, regional 318–19, 320

sequestration: of Egyptian properties 170; of foreign assets 23, 28, 165, 166, 168

services sectors: employment in 91; share of GDP (Gross Domestic Product) 87

Shafei, Zaki 236–37, 250

al-Shater, Khaled 313–14

Shindy, Wagih 37, 42

Sidqi, Aziz 169, 175, 214

Sinai, plans for agriculture in 45

situation rents 55

small and medium enterprises (SMEs) 47–48, 297, 304, 307

small and young firms 325–26

social consequences: of cronyism 298; of ERSAP 290–91; of infitah 219–21, 223–26, 265–66; of investment reallocations 152–53; of Nasser's policies 197, 201–202, 378n23, 379n24. *See also* regime survival concerns; social contract; social welfare

social contract 14, 264–65, 269, 273, 359

Social Fund for Development 55, 281–82

social versus private profitability 46–49

social welfare 52–53, 171, 194, 198–202, 305, 317. *See also* regime survival concerns; social contract

"soft infrastructure" 216

"software" of growth 316

South Korea: authoritarianism in 355; competitiveness in international market in 338–39; conglomerates in 366, 383n24; corruption in 354; development strategy of 130,

332–34, 348, 351, 352–53; economic growth in 9, 16–17, 332–34, 335–36; education in 340–42, 382n12; efficiency in 228; foreign aid to 344–45; foreign policy of 348; GNP growth 333; initial conditions in 353–54; knowledge-based policies of 342; planning in 367–68; public perception of reforms in 38, 342–43; SMEs in 339; work ethic in 339–40. *See also* GDP growth in East Asia, drivers of; South Korea, export policies in

South Korea, export policies in 335–45; contrasts between Egypt and South Korea 339–43; feasibility of model for Egypt 343–44; foreign aid 344–45; incentives and punishments 335–36, 381n8; selective incentives 337–39. *See also* South Korea

Soviet Union: aid sought from 184–85; Egyptian relations toward 4, 23; financing of High Dam by 153; investment in Egypt by 186–87; relations with U.S. 207–208, 215

stabilization programs: in 1960s 184, 198; in 1990s 44–45, 102–103

standard of living 16, 72, 141–42, 176, 182–83, 226, 265, 364

state role in economy, changes in under Nasser 162–88; central economic planning 172–83; expansion of control over economy 196–97; IFIs and Egypt 183–88; toward Arab socialism 162–72. *See also* industrial development under Nasser

steel plants 188, 191, 195. *See also* building materials industries

strategy, post-riots 261–70; blame-placing 261–62, 266; conflicting objectives of 268–70; problems identified 262–68

Strauss, Robert 60–61

structural changes in GDP 86–87, 176–77, 284–85

subsidies: creation of 95; critical role of 108–109; on energy 299, 303, 316; future targets of 320; implicit 264–65, 379n9; merits of questioned 264–65; percentage of budget of 102, 222–23; as placation 11–12, 126–27, 269, 380n10 (ch. 5); reforms of 251–52, 276, 288, 302; results of 13; strategy, post-riots 206; support for 47. *See also* IMF and World Bank in Sadat period; subsidy cuts (1977)

subsidy cuts (1977): cabinet decision for 246–48; consequences of 4–5, 57, 245–47; political risks of 59–60, 235–36, 239–41. *See also* IMF and World Bank in Sadat period; subsidies

Sudan 156, 184

Suez Canal: dues from 13; finance of construction 3, 92, 123–24; nationalization of 3–4

Suez Canal Authority 292–93

Suez Canal crisis: effect of on United Kingdom 4, 371n2; foreign policy changes following 23, 165–66; reason for 159–62; as turning point 168. *See also* Aswan High Dam

sustainable development strategy: vision to realization 320–22; Vision 2030 317–20

Taiwan 9, 16–17, 333–34, 345, 355. *See also* East Asian countries

targets without policies 179–80, 317–22

tariffs: history of 162; as impediment 114; in Mubarak period 291, 299, 303; in Nasser period 163; in Sadat period 222, 228; structure of 116–17; theory of 24–25

task ahead 323–68; challenge for policymakers 324–26; economic governance 345–68; GDP growth and its drivers 15–16, 334–45; strategies to meet challenges 327–34 taxation systems: agriculture tax 101; business profits 98, 163; in donor and recipient countries 64–65; economic rents 96–98, 269–70; equity in 98–99; indirect taxes 10–11, 98, 148, 236; inflation tax 99–100, 375n7; personal income tax 11, 98–99, 101; price administration 191–92; price control as 191–92; to promote private investment 163; sales tax 283; user fees 39–40; value-added tax (VAT) 98, 317, 375n6; weakness in 286. *See also* agrarian reforms; revenue issues; tariffs; taxes

taxes: 1952–2016 11; 1965–2016 14, 102; in Mubarak period 302; in Nasser period 187, 198; in post-Mubarak period 319–20; in Sadat period 236–37, 242, 247. *See also* agrarian reforms; revenue issues; tariffs; taxation systems

technology from Communist Bloc 155, 193–94, 215, 378n20

textile industry 191, 194–95, 293, 339, 378n19, 380n11. *See also* cotton production; cotton trade

30 March 1968 Paper 212–14, 217

time gap between costs and benefits of reform 41–46

tire industry 195

Toshka project 253

total factor productivity (TFP): in Egypt 7–10, 14, 87–88, 335, 371n5; in other countries 8–9, 334–35. *See also* productivity

tourism earnings 13, 279, 296–97, 315, 319

trade, domestic 148, 171

trade, international: 1952–2016 115–16, 128; direction of 153–55; in Mubarak period 274, 303; in Nasser period 151, 153–55, 169–71, 176, 186; in Sadat period 215–16, 218; during Second World War 162, 189

trade, wholesale 176

trade lobbies 372n7

trade unions 54, 292

transport sector 35

U.N. Security Council 160

UNCTAD (United Nations Conference on Trade And Development) 71

unemployment: 1952–2016 89–91, 106, 107; discouraged labor 90, 305, 308, 324, 374n2; and education 326; in Mubarak period 302, 304–305; in post-Mubarak period 307, 315, 324–26. *See also* employment rate; labor force; population, labor force, and unemployment

United Kingdom: effect of Suez Canal crisis on 4, 371n2; High Dam financing and 156–59; occupation of Egypt by 3, 92; in Suez Canal crisis 159–62; support for Free Officers 23; trade with Egypt 154

United States: aid sought from 184–85; debt relief 283; High Dam financing and 155–58; position of in Suez Canal crisis 159–62; relations with USSR 207–208, 215. *See also* foreign aid; U.S. assistance; USAID (United States Agency for International Development)

universities 182, 201–202

Upper Egypt 51, 108, 220, 239–40

upper poverty line (UPL) 105

urban, Egyptian definition of 138–39, 376n2

urbanization: and informal populations 111–12, 140–41; of population 136–41

U.S. assistance: after Free Officers revolution 22; aid-tying 70–71; complex relationship of 59–60; decrease in 13, 318–19; dilution of leverage from 65–67; disbursements 76–77; as inducements 28; military aid 65–67;

political aims of 154–58; supervision of projects 69. *See also* foreign aid

USAID (United States Agency for International Development): failed projects of 79–80, 374n33; methods for subsidy reform 250–51; strategic assistance by 232. *See also* foreign aid; U.S. assistance

U-statistic 363, 383n20

vehicle assembly plants 188, 191, 195

Vision 2030 317–22

vision plans, generally 320–22

wages and benefits 200–201. *See also* compensations; salaries and wages in public sector

waqf 21–22

war(s) 12, 218, 348–49; with Iraq (1991) 28, 127, 277, 281; with Israel (1973) 23–24, 207–208, 320; in Yemen (1960s) 154, 178, 187, 320. *See also* Second World War; Suez Canal crisis

Washington Consensus 327–31, 381n4, 381n5

water distribution 10, 101, 149–51. *See also* irrigation; Nile

water pricing 48, 101

West Germany 155, 252

Witte, Count Sergei 58, 373n20

Wolfensohn, James 274

World Bank: conditions for loans 59–60, 230–31, 234–36; cuts in aid 202–203; High Dam construction and 155–56, 158. *See also* IMF (International Monetary Fund); IMF and World Bank in Sadat period; international financial institutions (IFIs)

Yemen war (1960s) 154, 178, 187, 320

Yunes, Mahmoud 292–93

zaibatsu (conglomerates) 366, 383n24

Zaki, Hassan Abbas 212